*Communism and Nationalism*

# Communism and Nationalism

## Karl Marx Versus Friedrich List

### Roman Szporluk

New York    Oxford
OXFORD UNIVERSITY PRESS
1988

Oxford University Press

Oxford   New York   Toronto
Delhi   Bombay   Calcutta   Madras   Karachi
Petaling Jaya   Singapore   Hong Kong   Tokyo
Nairobi   Dar es Salaam   Cape Town
Melbourne   Auckland

and associated companies in
Beirut   Berlin   Ibadan   Nicosia

Library of Congress Cataloging-in-Publication Data
Szporluk, Roman.
Communism and nationalism.
Bibliography: p.   Includes index.
1. Nationalism and socialism.   2. Marx, Karl,
1818–1883—Views on nationalism.   3. List, Friedrich,
1789–1846—Views on nationalism.   I. Title.
HX550.N3S95   1988       320.5′32       87–10993
ISBN 0-19-505102-5

1 3 5 7 9 8 6 4 2

Printed in the United States of America
on acid-free paper

*For Mary Ann, Ben, Larissa, and Michael*

# Preface

In 1977 I began to teach a course at the University of Michigan called "Socialism and Nationalism." The course was based on the idea that in the historical epoch inaugurated by the French and Industrial revolutions, socialism and nationalism addressed very similar—if not identical—questions, but gave different answers to them, provided competing programs for their realization, and in general, offered alternative visions of the world. Thus the course granted "equal time" to these two world views, while most books and articles (and I suppose university courses) titled "Socialism, or Communism, or Marxism, and Nationalism" seemed really to be accounts of what socialists (Marxists, or Communists) said or thought *about* the National Question, nation, and nationalism.

My students were intrigued by the approach. They also proved to be very challenging and inspiring. They had known Marxists as people with ideas, some students told me, but nationalists? Nationalist thinkers?

To sustain my claim that nationalists did have ideas, I had to present evidence. I read the writings of nationalist "classics." It was then that I discovered for myself Friedrich List. I also realized that the conventional treatment of Marx and nationalism that begins with the years 1848–1849 must be wrong. Marx, born in 1818, presumably read newspapers as a young man; he therefore must have been aware of German nationalism and should have thought *something* about the economist List. But in the books on young Marx that I consulted, I found List to be mentioned only in passing, if at all, and nationalism, even German nationalism, to be treated marginally at best. Indexes to some of those books mentioned "narcissism" but not nationalism. Finally, when reading young Marx himself, I ran into his essay on List. Reference to it opens the introduction to this volume, and the essay as a whole is discussed in Chapter 3. This book is an original work, not one based on my lecture notes, but I was inspired by my students to write it.

Many of my debts are recognized in the text, notes, and bibliography. The bibliography is highly selective, but I have tried to acknowledge all those scholars on whose research I draw and whose findings I adopt. My general thinking on nationalism and socialism has been influenced especially strongly by three books: Karl W. Deutsch's *Nationalism and Social Communication*, which I first read in the late 1950s, and George Lichtheim's *Marxism: An Historical and Critical Study* and Ernest Gellner's *Thought and Change*, both of which I read in the mid-1960s. Needless to say, these authors bear no responsibility whatsoever for what I claim or imagine to have learned from them.

My more immediate debts are many and just as difficult to acknowledge properly. I have talked about Marx and List to anybody who would listen (and to some who would not). I learned much from my colleagues in the Department of History and at the Center for Russian and East European Studies at the University of Michigan. I received advice about specific points, suggestions for further reading, and encouragement from many, including Stephen J. Tonsor, Elizabeth L. Eisenstein, Roger F. Hackett, Alfred G. Meyer, Arthur P. Mendel, William G. Rosenberg, Ronald G. Suny, and David A. Hollinger. I benefited greatly from the discussions at the departmental Colloquium in Comparative History and at the Graduate-Student and Faculty Seminar in Soviet and East European Studies, where I presented my work in progress. J. David Singer, a member of the Political Science Department at the University of Michigan, and I discussed this project in a number of meetings, and he invited me to present my findings to the Study Group on World Politics, which he heads. Outside of Ann Arbor, I lectured on aspects of this book at Harvard, Indiana, McMaster, and York universities. Some of my ideas were first presented in my articles, "War by Other Means" (*Slavic Review*, 1985) and "Marx, List, Palacký" (*Cross Currents*, 1986).

Michael E. Geyer, now of the University of Chicago, encouraged this project from its inception and commented on an earlier version of the book. Frederic L. van Holthoon, of the Rijksuniversiteit, Groningen, critically read an early version while a visiting professor at Michigan. Geoff Eley and I have had frequent conversations about matters of mutual interest, which happen to include socialism and nationalism, and I have learned much from those discussions. But I am especially grateful to him for reading what I had thought was the final version of the book and for showing me, in a careful and detailed review, why it should not be. Raymond Grew also read the entire manuscript and raised questions that required rethinking of major points and that led to the rewriting of several chapters. I also thank Roman Solchanyk of Munich, Germany for his advice and comments as well as for his help in obtaining books and articles that I would have otherwise not seen.

Writing this book, I was constantly reminded of what an extraordinary institution the University of Michigan Library is. I am much indebted to its staff, and especially to Joseph A. Placek and Holde H. Borcherts. The Center for Russian and East European Studies has supported my research for many years, but its generous help in this project was critical. I am also grateful to my graduate assistants, Richard G. Johnson, Gregory L. Ketcham, Louisa Vinton, Irina Livezeanu, and Phillip C. Zane, as well as to Michael E. Moore who gave me valuable comments on the manuscript, and to Michelle Wynn who edited an early draft.

While grateful to all for their support and advice, I must make clear that none of the persons or institutions named above should be presumed to have approved of any statement this book contains.

Countless drafts and revisions were typed and retyped by the staffs of the Center and the History Department, and I am pleased to thank Darlene Breitner, Janet Rose, Jeanette Diuble, Connie Hamlin, Lorna Altstetter, Erika Engelhardt, and Lisa K. Szuma for their expert skill, as well as for their patience with revisions they must have thought would never cease.

It was both inspiring and pleasant to be associated with Oxford University Press in the course of working on this book. Nancy Lane encouraged me when it was still only a proposal. Marion Osmun has been an exemplary editor.

This book is dedicated to my wife, Mary Ann, and to our children, Ben, Larissa, and Michael.

*Ann Arbor, Michigan*                                                                    R.S.
*July 1987*

# Contents

"The workers have no country"
–*Karl Marx (1848)*

"Between the individual and humanity stands
the nation"
–*Friedrich List (1841)*

*Communism and Nationalism*

# 1

## Introduction

In March 1845 Karl Marx began to write a critical essay on *The National System of Political Economy*, a book published in 1841 by his contemporary, Friedrich List. He never finished his "List Critique." It remained unknown long after his death, until a Russian translation appeared in a Soviet historical journal in 1971.[1]

The "List Critique" is important both in the intellectual biography of Marx and as his theoretical statement on nation and nationalism, on which, it is commonly alleged, he failed to speak clearly and comprehensively. In fact, the "List Critique" is more explicit than anything Marx ever wrote on nationalism.

Conventional Marxian scholarship usually begins the review of Marx's stand on nation and nationalism with the position he and Engels formulated in 1848–1849. The scholar normally proceeds with an initial, brief, and somewhat embarrassed reference to *The Communist Manifesto* and its various statements—that national differences were disappearing, that one world literature was emerging, that the world market was subjecting backward nations to the rule of those more advanced, and, of course, that the workers "have no country." This review is followed, in a mood of relief, by an examination of the nationality problem in the European revolutions of 1848–1849, a problem that is viewed in light of the writings of Engels alone, especially his "Revolution and Counter-Revolution in Germany." In this work Engels spoke approvingly about the political aspirations of the "historical nations," or the Germans, Poles, and Hungarians, and correspondingly condemned such "nonhistoric" peoples as the Czechs, Croats, and other East Europeans.

Despite its wide acceptance, however, this approach remains problematic. First, in 1848 Marx was already thirty years old, an age that in those days was not considered young. By then, as is well known, Marx had managed to produce a considerable body of writing. Second, and more important, this conventional approach does not ask what the young Marx— that is, Marx *before* 1848—thought on the "German Question," which after all was a "nationality problem," too. Any answer to this question would be revealing of Marx's view of the world: The German Question was a major national problem in post–1815 and pre–1848 Europe. Whatever Marx thought about it, therefore, must be taken into account when one wants to elucidate the issue of Marx and nationalism. And yet, strangely, the writers on young Marx (and there are many of them) have consistently avoided this specific historical and biographical question about Marx and German nationalism—even when they have written (as most of them have) on Marx's own program for Germany.

This neglect is even stranger in view of the fact that anyone growing up in Germany during Marx's youth had to be aware of nationalism: German nationalism concerned itself not only with culture and politics, but also with economic questions, including industrialization. The last issue was the central concern of Friedrich List (1789–1846). It would have been very odd for Marx to have overlooked German nationalism and especially this aspect of German nationalism, or to have ignored List, "the most intelligent and optimistic of nationalist ideologues."[2] The publication of the "List Critique" makes it imperative, then, to begin the systematic study of Marx and the German Question, and of Marx and nationalism in general, before the year 1848.

Of course, this does not mean that before discovery of the "List Critique" nothing was known about Marx and Engels' view of List or about their assessment of the economic program of German nationalism. In a letter to Marx written in 1844, Engels remarked that it was "curious" that both he and Marx should have thought, independently of each other and at about the same time, of writing a critique of List. Engels added that he intended to discuss List "practically," but he expected ("from my knowledge of your personality") that Marx would deal with List's *"premises* rather than with his conclusions."[3]

It appears that Engels never wrote his own planned work on List. However, he referred ("practically") to List's program in his speeches at Elberfeld (February 8 and 15, 1845), a month before Marx began to write his "List Critique." Engels argued there that a social revolution in Germany would come inevitably and soon. This would happen without regard to whether Germany adopted any policy that was founded on the principle of private property, be it a policy that provided a moderate protective tariff, or that was based on free trade without restrictions, or that adhered to the recommendations of List. Engels insisted that "communism is, if not a historical, at any rate *an economic necessity for Germany.*"[4]

Even if Germany were to repeat the earlier industrial development of England, Engels argued, "sooner or later we should arrive at the point which England has now reached—namely, the eve of the social revolution. But in all probability it would not take as long as that." Also, economic competition between Germany and England would benefit neither German nor English industrialists and would inevitably produce "a *social revolution.*"

> With the same certainty with which we can develop from given mathematical principles a new mathematical proposition, with the same certainty we can deduce from the existing economic relations and the principles of political economy the imminence of social revolution.[5]

Such a future social revolution, Engels was sure, would implement "the principles of communism." No other outcome was possible.[6]

Thus, Engels dealt with the ideas of List "practically," as he said he would. And his supposition that Marx would concern himself with List's "premises" is, we now know, borne out in the "List Critique." As we shall see (Chapter 3), Marx viewed List and the German Question, and the nation in general, in a broader framework of his interpretation of capitalism.

By the time he first encountered the ideas of List, Marx, like Engels, had concluded that capitalism was a doomed system, deserving of condemnation on moral grounds, and simultaneously destined for an inevitable fall by the development of history itself. When Marx considered the future of Germany in his critiques of Hegel and List, this imminent fall of capitalism was the central premise of his argument.

In Marx's view, modern society consisted of two classes that were engaged in an irreconcilable conflict: the ruling class of the bourgeoisie or the capitalists and the exploited class of the proletariat, i.e., the industrial workers. That society itself was the product of a long historical development, of which the most recent and important phase had been inaugurated by the Industrial Revolution. The other central event in Marx's view of the modern world was the French Revolution. The theories and practice of 1789 and their consequences, as well as the Industrial Revolution, were all interpreted by Marx as aspects of one process—the rise of capitalism.

At the same time, Marx's critique of the capitalist system was formulated and articulated in the philosophical language that he had learned from classical German philosophers, Hegel in particular. When it finally took shape, Marxism was simultaneously a theory of history, economics, politics, and philosophy—and a program for the liberation of man that extended to all those areas. Marx postulated a connection between all spheres of human life, and his program dealt accordingly with all of them in a dialectical unity. Indeed, Marx claimed that his theory, while the result of his own intellectual endeavor, was also the reflection of objectively working historical forces and would therefore be carried out as a predestined outcome of historical development. Marx further thought that the proletariat was that "material force" whose historical task was to realize his philosophy.

When one bears all of this in mind, it is easy to see why Marx found the theories of List, particularly his view of history and his program for the future, not only objectionable but aberrant. The doctrine of List, Marx was convinced, contradicted everything then taking place in the development of society—before his, and List's, eyes. It was axiomatic to Marx that industrial progress intensified and sharpened the antagonism between the bourgeoisie and the proletariat, an antagonism that would in the immediate future explode in a violent revolution. List, in the meantime, preached class cooperation and solidarity in the building of a nation's power. Marx thought that the Industrial Revolution, and the concomitant rule of the bourgeoisie, promoted the unification of the world and obliterated national differences. (Communism, he thought, would abolish nations themselves.) List claimed that the same phenomenon, the Industrial Revolution, intensified national differences and exacerbated conflicts among nations.

While Marx saw the necessity of workers uniting across nations against the bourgeoisie, List called for the unification of all segments of a nation against other nations. Marx criticized the political ideas of 1789 and their realization in the modern capitalist state by arguing that political liberty was illusory: It ignored the realities of "society," in which private property reigned and in which man was oppressed by man. The task was to abolish politics altogether by carrying out a complete social revolution and thereby to free man as a human being. List also criticized the political theories and institutions of the West. The real basis for a political community for List was the community of a nation, which he defined by cultural (including linguistic) criteria, and to which he wanted to adjust political boundaries. But List concentrated his critique specifically on the rules that regulated the relations among nations, especially the rules of free trade. As we shall see, List considered free trade a cover-up for unequal relations among nations, just as Marx thought political liberty was an ideological cover for class oppression.

The most urgent and significant item on Marx's political agenda was the call for a revolution of the proletariat against the bourgeoisie. What was he to do when List came along with his absurd assertion that the most important task for the Germans was to unite against England so that their nation might equal and surpass her rival economically, culturally, and politically?

This distillation of the main points of disagreement between Marx and List should help introduce some of the questions a study like this is bound to provoke. How does one go about comparing and contrasting nationalism with Marxism and List with Marx? Does this work claim that List was an intellectual, especially philosophical, peer of Marx, or that nationalism matches Marxism in the breadth and depth of its world view? And does a theory of nationalism exist in the first place?

Most would agree that the history of nineteenth-century Europe, from the French Revolution and Napoleon to the outbreak of the First World War in 1914, must take nationalism into account. In recent decades, nationalism has proved to be an effective and successful rival of Marxism and communism. Indeed, when communism has defeated rival doctrines, it has owed its victory to the adoption of at least some of the principles of nationalism and to the fact that it has become national, indeed nationalist, itself. And to be sure, nationalism is undeniably a powerful force in the world today.

But even those who concede that nationalism is significant politically do not think that it is also intellectually important. What is the message of nationalism other than antipathy to foreigners and the determination to be ruled by "one's own people" (however these people are defined)? Does nationalism have a *Weltanschauung* to speak of—a conception of human nature, of history and society, a vision of world order? Are there philosophers of nationalism who are comparable to the intellectual giants of other philosophies? Is there such a philosophic representative for the nationalist alternative to Marxism?

We might begin to answer these questions by first clarifying the terms under which Marxism is accepted as a major political and intellectual force. Its importance is usually assessed according to its relation to the historical processes it interpreted and/or sought to bring about. The first of these processes was the Industrial Revolution, which exerted a powerful influence on economic, social, political, and religious life and which inspired and created new theories, beliefs, and movements. One of those theories and movements was Marxism. In George Lichtheim's view, Marxism was an alternative "historical counterpoint to the liberal integration," which had been another reaction, chronologically earlier, "to the challenge posed by the Industrial Revolution."(Conservatism was the third major type of response.)[7]

Along with the Industrial Revolution "and its repercussions in the theoretical sphere," Lichtheim includes the French Revolution and its impact on early nineteenth-century Germany as points of departure in his study of Marx and Marxism. Rather than focus on the ideas of Marx alone, Lichtheim also considers the actions and ideas of Marx's disciples and followers in the entire historical epoch up to the Russian Revolution of 1917. To understand Marx, Lichtheim argues, requires taking into account "those historical changes which he both predicted and helped bring about." Marxism was both "the theoretical reflection" of, and "the political agent" in, the process of social change after the French and Industrial revolutions. Marxism was "the theory of one particular kind of revolutionary movement . . . which arose from the impact of industrialism upon the highly stratified society of nineteenth-century Europe," and it provided a link between the French and the Russian revolutions.[8]

The necessity of treating the Industrial Revolution and its impact in connection with the French Revolution is widely accepted.[9] Trygve R. Tholfsen, for example, stresses that "what was decisive was the conjuncture of social, intellectual, and ideological developments." Not only Marxism but also other socialist critiques arose out of that "conjuncture" of the Industrial Revolution with the French Revolution. As people formulated their views of the world around them, many concluded at that time "that the principles of liberty and equality, and perhaps the 'postulate of a rational order,' required the transformation of the emerging industrial society into something radically different."[10] In this connection, Tholfsen quotes approvingly from J. L. Talmon, who observed that the French Revolution "conditioned men to experience and interpret" the social and economic changes caused by the Industrial Revolution "in a way that would have been quite unthinkable had the technological and social-economic changes taken place earlier." The Industrial Revolution by itself did not give rise to new ideas by simply "engendering new conditions."[11]

Those ideas about the industrial world, Talmon implies, were formulated in the intellectual and political setting created by the French Revolution. Similarly, it is worth quoting the words of François Furet, according to whom the French Revolution "invented a new type of political discourse and practice by which we have been living ever since." It placed "on the stage of history . . . a practical and ideological mode of social action unrelated to anything that came before."[12] Furet also speaks about two sets of beliefs forming "the very bedrock of revolutionary consciousness." One of them was the transformation of personal problems and moral or intellectual matters into political issues, with a corresponding belief in the amenability of human problems to a political solution. The second belief held that "since everything can be known and changed, there is a perfect fit between action, knowledge, and morality. . . . Henceforth, there was no limit to the beneficent possibilities of political action."[13]

After citing Furet's observation that the "seminal ideal" of the Revolution was that of the advent of a new age,[14] Tholfsen concludes by pointing out that "what France 'invented' in 1789 was not democracy, but rather the new revolutionary phenomenon, the new practical and ideological mode. . . . "[15]

All these observations, essential as they are for an understanding of the rise of Marxism, need to be borne in mind equally when one clarifies the genesis of nationalism. More immediately, by taking note of these aspects of the new outlook, we can recognize more easily the originality of Marx amidst those who responded, in their own different ways, to the new age. Marx's special claim to originality and distinction, it would seem, lay in his connecting these political and economic phenomena to, and interpreting them in terms of, a philosophical system he himself had created in response to the Hegelian system. The fusion of philosophy with politics and economics helps explain Marxism's spectacular historical failure as a practical program—but also its lasting intellectual vitality.

Since interpretations of the Industrial Revolution were shaped by philosophical and political ideas that were not themselves a product or "reflection" of the economic processes, it should cause no surprise that other theories treated the meaning and impact of the Industrial Revolution in ways quite different from those of socialism in general and Marxism in particular. In his study of nationalism, first published in 1931, Carlton J. H. Hayes noted that

> the Industrial Revolution is not necessarily an intellectual revolution. Of itself it is neither nationalist nor internationalist. It is essentially mechanical and material. It has merely provided improved means and greater opportunities for the dissemination of any ideas which influential individuals entertain. Now it so happened that when the Industrial Revolution began, nationalism was becoming a significant intellectual movement, even more significant than internationalism.[16]

Nationalist doctrines, Hayes pointed out, had been first formulated prior to the Industrial Revolution, "in an agricultural society, before the advent of the new industrial machinery,'' but they spread and succeeded only after ''the introduction of the new machinery and the transition from an agricultural to an industrial society.'' That ''marvelous improvement ... termed the Industrial Revolution,'' according to Hayes, made it possible for nationalist ideas ''to take hold.'' The impact of the Industrial Revolution ''paralleled the rise and spread of popular devotion to nationalism.''[17]

Developing this idea further, we might ''locate'' the birth of nationalism in its own historical ''conjuncture'' prior to the Industrial Revolution. This conjuncture included cultural trends, such as Romanticism in Germany, the ideas of the French Revolution, and certain developments in East Europe, especially the Polish Question. At a greater distance, it also included the invention of printing and the Protestant Reformation (see Chapter 6). All of these factors contributed to the formation of an intellectual and political climate in which the Industrial Revolution was interpreted from a nationalist perspective.

Hayes was one of the first scholars to have seen this. He noted, of course, that the economic liberalism of factory owners and the socialism of factory workers had been the two principal doctrines responding to the Industrial Revolution.[18] But Hayes also recognized that economic liberalism and Marxist socialism, though initially ''formulated as strictly economic doctrines,'' gradually acquired ''nationalist significance and became factors in the nineteenth-century development of nationalism.'' More originally, he even saw that specifically nationalist interpretations of the economy emerged and that those interpretations ultimately proved to be ''especially influential in the evolution of nationalism.''[19]

It is one of the central ideas of this study that nationalism—let us stress this point over and over again—was not a product of the Industrial Revolution, but rather had been born beforehand, and that a specifically *nationalist* reaction to the Industrial Revolution was not reducible to the liberal, conservative, or socialist position.

Those who limit themselves to identifying liberal, conservative, and socialist positions do not always remember that these classifications tacitly presuppose the existence of an established polity. Furthermore, such a perspective assumes that this polity is fairly well developed, for it consists of the bourgeoisie, the landed proprietors, and the industrial workers, whose respective interests these three positions or ideologies ''reflect.'' Leaving aside the crude reductionism involved in its assignment of ideologies to particular economic classes, this approach overlooks the fact that the nineteenth and twentieth centuries were periods when new national communities were being formed, when various premodern states, ethnic

groups, regional identities, and religious communities were being transformed into nations. While liberals, conservatives, and socialists indeed
responded to the Industrial Revolution within already existing societies
and polities, there were also nationalists who were engaged in establishing
new communities and who, in the process, asked how the Industrial Revolution affected the position of their respective nations—often nations in
the making—versus other nations.

This discussion has already provided numerous themes around which
to compare and contrast Marxism and nationalism. Yet another theme can
now be added. As people approached the challenges generated by the
Industrial Revolution in terms that were in one way or another informed
by the French Revolution, many of them realized that the two revolutions
implied different solutions to the question of authority and leadership in
society. The message of 1789 was of course liberty, equality, fraternity,
democracy, and sovereignty of the nation. The key questions raised by the
Industrial Revolution, however, concerned expert, specialist leadership:
They focused on the role of the manager, the scientist, the engineer, and
the entrepreneur. How was the economy's management by the bosses to
be reconciled with popular politics?

Marx thought that he had a solution for this problem, just as he had
for everything else, in his overall scheme of revolution. The liberals,
democrats, and conservatives also had their own ideas about who should
lead the nation, who should run the economy, and what the relationship
between politics and "civil society" should be. But so did the nationalists.

Bertrand Russell titled his history of the nineteenth century *Freedom
versus Organization, 1814–1914*, and explained in the preface that

> The purpose of this book is to trace the opposition and interaction of two
> main causes of change in the nineteenth century: the belief in FREEDOM
> which was common to Liberals and Radicals, and the necessity for OR-
> GANIZATION which arose through industrial and scientific technique.[20]

Nationalism—and here List is especially important and interesting—
had its own approach to the dilemmas created by the confrontation of
"freedom," the message of 1789, with "organization," the issue made
central by the rise of industry.

Although he did not put it in precisely these words, Alexander Gerschenkron touched on the same issue in a wider framework when in his
influential essay, "Economic Backwardness in Historical Perspective"
(1962), he evaluated the historical role of nationalism in general and of
List specifically. Gerschenkron argued that in England, where industrialization occurred first, rational arguments in favor of industrialization did

not need to be supported with "a quasi-religious fervor." However, in France, Germany, and Russia, which entered the path of industrialization after Britain, it was necessary to create "ideologies of delayed industrializations" as a "spiritual vehicle of an industrialization program"; a laissez-faire ideology was inadequate for that purpose. "In a backward country the great and sudden industrialization effort calls for a New Deal in emotions."

> To break through the barriers of stagnation in a backward country, to ignite the imaginations of men, and to place their energies in the service of economic development, a stronger medicine is needed than the promise of better allocation of resources or even of the lower price of bread. Under such conditions even the businessman, even the classical daring and innovating entrepreneur, needs a more powerful stimulus than the prospect of high profits. What is needed to remove the mountains of routine and prejudice is faith—faith, in the words of Saint-Simon, that the golden age lies not behind but ahead of mankind.[21]

According to Gerschenkron, the doctrines of Saint-Simon became the ideology of industrialization in France. (As we see, Gerschenkron does not lump England together with France under the colorless umbrella called "the West.") In Russia, Marxism assumed that role in the late nineteenth century, and in Germany, the doctrine of List served an analogous function.

> Friedrich List's industrialization theories may be largely conceived as an attempt, by a man whose personal ties to Saint-Simonians had been very strong, to translate the inspirational message of Saint-Simonism into a language that would be accepted in the German environment, where the lack of both a preceding political revolution and an early national unification rendered nationalist sentiment a much more suitable ideology of industrialization.[22]

Gerschenkron's scheme offers guidance on how one might handle some of the questions raised here, especially those regarding the historical role of nationalism and its interaction with Marxism. For Gerschenkron, nationalism and Marxism, along with the doctrine of Saint-Simon, were competing theories of industrialization and indeed were rival programs for a modern society.

If modern German historians had paid more attention to List and nationalism, and if they accordingly recognized that there has been a specifically nationalist response to the Industrial Revolution, they would not have blamed the German "bourgeoisie" for its alleged failure to act in conformity with what these historians assume was the only right way for the bourgeoisie to act. These scholars believe that under the original "Western" pattern of development the bourgeoisie had asserted itself firmly against feudalism and seized state power for itself, while the German bourgeoisie allegedly accommodated itself to the old regime, Junkers and all. In consequence, post–1871 Germany supposedly constituted a mixture of premodern politics with a modern economy. This German *Sonderweg* reflected a basic "abnormality" of nineteenth-century German history— and led straight to Hitler in the twentieth. David Blackbourn and Geoff Eley have subjected this ideological construct to a thorough scrutiny.[23]

For the purposes of our discussion, it is enough to note that the *Sonderweg* theory treats the history of a nation like Germany as an isolated and self-contained process. But if one remembers that the German bourgeoisie "saw its own future reflected" in Britain's "industrial prosperity,"[24] one will also recognize that the bourgeoisie believed its less developed country could attain that future only through competition with Britain. This, of course, required that it take this "external" factor into account in domestic politics as well, including the relations between classes, their economic goals, and political aspirations. Such was precisely the point List was making—and the one that Marx refused to recognize when in the 1840s he first formulated his charges against the German bourgeoisie. (See especially Chapters 3 and 4.) The alleged failure or betrayal of the German bourgeoisie was therefore a rational choice in an international framework.

Certain scholars before Gerschenkron also recognized List as a major figure in the history of nationalism and thought him important enough to merit comparison with Marx. As early as 1928, for example, Alfred Meusel published a comparative study of Marx and List.[25] Another scholar, Friedrich Lenz, the author of many List studies, discussed the economic theories of List and Marx in a book published in 1930.[26] Still another author, Karl Löwith, argued in 1941 that Hegel's "achievement in the study of history," "magnificent" though it had been, "was corrected in the nineteenth century by F. List and Marx, both of whom . . . sought with a quick grasp to shape their assumptions concerning the meaning for the world of the new technical and socioeconomic advances." Löwith agreed in his assessment of List with Johann Plenge, who in 1911 viewed List and Marx as the two thinkers who had responded to the realities of a new industrial age that had "shoved Hegel's system aside, showing more simple ways for thought."[27]

In more recent scholarship (1964), Eduard Heimann has also drawn attention to List as a key thinker deserving comparison with Marx. According to Heimann,

[List] did not content himself with making a general protest against the doctrine of free trade; he attacked it at its root. In fact, his criticism reads almost as if it were Marxian in inspiration. He did not discuss the validity of the theory *per se* or engage in what he regarded as a purely academic dispute about correct or faulty reasoning. Rather, he blamed the doctrine of free trade on the ground that it was inspired by special interests posing as the general interest, in other words, that it was what Marx later called an ideology.[28]

List criticized the classical school for purposely ignoring the fact that free trade among nations—which were of an unequal economic strength—affected them differently not only in economics but also in politics and culture. List's criticism of unequal relations between *nations* under free trade constituted, according to Heimann, a "precise parallel" to the criticism that Sismondi and, later, Marx raised regarding the impact of *domestic* laissez faire on individual *classes*.[29]

This is indeed a very important point that needs to be stressed: Like Marx, List believed that the economy remained in a close connection with politics, especially in the modern industrial era. List was an economist who not only saw a reciprocal connection between politics and economics but, like Marx, also linked economics to a broader intellectual structure, a *Weltanschauung* or an ideology, a view of history and society, and a program for the future. Unlike Marx, however, he constructed his *Weltanschauung* to reflect a *national*, not class-oriented, point of view.

At the same time, unlike other economic nationalists (about whom we shall speak later on), List based his program not on the state but on a "cultural nation"—that is, a community of language—for this was what the Germany of his time was. List recognized the role of the state, but that state was to be *national* first. On the basis of Germany's cultural identity, List advocated its economic modernization and political unification, and he accurately saw culture, politics, and economy as linked. For this reason, Hans Gehrig was right to call List the first among political economists who "wanted to raise through economic development a people that had been recognized as a cultural nation (*Kulturnation*) to a political nationhood."[30] There was nothing specifically "German" about List's doctrine. As Franz Schnabel observed, any people that wanted to become economically independent could use it.[31]

The distinguished List scholar, Edgar Salin, recognized this universal appeal and enduring relevance of List's ideas when, in 1962, he called him more topical and timely (*aktuell*) in our own time than ever before. On the occasion of the publication of his afterword to List's collected works (the Nazis had suppressed the afterword in 1935, when the final volume appeared), Salin recapitulated his assessment of List:

> No scholar of politics and no economist, with the exception of Tocqueville and Marx, had such a brilliant and prescient "insight into the future"—that is, into our present. Nobody should be writing about development of under-developed countries without first becoming an apprentice with that great forefather of the theory of growth and the politics of development.[32]

While we agree with these opinions, we go even further here: We argue that List's doctrine, linking culture, politics, and economy in a single comprehensive world view, comes closer than the thought of any other individual to capturing the essence of nationalism.

Friedrich Meinecke (1862–1954), Germany's foremost historian of the "idealist" school, considered socialism and nationalism to be "the two waves of the age" after the French Revolution, and he related their rise to the vast increase of population caused by the Industrial Revolution. Socialism was an ideology that enjoyed the support of the masses struggling for a better standard of living, said Meinecke, while nationalism "gathered its main body of adherents . . . from the educated middle class which was enriching itself." Meinecke thought that this middle class and its outlook had also been "a result of the transformations . . . which took place in the old European society after the end of the eighteenth century."[33]

Although he was out of sympathy with both, Meinecke admitted that the socialist and nationalist waves had each the right to claim "a deep historical justification": "They were . . . instinctive groping efforts to solve the human problems resulting from a population increase everywhere un-precedented in the history of the world."[34] Socialism, which had become a gospel for the masses, "surged up as a mighty wave which . . . swept over the traditional culture of the world." However, Meinecke pointed out that here also rose, in competition with socialism, "the second mighty wave"—the wave of nationalism.

> This second wave flooded crosswise over the first, more or less weakening or diverting it; its aim was not a fundamental social revolution but the increase of the political power of the nation. This second wave was none other than the nationalist movement of the nineteenth century.[35]

Salo Wittmayer Baron, the great historian of the Jewish religion, char-acterized the modern epoch in strikingly similar terms when he spoke of nationalism and class struggle as "determinant factors in the evolution of the modern world." Social revolution, he wrote, was "often dividing nations against themselves and transcending national boundaries." In its course, "it was vastly complicated by the simultaneous nationalist revolution, equally unprecedented in scope and intensity." Baron's further development of this idea offers a capsule overview of the agenda of this book:

> While the social revolution was growing ever more international in outlook and its most activist forces were marshaled under the flag of the socialist "International," the nationalist revolution was gaining some of its most substantial victories. In the name of the national principle Italy and Germany, long hopelessly divided, found a new unity and the map of Europe was constantly and forcibly redrawn. A new legitimacy was thereby secured for the most subversive and insurrectional movements in old and venerable empires embracing more than one nationality. Curiously, just when nationalism seemed to reach the apogee of its achievements, when during the First World War it succeeded in breaking up Austria-Hungary, Turkey, and Czarist Russia and in securing ever-wider recognition of the principle of "national self-determination," the socialist International achieved its first major victory in the Communist Revolution.[36]

If the argument presented here is valid, the conventional map of the correlation of intellectual and political forces in nineteenth-century Europe needs to be redrawn. This applies especially to the location of Marxism on that map. Conventionally, Marxism is seen as a challenge to classical political economy, which in turn is viewed as the ideology that legitimates the capitalist system. Marxism thus appears as a critique of capitalism from "within," a critique speaking on behalf of the society's underdog— the proletariat. What this approach overlooks is that historically Marxism was more than a critique of capitalist relations of production within one country. It was also a critique of nationality (and religion) and a program for the liberation of people from all "intermediate" identities that obstructed an individual's metamorphosis into a "world-historical personality." Marxism postulated the formation of the proletariat as a force that transcended national identities and that operated on a supranational scale. Because of this, from its earliest beginnings, Marxism viewed nationalism as a rival and an enemy.

Marxism's relationships—involving capitalism, communism, *and* national interests—were thus triangular, not bipolar, even though Marx himself and most of his followers understood nationalism as nothing more than an expression of the selfish economic interests of the bourgeoisie and denied that it represented a third party. But in reality, nationalism was such a third party on the battlefield where Marxism met capitalism. Nationalism was a response to the dominance of the advanced capitalist powers of the

West and a critique of the ideology of free trade in particular, and thus in a sense it was an ally of socialism. At the same time, however, it functioned as an alternative not only to classical, " cosmopolitan" capitalism but also to Marxism. As a rival of socialism, it promoted the formation of distinct national communities with their own economic and political interests—communities that emphatically included the workers. By doing so, it ran counter to the attempts of the socialists to build a solidarity of workers along supranational lines. When the Marxists condemned the state—any state, every state—as an instrument of class domination and prophesied that state's "withering away," the nationalists put forward the ideal of the national state.

Thus both Marxism *and* nationalism in the era between 1789 and 1917–1918 served, to repeat Lichtheim's phrase, as "the theory of one particular kind of revolutionary movement." Nationalism both interpreted the process of nation-building and was thus its "theoretical reflection"; at the same time, it functioned as the historical agent in that process. By analogy with Lichtheim's use of 1917 as the cutoff date in the history of Marxism, it is possible to see the years 1917–1918 as closing an epoch in the history of European nationalism as well. In that period, Marxism confronted nationalism, and Marxism evolved in that confrontation. At the same time, nationalism faced the challenge of Marxism and was in turn influenced by it.

# Part One

# 2

# Marx and Germany: The "Hegel Critique"

What was Marx's philosophical and political outlook in 1845 when he wrote his critique of List? Were his views already "Marxist" in the sense in which Marxism has been understood historically?

According to Engels, this was indeed the case: by then Marx had formulated the fundamental proposition that forms the nucleus of *The Communist Manifesto*. Writing in 1888, Engels claimed that by about 1845 Marx had reached the view that "in every historical epoch, the prevailing mode of economic production and exchange, and the social organization necessarily following from it, form the basis upon which is built up, and from which alone can be explained, the political and intellectual history of that epoch."

From this Marx further concluded, according to Engels, that "consequently the whole history of mankind . . . has been a history of class struggles, contests between exploiting and exploited, ruling and oppressed classes." Having thus satisfied himself about the nature of society—or we might say, having diagnosed both its "anatomy" or "morphology" (the interrelation of economic, social, political, and intellectual spheres), as well as its dynamics (the driving forces and direction of history)—Marx reached a comprehensive view about the synthesis of history and society. Specifically, he concluded that

> the history of these class struggles forms a series of evolutions in which, nowadays, a stage has been reached when the exploited and oppressed class—the proletariat—cannot attain its emancipation from the sway of the exploiting and ruling class—the bourgeoisie—without at the same time, and

once and for all, emancipating society at large from all exploitation, oppression, class distinctions, and class struggles.[1]

Thus on a diagnosis of the present that was based on an interpretation of the past, Marx formulated a program whose realization would constitute a leap into an entirely new stage in the history of humanity.

In an article written in 1885, Engels also recalled that by 1844 Marx had arrived at the view that

speaking generally, it is not the state which conditions and regulates civil society, but civil society which conditions and regulates the state, and consequently, that policy and its history are to be explained from the economic relations and their development, and not vice versa.[2]

A vast literature exists on the young Marx, on "Marx before Marxism" (to cite the title of a book by David McLellan), which traces the sources of Marx's political, philosophical, and economic views. Although these broader issues of Marx's outlook must be considered, we wish in this volume to clarify Marx's stand on nation and nationalism in particular. Let us focus, then, on those specific writings that help us to do so, but beforehand, two points relating to Marx's thought must be addressed.

First, in the early stage of his philosophical and political development, Marx had argued that his critique of the contemporary society was not a product of philosophical speculation but, on the contrary, something he arrived at by observing the existing conditions. Such a critique, accordingly, did not require philosophical system-building, nor the imposition of something external, but was a logical conclusion from what he saw, by just looking at the reality closely.[3] In that early critical period, Marx had not yet discovered the proletariat as the material force charged by history with the task of liberating man. As Leszek Kolakowski has pointed out, Marx's subsequent choice of the proletariat as that class which would liberate itself and society as a whole was the result of a "philosophical deduction rather than a product of observation."[4]

Second, the study of political economy came later; for Marx, the economy became the proving ground, the material base on which the realization of a philosophical project would be carried out. In 1842–1843 Marx had not yet become familiar with political economy, even though he claimed in 1859 that his concern with it had dated back to the time when he edited the *Rheinische Zeitung* (October 1842–March 1843). Marx allegedly had been concerned at that time with the debates on free trade and protection, but he wrote nothing on that particular topic. As Michael Evans notes, however, it is a little surprising that the editor of a liberal newspaper, the editorship of which had first been offered to Friedrich List, should have had nothing to say about the controversy inspired by List's defence of protection in his book *Das nationale System der politischen Ökonomie* published in May 1841.

Evans adds that Marx first refers to List in his "Contribution to the Critique of Hegel's *Philosophy of Right*: Introduction" (end of 1843–January 1844) and that only in March 1845 did Marx write his critique of List.[5] Thus it was at the time when he read List that Marx began to study seriously the problems of political economy. Paradoxically enough, Marx was introduced to political economy not by reading the Western classics on the subject, but by their chief German critic. As Gareth Stedman Jones notes, "until his unfinished essay on List, written early in 1845, Marx's references to modern industry had been cursory and descriptive."[6]

There are several reasons why, of the early works of Marx, "A Contribution to the Critique of Hegel's *Philosophy of Right*: Introduction" is uniquely suited for our purposes. It marks a major step in Marx's formulation of his mature position on the relationship between politics, law, philosophy, and economics. It is the first of Marx's works to assign to the proletariat the role of the liberator. It also shows how Marx treated the nation—in this important case, Germany—within what was to him a larger and more meaningful unit, that of "modern society" or "civilization." Finally, the "Contribution" is especially important to our project because it is the first work of Marx that alludes to the name of Friedrich List. Hereafter, we shall refer to it as the "Hegel Critique," even though there exists another, much longer work called "Contribution to the Critique of Hegel's *Philosophy of Right*," which might be confused with it.[7]

As Maximilien Rubel and Margaret Manale have noted, it is in the "Hegel Critique" that "Marx speaks for the first time of the proletarian 'class' and of the 'formation' of an industrial working class which is to act as a social emancipatory force," and therefore this work "represents, in a sense, the germ of the future *Communist Manifesto*."[8] Rubel and Manale further stress that this essay contains a "sociological" analysis of religion, the state, and law "as elements of the social superstructure."

> Religion is the point of departure and man the orientation for this discourse. It is man who creates religion, Marx began, and not vice versa: religion is man's theory of the world and his fantastic self-realization because he lives under conditions which prohibit him from realizing himself in the real world.[9]

They comment that just as Marx recommended that the "critique" of religion should be carried out by means of an analysis of the *real* world conditions, he also thought one should criticize the theory of the state and of right in the same manner. Marx did precisely that in his discourse on German philosophy and on German conditions.[10]

All these considerations justify extensive use of the "Hegel Critique." Marx began by saying that the criticism of religion, which "for Germany has been largely completed," "is the premise of all criticism."

> The basis of irreligious criticism is this: *man makes religion*; religion does not make man. Religion is indeed man's self-consciousness and self-aware-ness so long as he has not found himself or has lost himself again. But *man* is not an abstract being, squatting outside the world. Man is *the human world*, the state, society. This state, this society, produce religion which is an *inverted world consciousness*, because they are an *inverted world*. Re-ligion is the general theory of this world. . . . It is the *fantastic realization* of the human being inasmuch as the *human being* possesses no true reality. The struggle against religion is, therefore, indirectly a struggle against *that world* whose spiritual *aroma* is religion.[11]

This was immediately followed by that well-known passage in which Marx called religion "the opium of the people," and then by the declaration that "the abolition of religion as the *illusory* happiness of men, is the demand for their *real* happiness." Marx compared religion to the "illusory sun about which man revolves so long as he does not revolve about himself."

> It is the *task of history*, therefore, once the *other-world of truth* has vanished, to establish the *truth of this world*. The immediate *task of philosophy*, which is in the service of history, is to unmask human self-alienation in its *secular form* now that it has been unmasked in its *sacred form*. Thus the criticism of heaven is transformed into the criticism of earth, the *criticism of religion* into the criticism of law, and the *criticism of theology* into the *criticism of politics*.[12]

This was a very sweeping (not to mention ambitious) declaration of the importance of "history" and "philosophy" in the task of liberating man from "human self-alienation." Let us see where Germany fit in this overall endeavor.

As we shall see, Marx did not limit himself to making a general statement on the relation between politics, history, religion, and philos-ophy. He also analyzed the conditions in Germany and drew certain specific guidelines for practical action *there*. He explained that his work did not deal "directly with the original but with a copy, the German philosophy of the state and of right," precisely because it dealt with Germany.[13]

This was so because for Marx the fundamental fact was the backwardness of Germany. To deal with the status quo in Germany, he said, was to deal with an *anachronism*. Germany was lagging behind.

> Even the negation of our political present is already a dusty fact in the historical lumber room of modern nations. . . . If I negate the German situation of 1843 I have, according to French chronology, hardly reached the year 1789, and still less the vital centre of the present day.[14]

What conclusions did Marx draw from this fact of Germany's backwardness in social, economic, political, and cultural spheres? What prospects were there for liberation? Was there a solution for the problem, and if so, what was it?

One thing becomes evident very early in the argument. Marx did not believe in a specifically *German* solution of the German problem; rather, he compared Germany with the West. The struggle of the *ancien régime* against "a new world" in the advanced countries of the West had been "tragic," Marx said, because "there was on its side a historical error but no personal error." But the "present German regime," Germany's "modern *ancien régime*," is "the comedian of a world order whose *real heroes* are dead." To develop a critique of "modern social and political reality" and thus to arrive at "genuine political problems," one would have to "go outside the German status quo or approach its object indirectly."[15]

It was in this context that Marx commented in the "Hegel Critique" on Friedrich List's proposals for tariff protection for German industry. According to Marx, List (whom he did not name, except by means of a pun) showed what happened when one did *not* go "outside the German status quo" but instead tried to work out some specifically German solutions about what Marx thought was the central and universal problem of modern society (not just Germany): "The relation of industry, of the world of wealth in general, to the political world is a major problem of modern times." Marx continued:

> In what form does this problem begin to preoccupy the Germans? In the form of *protective tariffs*, the *system of prohibition*, the *national economy*. German chauvinism had passed from men to matter, so that one fine day our knights of cotton and heroes of iron found themselves metamorphosed into patriots. The sovereignty of monopoly within the country has begun to be recognized since *sovereignty vis-à-vis foreign countries* was attributed to it. In Germany, therefore, a beginning is made with what came as the conclusion in France and England. The old, rotten order against which these nations revolt in their theories, and which they bear only as chains are borne, is hailed in Germany as the dawn of a glorious future which as yet hardly dares to move from a cunning [in German: *listigen*, which is a pun on the name of List] theory to a ruthless practice. While in France and England

the problem is put in the form: *political economy* or the *rule of society over wealth;* in Germany it is put in the form: *national economy* or the *rule of private property over nationality.* Thus, in England and France it is a question of abolishing monopoly, which has developed to its final consequences; while in Germany it is a question of proceeding to the final consequences of monopoly. There it is a question of the solution; here, only a question of the collision. We can see very well from this example how modern problems are presented in Germany; the example shows that our history, like a raw recruit, has so far only had to do extra drill on old and hackneyed historical matters.[16]

The point of this elaborate diatribe can be summarized in simple, non-"Hegelian" language: It means that according to Marx, the abolition of the capitalist system in England and France had entered "the agenda," while in Germany people like List were trying to establish a capitalist system, pretending at the same time to be working for Germany's national independence, especially her economic independence. In the West, the "nations revolt in their theories" against what they perceive as the "old, rotten order"; in Germany, that order is not yet established.

Marx clearly believed that the program of establishing a *German* version of the system that in the West was already viewed as an obstacle to further development, as "chains," was a reflection of the backwardness of Germany. He hurried to point out that not everything in Germany remained on the low level of her *political* development. "If the *whole* of German development were at the level of German *political* development, a German could have no greater part in contemporary problems than can a *Russian.*" However, the Germans were not as backward as *that.* Unlike the Russians (whom by implication Marx excluded as participants in the world-historical process), the Germans were

> *philosophical* contemporaries of the present day without being its *historical* contemporaries. . . . When . . . we criticize, instead of *oeuvres incomplètes* of our real history, the *oeuvres posthumes* of our ideal history—*philosophy*, our criticism stands at the centre of the problems of which the present age says: *that is the question.* That which constitutes, for the advanced nations, a *practical* break with modern political conditions, is in Germany where these conditions do not yet exist, virtually a *critical* break with their philosophical reflection.
>
> The German *philosophy of right and of the state* is the only German history which is *al pari* with the *official* modern times.[17]

This striking statement deserves to be remembered, but unfortunately has often been overlooked by writers and followers of Marx. To paraphrase, he thought an economically and politically backward Germany had the most up-to-date philosophy. The *political* and practical conclusions Marx drew were based precisely on this backward character of the German "reality" *and* on the advanced level attained by German philosophy. The lesson Marx extracted from this condition of the "contemporaneity" of German philosophy with the advanced developments elsewhere was that Germany might as well go *beyond* trying to adjust its political and social conditions to the level attained by its philosophy (and the political order achieved in the advanced countries).

> The German nation is obliged, therefore, to connect its dream history with its present conditions, and to subject to criticism not only these existing conditions but also their abstract continuation. Its future cannot be restricted either to the direct negation of its real juridical and political circumstances, or to the direct realization of its ideal juridical and political circumstances. The direct negation of its real circumstances already exists in its ideal circumstances, while it has almost outlived the realization of its ideal circumstances in the contemplation of neighboring nations. It is with good reason, therefore, that the *practical* political party in Germany demands the *negation of philosophy*.[18]

The last sentence in the above quotation helps clarify Marx's further point about the need for "the *practical* political party" to understand that one "*cannot abolish philosophy without realizing it.*" At the same time, Marx pointed out that another philosophical school (equally mistakenly) "*believed that it could realize philosophy without abolishing it.*"[19] In Germany, neither of these procedures was sufficient alone. Because in politics "the Germans have *thought* what other nations have *done*" and thus "Germany has been their theoretical consciousness," Marx concluded that "the *status quo* of *German political science* expresses the *imperfection of the modern state* itself, the degeneracy of its flesh." On the other hand, the German political system represents "the consummation of the *ancien régime.*"[20] To interject once again, German "reality" remained behind that existing in the advanced countries, but *Marx's* thought had already advanced not only beyond Western ideas but also beyond those advanced conditions and even beyond the German philosophy that, according to Marx, was *al pari* with those conditions.

We would be digressing from our theme—though to do so would be intellectually attractive—if we pursued Marx's argument on the reasons why "the criticism of the speculative philosophy of right . . . leads on to *tasks* which can only be solved by *means of practical activity.*" For our proper topic, two points matter here. First, Marx says that it is asked: "Can Germany attain a practical activity *à la hauteur des principes*; that is to say, a revolution which will raise it not only to the *official level* of the modern nations, but to the *human level* which will be the immediate future of those nations?''[21] Second, Marx answers this question by stating that because in Germany "the *civilized deficiencies* of the *modern political world* (whose advantages we do not enjoy)" are combined with "the *barbarian deficiencies* of the *ancien régime* (which we enjoy in full measure),"

> *Germany, as the deficiency of present-day politics constituted into a system*, will not be able to demolish the specific German barriers without demolishing the general barriers of present-day politics.[22]

Translated from philosophical into practical language, this means that Marx advocated a revolution in Germany that would not simply aim at Germany's "catching up with the advanced nations of the West," so to speak, but would also perform the same task that even the advanced nations still had *ahead* of them at that moment: the liberation of men as *human* beings, not just a political liberation.

Superficially, it might seem that by posing the problem in this manner Marx wanted Germany not only to catch up with but also to surpass the leading nations. If our reading of his essay is correct, however, this was not his intention. Marx was concerned not with the liberation of Germans as Germans but with their liberation as human beings: "It is not *radical* revolution, *universal human* emancipation, which is a Utopian dream for Germany, but rather a partial, *merely* political revolution which leaves the pillars of the building standing."[23]

He argued that in Germany, unlike in France, the conditions for "a partial, merely political revolution" did not exist. In "merely political" revolutions such as those that took place in France, "a *section of civil society* emancipates itself and attains universal domination." This happens when a certain class "undertakes, from its *particular situation*, a general emancipation of society" and "emancipates society as a whole." For such an event to occur, "the whole of society" must be "in the same situation as this class."[24] The following quotation presents Marx's definition of the preconditions for such a partial political emancipation:

> For a *popular revolution* and the *emancipation of a particular class* of civil society to coincide, for *one* class to represent the whole of society, another class must concentrate in itself all the evils of society, a particular class must embody and represent a general obstacle and limitation. A particular social sphere must be regarded as the *notorious crime* of the whole society, so that emancipation from this sphere appears as a general emancipation. For *one* class to be the liberating class *par excellence*, it is necessary that another class should be openly the oppressing class. The negative signifi-

cance of the French nobility and clergy produced the positive significance of the *bourgeoisie*, the class which stood next to them and opposed them.[25]

In Germany, such conditions did not exist because no class was capable of acting as "a negative representative of society," and every class lacked that "generosity of spirit which identifies itself, if only for a moment, with the popular mind; that genius which pushes material force to political power, that revolutionary daring which throws at its adversary the defiant phrase: *I am nothing and I should be everything*."[26]

The German middle class, Marx further pointed out, did not dare "to conceive the idea of emancipation from its own point of view," because "the development of social conditions and the progress of political theory show that this point of view is already antiquated, or at least disputable."[27] Marx thus explicitly intimated that the German bourgeoisie somehow (but very realistically, according to him) sensed that its cause had already become *passé* without having ever triumphed.

Marx did not really explain (at least not in the reading of his work presented here) *why* the German bourgeoisie was so fatally incapacitated. One has to conclude that Marx's overall *historical* judgment was simply a deduction from his philosophical principles, his teleology, in which the perfect force of liberation, i.e., the proletariat, had to be contrasted with an opponent lacking any virtues whatsoever, i.e., the German bourgeoisie.

In France, according to Marx, the role of the liberator passes from one class to another "until it finally reaches the class which achieves social freedom," i.e., the proletariat. The proletariat organizes human life on the basis of social freedom, unlike its predecessors, who assumed "certain conditions external to man." In Germany, on the other hand, no social class "feels the need for, or the ability to achieve, a general emancipation." This led him to ask the central question, "where is there, then, a *real* possibility of emancipation in Germany?"

> *This is our reply*. A class must be formed which has *radical chains*, a class in civil society which is not a class of civil society, a class which is the dissolution of all classes, a sphere of society which has a universal character because its sufferings are universal, and which does not claim a *particular redress* because the wrong which is done to it is not a *particular wrong* but *wrong in general*. There must be formed a sphere of society which claims no *traditional* status but only a human status, a sphere which is not opposed to particular consequences but is totally opposed to the assumptions of the German political system; a sphere, finally, which cannot emancipate itself without emancipating itself from all the other spheres of society, without, therefore, emancipating all these other spheres, which is, in short, a *total loss* of humanity and which can only redeem itself by a

*total redemption of humanity*. This dissolution of society, as a particular class, is the *proletariat*.[28]

Marx acknowledged that the proletariat was only beginning to form in Germany under the impact of industrial development. Using terms widely current in the 1840s in literature devoted to the question of "pauperism" (*Pauperismus*), Marx defined or described the proletariat as "poverty *artificially produced*, . . . the mass resulting from the *disintegration* of society, and above all from the disintegration of the middle class."[29] But despite the proletariat's relative youth and evident and overwhelming weakness, Marx was optimistic. He did *not* say that the proletariat was as yet not ready to address itself to the fundamental questions of the times. On the contrary, Marx emphatically affirmed the crucial role the proletariat would play and the universal mission it would perform in liberating humanity.

> When the proletariat announces the *dissolution of the existing social order*, it only declares the secret of its own existence, for it *is* the *effective* dissolution of this order. When the proletariat demands the *negation of private property* it only lays down as a *principle for society* what society has already made a principle *for the proletariat*, and what the *latter* already involuntarily embodies as the negative result of society. Thus the proletarian has the same right, in relation to the new world which is coming into being, as the *German king* has in relation to the existing world when he calls the people *his* people or a horse *his* horse. In calling the people his private property the king simply declares that the owner of private property is king.
>
> Just as philosophy finds its *material* weapons in the proletariat, so the proletariat finds its *intellectual* weapons in philosophy. And once the lightning of thought has penetrated deeply into this virgin soil of the people, the *Germans* will emancipate themselves and become *men* [i.e., human beings].[30]

Marx concluded that this kind of emancipation was "only possible *in practice* if one adopts the point of view of that theory according to which man is the highest being for man"—that is, communism. Germany's emancipation from the "Middle Ages" would be possible only if it emancipated itself also "from the *partial* victories over the Middle Ages," which presumably meant the kind of political development that had taken place in France through a succession of revolutions.

> In Germany *no* type of enslavement can be abolished unless *all* enslavement is destroyed. Germany, which likes to get to the bottom of things, can only make a revolution which upsets *the whole order* of things. The *emancipation of the German* is the *emancipation of the human being*. *Philosophy* is the *head* of this emancipation and the *proletariat* is its *heart*. Philosophy

can only be realized by the abolition of the proletariat, and the proletariat can only be abolished by the realization of philosophy.

When all the inner conditions ripen, *the day of German resurrection will be proclaimed by the crowing of the Gallic cock.*[31]

In other words, as Robert Tucker has observed (and all commentators on Marx agree), the last sentence means that "the future German revolution will be sparked by revolutionary developments in France."[32]

Although Marx linked the German revolution to the revolution in France and by implication made it a part of the international revolution he was to envision in later work, the "Hegel Critique" came closer than any of his writings to advancing the idea of some kind of "socialism in one country," a "national communism," perhaps. What would happen, one wants to ask, if the communist seizure of power in Germany had occurred *without* revolution in the West? Such questions are understandable in light of the Russian experience after 1917. However, there is no basis for supposing that Marx expected, let alone favored, such an outcome. As we shall see, he considered the proletariat to be a universal, supranational, and cosmopolitan force, quite unlike any class previously known in history. And let us also not forget the obvious: In the "Hegel Critique," Marx did not say a word in favor of an "emancipation" of "Germany" that would realize any German nationalistic goals, such as establishment of a single state in place of the then existing thirty-eight Germanies. Instead he was after the abolition of *the state.*

# 3

# Marx and Germany: The "List Critique"

While the "Hegel Critique" reveals Marx's vision of the liberation of man within the specific historical context of Germany in her relation to England and France, the "List Critique" provides a detailed elaboration of the Marxian position on the German Question by focusing specifically on German nationalism. We learn from it what Marx thought of his "competition" insofar as the making of plans for Germany's future was concerned; it goes without saying at this time that German nationalism produced its own ideas on what kind of liberation the Germans needed.

As we shall see, Marx perceived nationalism as a bourgeois ideology and viewed List as a spokesman for the German bourgeoisie, which had its own vision of the future and was working for its realization. What did Marx think about that vision and about the prospects of its realization?

According to the "List Critique," the aim of the German bourgeois, as represented by List, was to establish the domination of "industry," by which, at that time, Marx meant particularly *capitalist* industry or capitalism in general. However, Marx continued, the German bourgeois was doing this "precisely at the unsuitable moment when the slavery of the majority resulting from this domination has become a generally known fact." The German bourgeois had not yet "achieved the development of industry," but a proletariat did exist that "already advances claims, and already inspires fear." The "awareness of the death of the bourgeoisie has already penetrated the consciousness even of the German bourgeois," Marx claimed. In one of his literary references, Marx said: "The German bourgeois is [like] the *knight of the rueful countenance*, who wanted to introduce knight-errantry just when the police and money had come to the fore.''[1]

As we have observed, Marx was aware of the backwardness of Germany in relation to the West. He thought that such backwardness revealed itself in the poverty of political aspirations and intellectual outlook of the German bourgeoisie. Let us note at the outset that there is not the slightest hint anywhere in the ''List Critique'' that a ''national bourgeoisie,'' because it fought for capitalism in a backward country still dominated by feudalism, might therefore be progressive and thus deserving of support on the part of Communists. As the ''Hegel Critique'' has shown us, Marx anticipated what his successors, such as Trotsky, Lenin, and their late-twentieth-century followers, would much later call ''uneven development,'' from which they would draw political conclusions that justified tactical alliances with their own national bourgeoisie against imperialism. To repeat, Marx did account for all those phenomena that fifty (or more) years later, at the turn of the twentieth century, his followers would present as something new and that therefore demanded a different treatment from that recommended by ''the classics,'' i.e., Marx and Engels in their later, mature years.

The ''List Critique'' shows us that Marx, writing in 1845, was absolutely merciless in his assessment of the German bourgeoisie. It is clear that his comments on the German case reveal more than just his stand on the German Question in a certain specific moment. Two long quotations express his position better than any summary or paraphrase could hope to do. The first quotation places the German bourgeoisie in a comparative setting with the West and proclaims that in principle a backward country like Germany cannot make an original contribution to the development of economic thought.

> The German bourgeois comes on this scene *post festum* . . . it is just as impossible for him to advance further the political economy exhaustively developed by the English and French as it would probably be for them to contribute anything new to the development of philosophy in Germany. The German bourgeois can only add his illusions and phrases to the French and English reality. But little possible as it is for him to give a new development to political economy, it is still more impossible for him to achieve in practice a further advance of industry, of the by now almost exhausted development on the present foundations of society.[2]

Thus, a priori, Marx dismissed as reactionary all attempts, such as those of List, to develop an economic theory that reflected the national needs of less developed countries in their transition to capitalism and in their opposition to advanced capitalist countries.

The above passage both denies the possibility that an independent theoretical contribution could be made by German economists adhering to the principle of capitalist political economy and rejects the prospect that Germany could become a capitalist country. As his comments on Western conditions reveal, Marx also thought that the transition to communism would be the next historical task, but that it could not take place "in one country" alone. The following passage summarizes Marx's view of the historical process, which was to him a universal, worldwide process in which humankind was the agent.

> To hold that every nation goes through this development [of liberation from capitalism] internally would be as absurd as the idea that every nation is bound to go through the political development of France or the philosophical development of Germany. What the nations have done as nations, they have done for human society; their whole value consists only in the fact that each single nation has accomplished for the benefit of other nations one of the main historical aspects (one of the main determinations) in the framework of which mankind has accomplished its development, and therefore after industry in England, politics in France and philosophy in Germany have been developed, they have been developed for the world, and their world-historic significance, as also that of these nations, has thereby come to an end.[3]

Marx did not admit the possibility of a national road to capitalism, which List was trying to find, and had nothing to say in favor of socialism in one country, because capitalism and communism were worldwide systems and could be treated only in a supranational setting. Marx's basic argument, therefore, was that it is pointless to ask such questions as, "At what stage of development is Germany in comparison to France or England?" and "What should the Germans do in order to attain England's stage of economic or political development?"

As one ponders the passage just cited, one is tempted to exclaim: "If only the Russians had known this! They would surely have saved themselves the argument about whether it was possible or not for their country to skip stages in its historical development!" Indeed, they would have saved themselves this argument, but only if they had first given up their concern for Russia and had thought of themselves as members of the entire human race. In that case, the question of Russia's standing in comparison with Germany or France would not have arisen, and nobody would have thought of Russian solutions to Russian problems.

List, unlike Marx, based his entire argument on the idea that nations are the basic units into which the human race is divided and that they develop by passing through clearly definable stages. List recognized that a nation's evolution was vitally affected by its relations with other nations, and in this sense his history was indeed global or international, but he insisted that a nation that wanted to survive as an independent entity had to "[go] through this development internally." In other words, it had to do precisely what Marx thought was an "absurd" idea to do.

On List's premises, it was imperative to compare Germany's level of development with that attained by England and to view Germany as (to use a contemporary term) a "developing country" that was suffering economically and politically as a party engaged in "unequal exchange" with a highly developed England. Thus List viewed the German problem in an international context that included countries in various stages of development—that is, *Germany*, on the one hand, and England, so far the only fully modern country, on the other.

To Marx, the problem was completely different; *capitalism*, which he called "industry" (a term he used in a socioeconomic rather than a technological sense), was the real exploiter, not England.

> England's industrial tyranny over the world is the domination of industry over the world. England dominates us because industry dominates us. We can free ourselves from England abroad only if we free ourselves from industry at home. We shall be able to put an end to England's domination in the sphere of competition only if we overcome competition within our borders. England has power over us because we have made industry into a power over us.[4]

Marx went on to say that the German bourgeois, for selfish reasons of course, advanced a completely different interpretation of the problem when fighting against the English and French bourgeoisie. The German bourgeois did so under the name of "nationality," but to Marx "nationality" was a fraud and a disguise for the capitalist's cynical materialism. Marx thought that List's theory was an attempt to modify the principles of political economy and their application in relations between developed and developing countries (these terms are anachronistic but their meaning fully corresponds to what List was arguing), for the advantage of the latter, particularly Germany. (This modification involved the idea of national interest as something that was distinct from the interest of the individual capitalist or indeed from the class as a whole.) Marx characterized the attempts to bring in "higher principles" in the following way:

> The German idealizing philistine who wants to become wealthy must, of course, first create for himself a new theory of wealth, one which makes wealth worthy of his striving for it. The bourgeois in France and England see the approach of the storm which will destroy in practice the *real* life of

what had hitherto been called wealth, but the German bourgeois, who has
not yet arrived at this inferior wealth, tries to give a new, "spiritualistic"
interpretation of it. He creates for himself an "idealizing" political economy,
which has nothing in common with profane French and English political
economy, in order to justify to himself and the world that he, too, wants to
become wealthy. The German bourgeois begins his creation of wealth with
the creation of a high-flown hypocritically idealizing political economy.[5]

With List's various protectionist measures in mind, Marx further argued
that the "German philistine" wanted "the laws of competition, of exchange value, of huckstering, to lose their power at the frontier barriers
of his country!" The German bourgeois accepted

the power of bourgeois society only insofar as it is in accord with *his interests*,
the interests of his class! He does not want to fall victim to a power to which
he wants to *sacrifice* others, and to which he sacrifices himself inside his
own country! Outside the country he wants to show himself and be treated
as a different being from what he is within the country and how he himself
behaves within the country! He wants to leave the *cause* in existence and
to abolish one of its *effects*![6]

Marx saw List's simultaneous support of free trade *within* a united
Germany and defense of external tariffs as contradictory: The "German
philistine" wants to exploit the proletarians of his country, "but he wants
also not to be exploited outside the country." The idea of "nation" did
the trick:

He puffs himself up into being the "nation" in relation to foreign countries
and says: I do not submit to the laws of competition; this is contrary to my
national dignity; as the nation I am being superior to huckstering. . . . Within
the country, money is the fatherland of the industrialist.[7]

Marx found this impossible; the German bourgeois must understand
that "selling oneself out inside the country has as its necessary consequence
selling out outside." Marx questioned whether the state, which the bourgeois wants to subordinate to himself inside the country, would be able
to "protect him from the action of bourgeois society outside the country."[8]
This subject of economic power inside and outside a country raised
the broader question of whether the bourgeoisie as a class had common
interests that transcended national boundaries, and if so, what those interests were. Marx responded by saying that the general interests of the
bourgeoisie were identical interests; as a class, they were "just as the *wolf*
as a *wolf* has an identical interest with his fellow wolves, however much
it is to the interest of each individual wolf that he and not another should
pounce on the prey."[9]

> However much the individual bourgeois fights against the others, as a *class* the bourgeois have a common interest, and this community of interest, which is directed against the proletariat inside the country, is directed against the bourgeois of other nations outside the country. This the bourgeois calls his *nationality*.[10]

But Marx did not specify how and why it should be possible for *some* bourgeois to agree on a common interest against *other* bourgeois, and why the basis for union and separation should be nationality, for example, German nationality. Obviously, an economic factor was not the only determinant of national unity. Had Marx admitted as much, he would have recognized that nationality could not be wholly reduced to class economic interests. He preferred not to allow that there was more to the unity of the German nation than the selfish class interest of the German bourgeoisie. But had he been consistent, he would have recognized that a segment of the bourgeoisie defined *nationally* could not have an identical *economic* interest against the rest of that class. Surely *some* German bourgeois actually benefited from a free-trade relationship with foreign countries even if free trade hurt *other* (perhaps most) German capitalists? If the former sacrificed their *economic* advantage in the name of *national* interest, were they acting primarily out of *class* motivations?

Marx did not ask such questions. When he compared "the German bourgeois" with a wolf among wolves, or with a pack of wolves competing with other packs of wolves for (the proletarian) prey, he did not think it possible that one day the "German wolves" might make a deal with their fellow German "sheep" against foreign "wolves" and "sheep." He did not envisage the proletariat succumbing to nationalistic temptations proffered by the bourgeoisie. The "List Critique" mentioned no such possibility. On the contrary, it contained the following categorical declaration:

> The nationality of the worker is neither French, nor English, nor German, it is *labour, free slavery, self-huckstering*. His government is neither French, nor English, nor German, it is *capital*. His native air is neither French, nor German, nor English, it is *factory air*. The land belonging to him is neither French, nor English, nor German, it lies a few feet *below the ground*.[11]

This is as explicit a statement on the nature of the proletariat's relationship to nation as anyone could ask for, and it deserves to be elevated to the status of the better known words on the same subject in *The Communist Manifesto*.

However, Marx's comments on the relation of the bourgeoisie in a backward country (such as Germany in the 1840s) to the ideology of nationalism are no less significant. He claimed, as we have noted, that nationalism is the viewpoint of the bourgeoisie in a backward country that wants to be protected from the more advanced and more powerful bourgeoisie abroad. This bourgeoisie wants freedom to exploit the proletariat at home without having to compete in such exploitation with foreign bourgeoisie. The motives of the "national" bourgeoisie are thus presented as completely "materialistic" and selfish. Its ideas and ideals are a cover-up for the drive for money, for wealth—"money is the fatherland of the industrialist." Theories such as List's are ideological masquerades deliberately set up to mislead. The ideology of the German bourgeoisie as represented by List is full of "spiritual" talk about principles, religion, and the sacrifice for the common good. But in fact, Marx felt, the policies recommended by List would allow the German bourgeois "to *exploit* his *fellow countrymen*, indeed exploit them even *more* than they were exploited from abroad," because protective tariffs require sacrifices from the consumers.[12]

Marx observed that List's theory was designed, among other purposes, to convince the ruling class "whose permission the German bourgeois thinks he requires for his emancipation."[13] Marx thus acknowledged that since in Germany the bourgeoisie did not control the state, it needed the support of those in power: "The bourgeois wants protective tariffs from the state in order to lay his hands on state power and wealth." Marx was not taken in by List's willingness to recognize the state as a guiding force in the nation's economic life; he viewed it as a ruse on the bourgeoisie's part. Precisely because in Germany, "unlike in England and France, he [the bourgeois] does not have state power at his disposal and therefore cannot arbitrarily guide it as he likes," the bourgeois "has to resort to requests, [and] it is necessary for him in relation to the state, the activity (mode of operation) of which he wants to control for his own benefit, to depict his demand from it as a *concession* that he makes to the state, whereas [in reality] he demands *concessions* from the state."[14]

> Therefore, through the medium of Herr List, he [the German bourgeois] proves to the state that his theory differs from all others in that he allows the state to interfere in and control industry, in that he has the highest opinion of the economic wisdom of the state, and only asks it to give full scope for its wisdom, on condition, of course, that this wisdom is limited to providing "strong" protective tariffs. His demand that the state should act in accordance with his interests is depicted by him as recognition of the state, recognition that the state has the right to interfere in the sphere of civil society.[15]

In this respect, too, the behavior of the German bourgeoisie was quite unlike that of the West European bourgeoisie, and as expected, was very unflattering to the Germans: "What would have become of the English and French bourgeoisie if it had first to ask a high-ranking nobility, an esteemed bureaucracy and the ancient ruling dynasties for permission to give 'industry' the 'force of law'?"[16]

Marx further contrasted List's "humble attitude to the nobility, the ancient ruling dynasties and the bureaucracy" with his "audacious" opposition to the French and English political economy. List opposed the English because, headed by Adam Smith, they "cynically betrayed the *secret* of 'wealth' and made impossible all illusions about its nature, tendency, and movement." In other words, Western political economy, however bourgeois, was too honest for the taste of the German hypocrite. "For since the German bourgeois is concerned with protective tariffs, the whole development of political economy since Smith has, of course, no meaning for him, because all its most outstanding representatives presuppose the present-day bourgeois society of competition and free trade."[17]

In Marx's opinion, the Listian argument about the national interest and the development of "productive forces" constituted a retrogression, a retreat from the intellectual and analytical levels attained by the bourgeois political economy of Adam Smith. Marx noted approvingly that the earlier "scientific spokesmen of political economy," having spoken for the English and French bourgeoisie with a "frank, classic cynicism," had "elevated wealth into a god and ruthlessly sacrificed everything else to it, this Moloch, in science, as well." This stood in sharp contrast to "the idealizing, phrase-mongering, bombastic manner of Herr List, who in the midst of political economy despises the wealth of 'righteous men' and knows loftier aims."[18] To repeat our earlier comment, Marx gave no hint that what List proposed to do in Germany might be progressive or relatively progressive in view of Germany's backward condition as compared with Britain or France. (Marx changed his view on this score in the 1860s–1870s, however, when he accepted the fact that Germany would become a capitalist country.)

Marx thought that the German bourgeoisie's goal was to attain the level reached in the West: "The whole desire of the bourgeoisie amounts, in essence, to bringing the factory system to the level of 'English' prosperity and making industrialism the regulator of society, i.e., to bringing about the disorganization of society."[19] He did not think this was a goal worth pursuing and spoke with contempt about "the wretched individual who [in his outlook] remains within the present system, who desires only to raise it to a level which it has not yet reached in his own country, and who looks with greedy envy on another nation that has reached this level."[20] Marx questioned the right of those who (like List) advocated this

kind of national development to depict it as one promoting "the development of man's abilities and man's mastery of the forces of nature."

> This is just as *vile* as if a slave-driver were to boast that he flourished his
> whip over his slaves in order that the slaves should have the pleasure of
> exercising their *muscular power*. The German philistine is the slave-driver
> who flourishes the whip of protective tariffs in order to instil in his nation
> the spirit of "industrial education" and teach it to exercise its muscular
> powers.[21]

Marx made it clear that there *was* an alternative to "industry." It *was*
possible to view "industry" as something involving more than "sordid
huckstering interest":

> Industry can be regarded as a great workshop in which man first takes
> possession of his own forces and the forces of nature, objectifies himself
> and creates for himself the conditions for a human existence.[22]

When one regards industry in this light, however, "one *abstracts* from
the *circumstances* in which it operates today, and in which it exists *as
industry*; one's standpoint is *not* from within the industrial epoch, but
*above* it." Such a historical standpoint looks beyond what industry "is
for *man* today" and sees "what present-day man is for *human history*,
what he is historically." This view therefore recognizes not *"industry* as
such" but "the power which industry has without knowing or willing it
and which *destroys* it and creates the basis for a *human* existence."[23]

To look at "industry" in *this* way, Marx continued, is to recognize
that "the hour has come for it to be done away with, or for the abolition
of the material and social conditions in which mankind has had to develop
its abilities as a slave."[24]

Thus there stood against the bourgeoisie, as its enemy and its slave,
not only the proletariat (and "in the shape of the proletariat the power of
a new order") but also the "forces of nature" themselves.

> The forces of nature and the social forces which industry brings into
> being (conjures up), stand in the same relation to it as the proletariat. Today
> they are still the slaves of the bourgeois, and in them he sees nothing but
> the instruments (the bearers) of his dirty (selfish) lust for profit; tomorrow
> they will break their chains and reveal themselves as the bearers of human
> development which will blow him sky-high together with his industry, which
> assumes the dirty outer shell—which he regards as its essence—only until
> the human kernel has gained sufficient strength to burst this shell and appear
> in its own shape. Tomorrow they will burst the chains by which the bourgeois
> separates them from man and so distorts (transforms) them from a real social
> bond into fetters of society.[25]

When he considered the prospects of human liberation and of an interaction involving the forces of nature, technology (which was "industry" without the bourgeoisie), and social classes such as the proletariat and the bourgeoisie, Marx made the comment quoted earlier (identified in note 3 of this chapter) on the senselessness of imagining that such matters could be resolved by individual nations acting on their own, with each passing "internally" through the necessary stages of human development: "To hold that every nation goes through this development internally would be . . . absurd." In the framework Marx adopted, German nationalism, because it wanted Germany "to go through" the development of England, was precisely this: an attempt to preserve or introduce the system of exploitation, of slavery.

It is not altogether surprising that Marx had only harsh words for the thinker who would propose a system justifying such a program of enslavement at the moment when *real* liberation was a real prospect. Obviously, List—as the leading spokesman for the German bourgeoisie, a social class that had "missed the boat"—was trying to appear on the stage after the play had ended (*"post festum"*) and therefore could not have a very original mind. Indeed, this was just what Marx thought about List. List was an inferior thinker who "despite all his boasting . . . has put forward *not a single proposition* that had not been advanced long before him not only by the defenders of the prohibitive system, but even by writers of the 'School' invented by Herr List. . . . Only the illusions and idealizing language (phrases) belong to Herr List."[26] According to Marx, "not a single basic idea" in List's book "has not been first stated, and better stated," in the book by François Ferrier, *Du gouvernement considéré dans ses rapports avec le commerce,* published in Paris in 1805.[27]

But, Marx noted, Ferrier, who had been a customs official under Napoleon, had defended the Continental System. This circumstance stopped Marx from further comparing List and Ferrier's intellectual capacities and led him to the more significant consideration of the relative strengths and merits of the political causes for which Ferrier and List spoke.

> The difference between Ferrier and List is that the former writes in support of an undertaking of world-historic importance—the Continental System, whereas the latter writes in support of a petty, weak-minded bourgeoisie. . . . all that remains as his share is empty *idealizing*, the productive force of which consists in words—and the clever hypocrisy of the German bourgeois striving for domination.[28]

So much for the cause of national unification and economic modernization of Germany—some practical results of which Marx would live long enough to see with his own eyes.

After 1845, Marx returned to issues raised by List on several occasions without ever reconsidering his original judgment on the List system. Thus he referred to Listian concerns in September 1847, in two speeches on free trade and protectionism. In one speech, he distinguished between protectionists like Gustav von Gülich, who wanted to prevent the entry of foreign industrial goods and at the same time to hinder the growth of national industry in order to save handicraft production, and protectionists like List, who did not protect "small industry, handicraft proper." Marx asked, "Have Dr. List and his school in Germany by any chance demanded protective tariffs for the small linen industry, for hand loom-weaving, for handicraft production?" No, Marx replied, they simply wanted "to oust handicraft production with machines and patriarchal industry with modern industry." In short, they wished "to extend the dominion of the bourgeoisie, and in particular of the big industrial capitalists." Accordingly, their program accepted the decline of small industry, the petty bourgeoisie, and the small farmers "as a sad and inevitable . . . occurrence" that was at the same time necessary for the industrial development of Germany.[29]

If they were honest, Marx said, the protectionists proper (i.e., other than those of the Gülich persuasion) would tell the workers that "it is better to be exploited by one's fellow countrymen than by foreigners." Marx did not expect the working class even to accept this "solution," because it was "indeed very patriotic, but nonetheless a little too ascetic and spiritual for people whose only occupation consists in the production of riches, of material wealth."[30]

Marx rejected as self-contradictory the argument of those who suggested that the national capital, strengthened in opposition to foreign capital, would be "small and weak in opposition to the working class" and therefore amenable to social reform favorable to workers within the country. It was a delusion to expect such reform to occur. "In general, social reforms can never be brought about by the weakness of the strong; they must and will be called to life by the strength of the weak."[31]

In a second speech that month, Marx voiced no illusions about what free trade would do to the condition of workers: "The lowest level of wages is the natural price of the commodity of labour . . . [under free trade] all commodities will be sold at a cheaper price."

> You have to choose: Either you must disavow the whole of political economy as it exists at present, or you must allow that under the freedom of trade the whole severity of the laws of political economy will be applied to the working classes. Is that to say that we are against Free Trade? No, we are for Free Trade, because by Free Trade all economical laws, with their most astounding contradictions, will act upon a larger scale, upon a greater extent

of territory, upon the territory of the whole earth; and because from the uniting of all these contradictions into a single group, where they stand face to face, will result the struggle which will itself eventuate in the emancipation of the proletarians.[32]

There were certain new formulations on January 9, 1848, when Marx spoke again on free trade. He insisted that free trade meant in reality "freedom of Capital" and that its "only result will be that the antagonism of these two classes (bourgeoisie and proletariat) will stand out more clearly." He was sure it would not establish a universal brotherhood.[33] At the same time, he claimed, with reference to the plight of both the East and West Indies in the international trade, that the free traders "cannot understand how one nation can grow rich at the expense of another."[34] The implication is that he himself understood how this was so. If he did understand, he had changed his position from that expressed in the "List Critique" in which the possibility of international exploitation was explicitly denied—that is, England did not exploit Germany, but rather the bourgeoisie exploited the workers.

Also in this speech Marx conceded that protectionism might help develop free competition within a country but insisted that nevertheless it would make the protectionist country in fact dependent on the world market.

> The Protective system is nothing but a means of establishing manufacture upon a large scale in any given country, that is to say, of making it dependent upon the market of the world; and from the moment that dependence upon the market of the world is established, there is more or less dependence upon Free Trade too.[35]

There is a faint hint here of the possibility that perhaps a case could be made for the existence of a "relatively progressive national bourgeoisie" in a "developing country" struggling against "imperialism." But Marx left this possibility for his successors to consider more fully.[36] To avail oneself of this possibility, one would have to accept "the nation" as a value in itself; Marx did not do that. His own emphasis and overall assessment were different.

> Generally speaking, the Protective system in these days is conservative, while the Free Trade system works destructively. It breaks up old nationalities and carries antagonism of proletariat and bourgeoisie to the uttermost point. In a word, the Free Trade system hastens the Social Revolution. In this revolutionary sense alone, gentlemen, I am in favor of Free Trade.[37]

In Marx's scheme of things, capitalism was a doomed system when viewed, as Marx insisted it should be viewed, in terms of world history.

At first, as in the "List Critique," he thought a program to build capitalism in one country was bound to fail if it tried to emancipate that country from the workings of the world capitalist market; the state, on which the bourgeoisie in Germany counted as its protector abroad and liberator at home, would not be able to resist the world market. By 1848, he modified his view of the potential of protectionism and granted that it might have a temporary effect. But that would only pave the way for free trade in any event. He did not think that nationalism stood for anything other than a class interest of the bourgeoisie, and he was quite sure that what others called "national liberation" stood in the way of real liberation. The Germans needed to be liberated as *human beings*.

# 4

## Nation and Revolution: Marx and Engels, 1845–1848

After the "List Critique," but before *The Communist Manifesto*, Marx and Engels continued to work out their stand on the questions of nationality and the role of the national factor in history and politics in relation both to class conflict and to what they understood by the liberation of the individual as a human being. An examination of those issues in selected writings from 1845–1848 makes it possible to link Marx's earlier formulations with the comprehensive and systematic statement found in the *Manifesto*.

In criticizing List, Marx recognized, as we have seen, that the bourgeoisie was divided into separate national units, such as the German bourgeoisie. The latter fought for its interests against its French and British class comrades while exploiting or seeking to exploit the proletariat just as any bourgeois would. Marx never quite explained why, if "big industry created everywhere the same relations between the classes of society, and thus destroyed the peculiar individuality of the various nationalities," at the same time "the bourgeoisie of each nation still retained separate national interests."[1]

While he recognized the bourgeoisie's nationalism, Marx was quite sure that in the proletariat "big industry created a class which in all nations has the same interest and with which nationality is already dead."[2] The proletariat was completely unlike any other class, as it was "the class which no longer counts as a class in society, is not recognized as a class, and is in itself the expression of the dissolution of all classes, nationalities, etc., within present society." Similarly, a revolution carried out by the proletariat would be unlike any previous revolution. In all previous revolutions, "the mode of activity always remained unscathed and it was only a question of a different distribution of this activity, a new distribution of labour to other persons." The proletarian, or communist, revolution, on the other hand, "is directed against the preceding *mode* of activity, does away with *labour*, and abolishes the rule of all classes with the classes themselves."[3]

When he compared the history of Germany with that of France, Marx passed a very unfavorable judgment on the failure of the German bourgeoisie to speak up, if only for a brief moment, for the whole society, not merely for its own narrow, sectarian, and selfish interest. He went even further and denied that the German bourgeoisie had *any* future in view of the fact that capitalism had outlived itself in terms of world-historical development. At the same time, Marx did not allow any possibility that the German proletariat might instead become the national force that the bourgeoisie did not become. On the contrary, he repeatedly stressed that the mission of the proletariat was to destroy not only class divisions derived from private property, but also nationality.

The same thought is to be found in Engels. Thus, in an article written in 1845, Engels said that the bourgeoisie had in each country "its own special interests, and since these interests are the most important to it, it can never transcend nationality." The proletariat, on the other hand, would be able—indeed, had already begun—to "fraternize on an international scale."

> But the proletarians in all countries have one and the same interest, one and the same enemy, and one and the same struggle. The great mass of proletarians are, by their very nature, free from national prejudices and their whole disposition and movement is essentially humanitarian, antinationalist. Only the proletarians can destroy nationality, only the awakening proletariat can bring about fraternization between the different nations.[4]

The passage we just quoted is the version that was "improved" from the original German by the Moscow publishers of the current edition of Marx and Engels' works. Engels *really* said (in the second sentence quoted) that the proletariat is "essentially humanitarian, antinational."[5]

There were times, however, for example in 1847, when Marx admitted that an international solidarity of the bourgeoisie, a bourgeois brotherhood of nations, did exist after all. Such a "brotherhood," of course, was "the brotherhood of the oppressors against the oppressed, of the exploiters against the exploited." Just as "the bourgeois class of one country is united by brotherly ties against the proletariat of that country, so the bourgeois of all countries, despite their mutural conflicts and competition on the world market, are united by brotherly ties against the proletariat of all countries.''[6]

But this applied of course to the bourgeoisie, a small and, according to Marx's analysis of capitalism, constantly shrinking segment of the population whose solidarity was based on a shared exploitation of the workers. What about the international (or transnational) solidarity of the working people? What was *it* based on?

"For the peoples to be able truly to unite," Marx explained, "they must have common interests." But for this to happen, "the existing property relations must be done away with, for these property relations involve the exploitation of some nations by others." Only the working class was concerned with bringing about "the abolition of existing property relations." This meant that the liquidation of national exploitation could not be achieved within the framework of capitalist relations of property (which, as we shall see, List hoped could be done if his policies were adopted). Accordingly, Marx argued that the "victory of the proletariat over the bourgeoisie is at the same time, victory over the national and industrial conflicts which today range the peoples of the various countries against one another in hostility and enmity. And so the victory of the proletariat over the bourgeoisie is at the same time the signal of liberation for all oppressed nations.''[7]

What about those peoples who had not *yet* been conquered by the bourgeoisie? On this issue we have a clear statement by Engels, whose views may be quoted here as they appear to be those of Marx as well. In an article of January 1848, Engels praised the then ongoing French conquest of Algeria, despite the "highly blameable" methods of the French: "The conquest of Algeria is an important and fortunate fact for the progress of civilization.''[8]

> And if we may regret that the liberty of the Bedouins of the desert has been destroyed, we must not forget that these same Bedouins were a nation of robbers. . . . All these nations of free barbarians look very proud, noble and glorious at a distance, but only come near them and you will find that they, as well as the more civilized nations, are ruled by the lust of gain, and only employ ruder and more cruel means. And, after all, the modern *bourgeois*, with civilization, industry, order, and at least relative enlightenment following him, is preferable to the feudal lord or to the marauding robber, with the barbarian state of society to which they belong.[9]

The liberation of nations depended then on the progress of the proletarian cause against capitalism. As summarized by Engels, Marx said in a speech commemorating the seventeenth anniversary of the Polish revolution of 1830: "England would give the signal for the deliverance of Poland. . . . The success of other European democrats depended on the victory of the English Chartists; therefore Poland would be saved by England."[10] Because in England the antagonism between the proletariat and bourgeoisie was sharpest, "the decisive struggle" was inevitable there. Marx expected that therefore "in all probability the fight would begin" in England and that it "would end with universal triumph of democracy . . . which would also break the Polish yoke."[11]

Marx thought that "Poland must be liberated not in Poland but in England" and insisted that the victory of the English workers over the bourgeoisie would be "decisive for the victory of all the oppressed over their oppressors." Directly addressing the Chartists, he declared: "Defeat your own internal enemies and you will then be able to pride yourselves on having defeated the entire society."[12]

Why was the struggle between the bourgeoisie and the proletariat the most intense in England? Why was England so important for the whole world? Marx answers: "Because in England, as a result of modern industry, of the introduction of machinery, all oppressed classes are being merged together into a single great class with common interests, the class of the proletariat." For the same reason, "all classes of oppressors" merged "into a single class, the bourgeoisie." "The struggle has thus been simplified and so it will be possible to decide it by one single heavy blow." It was owing to "machinery" that the differences within the working people were eliminated through the leveling of the living standards of all workers, that is, "without machinery no Chartism, and although machinery may temporarily worsen your position it is nevertheless machinery that makes our victory possible."[13]

Marx pointed out that the same process was occurring in Belgium, America, France, and Germany. Modern technology ("machinery") has been evening out "the position of all workers and daily continues to do so more and more; in all these countries the workers now have the same interest, which is the overthrow of the class that oppresses them—the bourgeoisie." "Machinery" lay behind the "identification of the party interests of the workers of all nations." This process thus marked "an enormous historical advance." The condition of the workers of all countries was the same and so were their interests and their enemies. It followed from this that the workers must "fight together, they must oppose the brotherhood of the bourgeoisie of all nations with a brotherhood of the workers of all nations."[14] The revolution would clearly be international.

In "Principles of Communism," which Engels wrote in October 1847 and which was used by Marx in writing *The Communist Manifesto*, the following question was asked: *"Will it be possible for this revolution to take place in one country?"*

This was answered with a firm negative. "Large-scale industry, already by creating the world market, has so linked up all the peoples of the earth, and especially the civilized peoples, that each people is dependent on what happens to another." It was further explained that "large-scale industry" in "all civilized countries" transformed the bourgeoisie and the proletariat into "the two decisive classes of society" and their struggle into "the main struggle of the day."

> The communist revolution will therefore be no merely national one; it will be a revolution taking place simultaneously in all civilized countries, that is, at least in England, America, France and Germany. . . . It will develop more quickly or more slowly according to whether the country has a more developed industry, more wealth, and a more considerable mass of productive forces. It will therefore be slowest and most difficult to carry out in Germany, quickest and easiest in England. It will also have an important effect upon the other countries of the world, and will completely change and greatly accelerate their previous manner of development. It is a worldwide revolution and will therefore be worldwide in scope.[15]

Engels conceded that the differences between individual countries in the revolutionary process might be quite serious. For example, in Germany, where the struggle between the absolute monarchy and the bourgeoisie was yet to come, the Communists would at first support the bourgeoisie and then try to overthrow it.[16]

To some extent, Engels contradicted an earlier stand of Marx: In his "List Critique," Marx had doubted whether the bourgeoisie would make a bid for power in Germany at all. Engels' view was also different from that presented in *The Communist Manifesto*, which saw the communist revolution as the *immediate* task facing Germany precisely because Germany was more backward than the West. To some extent this contradiction is not surprising: Marx and Engels did not see eye to eye on all questions. Engels, for example, tended to be more willing to recognize the importance of matters relating to nationality. There was, however, no serious divergence of their views on the revolution: On that issue, both Marx and Engels were strictly internationalist.

As we shall see, Marx retained his international vision as he considered the revolutionary prospects in light of the events of 1848. By the end of that year, he had realized that social, political, as well as national and international issues and conflicts were interrelated in ways he had not anticipated before. Even then, however, he did not modify or revise his strategic assessment of the role of the national factor in European politics, although he modified somewhat the grand scenario that involved England as the main actor. On December 31, 1848, Marx wrote an article for the January 1, 1849 issue of the *Neue Rheinische Zeitung*. He declared in it that the most crucial of all the multiple lines of conflict was the revolutionary struggle in France: "The liberation of Europe, whether brought about by the struggle of the oppressed nationalities for their independence or by overthrowing feudal absolutism, depends therefore on the successful uprising of the French working class." He further argued that the English bourgeoisie would try to "thwart" any such upheaval in France by taking part in a European war that "will be the first result of a successful workers' revolution in France."

> England will head the counter-revolutionary armies, just as it did during the Napoleonic period, but through the war itself it will be thrown to the head of the revolutionary movement and it will repay the debt it owes in regard to the revolution of the eighteenth century. [That is, England will atone for its past role as the main enemy of the American and French revolutions.][17]

Marx thought that because of England's importance, a *"European war"* involving England would be a world war "waged in Canada as in Italy, in East Indies as in Prussia, in Africa as on the Danube." Only a war like that "can overthrow the old England" by providing the Chartists, "the party of the organized English workers, with the conditions for a successful rising against their gigantic oppressors." Then, after the Chartists had taken power, the social revolution would pass "from the sphere of utopia to that of reality."

The importance of the English proletariat was a reflection of the role England had acquired in the modern world. Marx called England "the country that turns whole nations into its proletarians, that takes the whole world within its immense embrace, that has already once defrayed the cost of a European Restoration." It was also the country of most acute and sharp class contradictions.

> *England* seems to be the rock against which the revolutionary waves break, the country where the new society is stifled even in the womb. England dominates the world market. A revolution of the economic relations in any country of the European continent, in the whole European continent without England, is a storm in a teacup. Industrial and commercial relations within each nation are governed by its intercourse with other nations, and depend on its relations with the world market. But the world market is dominated by England, and England is dominated by the bourgeoisie.[18]

Marx concluded his article as follows: "The table of contents for 1849 reads: REVOLUTIONARY RISING OF THE FRENCH WORKING CLASS, WORLD WAR."[19]

In a revealing phrase quoted earlier, Marx told the English Chartists that if they were to defeat their "internal enemies" they would be able to pride themselves on "having defeated the entire society." That "entire society" clearly referred to the world capitalist system, the world held together by the capitalist market. This is a point of central importance in any attempt to understand Marx's view of the role of the state and nationality in history. For him, the real unit of history, and therefore the unit of historical analysis, was the whole of human society, not any of its segments divided by geographic, political, or linguistic criteria. He did not believe in a "revolution in one country" because he recognized no "history in one country." In other words, Marx did not think that national or state boundaries imposed a meaningful restraint on the operation of those larger causal factors that gave rise to such events as revolution. He did not think therefore that a state or a nation constituted an entity that could be analyzed within itself.

Marx's evaluation of the German bourgeoisie (and of the German Revolution of 1848, as compared with the earlier revolutions in France and Britain) was consistent with his conception of history. To him, history was world history, a process in which local and national developments formed only a part and an admittedly insignificant part—unless, that is, a nation happened to find itself, during a certain turning point in world history, at the head of the progress of all humanity.

Such a historically important role had been played by the revolutionary bourgeoisie in the West, to which the German bourgeoisie, in Marx's view, represented such a pitiful contrast. Marx stressed that the revolutions of 1648 and of 1789 "were not *English* and *French* revolutions, they were revolutions of a *European* type."

> They did not represent the victory of a *particular* class of society over the *old political order*; they proclaimed *the political order of the new European society*. The bourgeoisie was victorious in these revolutions, but the *victory of the bourgeoisie* was at the time *the victory of a new social order*, the victory of bourgeois ownership over feudal ownership, of nationality over provincialism, of competition over the guild, of the division of land over primogeniture, of the rule of the landowner over the domination of the owner by the land, of enlightenment over superstition, of the family over the family name, of industry over heroic idleness, of bourgeois law over medieval privileges. The revolution of 1648 was the victory of the seventeenth century

over the sixteenth century; the revolution of 1789 was the victory of the eighteenth century over the seventeenth. These revolutions reflected the needs of the world at that time rather than the needs of those parts of the world where they occurred, that is, England and France.[20]

In the same terms, Marx also contrasted the German Revolution with the February 1848 revolution in France. The latter, he said, "actually *abolished* the constitutional monarchy and nominally *abolished* the rule of the bourgeoisie. The Prussian revolution in March was intended to *establish* nominally a constitutional monarchy and to *establish* actually the rule of the bourgeoisie. Far from being a *European revolution* it was merely a stunted after-effect of a European revolution in a backward country." The German Revolution "instead of being ahead of its century . . . was over half a century behind its time. . . . It was not a question of establishing a new society, but of resurrecting in Berlin a society that had expired in Paris."[21]

Marx's writing of the 1848–1849 period contains many harsh and contemptuous strictures addressed to the German bourgeoisie. But Marx apparently did not consider that if the German bourgeoisie was as feeble, sluggish, and timid as he insisted it was when it "confronted feudalism and absolutism," its behavior was perfectly sound from *its* own class point of view. Why should the bourgeoisie have speeded up its demise by acting more boldly? Marx himself admitted the bourgeoisie already "saw menacingly confronting it the proletariat and all sections of the middle class whose interests and ideas were related to those of the proletariat." The following description of the German bourgeoisie's behavior (assuming that Marx's "facts" are right) would suggest that it acted very sensibly, in accordance with its class interest. (Or should a class be blamed for not acting against its vital interests?)

> Unlike the French bourgeoisie of 1789, the Prussian bourgeoisie, when it confronted the monarchy and aristocracy, the representatives of the old society, was not a class speaking for the *whole* of modern society. It had sunk to the level of a kind of *social estate* as clearly distinct from the Crown as it was from the people. . . . From the first it was inclined to betray the people and to compromise with the crowned representative of the old society, for it itself already belonged to the old society; it did not represent the interests of a new society against an old one, but renewed interests within an obsolete society.[22]

Marx's strictures against the German bourgeoisie can only make sense if one recognizes that there was nothing "national" in the class itself or its conduct. We may well imagine that he would have been even more critical of the Italian, Spanish, or Russian bourgeoisies had any of them come to his attention then. The German bourgeoisie was feeble, backward, and contemptible because *no* bourgeoisie could take significant action once the English and French bourgeoisie had performed their world-historical mission in the seventeenth and eighteenth centuries respectively. The German bourgeoisie was condemned because the proletariat, its historic successor, was already on the stage as a distinct force.

This was to be seen not necessarily in the German context, but rather when examining the world at large or "civil society." "Civil society is the true source and theatre of all history," Marx wrote in *The German Ideology*.

> How absurd is the conception of history held hitherto, which neglects the real relationships and confines itself to high-sounding dramas of princes and states. . . . Civil society embraces the whole material intercourse of individuals within a definite stage of the development of productive forces. It embraces the whole commercial and industrial life of a given stage and, insofar, transcends the State and the nation, though, on the other hand again, it must assert itself in foreign relations as nationality, and inwardly must organize itself as State.[23]

Marx never managed to explain *why* and in what circumstances civil society "must assert itself . . . as nationality." But there can be no doubt that he considered nationality to be a minor factor, a "dependent variable," in the process of social development. He had been aware of the backwardness of Germany before 1848, but he was not prepared to recognize that the contradiction between the state of "Germany" and the state of the more advanced part of the world was important or meaningful in a *national* sense. "Germany" belonged to a larger whole. On the contrary, he did recognize a peculiar spatial form of the contradiction of "existing social relations . . . with existing forms of production" that "can also occur in a particular national sphere of relations through the appearance of the contradiction, not within the national orbit, but between this national consciousness and the practice of other nations, i.e., between the national and the general consciousness of a nation (as we see it now in Germany)."[24]

In other words, the problem in Germany was to free the "general consciousness" of the nation, which it shared with the advanced world, from its "national" component, which Marx obviously identified as German backwardness exemplified by the German bourgeoisie. And the German bourgeoisie was backward because it was to be replaced by the already existing worldwide proletariat.

The proletariat's mission was not to liberate nations in order to make them live in isolation from each other, but to liberate people as "world-historical" individuals, as persons engaged in "world-historical activity," which raised them above narrow identities and ties. The force that enslaved individuals was a worldwide phenomenon as well. As Marx put it, "separate individuals have, with the broadening of their activity into world-historical activity, become more and more enslaved under a power alien to them . . . , a power which has become more and more enormous and, in the last instance, turns out to be the *world market*."[25]

That society dominated by the world market would be overthrown "by the communist revolution . . . and the abolition of private property which is identical with it." The liberation of the individual would be accomplished "in the measure in which history becomes transformed into world history."

> Only then will the separate individuals be liberated from the various national and local barriers, be brought into practical connection with the material and intellectual production of the whole world and be put in a position to acquire the capacity to enjoy this all-sided production of the whole earth (the creations of man). *All-round* dependence, this natural form of *world-historical* co-operation of individuals, will be transformed by this communist revolution into the control and conscious mastery of these powers, which, born of the actions of men on one another, have till now overawed and governed men as powers completely alien to them.[26]

When we bear in mind this conception of individual liberation as a "world-historical" agent, we can understand why Engels spoke in the following terms about the future of nations under communism in his "Draft of a Communist Confession of Faith," written in June 1847:

> Question 21: *Will nationalities continue to exist under communism?*
> Answer: The nationalities of the peoples who join together according to the principle of community will be just as much compelled by this union to merge with one another and thereby supersede themselves as the various differences between estates and classes disappear through the superseding of their basis—private property.[27]

The future of nations was to be exactly the same as that of religion:

> Question 22: *Do Communists reject the existing religions?*
> Answer: All religions which have existed hitherto were expressions of historical stages of development of individual peoples or groups of peoples. But communism is that stage of historical development which makes all existing religions superfluous and supersedes them.[28]

Both religion and nationality were, for Marx, forms of false consciousness that prevented mankind from developing its real human nature.

As is evident especially in "On the Jewish Question," Marx did not think that freedom of religion, while preferable to religious oppression or dis-crimination, was the proper solution to the problem of religious belief. Nor did he think that "political emancipation from religion"—that is, the establishment of a secular state—was enough: Instead of enjoying religious freedom, people should be freed "from religious conceptions," "freed from religion."[29] As McLellan puts it, "For Marx, the question of Jewish emancipation had become the question of what specific *social* element needs to be overcome in order to abolish Judaism."[30]

It was clear to Marx that political emancipation would not result in the freedom of human beings as human beings:

> The *political* emancipation of the Jew or the Christian—of the *religious* man in general—is the *emancipation* of the state from Judaism, Christianity, and *religion* in general. The *state* emancipates itself from religion in its own particular way, in the mode which corresponds to its nature, by emancipating itself from the *state religion*; that is to say, by giving recognition to no religion and affirming itself purely and simply as a state. To be *politically* emancipated from religion is not to be finally and completely emancipated from religion, because political emancipation is not the final and absolute form of *human* emancipation.
>
> The limits of political emancipation appear at once in the fact that the *state* can liberate itself from a constraint without man himself being *really* liberated; that a state may be a *free state* without man himself being a *free man*.[31]

Political emancipation, Marx argued further in "On the Jewish Ques-tion," treats the human being in a dual capacity: As a member of civil society he is "an *independent* and *egoistic* individual," while as a *citizen*, the individual is supposed to be a "moral person." This dualism had to be abolished.

> Human emancipation will only be complete when the real, individual man has absorbed into himself the abstract citizen; when as an individual man, in his everyday life, in his work, and in his relationships, he has become a *species-being*; and when he has recognized and organized his own powers (*forces propres*) as *social* powers so that he no longer separates this social power from himself as *political* power.[32]

One might have concluded from this that, according to Marx, just as a "merely political" revolution and political emancipation would not free the Jews from Judaism or the Christians from Christianity, so the estab-lishment of a united Germany would not emancipate the Germans from "Germanism," that is, nationality. But Marx's treatment of the Jews and

Christians, or the Jews and Germans, was not even-handed. As we saw in Chapter 3, Marx used fairly strong language in his discussion of the German Question. But he spoke in those strong terms (never mind that he did not actually *publish* his piece) about German national*ism*. About the Jews as a people, a religion, or a nationality, Marx spoke in a highly abusive, venomous language that one might expect to find in a racist tract. He did this in an article that he *did* publish. He heaped abuse on the Jewish religion, and he called the Jews a *"chimerical* nationality."[33] We must therefore conclude, leaving Marx's psyche for a biographer to explain, that for Marx as a writer on history and society Jewry represented a phenomenon destined not only for political dissolution (the Jews did not have a state in Marx's time, nor was there a Jewish nationalist movement to catch his attention), but also for disappearance as a spiritual and cultural entity. In this sense, the Jews belonged in the same class as the Czechs (see Chapter 11).

In general, Marx's approach to religion and nationality was exactly analogous to his conception of politics. It is a central point of the Marxist theory of history and society that all politics, including democratic politics, presupposes coercion and domination. Real freedom would transform the *citizen*—that is, the member of a political community—into a human being. The success of the communist revolution, Engels said, would be identical to the establishment of a democratic constitution.[34] But he might have added that the constitution would be followed by the abolition, or "transcendence," of democracy. No paradox, let alone a Machiavellian ruse, therefore exists either in Marx and Engels' proclamation of the liberation of nations in the communist revolution or in their expectation that, so "liberated," nations would disappear.

Two questions relating to Marx's treatment of state and nationality should be further pursued here: First, Marx's view of the role of political and ethnic factors in the operation of modern society, including the reciprocal relationship that economy, politics, and culture have to each other; and second, his idea of emancipation as release from national and political, as well as religious, ties.

It is commonplace to say that Marx failed to develop a political theory based on his general theory of history and society. We have already said that just as often Marx has been found wanting in explaining what exactly he thought the nature of nationality was. He never found time to present his understanding of these subjects in the overall frame of his *Weltanschauung*. In 1845, he actually planned to write a book dealing with these questions, but all we have is an outline of the contents of the proposed work. Here is that outline, which, as Hal Draper puts it, is "tantalizing in its intimation of what might have been written":

> (1) The *history of the origin of the modern state* or the *French Revolution*. The self-conceit of the political sphere—to mistake itself for the ancient state. The attitude of the revolutionaries toward civil society. All elements exist in duplicate form, as civic elements and [those of] the state. (2) The *proclamation* of the *rights of man* and the *constitution of the state*. Individual freedom and public authority. *Freedom, equality* and unity. Sovereignty of the people. (3) *State* and *civil society*. (4) The *representative state* and the *charter*. The constitutional representative state, the democratic representative state. (5) *Division of power*. Legislative and executive power. (6) *Legislative power* and the legislative bodies. Political clubs. (7) *Executive power*. Centralisation and hierarchy. Centralisation and political civilisation. Federal system and industrialism. *State administration* and *local government* (8a) *Judicial power* and *law*. (8b) *Nationality* and the *people*. (9a) The *political parties*. (9b) *Suffrage*, the fight for the *abolition* of the state and of bourgeois society.[35]

Marx's critique of Hegel, Hobsbawm notes, "forms the first and last occasion on which Marx's analysis operates systematically in terms of constitutional forms, problems of representation, etc." Hobsbawm adds that Marx never tried to carry out the plan mentioned above, "which was also conceived in these terms, but specifically identified the origin of the modern state with the French revolution and its abolition with the end of the bourgeois society (under the heading '*Suffrage*')."[36]

Had Marx written that book, perhaps he would have clarified the relation of the state in modern times—that is, the nation-state—to the world market, which he understood to be an international, or rather "transnational," force. As we recall, Marx claimed that the bourgeois revolutions in England and France had not been national in their impact and significance, but instead had been "European," that is, international. He also believed, and this was a central theme of the "List Critique," that the world market was stronger than any bourgeoisie, or bourgeois state, in a national framework such as Germany. We know that Marx severely underestimated the prospects of German nationalism against the advanced nations of the West. As a historian, he appears to have been equally mistaken in speaking about international bourgeois revolutions. To speak that way, one had to underestimate the power of the state and the significance of national boundaries. In this connection, Anthony Giddens helps to clarify some of the issues considered here. Giddens argues that "while an international proletarian revolution may have seemed to some a possible scenario . . . , an international bourgeois revolution never was.'' This was so, according to Giddens, because the nation-state became ''the crucible of power'' in Western Europe and the United States beginning in the eighteenth century. That state delimited the territorial unit within which social, political, and economic change, including industrialization, took place. ''It is crucial in this that the bourgeois classes were 'national bourgeoisies': in other words, that the political revolutions of seventeenth-eighteenth century Europe were made within an already constituted state system.''[37]

As one looks at Marx's predictions and the premises on which they rested, one is inclined to admit the force of Giddens' remarks. Indeed, Marx paid what appears to be quite inadequate attention to the legal and administrative structures within which the rise of capitalism, especially the emergence of modern industry, had taken (or was taking) place. Giddens may be right when he says that ''capitalism does not, as Marx tended to think, sweep away all significantly competing forms of socio-political and cultural organization.'' He may be also right to stress that ''the conjunction between the rise of capitalism and the absolutist state system produced a system of nation-states that . . . is integral to the world capitalist economy— which is at one and the same time a world military order.''[38]

A good example of how far contemporary *Marxist* thinking has deviated from Marx's thought on the question of state and the rise of capitalism is provided by Claudia von Braunmühl. She does not find it in any way ideologically awkward to admit that after England,

> once the world market had come into being, and once the capitalist mode of production was established, the remaining European states were compelled to open up to them on pain of economic stagnation or the loss of the material basis of their authority; where the social preconditions were lacking, this opening up was achieved through the active involvement of the state apparatus which owes to a large extent its specific shape and its specific location in class society to just those interventions in the service of the establishment of capitalist relations of production.[39]

In other words, to this contemporary theorist, it is not in the least subversive of Marxist orthodoxy to see the state as the force that plants and directs capitalism in a society not yet capitalist, not yet ready for capitalism.

> Whereas England was in world market competition with states which were still at the stage of an almost pure merchant capitalism, the European states were confronted in both domestic and external markets by a technologically superior competitor with extensive world market connections which was permanently in a position to effect value transfers through profitable

unequal exchange. They were thus forced, on the one hand, to create a complex of production and circulation subject to their own control and protected as far as possible from external influences by means of protective tariffs, and on the other, to revolutionize economic and social relations in order to introduce capitalist relations and promote the development of competitive conditions of production, or in a word, to develop a national capital which would be competitive on the world market.[40]

To see the precapitalist state as developing "national capital" and revolutionizing its domestic social relations in order to protect its political independence from foreign powers may be good history in our time, but it is not what Marx saw, or thought possible, when he exposed the ideas of List. That such views as those quoted above are now considered Marxist is an indication of how far the thinking of contemporary Marxists has moved away from Marx and how much it has assimilated the Listian way of looking at the world. This is not a question of having found minor errors in Marx on various matters of fact; indeed, it would be very odd had Marx not emerged mistaken on such matters. Rather, we are dealing here with issues fundamental to Marxism—issues involving the relationship between politics and economy, class and nation, "center" and "periphery."

Marx did not recognize the creative role the state would play in promoting economic and social change in developing countries. Nor did he show that he understood the political implications of the cultural and political nationalism that began at the time of the French and Industrial revolutions and that is associated with Herder and Rousseau. There is hardly any evidence that Marx grasped the role of the French Revolution in spurring the emergence of a modern French nationalism or in inspiring nationalism in other lands. This neglect was of course symptomatic of his overall treatment of nation and nationalism. Z. A. Pelczynski notes that while Marx and Engels acknowledged the strength of nationalism in their time, for example in Ireland and Poland, and while they supported the Poles in their struggle for independence, their interest in nationalism was practical, not theoretical.

> They viewed it as a political force to be taken into account in analyzing the strength of class forces and in charting the revolutionary strategy of the proletariat in different countries, not as a phenomenon to be explained systematically in terms of definite economic and social conditions, still less of course in terms of cultural, historical and traditional factors having their own logic of development. They had no explanation, for instance, of *why* Polish patriotism in the nineteenth century was so intense and manifested

itself in frequent uprisings against foreign powers, although they noted and praised it often in their writings.[41]

Pelczynski declares that "the failure of marxism [sic] to acquire a coherent and developed theory of nationalism, either of an empirical or a normative kind, is unquestionable."[42]

Perhaps Marx's concept of human nature and of human liberation is the key to his (and Marxism's) myopia in matters relating to politics and nationality. It may well be that his philosophy determined what Marx the historian and sociologist saw and how he interpreted it. Pelczynski asks:

> How ... could Marx, who was such an acute observer of contemporary history as well as a social theorist of genius, have been so theoretically unconcerned about one of the dominant political phenomena of nineteenth-century Europe, and apparently blind to its significance for world history?[43]

Pelczynski answers, after an elaborate and subtle argument, that Marx's position was largely influenced by his adherence to Hegel's concept of nation, which Marx nevertheless modified substantially for his own purposes. According to Pelczynski, Hegel saw modern man as both a member of the "civil society" and of a "specific, historically formed national community existing within a political framework." It was in the latter community that man reached "the height of ethical life." Marx shared Hegel's conception of nationality as a political entity and, like Hegel, did not think of nationalities as "merely cultural, ethnic or linguistic communities." But he denied that the modern state was a political *community*, which was what Hegel thought.[44]

Marx's thought on such fundamental questions as the role of labor in the development of society in history paralleled that of Hegel. However, Marx and Hegel disagreed on "the centrality of the economic aspect of society." Marx treated family and politics as aspects of economic relations "determined by and subordinated to the central productive activity in society, which is work"; Hegel saw economic life in a "wider context of ethical, religious, legal and political life, a context which is itself under the influence of history, tradition and nationality."[45]

Marx modified the Hegelian conception of civil society by narrowing its meaning to the sphere of production and exchange, which according to Marx was the area in which human nature revealed itself. Marx, according to Pelczynski, held that people's political consciousness and national characteristics were "not essential features of their human nature. In all epochs of history, not just the bourgeois one, the notion of political community and national identity is an illusion and false consciousness."[46]

Hegel's conception of nation was political and thus was closer to the ideas of Montesquieu and Rousseau than to those of the German Romantics and the Historical School. Hegel cared little for ethnic or linguistic unity. But even so, his recognition of the role of the state and law provided him with "a substantial theoretical basis for appreciating the significance and persistence of a whole range of socially and historically important phenomena." Marx lacked that basis, as Pelczynski notes:

> The rejection of the conception of the state as a sovereign national community left Marx and Engels without such a theoretical basis or at least with a highly limited one. The conception of civil society [in Marx] is . . . grounded in a universalistic, cosmopolitan and rather abstract view of man and society; its basic categories, especially its narrow version as 'the system of needs', such as need, labour, relations of production, classes and capital, may be discussed without reference to national factors. They certainly presuppose the concept of some kind of state power in the sense of a coercive apparatus for the maintenance of law, order and independence, but not the idea that state power is generally a product of a historically formed nation and that it often serves as an instrument for the protection of national values or of national self-assertion.[47]

Pelczynski concludes that in conformity with their narrowly defined conception of civil society, Marx and Engels considered class consciousness and solidarity to be those forces that would bring about the liberation of man from the corrupting influences of private property and would launch a new community, "the classless, stateless and nationless community of free producers," which would be global in scope.[48]

Leszek Kolakowski argues along the same lines, as do many other contemporary writers on Marx's political and philosophical ideas. Kolakowski stresses that contrary to the assertions of Marx's opponents, Marx did not advocate or envisage "the extinction of individuality or a general levelling for sake of the 'universal good.' " (That was in other socialist and communist utopias and programs, but not in Marx's plan.)

> To Marx . . . socialism represented the full emancipation of the individual by the destruction of the web of mystification which turned community life into a world of estrangement presided over by an alienated bureaucracy. Marx's ideal was that every man should be fully aware of his own character as a social being, but should also, for this very reason, be capable of developing his personal aptitudes in all their fullness and variety. There was no question of the individual being reduced to a universal species-being; what Marx desired to see was a community in which the sources of antagonism among individuals were done away with.[49]

The "web of mystification" Marx wanted to destroy included not only those bonds arising out of class division and exploitation, but also religious and national ties.

> Marx's basic principle is that all mediation between the individual and mankind will cease to exist. This applies to all constructions, rational or irrational, that interpose themselves between the individual and his fellows, such as nationality, the state, and law. The individual will voluntarily identify himself with the community, coercion will become unnecessary, the sources of conflict will disappear.[50]

This conclusion of Kolakowski agrees with that reached by Michael Löwy after a different line of argument. According to Löwy, Marx's pre-1848 writings contain a "cosmopolitic/internationalist . . . projection of a *world city*, a universal *Gemeinschaft*."[51]

Four or five drafts ago, this chapter was a transition piece linking the "List Critique" discussed in Chapter 3 with *The Communist Manifesto* to be examined in Chapter 5. In its present form, however, this chapter does more than take care of the subject of Marx and nationality from 1845 to 1848. It raises questions inspired by that subject that are related to more fundamental and more general aspects of Marx's world view. Our discussion suggests, for example, that Marx's anti-statism—his conviction that the state was a parasitical force—may have been reinforced, if not directly inspired, by his reaction to the specifically German conditions under which, in Marx's time, thirty-eight sovereign governmental machines operated in *one* linguistic and cultural space. (The nationalists, who too did not like this, wanted to reduce the number of states to one; Marx thought that even one was one too many and proclaimed the abolition of the state altogether.) This chapter also suggests that there is a basic unity in Marx's treatment of both the Jewish Question and the German Question, and that, in view of his treatment of Hegel and List, a fundamental consistency exists in his approach to politics, religion, and nationality. Furthermore, the "Marx and Hegel" theme appears in a new and interesting light when one examines the place of the nation in Marx's thought and compares his position with Hegel's.

This chapter raises other issues, too, including some that lie at the center of current Marxist discussion—for example, the role of the state in developing societies or the more general question of the relation between the political sphere on the one hand and economy and culture on the other. To some of those topics we shall return in the next chapter, which is devoted to Marx's synthesis of history, politics, and the future—*The Communist Manifesto*.

# 5

# *The Communist Manifesto*

A good way to read *The Communist Manifesto* is to bear in mind that its author, Karl Marx,[1] was in a hurry to leave the writing desk for the battlefield. He did not have the time, indeed he saw no *need*, to write the "Big Book," to construct a system in support of his program. Marx was sure that he had unraveled the mysteries of the past and had found the key to the future of humanity; everything was perfectly clear. The principles of communism, he said in the *Manifesto*, are not something "invented, or discovered, by this or that would-be universal reformer. They merely express, in general terms, actual relations springing from an existing class struggle, from a historical movement going [on] under our very eyes."[2]

The Marx of the *Manifesto* clearly was the same Marx who just a few years earlier had concluded his "Theses on Feuerbach" with the following sentence:

> The philosophers have only interpreted the world, in different ways; the point is to *change it*.[3]

Little did the author of *The Communist Manifesto* imagine that the major effort of the remaining part of his life would be devoted to the writing of a big book—that is, to the process of interpreting the world all over again. Nor did he suspect that the first volume of that book would not appear until almost twenty years later, in 1867, and that the project would still remain unfinished at the time of his death in 1883.

When he wrote the *Manifesto*, Marx hardly thought that the revolution would have to wait until complex questions of political economy had been resolved in detail and with precision. His tone and mood were confident and optimistic. The style of the document reflects this perfectly, and the reader, whether persuaded by the argument or not, is unfailingly impressed by its sweeping and daring vision. "What a work! It never fails to astonish when you come back to it," a distinguished French historian is said to have exclaimed upon hearing it read in an admittedly unusual setting: a German prisoner-of-war camp in 1943.[4] A more detached but certainly no less distinguished commentator, Isaiah Berlin, sees in this "unique masterpiece" a "most arresting exposition" of Marx's views.[5]

This chapter does not aim to contribute to the exegesis of this most famous, most read, and most influential of Marx's works, which to this day continues to engage lively scholarly interest.[6] Rather, it attempts to show where nation belongs in the broader framework of Marx's world view, as Marx himself sketched it in that unique exposition of his total system.

The author of the *Manifesto* had confronted the question of nationalism earlier, as we have observed in the preceding discussion. His comments about it, therefore, were neither random remarks nor asides, but were rather the result of careful consideration. In his introduction to *The Communist Manifesto*, Harold Laski argues that Marx's reference to protective tariffs "is primarily a thrust at Friedrich List— who had died only the year before—and his system of German national economy based upon a closed customs union as the unit of prosperity." Laski (who is the only writer to have noticed an anti-List message in the *Manifesto*) suggests that this reference further links the *Manifesto* to American economic literature, especially Alexander Hamilton's *Report on Manufactures* (1791) and the writings of Henry C. Carey, to which Marx and Engels "gave careful attention."[7] If Laski is right, as I think he is, *The Communist Manifesto* is more than a frontal and comprehensive attack on the bourgeoisie and "classical capitalism." It is also an "antinationalist manifesto" by someone who had confronted German nationalism through the works of its main spokesman—Friedrich List.

Seemingly random and marginal remarks about nations are scattered throughout the text of the *Manifesto*. But it would be a mistake to isolate them from the main line of argument. Let us instead elicit from the argument those components that are essential for an understanding of Marx's position on nation. First of all, there is the central statement of Marx's conception of history: "The history of all hitherto existing society is the history of class struggles."[8] Elsewhere in the text, the same idea appears in somewhat different phrasing: "The history of all past society has consisted in the development of class antagonisms, antagonisms that assumed different forms at different epochs.''[9] These epochs were as follows:

> Freeman and slave, patrician and plebeian, lord and serf, guild-master and journeyman, in a word, oppressor and oppressed, stood in constant opposition to one another, carried on an uninterrupted, now hidden, now open fight, a fight that each time ended, either in a revolutionary reconstitution of society at large, or in the common ruin of the contending classes.[10]

Many think that according to Marx historical change was an uninterrupted move upward. Let us note in passing, therefore, that in the quotation above Marx recognized that class conflict in certain historical situations may result ''in the common ruin of the contending classes.'' However, it is only fair to add that this remark, in the overall context of the *Manifesto*, must have been a side reflection. Certainly it left little mark on the Marxists' attitude toward history and politics, for their outlook remained fundamentally optimistic. (Only the nuclear age impressed on most, but not all, of them the idea that class conflict might end badly for all.)

But as a matter of fact, even Marx's general formula on what history is about has not been followed up by Marxist historians: few among them appear to have taken up the clue of the *Manifesto* and written a history of the world as a history of classes and class conflicts. Marxists, like all other historians, have written histories that conceive of states and nations as constant and lasting units and have treated classes as entities operating *within* national or state boundaries, which they thus assume to be more important.

For Marx, the whole of humankind was *the* unit of history and therefore *the* unit of historical study. Social classes were the proper actors in the historical process. If he implied anything, it was that nations, empires, states, religions, cities, etc., were secondary phenomena or forces that needed to be studied and evaluated in the context, and from the perspective, of their place in class relations and in the class struggle occurring on a global scale. (This idea also appeared, as noted in Chapter 4, in *The German Ideology*, where Marx spoke of ''civil society'' as the real ''stage'' of human history.) Turning from history to the present, Marx stressed that the modern, contemporary society was also divided into antagonistic classes. Modern society ''has but established new classes, new conditions of oppression, new forms of struggle in place of the old ones.'' However, unlike previous epochs, in which class relations had been very complex, ''the epoch of the bourgeoisie . . . has simplified the class antagonisms.'' Society was becoming ever more divided ''into two great hostile camps,

into two great classes directly facing each other—bourgeoisie and proletariat.'' In the Middle Ages, on the other hand, there had been feudal
lords, vassals, guild-masters, journeymen, apprentices, and serfs.[11]

Marx admitted that the process of this simplification, or better still,
polarization, of class relations was not yet completed; there still existed
''the lower strata of the middle class: the small tradespeople, shopkeepers,
and retired tradesmen generally, the handicraftsmen and peasants.'' Their
days were numbered, however.

> All these sink gradually into the proletariat, partly because their diminutive
> capital does not suffice for the scale on which modern industry is carried
> on, and is swamped in the competition with the large capitalist, partly because
> their specialized skill is rendered worthless by new methods of production.
> Thus the proletariat is recruited from all classes of the population.[12]

Elsewhere in the *Manifesto*, Marx noted that while the Communists
proposed to abolish ''bourgeois property,'' there was no need for them to
proclaim the abolition of the petty artisan or peasant property: ''The development of industry has to a great extent already destroyed it, and is
still destroying it daily.''[13]

The actual constellation of forces in the modern society, therefore,
included the bourgeoisie, the proletariat—which ''of all the classes that
stand face to face with the bourgeoisie today . . . alone is a really revolutionary class''—and the ''other classes [that] decay and finally disappear
in the face of modern industry.'' (By contrast, the proletariat was industry's
''special and essential product.'') Marx specifically included the small
manufacturer, the shopkeeper, the artisan, and the peasant among those
who ''fight against the bourgeoisie, to save from extinction their existence
as fractions of the middle class. They are therefore not revolutionary but
conservative. Nay more, they are reactionary, for they try to roll back the
wheel of history.''[14]

If class polarization was one novel feature of modern society, internationalization or globalization—that is, unification on a world scale—was
the other. This process of global unification expressed itself in the formation
of a world market, which Marx considered as a great turning point in
history.

> The world market, for which the discovery of America paved the way
> . . . has given an immense development to commerce, to navigation, to
> communication by land. This development has, in its turn, reacted on the
> extension of industry; and in proportion as industry, commerce, navigation,
> railways extended, in the same proportion the bourgeoisie developed, in-

creased its capital, and pushed into the background every class handed down from the Middle Ages.[15]

Economic necessity—"the need of a constantly expanding market for its products"—forced the bourgeoisie to operate worldwide. "It must nestle everywhere, settle everywhere, establish connections everywhere."[16] In the process, the bourgeoisie "has played a most revolutionary role in history," destroying old relationships, values, beliefs, rules, and regulations.

> The bourgeoisie . . . has resolved personal worth into exchange value, and in place of the numberless indefeasible chartered freedoms, has set up that single, unconscionable freedom—Free Trade.[17]

In place of old values and usages, Marx repeated the same point in another context, came "free competition accompanied by a social and political constitution adapted to it, and by the economic and political sway of the bourgeois class."[18]

All of this, we must remember, was taking place globally, according to Marx. Did that mean that in the process some *nations* would establish dominion over other *nations*? The rule of the bourgeoisie, Marx said, would express itself in the establishment of the rule of "towns" over "the country." The rise of "enormous cities" would allow a portion of the village population to find rescue "from the idiocy of rural life." Marx developed this thought further and said that the bourgeoisie, besides making "the country dependent on the towns . . . has made barbarian and semi-barbarian countries dependent on the civilized ones, nations of peasants on nations of bourgeois, the East on the West."[19]

If one were to transpose Marx's idea concerning the future of the peasants as a class and his conception of "nations of peasants," one might conclude that he envisaged the disappearance of those nations or their absorption in "bourgeois" nations. But this does not seem to be what the *Manifesto* meant. Rather, it would appear that, according to Marx, when the bourgeoisie of the advanced part of the world established its influence in the rest of the globe, it would not impose one *nation's* rule over other *nations* as *nations*.

> The bourgeoisie, by the rapid improvement of all instruments of production, by the immensely facilitated means of communication, draws all nations, even the most barbarian, into civilization. . . . It compels *all nations*, on pain of extinction, to adopt the *bourgeois* mode of production; it compels them to introduce what it calls civilization into their midst, i.e., to become bourgeois themselves. In a word, it creates a world after its own image.[20]

In a sharp contrast to the nationalist world view, Marx does *not* say that nations of the world were becoming more like England, France, or the Netherlands; instead, they were becoming "bourgeois." Implicit in this stand was the idea that bourgeois nations too were becoming less "national." Marx actually admitted something like this directly when he said that through its exploitation of the world market, the bourgeoisie had "given a cosmopolitan character to production and consumption in every country." The rise of a cosmopolitan economy was making reactionaries angry, Marx continued, because it drew "from under the feet of industry the national ground on which it stood." The new world economy was destroying "all old-established national industries." It is clear that Marx identified national industries with the premodern era and regarded modern industry and commerce, under which wares were delivered to "distant lands and climes," as non-national.[21]

Marx clearly said that the following process of what we might call internationalization was taking place in all countries:

> National differences and antagonisms between peoples are vanishing gradually from day to day, owing to the development of the bourgeoisie, to freedom of commerce, to the world market, to uniformity in the mode of production and in the conditions of life corresponding thereto.[22]

The conclusion that Marx intended his statement to apply especially to the advanced nations (with the implication that the others would join in as they became drawn into international exchange) is further supported by the following:

> In place of the old local and national seclusion and self-sufficiency, we have intercourse in every direction, universal inter-dependence of nations, and as in material, so also in intellectual production. The intellectual creations of individual nations become common property. National one-sidedness and narrow-mindedness become more and more impossible, and from the numerous national and local literatures there arises a world literature.[23]

Thus we see that Marx did not say that *English* literature was driving out German or French or Indian literatures any more than he said that the *English* (or French or Dutch) way of life was being imposed on other nations. Instead, he said that a *world* (not English) literature would emerge in place of national literatures and that a *bourgeois* way of life would eliminate national modes of life. To repeat, for Marx "national" was synonymous with "premodern."

It would have been logical, in light of his argument, for Marx to speak of the rise of an international or transnational bourgeoisie and of the demise of the older national bourgeoisie of individual countries. However, Marx seems to have assumed that the bourgeoisie would remain divided into national units. One passage in the *Manifesto* states that the bourgeoisie "finds itself involved in a constant battle. . . . at all times with the bourgeoisie of foreign countries."[24] In another place, we read that "the proletariat of each country must, of course, first of all settle matters with its own bourgeoisie."[25] This sentence is preceded in the text by the statement that "though not in substance, yet in form, the struggle of the proletariat with the bourgeoisie is at first a national struggle."[26] Similarly, later on, Marx explains that "since the proletariat must first of all acquire political supremacy, must rise to be the leading class of the nation, must constitute itself *the* nation, it is, so far, itself national, though not in the bourgeois sense of the word."[27]

In a recent book, Benedict Anderson draws attention to Marx's statement, quoted above, on the "proletariat of each country" and "its own bourgeoisie." He warns: "In any theoretical exegesis, the words 'of course' should flash red lights before the transported reader." This occasion inspires Anderson to make a broader comment on the question of Marxism and nationalism. He notes that "nationalism has proved an uncomfortable anomaly for Marxist theory and, precisely for that reason, has been largely elided, rather than confronted." Anderson sees evidence of this in "Marx's own failure to explicate the crucial pronoun" ("its own bourgeoisie"). He further points out that for over a century Marxists have used the concept of "national bourgeoisie," but have not made "any serious attempt to justify theoretically the relevance of the adjective." They have not explained why "*this* segmentation of the bourgeoisie—a world-class in-so-far as it is defined in terms of the relations of production, [is] theoretically significant."[28]

Anderson's criticisms are well taken and present a serious question to contemporary Marxists. As for Marx in 1847–1848, he appears to have used those expressions quite casually, without attaching theoretical or practical significance to the more basic fact tacitly acknowledged: the continued existence of separate states. But if political forms and structures are a reflection and an instrument of economic relations, why should separate states survive the conditions of a *world* market? Why should a unitary world economy not produce for its own convenience a "corresponding" political "superstructure"?

One answer would be that Marx did not think the world economy needed a single state. He must have thought the unhindered operation of the world economy and the free functioning of a world market were secured by free trade, and he took for granted its continued existence. (This assumption is not contradicted by his reference to "one customs tariff," because it appears in a context in which he describes how heretofore isolated provinces of one state were unified by means of establishing "one code of laws, one national class interest, one frontier, and one customs tariff.")[29]

Secondly, he really did not think that capitalism had much time left. The proletarian revolution was imminent, and whatever ambiguity may have remained in Marx's view of the national character of the bourgeoisie, he had no doubts whatsoever that the proletariat was above nationality and nationalism.

"The working men have no country. We cannot take from them what they have not got."[30] These famous and much quoted words are not simply a comment on *material* poverty or legal and *political* status of the proletarians. Rather, they should be seen in conjunction with Marx's other statements in the *Manifesto*, as well as in his earlier works. They appear in the *Manifesto* next to the statement proclaiming that national differences are disappearing. They are then followed by this prediction: "The supremacy of the proletariat will cause them [national differences and antagonisms] to vanish still faster. United action, of the leading civilized countries at least, is one of the first conditions for the emancipation of the proletariat." When this happens, then "the exploitation of one nation by another" will cease, as will the exploitation of one individual by another. Similarly, the hostility between nations will be removed "in proportion as the antagonism between classes within the nation vanishes."[31] What Marx meant, but did not say, was that hostility between nations will disappear together with the nations *themselves*.

To what qualities and circumstances of its life did the proletariat owe its freedom from national limitations? Marx presented a very gloomy and depressing picture of the condition of the proletariat under capitalism—a condition that would appear most unlikely to stimulate the sentiment of international solidarity or to produce the realization of interests that transcended the local, let alone national, confines. Thus we find in the *Manifesto* that both the serf and the petty bourgeois under feudalism, as a members of an oppressed class, were guaranteed certain conditions for the continuation of their existence. Such a condition for the class member was in contrast to the condition of the modern worker, who lacked such guarantees:

> The modern laborer, on the contrary, instead of rising with the progress of industry, sinks deeper and deeper below the conditions of existence of his own class. He becomes a pauper, and pauperism develops more rapidly than population and wealth.[32]

This shows, Marx continued, "that the bourgeoisie is unfit any longer to be the ruling class in society, and to impose its conditions of existence upon society as an overriding law." The proof of the bourgeoisie's incompetence lay in its inability "to assure an existence to its slave within his slavery." The bourgeoisie "cannot help letting him sink into such a state. . . . It has to feed him, instead of being fed by him. Society can no longer live under this bourgeoisie, in other words, its existence is no longer compatible with society."[33]

It would appear that this describes the transformation of the proletariat into a *Lumpenproletariat*, to which Marx made reference earlier in the text as "the 'dangerous class,' the social scum (*Lumpenproletariat*), that passively rotting mass thrown off by the lowest layers of old society." That "social scum," according to Marx, "may, here and there, be swept into the movement by a proletarian revolution; its conditions of life, however, prepare it far more for the part of a bribed tool of reactionary intrigue."[34]

Such a vision of the future of the working class presents only one side of Marx's overall picture. It is admittedly the one that is often forgotten. As Alfred G. Meyer has noted, "The concept of the *Lumpenproletariat* indicates that Marx had two theories of the working class, one totally the opposite of the other."[35]

Apart from the *Lumpenproletariat*, what was the other side of Marx's view of the working class? What was his other theory? Given the terrible circumstances and conditions of bourgeois domination, what saved the workers or most of them from becoming "declassed"?

First of all, Marx believed that the advance of industry replaced the isolation of workers that was caused by competition—the condition of wage labor ("wage labor rests exclusively on competition among workers")— with "their revolutionary combination due to association." In this context, Marx said that "the bourgeoisie . . . produces . . . its own grave-diggers," and he proclaimed the "fall of the bourgeoisie and the victory of the proletariat . . . equally inevitable."[36]

Marx stressed that competition between the workers was the principal obstacle to the "organization of the proletarians into a class, and consequently into a political party." For him, the history of the proletariat was in large measure the story of the formation of an "ever expanding union of the workers." The improved means of communication, especially railways, facilitated contact among workers in different localities, and this in turn helped "to centralize the numerous local struggles . . . into one national struggle between classes. But every class struggle is a political struggle."[37] One of the political goals of the struggle was "legislative recognition of particular interests of the workers," which could be achieved by taking advantage of divisions within the bourgeoisie. (One example of such a success was the approval of the Ten-Hour Bill in England, Marx noted.)[38]

Marx also thought that the proletariat benefited from the political experience that it gained in helping the bourgeoisie with its struggle against the aristocracy, against certain reactionary sections of the bourgeoisie itself, and against the foreign bourgeoisie. In those battles, the bourgeoisie was compelled "to drag [the proletariat] into the political arena. The bourgeoisie itself, therefore, supplies the proletariat with its own elements of political and general education, in other words, it furnishes the proletariat with weapons for fighting the bourgeoisie."[39]

The proletariat also gained "fresh elements of enlightenment and progress" when sections of the ruling class were "precipitated into the proletariat" by industrial advance.[40]

Finally, and most interestingly from the point of view of Marx's theory of history, it was apparently possible for certain members of a class to defy the very laws of social gravitation that Marx himself proclaimed in the same *Manifesto*. When the class struggle "nears the decisive hour," he said,

> a small section of the ruling class cuts itself adrift, and joins the revolutionary class, the class that holds the future in its hands. Just as, therefore, at an earlier period, a section of the nobility went over to the bourgeoisie, so now a portion of the bourgeoisie goes over to the proletariat, and in particular, a portion of the bourgeois ideologists, who have raised themselves to the level of comprehending theoretically the historical movement as a whole.[41]

Thus, Marx expressly stated that it was possible for some "bourgeois ideologists" to join the proletariat not as a result of a change in their social and economic position but by means of a conscious and free decision based on their superior understanding of "the historical movement as a whole." In other words, some bourgeois ideologists could see the reality and were free from the constraints and distortions to which the bourgeoisie as a whole class was subject by virtue of its objective historical situation.

This significant and revealing admission that certain, rather exceptional, members of a class could perceive reality objectively should be borne in mind when one considers the Marxian concept of the identity and role of Communists in the proletarian movement. Marx denied that the Communists formed "a separate party opposed to other working-class parties," and he proclaimed that they had "no interests separate and apart from those of the proletariat as a whole." They did not advance any "sectarian principles of their own, by which to shape and mould the proletarian movement."

What *did* they do, then?

> The Communists are distinguished from the other working-class parties
> by this only; 1. In the national struggles of the proletarians of the different
> countries, they point out and bring to the front the common interests of the
> entire proletariat, independently of all nationality. 2. In the various stages
> of development which the struggle of the working class against the bourgeoi-
> sie has to pass through, they always and everywhere represent the interests
> of the movement as a whole.
>
> The Communists, therefore, are on the one hand, practically, the most
> advanced and resolute section of the working-class parties of every country,
> that section which pushes forward all others; on the other hand, theoretically,
> they have over the great mass of the proletariat the advantage of clearly
> understanding the line of march, the conditions, and the ultimate general
> results of the proletarian movement.
>
> The immediate aim of the Communists is the same as that of all the
> other proletarian parties: Formation of the proletariat into a class, overthrow
> of bourgeois supremacy, conquest of political power by the proletariat.[42]

This enumeration inspires more questions than it provides answers.
What enabled the Communists, but presumably not the others, to perceive
the interests of the entire proletariat independently of nationality? What
vantage point helped the Communists, unlike the others, to achieve a
position from which they could "represent the interests of the movement
as a whole"? Was this not a claim to a position of superiority and leadership
in the movement? What did the Communists do to make themselves, and
how did they convince the others that they were, "the most advanced and
resolute section of the working-class parties" so that they could then push
forward "all others"? In what ways did they gain their theoretical "advantage of clearly understanding" the direction, conditions, and end results
of the movement, an advantage the majority of the workers were denied?
And finally, who verified that their claims to all those qualifications were
justified? Is it only the wisdom of hindsight that makes a late-twentieth-
century reader ask all these questions and see in the Marxian pronounce-
ment the first formula for a Leninist party?
Let us set aside those questions that are inspired by the historical
experience of hindsight. Let us concentrate instead on the text of the
*Manifesto* itself and see whether it provides any clues about the true identity
of those so-called "Communists." Consider, first of all, that Marx insisted
on the role of political and educational factors in the formation of the
proletariat as a class (instead of a mass of paupers, which it would have
been without the political organization, experience, and so on). Secondly,

take also into account Marx's striking admission that bourgeois ideologues under certain circumstances would join the proletarian cause. Given these considerations, is it unhistorical to suppose that Marx's Communists were more likely than not to be something other than workers?

Such a supposition is reinforced by a reading of the *Manifesto*'s concluding section, "Position of the Communists in Relation to the Various Existing Opposition Parties." Before indicating specifically what the Communists do or will do in individual countries, the *Manifesto* lays out as a general rule that

> the Communists fight for the attainment of the immediate aims, for the enforcement of the momentary interests of the working class; but in the movement of the present, they also represent and take care of the future of that movement.[43]

In accordance with this, the Communists in Germany "fight with the bourgeoisie whenever it acts in a revolutionary way, against the absolute monarchy, the feudal squirearchy, and the petty bourgeoisie."[44] At the same time, however,

> they never cease, for a single instant, to instill into the working class the clearest possible recognition of the hostile antagonism between bourgeoisie and proletariat, in order that the German workers may straightway use, as so many weapons against the bourgeoisie, the social and political conditions that the bourgeoisie must necessarily introduce along with its supremacy, and in order that, after the fall of the reactionary classes in Germany, the fight against the bourgeoisie itself may immediately begin.[45]

The next paragraph explains why Germany is especially important to the Communists:

> The Communists turn their attention chiefly to Germany, because that country is on the eve of a bourgeois revolution that is bound to be carried out under more advanced conditions of European civilization and with a much more developed proletariat than what existed in England in the seventeenth, and in France in the eighteenth century, and because the bourgeois revolution in Germany will be but the prelude to an immediately following proletarian revolution.[46]

Clearly, all this could be understood only by those whose political and historical vision extended beyond Germany. Is it too audacious to decipher Messrs. Marx and Engels (plus a few friends) behind the code name "Communists"?

It is obvious in light of the above that the bourgeoisie did not have much of a future in Germany. In this respect, Marx did not change his earlier assessment of its prospects. However, the *Manifesto* devotes a fair amount of attention to another program for Germany, which must mean that Marx thought that program to be of some importance. Let us see what it was and what Marx thought of its prospects.

Many readers and writers tend to view the third part of the *Manifesto*, "Socialist and Communist Literature," as quite boring and definitely unimportant. Some editions omit it altogether. And yet it is significant because it reveals those currents that Marx in his time deemed important enough to expose. For our purposes, it is not necessary to pay attention to his comments on the French and English figures and ideas. Let us concentrate on just one current, which Marx termed "German or 'True' Socialism."

By placing it, along with two other currents, under a larger heading of "Reactionary Socialism" (there were also sections on "bourgeois socialism" and "critical-utopian socialism and communism"), Marx located "German socialism" among the reactionary classes (as he called them), which included the petty bourgeoisie, the peasants, etc. His point of departure was to note that while in France the body of socialist and communist literature had arisen in a society ruled by the bourgeoisie, such literature had been introduced to Germany when the bourgeoisie "had just begun its contest with feudal absolutism."[47] But while ideas moved easily from France to Germany, "French social conditions had not immigrated along with them." Because of the difference in the actual conditions of the two countries, the demands of the French Revolution were transformed in Germany into philosophical categories and concepts by German philosophers. The later French socialist and communist literature was likewise "completely emasculated."

> Since it ceased in the hands of the German to express the struggle of one class with the other, he felt conscious of having overcome "French one-sidedness" and of representing, not true requirements, but the requirements of truth; not the interests of the proletariat, but the interest of human nature, of man in general, who belongs to no class, has no reality, who exists only in the misty realm of philosophical fantasy.[48]

This was not politically irrelevant "philosophizing," though. As the struggle of the bourgeoisie against feudalism intensified, "German Socialism . . . gradually lost its pedantic innocence"; it was used by the old reactionary regimes in their struggle against liberal ideas and programs. "True" socialism thus was used by the reactionaries to attack liberalism, bourgeois competition, representative government, bourgeois liberty and equality, and so on, in order to persuade the masses that they "had nothing to gain, and everything to lose, by this bourgeois movement." The German critics "forgot that the French criticism . . . presupposed the existence of modern bourgeois society," which Germany did not have.[49]

German socialism not only "served the governments as a weapon for fighting the German bourgeoisie," but also

> directly represented a reactionary interest, the interest of the German Philistines. In Germany the petty bourgeois class, a relic of the sixteenth century, and since then constantly cropping up again under various forms, is the real social basis of the existing state of things.
>
> To preserve this class, is to preserve the existing state of things in Germany. The industrial and political supremacy of the bourgeoisie threatens it with certain destruction—on the one hand, from the concentration of capital; on the other, from the rise of a revolutionary proletariat. "True" Socialism appeared to kill these two birds with one stone. It spread like an epidemic.[50]

It is no longer important whether Marx's specific characterizations or charges were justified, whether, for example, German socialism in fact "proclaimed the German nation to be the model nation, and the German Philistine to be the typical man."[51] To the historian of Marxism and of nationalism, German socialism as depicted by Marx appears to have been an attempt, undertaken in the 1840s, to find a place in a changing society for those social groups that Marx saw destined to be destroyed by capitalism: the small bourgeoisie, the craftsmen, and the peasants. This kind of "socialism," Marx pointed out, proclaimed "its supreme and impartial contempt of all class struggles."[52] (At the same time, this presupposed, although Marx did not bother to note it, a national interest and national solidarity common to all classes.) Marx certainly agreed with Engels, who declared that

> the fraternisation of the nations, as it is now being accomplished everywhere by the extreme, proletarian, party against the ancient elementary national egoism and the hypocritical, privately egoistic cosmopolitianism of free trade, is more valuable than all German theories on true socialism.[53]

On the eve of 1848, Marx was certain that not only was the solution sought by German socialism impossible, but that a bourgeois revolution would at best be short-lived in Germany, and that almost immediately a proletarian revolution would follow.

But Marx's predictions did not materialize. As it is now possible to see, his contemporaries, whose views he attacked under the German socialist label, had been groping for a formula or program that emerged in Russia in the guise of populism several decades after 1848. Later on, in this century, that idea would win wide support in the Third World, where it would be known as *the* Marxist view, too. . . .

In Marx's historical scenarios, however, the prospect of a national alliance of the proletariat with the peasantry, which to him was more reactionary than the bourgeoisie itself, was unthinkable.

Clearly, Marx has been proven wrong. But more needs to be said if we are to understand exactly what happened. Before we move on to a comprehensive and systematic examination of nationalism, a few brief points may be appropriate now, at the close of this part of the book.

First, Marx was neither alone nor really mistaken when he felt that the conditions in pre–1848 Europe were in a state of flux or crisis, not only economically and socially, but also in terms of religion and politics. People felt that the world was undergoing a profound transformation and that some new comprehensive solution—whether religious, philosophical, or scientific—was about to emerge in response to that crisis. Such sentiments and opinions were in evidence among radicals and conservatives, revolutionaries and reformers alike.[54]

Second, Marx and virtually all of his contemporaries, regardless of whether they were left or right politically, shared his myopia about nationalism. They failed to notice that it had already become a major force that mobilized the masses around its goals and ideals. Even when Marx actually took note of nationalism, which he did in his response to List, for example, he did not appreciate that it was more than an intellectual or political current. As we shall see, nationalism was changing the actual social reality—including those aspects of it that Marx assumed to be immune to change. Although nationalism, according to Isaiah Berlin, "dominated much of the nineteenth century in Europe" and proved to be even more powerful in our time, most influential nineteenth-century thinkers neither recognized its force nor "foresaw its future."[55]

# Part Two

# 6

## *Nationalism before List*

Some of the most influential contemporary writers on nationalism have asserted that nationalist doctrines contain little or no intellectual content. Hugh Seton-Watson, for example, has said that there is "little point in trying to analyse nationalism itself as an ideology." "Its essence," he wrote, "is very simple: it is an application to national communities of the Enlightenment doctrine of popular sovereignty. . . . The rest of nationalist ideology is rhetoric."[1] Ernest Gellner has declared that there simply are no "texts" worth discussing when one considers nationalism. In his view,

> [nationalist] thinkers did not really make much difference. If one of them had fallen, others would have stepped into his place. . . . No one was indispensable. The quality of nationalist thought would hardly have been affected much by such substitutions. Their precise doctrines are hardly worth analyzing.[2]

Benedict Anderson sees one of the paradoxes of nationalism in the disparity between the " 'political' power of nationalisms" and "their philosophical poverty and even incoherence." He too states that "unlike other isms, nationalism has never produced its own grand thinkers: no Hobbeses, Tocquevilles, Marxes, or Webers." He recommends that nationalism should not be classified as an ideology—and thus thought comparable to fascism or liberalism—but rather viewed alongside such categories as "kinship" and "religion."[3]

In a recent article, William H. Sewell, Jr., takes a more positive view of nationalism as an ideology and makes constructive suggestions for how one might go about identifying the content of nationalist doctrine. Sewell points out that traditionally scholars writing on ideology focused their attention on "highly self-conscious, purposive individuals attempting to elaborate or enact 'blueprints' for change." More recently, however, attention has shifted to "the relatively anonymous and impersonal operation of 'ideological state apparatuses,' 'epistemes,' 'cultural systems,' or 'structures of feeling.' . . . " Now, when scholars study "the coherence and the dynamics of an ideological formation," they are interested in "the interrelations of its semantic items," and they find them "in their relation to social forces, not in the conscious wills of individual actors." Sewell approves of this approach because he thinks that indeed "ideologies are . . . *anonymous* or transpersonal." The consciousness of no single individual actor, not even "a Robespierre, a Napoleon, a Lenin, or a Mao," can ever contain "the whole of an ideological structure (with its inevitable contradictions and discontinuities)." An ideological structure is not a "self-consistent 'blueprint'" but rather "an outcome of the often contradictory or antagonistic action of a large number of actors or groups of actors." [4]

It is this understanding of ideology that Sewell recommends for historians as they seek to elucidate the role of ideas in history. Reflecting on the impact of the French Revolution (which is the main subject of his article), Sewell considers nationalism and the new concept of revolution as the "two most significant unanticipated outcomes" of that revolution. He insists, however, that he understands nationalism to have been "an anonymous discourse that arose out of the demands of the situation and the possibilities of pre-existing ideology rather than being formulated systematically by some theoretician."[5]

By contrast, this study stresses the original insights of major nationalist thinkers (that is, insights that have eluded thinkers of other schools) and therefore does not share Sewell's position regarding the extent of "anonymity" in nationalist doctrine. However, this does not mean to deny that conventional historical events, especially the French Revolution, have played a major, albeit somewhat "anonymous" (in Sewell's meaning of the word), role in the rise of nationalism as an *ideology*. The French Revolution did create the first modern nation in Europe, and it accomplished this through a variety of measures that deliberately aimed at such an outcome. Those measures included the promotion of French in populations that had customarily spoken other languages. In support of this linguistic policy, it was argued that French was the "language of liberty" and that those other tongues spoken in France by the Provençals, Basques, Corsicans, Flemings, Alsatians, and so on, were means to perpetuate "the reign of fanaticism and superstition . . . the domination of priests and aristocrats.''[6]

The new state created by the revolution expanded its role in such areas as education and social welfare, which had previously been the responsibility of the church. The revolution proclaimed that care for the poor, the sick, and the old would be among the responsibilities of the national government. "The Jacobins," Carlton J. H. Hayes writes, "in their anxiety to assure equality among citizens and to unite the whole nation in enthusiastic loyalty to the republic, thought of economics in terms of national policy."[7] Some of the leaders, such as Barére, proclaimed national interest to be "a pater familias, foreseeing and industrious" and proposed "a system of national works, on a grand scale, over the whole territory of the Republic."[8] Thus, even if reality fell far short of the ideal, the revolution clearly pursued a program of what in our time is called "nation-building."

The French example became the model that nationalists in other parts of the continent consciously emulated. In this sense, it exerted a powerful but paradoxical intellectual impact. Besides serving as a model, the French contributed to the rise and spread of nationalism through their direct military and political impact in Germany, Italy, Poland, and elsewhere. In some places, most notably in Poland, the French helped support a local nationalism that was pro-French. In other places, they provoked an anti-French nationalism—an attitude that was different from an old-style dislike of foreigners and from the dynastic loyalism known in prerevolutionary times. During the Napoleonic era, the enemies of French power resorted to arguments that owed their origins to the French. This happened because the French Revolution had proclaimed *universal* principles but failed to practice them as its influence extended abroad. In this sense, it is indeed true that modern nationalism is a *product* of the French Revolution and as a concept was born out of the failure of the revolution's universalism.[9] The last period of Napoleon's reign, for example, is known in German history as one of the "Wars of Liberation," that is, *national* liberation. This was not what the monarchs of the *ancien régime* thought of the opposition to Napoleon, however. In Russia, the war with Napoleon contributed to the formation of a modern national consciousness that was distinct from the traditional attitudes instilled by the government toward the authority of the tsars.

Some efforts of the French Revolution had been anticipated by individual thinkers whose philosophical, historical, and political reflections contributed to the formation of nationalist ideology. It is necessary to mention Jean-Jacques Rousseau (1712–1778) among those thinkers who, if not outright nationalist theorists, were major contributors to theories of nationalism. Rousseau's "Constitutional Project for Corsica" (1765) reveals a very central feature of nationalism:

> We have already done our best to level the site of the future nation: let us now try to sketch upon this site a plan of the building to be erected. The first principle to be followed is the principle of national character; if it did not [have it], we should have to start by giving it one.[10]

Rousseau further developed this approach by combining cultural features with politics in his essay of 1772, "Considerations on the Government of Poland." He called on the Poles to develop a universal program of national education as a guarantee for survival. "You may not prevent [your enemies] from swallowing you up," he told the Poles, but "if you see to it that no Pole can ever become a Russian, I guarantee that Russia will not subjugate Poland."[11] In other words, Rousseau argued that a nation defined as a cultural or spiritual community could survive even foreign rule.

Rousseau was the first among modern thinkers to argue that a nation exists independently of the state, or as Alfred Cobban summarizes Rousseau's view, "that a national character is a natural and unfailing attribute of every people." Rousseau postulated a link between culture and politics, as his comments on Poland and Corsica indicate. He saw in culture— language, history, laws, and customs—a political weapon and force and in certain circumstances charged the government with the task of *creating* a national culture. Thus Rousseau proclaimed a two-way relationship between culture and politics and anticipated the nation-building activity of the modern state.[12]

Rousseau's argument, Eric Hobsbawm points out, was "taken up by the French Revolution." The "nation," as understood by Rousseau, was the "sovereign people." Such a people, according to Hobsbawm,

> cannot tolerate intermediate and sectional interests and corporations between itself and its members. But by implication this very elimination of other centres of loyalty makes the relation of loyalty of citizen to "nation" the only valid, and therefore the strongest, of his emotional-political commitments. It is the content of the "civic religion" which the community needs. There is no difference between "*Gemeinschaft*" and "*Gesellschaft*," because the only valid " *Gemeinschaft*" is the *Gesellschaft*, organised as the polity. Free man equals citizen. It is irrelevant that Rousseau himself did not think in terms of modern nation-states, for such arguments were applied to them.[13]

Rousseau understood very well that the national state, unlike its dynastic predecessor, would want not only to be obeyed but also to be loved.

It is not essential to prove that Rousseau actually exercised a direct influence on events. What matters is that Rousseau, according to Alfred Cobban, "was more conscious than others of the stirrings in the air, of the springtime of a new world, and that he not only wrote the words that spelt the doom of the *ancien régime*, but also prophesied the national state of the future which was to take its place."[14]

Edmund Burke (1729–1797) developed another kind of argument in support of the cause of nationality, but he also agreed with Rousseau that emotional factors played a crucial role in modern politics.[15] In opposition to the political theories and practices of the French Revolution, which he condemned as rationalist, abstract, and thus neglectful of the realities created by historical development, Burke proclaimed the rights of historically grown nations. (Unlike Herder, Burke saw that the essence of nation resided more in laws and institutions than in the facts of folklore and ethnology.) His approach may be illustrated by comparing the causes he disapproved of—e.g., the French Revolution—with those he supported: the English Revolution of 1688; the American Revolution of 1776; the Polish reforms and the Polish struggles against Russia, Austria, and Prussia; Indian resistance to the British; and the Corsican revolt against France. In all those cases, Burke saw the struggle of authentic communities—authentic because they were historically grown—against a brute force that had no right to impose itself on them except by sheer virtue of its power.

Conventionally, Burke's nationalism is called conservative, and up to a point this is a correct designation. But when it is examined more closely, it also appears, perhaps paradoxically, to have been revolutionary. Like Rousseau, Burke affirmed the right of nations to defy those rulers who did not meet certain requirements set by the nations concerned. In other words, the fact that an authority existed was not sufficient reason to obey it.

The case of Poland shows the revolutionary implications of Burke's position. The Polish nationalism that Burke supported was not a reactionary or restorationist movement; the Poles were not challenging the status quo in order to reestablish the destroyed old order but rather to create something that combined the old with the new institutions. (They had begun to develop this synthesis before they were deprived of their independence.) Metternich, who some years later said that "Polonism is Revolution," correctly grasped this revolutionary character of Polish nationalism.[16]

The Poles lost their independent state, which had been uninterruptedly in existence for many centuries, precisely at that historical juncture which we have identified as the moment when modern nationalism was born; the

French Revolution and the era of Rousseau and Burke. In the years preceding the final partition of Poland (1795), major educational reforms were
carried out, resulting in the creation of a number of elementary and secondary schools that used Polish as the language of instruction (Latin had
been dominant until then). There was a flowering of periodical presses,
professional theaters, and book publishers through which domestic and
foreign affairs were discussed. By the early 1790s, the change in the public
mood had become broad and deep enough to enable the reform forces in
the parliament to attempt major constitutional changes (the Constitution
of May 3, 1791).

After the partitions, Polish nationalists looked back to 1791, that is,
to the constitutional revolution against the old Poland, as the point of
departure in their struggle for a new Poland. Polish nationalism was thus
predominantly political and reformist in its concerns and goals. In the
absence of national political institutions, however, literature and art began
to play an increasingly important role in maintaining the national identity
and in spreading national sentiment to those segments of the population,
most notably the peasantry, which the old Poland had excluded from
participation in national affairs. To those elements, Polish nationalism
carried both a cultural and a political message. These basic facts of Polish
history should make it easier to appreciate Lord Acton's comment, made
more than a hundred years ago, about the international importance of Polish
nationalism. Very much like Edmund Burke before him, Acton stressed
that the partition of Poland was "an act of wanton violence, committed
in open defiance not only of popular feeling but of public law. For the
first time in modern history a great State was suppressed, and a whole
nation divided among its enemies." But Acton saw the other aspect of the
Polish crisis, too:

> This famous measure, the most revolutionary act of the old absolutism,
> awakened the theory of nationality in Europe, converting a dormant right
> into an aspiration, and a sentiment into a political claim. . . . Thenceforward
> there was a nation demanding to be united in a State,—a soul, as it were,
> wandering in search of a body in which to begin life over again; and, for
> the first time, a cry was heard that the arrangement of States was unjust—
> that their limits were unnatural, and that a whole people was deprived of
> its right to constitute an independent community.[17]

The Poles were able to awaken the theory of nationality in Europe
precisely because they had been deprived of their independent statehood,
which they had enjoyed for centuries, at exactly that moment when they
were becoming a modern nation, a contemporary of the new age of sov-

ereignty of the people. For this reason, the Polish case deserves to be placed alongside the French Revolution as a major historical event that had a direct ideological significance in the history of nationalism. Understandably, the Polish message was appreciated warmly by the early intellectuals from those "awakening" nations of Central and Eastern Europe that lacked a history as glorious as Poland's but that could boast an authentic folk culture. These intellectuals argued (as Lord Acton recognized) that they, too, represented a people with its own language, culture, and "soul." Thus, while the Poles were unique, they became a role model whose cause, resting on a combination of political and cultural arguments, could be imitated. Acton, no friend of nationalism, recognized this clearly; Marx and Engels, as we shall see, did not.

Having thus recognized in Poland the other major historical event (besides the French Revolution) to play an ideological role in the rise of modern nationalism, let us return to individual nationalist thinkers. Before List, the most important among them was, without a doubt, Johann Gottfried Herder (1744–1803).

Before discussing Herder's views, it is first necessary to situate him and his "Germany" in a historical perspective. This means going back in time to periods preceding even the French Revolution, the partitions of Poland, and the Industrial Revolution in order to acknowledge those earlier but major events in European history that created the essential preconditions for the formation of a nationalist world view. We note, accordingly, that before the eighteenth century *the state* had come to be viewed as an agent and instrument of public improvement. In the era of nationalism, the adjective "public" was redefined to mean "national," and the scope of the state's functions was widened, but in actuality, the idea of the state as a creative force had emerged before nationalism. Furthermore, large-scale cultural communities, based on modern, standard languages, had also been formed in Western Europe before industrialization created a new set of ties and before the French Revolution invented a new politics.

In fact, the formation of those cultural communities can be traced back to the printing revolution of Gutenberg and the Protestant Reformation of Luther. This point has been forcefully made by Benedict Anderson in his *Imagined Communities*. Anderson points out that in medieval Western Europe, Latin, a dead language, was a sacred medium on which the European community was based and which was used for communication with God; Latin was the only language taught in medieval Europe. Western Christianity constituted a "great religiously imagined community" based on that sacred script-language. In that community, a "bilingual intelligentsia, by mediating between vernacular and Latin, mediated between earth and heaven." Anderson calls that intelligentsia a "trans-European Latin-writing clerisy." That medieval "imagined community" began to disintegrate under the pressure of two developments: an increased knowledge of the non-European world and the invention of printing. The former, according to Erich Auerbach (whom Anderson quotes), "abruptly widened the cultural and geographic horizon and hence also the men's conception of possible forms of human life." The latter precipitated the decline of Latin. The conception of time itself changed, leading to the abandonment of the previously dominant "conception of temporality in which cosmology and history were indistinguishable." A new conception of time and a new secular outlook emerged to replace the old.[18]

It was then that modern nations began to form. "A half-fortuitous, but explosive, interaction between a system of production and productive relations (capitalism), technology of communications (print), and the fatality of human diversity" (which Anderson also refers to as the "fatality of Babel") made nation a new kind of imagined community imaginable for the first time. Print-languages, he further argues, "laid the bases for national consciousness" in three ways. First, they created "unified fields of exchange and communications below Latin and above the spoken vernaculars." Second, languages became standardized. Third, certain print-languages acquired "a new politico-cultural eminence" when they became official languages of powerful monarchs and their courts; in the meantime, other print-languages were reduced to (or they retained) the status of "substandard" languages because they lacked political support. Although "mutual incomprehensibility" of languages had been "historically of only slight importance," it gained strong cultural and political significance after the introduction of print and the resultant formation of "monoglot mass reading publics."[19]

The Protestant Reformation also had an important effect on the rise of nations and, in the longer run, indirectly, on the rise of nationalism. The translation of the Bible into a vernacular was especially significant. The abolition of a separate class of priests as intermediaries between the believers and God accompanied (perhaps made possible?) the elevation of vernaculars to a status previously reserved for Latin. (One is tempted to say that Luther's replacement of Latin with the vernacular made it possible for everybody to "dial" God directly, without an "operator"—the priest.) Luther in combination with Gutenberg legitimized different, "national" roads to salvation. It was in German, not in Latin, that Luther uttered his famous "Here I stand; and I can do no other." Luther's "paradigmatic declaration"—his "grandiloquent gesture at the birth of conscience"[20]—

was performed in a medium that was deemed more "natural" than Latin for declarations of this importance. The belief that one language rather than another is a more adequate—more authentic—medium for expressing an individual's most profound feelings and thoughts lay at the heart of the doctrine of nationalism when it was formulated in the late eighteenth century.

But the printing revolution also influenced and benefited the state. Printing allowed the state to expand its control over its subjects on a previously unthinkable scale (storage and transfer of information, increased surveillance, standardization of regulations, accounting, etc.). At the same time, the state, previously based on divine sanction, began to evolve toward modern secular concepts of legitimacy.[21]

These developments also created a new kind of personality—the kind of individual who could function in a secular state and/or in that new language community brought about by the printing revolution and the Protestant Reformation. Although before the printing press there were individuals possessed of a "literate culture," which they owed to their ability to read and write, they were extremely few. The printing press, as A. J. Polan puts it, "turns the privilege of a few into the possession of the many, and thus implants literate culture as the dominant mode of thought for entire societies."[22]

Individuals of this kind were the ones who, in certain historical situations or conjunctures, were capable of conceiving and/or adopting the ideas of nationalism. Gale Stokes, who has discussed the connection between nationalism and individual psychology, argues that "the development of interdependent economic systems has led to the creation of, in almost all members of society rather than in just a few, a cognitive state which is especially well suited to responding to the appeals of nationalism." He calls such individuals "operational" and the quality they possess "operationalism." Such individuals are capable of abstract, logical thought and are "able to apply the fundamental rules of category, hierarchy, function, and so forth to the world" *and* to their words. Historically, when large numbers of people were drawn to new uses of language, they became interested in language and felt "comfortable among people who manipulated abstractions in a readily understandable way. The linguistic nation, not some larger group and not some smaller group, offered the most satisfying community to persons who were operational."[23]

In an argument that parallels Polan and Stokes', James J. Sheehan has related the rise of nationalism to an increase in the number of persons whose social ties were "linear," a word he adopts from Edward Whiting

Fox. "Linear," Sheehan explains, signifies those "relations among people
who do not necessarily live near to one another, but who do share some
social position, commercial interest, or cultural proclivity which links them
across space."[24]

We conclude that in general nationalism emerges in a society that (as
in Germany, for example) has been influenced by the printing revolution
and its product, "typographical culture," to produce educated individuals
capable of viewing "their nation's" position in relation to the world outside. It is those initially quite rare individuals who first conceive the idea
of a "nation" and then conclude that its political and economic conditions
lag behind its cultural potential, as well as behind the political, economic,
and cultural achievements of other—advanced—nations. Thus nationalism
takes as its point of departure a nation's relative advancement in education
and culture, as demonstrated by the fact that intellectuals capable of nationalist thinking are present. On this foundation, a nation then organizes
a political movement to establish a new state or to win over an already
existing state for the cause of its political, social, and economic advancement. It is an essential precondition of nationalism as a doctrine that
advanced communities—nations—already exist with which to compare the
inferior condition of one's own homeland. The *premodern* state does not
initiate such programs on its own; they are first put forward by nationalist
thinkers and agitators who argue in the name of "the national interest."[25]
It is a central aspect of their argument to point out that elsewhere—in "the
West" (England, France)—there already *exist* nations that meet the criteria
of progress.

Before such a political nationalism can emerge in an underdeveloped
society, however, it is necessary to formulate the idea of cultural nationalism. And in Germany, the central, seminal figure to perform that cultural
task was Herder. Thus it is not enough to see Herder as a preacher of the
virtues of the natural man and of the simple, rural community, or as
someone who idealized folklore, song, legends, and tales (what we call
oral culture and tradition). Herder was also a product of a "print culture"
and belonged to the literate class of the intelligentsia that shared a modern
medium of communication and creativity—the standard German language.
No less importantly, Herder was charged with a strong sense of individual
freedom and responsibility—a Protestant ethic par excellence—even
though at the same time he affirmed the necessity of belonging to a group.
According to F. M. Barnard, the distinguished Herder scholar, Herder saw
the essence of man in *freedom*. Barnard quotes the following passage from
"Essay on the Origin of Language" (1772) to illustrate Herder's understanding of man as fundamentally different from all other living beings:

Man alone has made a goddess of *choice* in place of *necessity* . . . he can weigh up good against evil, truth against falsehood; he can explore possibilities and choose between alternatives. . . . Even when he most despicably abuses his freedom, man is still king. For he can still choose, even though he chooses the worst; he can rule over himself, even if he legislates himself into a beast.[26]

According to Barnard, Herder believed that men could arrive at "this consciousness of freedom" through language as the "vital medium": "It is Herder's central thesis that language is first and foremost an indispensable requirement for the operation of the human mind, an integral part of thought."[27] This emphasis on the central role of language explains why Herder thought that "to belong to a given community . . . is a basic human need no less natural than that for food or drink or security or procreation."[28]

This emphasis on belonging did not deny—on the contrary, it assigned to—the individual a creative role. Herder's outlook considered the individual's self-realization to be the normal mode of the group's existence. (Isaiah Berlin calls this aspect of Herder's thought "expressionism," while Roger Hausheer prefers "expressivism.")[29] Herder wrote, "a poet is a creator of a people; he gives it a world to contemplate, he holds its soul in his hand." He also wrote, "we live in a world we ourselves create." Berlin, who quotes these sentences, observes that Herder also thought that the poet (and man in general) was "to an equal extent created by" his people and his world. Although Herder's ideas were "inflated into extravagant metaphysical shapes" by some later German thinkers, says Berlin, "they are equally at the source of the profoundest sociological insights of Marx and the revolution in the historical outlook that he initiated."[30]

Herder's expressionism was directly opposed to "the central doctrine of the Enlightenment," which held that "the rules in accordance with which men should live and act and create are pre-established, dictated by nature herself."[31] His view of language and nationality likewise contradicted the doctrines of the Enlightenment, which, although secular, shared with the old revealed religion the belief in the uniformity of human nature. As Alfred Cobban puts it:

> While most of the *philosophes* admired the classical spirit of patriotism, they disliked national differences, ignored the existence of nationality as a historical force, and if they had been aware of any general claim to national independence would certainly have repudiated a right based on nothing more than sentiment and tradition.[32]

The Enlightenment denied the Christian doctrine of original sin and believed in the natural goodness of man—or at least in the possibility of making man good through proper educational or political measures.[33]

Herder, in opposition to the dogmas of the Enlightenment, "believed that to understand anything was to understand it in its individuality and development." To achieve such understanding, it was necessary to take into account "the outlook, the individual character of an artistic tradition, a literature, a social organisation, a people, a culture, a period of history."[34]

We might therefore say that philosophically Herder challenged René Descartes' (1596–1650) famous *cogito* argument "I think, therefore I am." Herder responded, although not in these words, with "But I am what I speak." His successors, if not Herder himself, drew the further conclusion: "Since I speak differently from others, I also think differently, and *am* different, and therefore I should be governed differently from them."[35]

While Herder extolled the diversity of the human race, he "supposed that different cultures could and should flourish fruitfully side by side like so many peaceful flowers in the great human garden," and even more importantly, he postulated a fundamental equality and equivalency of all cultures and peoples. Berlin argues that Herder "rejected the absolute criteria of progress then fashionable in Paris: no culture is a mere means towards another; every human achievement, every human society is to be judged by its own internal standards." While "for Voltaire, Diderot, Helvetius, Holbach, Condorcet, there is only universal civilisation, of which now one nation, now another, represents the richest flowering," Berlin argues further, "for Herder there is a plurality of incommensurable cultures."[36]

It seems, however, that Berlin overemphasizes Herder's view of incommensurability of cultures. Herder's conception of human development was dialectical; conflict among nations, as well as intercommunication and cross-fertilization of cultures, played a central role in it. Thus he held that kinship groups transformed themselves into nations and that nations (and languages) came to differ from each other not because of climate or geography, but "largely [because of] internal factors such as dispositions and attitudes arising from relations between families and nations. Conflict and mutual aversion, in particular, have greatly favored the emergence of language differentiation." He also insisted that the cause of divisiveness was *not* "a matter of clashing material interests . . . but a matter of collective opinion and tribal honour."[37]

Thus Herder clearly thought that nations arose historically out of a "communication breakdown," as we would put it today, within already existing groups. However, if conflict was the initial spurt to the formation of a community, Herder's view of the history and development of nations attached a central importance to their interacting with, and learning from, one another after they had been formed. Just as individuals develop only by interacting with other individuals, Herder insisted, so groups develop "among other groups." As he wrote in his "Essay on the Origin of Language," originally published in 1772:

> Have we Germans not learned most of what we know as a "civilized nation" from other peoples? Indeed we have. In this and in many other such cases nature has forged a new chain of transmission, from nation to nation. Arts, sciences, languages, the totality of social cultures, have been developed and refined in a powerful progression in this very manner. This international transmission of social cultures is indeed the *highest form of cultural development which nature has elected.*
>
> We Germans would, like the Indians of North America, still be living contentedly in our forests, waging cruel wars as heroes, if the chain of foreign cultures had not pressed in upon us and, with the impact of centuries, had not forced us to join in. Roman civilization hailed from Greece; Greece owed its culture to Asia and Egypt; Egypt to Asia, China perhaps to Egypt, and so on; thus the chain extends from its first link to the last and will one day encircle perhaps the whole world. . . . Let the nations freely learn from one another, let one continue where the other has left off. . . . Egyptians, Greeks, Romans, and some modern nations, merely carried on and developed the heritage handed down to them. Others, such as Persians, Tartars, Goths, and Papists arrived on the scene to destroy and lay waste what the former had created. Yet this only helped to stimulate new activity and new creations upon the debris of the old. . . . [38]

How did Herder's ideas, of which this is only an incomplete account, sound—what "message" did they convey—in his time?

First, by stressing the language, culture, customs, and ways of life as the defining characteristics of a nation, Herder affirmed the primacy of culture, broadly defined, over political organization. Even though he himself was not directly involved in politics, it did not take long for some of Herder's compatriots to conclude that the political status quo, under which several hundred sovereign entities—kingdoms, duchies, grand duchies, free cities, margravates, bishoprics, and so on—functioned on German soil, was out of tune with "Germany" understood as a cultural community. Nationalism viewed those states in relation to the nation in a way analogous to Marx's treatment of the state in relation to society. The relations of domination, nationalism implied, were in conflict with the relations of communication in "Germany." In due course, men emerged who would argue that this contradiction ought to be resolved (transcended) by adjusting the former to the latter, i.e., by the establishment of a unified German state.

Second, in Herder's cultural nationalism, there was no belief in the self-sufficiency and cultural autarky of a nation. Herder's concept of a nation and national culture was historical, "developmental," and based on the presupposition that a nation's intimate relations with other nations were a condition of its own growth.

Third, Herder criticized the domination by one nation and culture over another nation and culture because for him alien rule (which included culture domination) was the most objectionable expression of alienation. Herder especially resented French dominance because it sought to *impose* its own standards and values on others and, while doing so, falsely presented these French "products" as universal or "cosmopolitan." Herder denied, as a matter of principle, that such cosmopolitanism or universalism was possible.

Fourth, Herder and his German contemporaries were aware that French culture, including language, owed its dominant and privileged position in no small measure to its association with the French state, to the fact that France was a powerful country. They resented this element of coercion in French influence. It was not hard for Herder's successors to conclude that while culture was indeed autonomous, it depended for its normal growth on political arrangements, and that ultimately political independence was required to prevent foreign domination over domestic culture.

Fifth, under Herder's inspiration, German nationalists (and other nationalists after them) began to view relations between nations in terms of an "unequal exchange" or "uneven development." They thought that the condition of one nation was adversely affected by the terms under which its relations with other nations were conducted. Herder was the first to suggest this view with reference to culture. Later thinkers and activists extended it to politics and economics as well and indeed postulated a linkage between politics, economics, and culture as spheres in which nations interacted and competed with each other. They introduced the idea of stages of development by which one nation could be judged as more or less "developed" or "backward" than others. Herder's concept of a national culture emphasized the importance of learning from others. As we shall see, this idea would be central in the thought of Friedrich List, particularly in his *National System of Political Economy* (1841).

Finally, Herder's charges against French claims to cosmopolitanism may have been one of the earliest formulations of the idea of "ideology." List would subsequently raise an identical charge against Britain by arguing that the doctrine of free trade, which the British had pronounced cosmopolitan and therefore equally beneficial to all humanity, was in actuality biased to favor England's selfish interest. List pointed out that this was so because nations were not at the same stage of development as England.

(At a further remove, a similar doctrine of ideology would become a distinct feature of Marxism.)

As one recognizes Herder's seminal role in creating the nationalist world view, it is important not to attribute to him more insight into the problematics of the modern world than can be reasonably supported by the evidence. Most notably, while Herder fully recognized the connection between action and speech, he underestimated, if not outright ignored, "the influence of work" in human life. (He did this despite his obvious familiarity with the life of ordinary working people.) That neglect, Berlin says, "was made good much later under Saint-Simonian and Marxian influence."[39]

Berlin's comment might seem to imply that only socialism—but not nationalism—corrected Herder's neglect. In fact, this has not been the case, as the following chapters will show. But before we can see how nationalism as well made good this neglect, it is necessary to ask about the general content of nationalist doctrine. As is well known, every nationalism claims to speak for a unique nation endowed with its unique virtues and faced with its unique problems. It is easy to conclude, therefore, that there is no nationalist "algebra" behind the "arithmetic," that there is no general content in nationalist theory, no *generic* nationalism. Among contemporary writers, Anthony D. Smith has achieved a real breakthrough in the study of nationalism by proposing to extract what he calls the "core doctrine" of nationalism from the various forms in which nationalism appears. Smith is especially concerned with separating the propositions of the core doctrine—let us call it generic nationalism—from what he calls the "German organic version," which has been long regarded as *the* representative form of nationalism. But according to Smith, identifying the notions of the German organic version with nationalism in general is a mistake. The core doctrine of nationalism includes the belief that "humanity is naturally divided into nations"; that nations have their "peculiar character"; that all political power is derived from the nation; that "men must identify with a nation" for their freedom and "self-realization"; that nations require their own states for fulfillment; that the nation-state has the highest claim to men's loyalty; and finally, that the nation-state is the condition of "global freedom and harmony."[40]

Nationalism "fuses three ideals," says Smith: national self-determination, "national character and individuality," and "the vertical division of the world into unique nations." Nationalism does not prescribe how self-determination should be carried out, nor does it define the content in which national individuality should express itself. Smith stresses the "doctrinal sketchiness" and "the multifarious nature" of nationalist goals and activities.[41] However, he believes that behind the "more extravagant and ambitious interpretations of specific writers," it is possible to discover the "assumptions common to most examples generally included under the rubric of 'nationalism,' a kind of *sine qua non* for all nationalists." He emphasizes that the "accretions" to the core doctrine are different in the various versions of nationalism because they reflect the specific conditions and aspirations of particular groups, and—we might add—the personal contributions of individual thinkers.[42]

Even though the nationalist ideal lacks "a central tradition, single prophet or biblical text or canon," Smith continues, all versions of nationalism are interrelated. He notes that nationalism has survived many transformations in facing the challenges of several powerful rivals in both the nineteenth and twentieth centuries. More specifically, there is in nationalism an enduring unity that has enabled it to face "millennial, fascist, racist and communist movements" in this century, just as, in the nineteenth century, it had met the criticisms from the religious and liberal democratic camps, as well as from the Marxist camp. Nationalism "has always outlasted them, showing itself to be more attractive, more flexible and more tenacious than its competitors."[43] Smith admits that "nationalism does not have a complete theory of social change or political action" and that, therefore, it requires "supporting theories,"[44] but he insists that in complexity and comprehensiveness nationalism can be compared with Marxism. Nationalism inverts "the 'base-superstructure' metaphor of the Marxists," says Smith, and on the cultural base of history and language builds "the 'corresponding' . . . economic, class and bureaucratic superstructures."[45]

Let us now summarize, without repeating the argument as it was presented, the main conclusions of this chapter. The Europeans began to think of themselves—became *capable* of thinking of themselves—as members of national communities under the influence of print-culture and the Protestant Reformation, with their profound religious, psychological, intellectual, and political consequences.[46] After Gutenberg and Luther, a new kind of individual, as well as a new kind of cultural and political community, emerged in Europe. The preconditions for the rise of nationalism thus appeared. The French Revolution contributed directly to the formation of nationalism when, by *design*, it created a modern nation in France and when it exerted a political and intellectual impact beyond France. Polish resistance also helped to make nationalism an intellectual-cum-political force as Poland became the classic case of a *nation* fighting for a *state*.

Nationalism as a world view, an ideology in the sense proposed by

Sewell, took shape in the writings of thinkers like Rousseau, Burke, and Herder. These individuals reflected on changes that were taking place in the world around them. They asked questions about human nature, about the relation of the individual to his or her group, and they even tried to discover what kind of association was most compatible with human nature as they understood it. Their discourse extended over culture broadly defined—language, literature, religion, history, law, and politics. They also asked about how foreign rule affects the psychological, moral, and intellectual make-up of individuals who belong to a dependent nation. Their very "unstructured" reflections did not easily fit within the traditional discourse of academic disciplines. (Indeed, as we shall see in Chapter 10, nationalism saw the emergence of—gave birth to?—new academic fields, for example, ethnography.) Earlier thinkers knew cities and city-states, principalities, kingdoms, and empires: In a world that itself was changing, the nationalists observed the making of new communities—nations.

We can readily agree, therefore, that early nationalism was a complex and comprehensive ideology, as Smith claims for nationalism in general. But preoccupied with culture and politics, the eighteenth-century nationalists had neglected the economic sphere in spite of the fundamental transformation of the economic way of life—the process we now call the Industrial Revolution—that had begun in Britain in the second half of that century. Sooner or later, however, European nationalists had to react to industrialization, and among those who did so was Friedrich List. It was List who linked the economic aspect of a nation's life to the nation's culture and politics in a synthesis that enabled nationalism to compete successfully with its rivals, including Marxism. If we cannot say about him that he inverted (to use Smith's phrase) "the 'base-superstructure' metaphor of the Marxists," it is only because List produced his system before Marx.

# 7

## *Friedrich List: 1789–1846*

Friedrich List, whose *National System of Political Economy* Marx criticized in 1845, was a public figure of considerable renown between the Congress of Vienna (1815) and the 1848 revolution. Accounts of the German Question in the ''pre-March era'' (i.e., pre–1848) emphasize List's role in the movement for economic and political unification of Germany. He is also remembered as an early and enthusiastic promoter of the railroad, to which he attributed both economic and political importance. The precise date of his birth is not known, but he was baptized Daniel Friedrich on August 6, 1789.[1] He was called Fritz and used only Friedrich as his given name. He was the eighth child (second son) of Johannes List and Maria Magdalene (Schäfer) List. In his time, he was a government official and a political prisoner, a university professor, a businessman, and a farmer, an editor and a lobbyist, an émigré and a diplomat.

For a number of years, he lived in the United States. He wrote and lectured there, owned a business, edited a newspaper, took part in political struggles, and was nominated for a diplomatic appointment to his homeland for his efforts on behalf of Andrew Jackson's successful campaign for president. After List's return from the United States, he lived for several years in France and traveled widely throughout Europe.

List's hometown, Reutlingen, in the historic region of Swabia, was a free Imperial City at the time of his birth. This means it was one of those several hundred virtually autonomous entities that composed ''Germany,'' or to be precise, the Holy Roman Empire of the German Nation, before the Napoleonic wars. Eighteenth-century Germany included powerful European states like Prussia and the hereditary lands of the Habsburgs (Austria, Bohemia, and Moravia), as well as a number of intermediate states (for example, Bavaria and Saxony) and a much larger number of smaller entities, including many similar to Reutlingen in size, population, and importance. And yet, Reutlingen recognized only the supreme authority of the Emperor and was autonomous in its affairs.

List's father was a tanner who at various times held municipal posts in his hometown, once serving, for example, as a city councilman. Friedrich List received his preliminary instruction in a local school (his biographers note he was not a good student) and was then apprenticed in his father's business, which he did not like and soon gave up. Some biographers claim the young Friedrich strongly disliked the strenuous effort this work required and mention that he questioned why the energy of the river could not be harnessed to make machines do the job instead. This may well be a retrospective and hagiographic tribute to a pioneer of modern industry, but there is no question that List's father gave up on him as a prospective successor in the family business.

In 1805, at age sixteen, List left home to become a junior clerk (*Schreiber*) in the Württemberg bureaucracy. In the meantime, Reutlingen had lost its independence and had become part of Württemberg, a principality Napoleon expanded and raised to the status of a kingdom. When this happened, the number of German "states" was drastically reduced in consequence of the Napoleonic wars. (In 1806, the Holy Roman Empire itself ceased to exist.)

For the next several years, List had a succession of government jobs in several cities of the kingdom. He studied law and public administration, taking time off only for family reasons (because of the deaths of his father and elder brother), and by 1817 he rose to the post of Director of Finance in the Ministry of the Interior of Württemberg. As a government official, List took a broad view of his profession. He wrote several memoranda recommending administrative reforms, and he became involved in the political struggle in Württemberg then being waged between the forces of reform, with which he sided, and those of reaction. One of List's major concerns was university reform, and he especially advocated improvements in the training of government officials. For a brief period (1818–1819), even though he did not have a university degree, he held a professorship of public administration at the University of Tübingen. This was a new subject not only in Tübingen but in Germany as a whole, and List was one of the officials who first proposed that a new school of public administration be founded at the university. He owed his post to the liberal minister of education, Karl-August von Wangenheim; the other professors thought List lacked the qualifications. However, he lost the position soon after the minister's fall, because of the enmity of his political opponents. In May 1819 he formally resigned his academic post and was also dismissed from Württemberg civil service for his political activities "abroad" (i.e., in other parts of Germany).

For, in those years, List had begun to speak up on general German public issues in the press. In one article, published in 1817, he recommended radical changes in the constitution of the German Confederation, which, as constituted at the Congress of Vienna, lacked an effective central government. He proposed a national parliament in place of the existing loose assembly, as well as an army, a supreme court for Germany, and "federal institutions to foster the arts, science and education."[2]

In 1819, List directly entered the German national scene when he became one of the founders of the Union of German Merchants and Manufacturers in Frankfurt. He was elected to be the Union's secretary and advisor (*Konsulent*), as well as the editor of its weekly journal. (That journal, *Organ für den deutschen Handels—und Fabrikantenstand*, existed from 1819 to 1821.) List looked back upon that period more than twenty years later when he was writing the preface to his *National System of Political Economy*. The story of the book, he said, was the story of half of his life.[3] Remembering those early years, he wrote:

> In 1819 all Germany teemed with schemes and projects for new political institutions. Rulers and subjects, nobles and plebeians, officers of State and men of learning, were all occupied with them. Germany was like an estate which had been ravaged by war, whose former owners on resuming possession of it are about to arrange it afresh. Some wanted to restore everything exactly as it had been, down to every petty detail; others to have everything on a new plan and with entirely modern implements; while some, who paid regard both to common sense and to experience, desired to follow a middle course, which might accommodate the claims of the past with the necessities of the present. Everywhere were contradiction and conflict of opinion, everywhere leagues and associations for the promotion of patriotic objects.[4]

In an attempt to put some order into a confusing picture, we might say that, in the post–1815 period, educated and nationally aware Germans in the thirty-eight states composing the German Confederation were preoccupied with one or the other (or both) of the following issues. On the one hand, there were those who sought ways to bring about a political unification of Germany, preferably in a constitutional state with liberal institutions. Political aspirations of this kind ran directly counter to the existing order and were resolutely opposed by the leading statesman of the period, Austria's Chancellor Clemens von Metternich. On the other hand, some nationally aware Germans concentrated their attention on the development and cultivation of a broadly defined German culture. They saw the essence of nationality in history, beliefs, legal and social customs, poetry, and music. Such interests and pursuits did not openly challenge the existing political order. However, these proponents of Germany's "cultural nationalism," by emphasizing the common ethnic features of the inhabitants of Prussia, Bavaria, Saxony, and Austria, inevitably played down the differences among the latter states as against the postulated common German elements. Thus it may be said that cultural nationalism provided an indirect support for the cause of the political activists.

In his youth, Friedrich List shared the ideas and values of those political and cultural nationalists, as shown by his reform plans for the German Confederation. However, he brought into nationalist thought and politics a new component or dimension—to wit, the idea of "Germany's" *economic* unity. List's program was novel and highly original, for it took as its premise the rise of industrialism following the Industrial Revolution in Britain and also accepted the political ideas and ideals of the French Revolution. His originality can be best appreciated when one first examines the reactions of his German nationalist predecessors and contemporaries to the phenomenon of modern industrialism. (Let us note in passing that there was no *single*, automatic nationalist response to the Industrial Revolution. Had there been one, individual thinkers would indeed not have mattered. But they did.)

Some of those German nationalists were aware of the development of modern industry in Britain and responded by condemning its practices and theories as a threat to German nationality. Accordingly, they recommended that Germans avoid modern industry. On this issue, German nationalists followed Edmund Burke's highly critical view of modern economic science. Burke had disapproved of the science of economics and of the new realities it interpreted, because it considered the *individual* to be the basic factor in the economic process; Burke, however, believed that a historically formed group was more important to that process than the individual. The German (and other) Romantics of Burke persuasion condemned the modern industrial society—we are speaking of early capitalism—as the cause of poverty, alienation, destruction of familial and other ties, and so forth. Against this bleak picture of modern urban and industrial life, of a society with competing individuals, the Romantics put forth an idealized image of the old, integrated "community." (Marx dealt with some similar arguments in the third part of *The Communist Manifesto*.)

Adam Müller (1779–1829) was a Burke disciple and the leading exponent of "economic Romanticism" in Germany. According to Henry

William Spiegel, "Müller extolled the corporate state and other medieval institutions and suggested their restoration." Müller opposed "the liberal commercialism of the modern age" and contrasted it with what he held to be "higher spiritual values" derived from authority, tradition, and religion. He elevated the state to the status of "a mediator between man and God."[5]

Spiegel further points out that Müller had been an early critic of capitalism because it posed a threat to the absolute state, which he supported. Müller believed that free enterprise and competition caused "disorder and loosen(ed) the traditional personal ties," and he objected to free trade because it destroyed "the ideal of a self-sufficient and independent state." Müller even opposed the abolition of serfdom, which in his time still survived in the eastern parts of Germany.[6]

Scholars are divided on List's relation to his German predecessors and contemporaries on the issue of economics. Some, like Alexander Gray, think that List borrowed from Müller.[7] Others, notably Charles Gide and Charles Rist, question this and point out that List was acquainted with Müller's ideas, but that his nationalism had other sources: "To be a German writer in the Germany of the nineteenth century was quite enough to imbue one with the idea of nationality."[8] More recently, Joseph Finkelstein and Alfred L. Thimm see Müller as one of the founders of modern German conservatism and also as "a key figure in the emergence of an anticapitalism of the right." This assessment sharply contrasts with their view of List:

> A far greater personality than Müller was the rebel politician and economist Friedrich List. . . . Although he is commonly referred to as a "nationalist," List had very little in common with Müller. List rejected completely Müller's regressive, dark, "back to medievalism" type romanticism. The future of Germany lay in the dynamic growth of progressive capitalism. It is easy to think of List as being very much at home among the supporters of the early New Deal, or with any stretch of the imagination, in the coterie of followers of President Johnson's Great Society.[9]

Arcadius Kahan surmises that List "probably borrowed more from Müller than from Hamilton" (about whom we shall speak shortly). However, Kahan provides a summary of the German Romantic position, especially Müller's position, that makes it easy to see that List was different from Müller and the other German Romantics. The Romantics, says Kahan, represented a reaction against the classical political economy that "could not be directed purely against the economic analysis, but had to include a reexamination of the underlying principles." He further argues that this reaction "became a part of the reaction against the philosophy of the eighteenth century Enlightenment."[10] The critics of the classical school, Kahan says,

> viewed the economy as a social institution shaped only to a small extent by the direct economic interests of its individual participants and to a much greater extent by the traditions, spirit, culture, and historical conditioning of large distinguishable and defined groups like nations, classes, etc.[11]

Another major German nationalist critic of capitalism was Johann Gottlieb Fichte (1762–1814). Fichte also placed the economy beneath the state, just as he perceived the individual to be subject to the authority of the community. For example, the right of an individual to practice an occupation was to be subject to the community's evaluation of his performance and could be revoked if the individual had been found deficient. Insofar as international economic relations were concerned, Fichte advocated a closed national industrial system. In his book, *The Closed Commercial State (Der geschlossene Handelsstaat)*, he proposed to make the national state fully independent economically from all other states and recommended that it close its frontiers to foreign trade. Whatever foreign trade was necessary would be conducted by the state itself. Fichte also proposed that at home the state would be the regulator of the economy and would both assign work to and determine the wages of all persons. On the other hand, all citizens would be guaranteed by the state "the right to work."[12]

When German economic thought of the early nineteenth century was critical of modern economic practices in the West (such as industrialization), when it rejected the values and principles underlying the new economy—for example, individualism—and denied the autonomy of the economic sphere from the political and from the state, it could draw on an earlier German philosophical and administrative ("cameralist") tradition. In that tradition, "the state" had been extolled as a moral entity, as the embodiment of moral values. Critics of Western individualism, nationalism, and democracy supported their views on the authority of the state by drawing from Hegel's philosophy.[13]

List did not reject the German tradition of respect for the state, but to him, the state was the guiding force in the process of intellectual, political, economic, and social change. In this he continued, and also modified, a tradition of German legal and political thought that went back to the late seventeenth and eighteenth centuries, when Christian Thomasius and Christian Wolff spoke in favor of an independent role for public authority. List made an original contribution to this particular tradition, however, by advocating "the nationalization" of the state and the transformation of society into an industrial and commercial nation under the state's aegis.[14]

What really distinguished List from those German jurists and instead drew him closer to Saint-Simon was his enthusiasm for modernity in science, technology, and manufacturing. Like Saint-Simon, List was an ideologist of industrialism and industrialization. At the same time, he subordinated the economy to a noneconomic entity—nation—and wanted the economy to serve the nation. It is evident that Saint-Simon influenced List's "industrialism," but he, unlike List, did not believe in a *national* state led by a *national* elite in charge of modern industry. On the contrary, Saint-Simon thought industrialism and science implied the "withering away" of the (national) state and of nationality, both of which would be replaced by a new supranational organization under a scientific authority.[15]

This interpretation of List's intellectual affinities agrees with the argument of Erna Schulz, who in a study published in 1937 argued that List's sense of the historical was "dramatic": Unlike Otto von Ranke, the famous German scholar who said that the task of history was to describe the past "as it really happened" (*wie es eigentlich gewesen* ), List was interested not in what "really happened" but in what *can* happen. Schulz placed List's intellectual development in the context of his legal studies at Tübingen, and she stressed the similarities between List's ideas and those of such Enlightenment thinkers as Montesquieu. "As a political character, List stands more closely to the activism of the Enlightenment than to the contemplative and reflective attitude of Romanticism."[16] List was neither an economic historian nor an economic theorist, she argued; the dominant feature of his talent was "the sense for the political."[17]

As we see, List was not the first German nationalist to treat the economic sphere in light of a nationalist doctrine, but he was the only one who *welcomed* the Industrial Revolution and its political, social, and cultural consequences. While he shared Müller's belief in a national community that was not itself economically defined, his economic and political views were directly opposed to Müller's or Fichte's.

As List adopted a nationalist view, he rejected the dominant free trade economic theory that had been developed in the West to explain and legitimize the new order. He had begun to question the validity of this theory as early as 1820 or even before that date, as he himself recalled many years later.[18] At first, List remembered, he had been of a divided mind regarding free trade. He saw the benefits accruing from free trade, but was also aware of the gains derived from protection. He settled his uncertainty when he concluded that free trade would be right if all nations followed its principles. But it is clear that List did not stop at this conclusion in the end. Nation was the overriding value for List, above "individualism" and above "humanity," but nations were not equally developed. Free trade was bound to affect them differently, depending on their level of development or the "stage" in their evolution. A nation's economic policies had to vary depending on this circumstance. But to treat economics in this way required an extension of one's analysis beyond economics per se. Why should nation be given such preferential treatment when List himself accepted the subordination of regional interests to those of the whole in the framework of states? Obviously one had to prove that nation was a noneconomic value or more than an economic value. This meant treating nation as a phenomenon in the sphere of culture as well. It also meant that economics should be treated as a policy science. The question of whether or not a nation needed certain economic measures, or even more importantly, the determination of what the national interest *was* in any particular historical moment, was a political matter to be decided and implemented by that state. What was the proper relationship between "society," including businessmen, and the state? List had no doubt that commercial policy was the proper business of the government.[19]

These were issues of the highest theoretical and practical importance, but as List later confessed, instead of developing his ideas through further research, his practical "spirit" or "instinct" (*Sinn*) led him to attempt putting them into practice just as they were forming in his mind. "I was still young." (*Ich war noch jung.*)[20] And thus, in 1819, at about the same age at which Marx would many years later compose a *Manifesto* for the Communist League, Friedrich List turned to the industrialists and merchants with an exhortation (though not in precisely these words): "Businessmen of All Germanies, Unite!" (He must have thought then that while the philosophers had interpreted the German spirit in various ways, the point was to change Germany.)

Unlike Marx, however, List did not call for revolution, but for reform. Instead of preaching a violent overthrow of the existing structures, List wanted to give them a new life and a new sense of purpose. He decided to avail himself of a dormant provision in the German Diet's constitution, one of whose articles, in his words, had "expressly left the door open for the establishment of a national commercial system. This article appeared to me to provide a basis on which the future industrial and commercial prosperity of the German Fatherland might rest."[21]

The Union of German Merchants and Manufacturers invoked this provision to justify its program, and in April 1819, it submitted to the Diet a petition written by List. In it, the Union called "for the removal of all custom-duties and tolls in the interior of Germany, and the establishment of a universal German system founded on the principle of retaliation against foreign states.''[22] This objective was repeated in the concluding section of the petition.

> We think that we have brought forward sufficient reasons to prove to your august assembly that only the remission of the internal customs, and the erection of a general tariff for the whole Federation, can restore national trade and industry or help the working classes.[23]

After a reference to the sufferings of the German manufacturers, most of whom ''are either entirely ruined or drag on a precarious and burdensome existence,'' and to the merchants, who ''have almost lost their occupation,'' the petition asked about the causes of this deplorable situation.

> The ruinous condition of German trade and manufactures must be due either to individuals or to the conditions of society. But who can reproach the German with the lack of talent or industry? Is he not proverbial for these qualities among all the nations of Europe? Who can deny his enterprise? Did not those towns which now serve as the instruments of foreign competition once conduct the trade of the world? It is only in the faults of the social organization that we can find the cause of evil.[24]

Then came a broader philosophical reflection:

> Rational freedom is the first condition of all human development, whether physical or mental. As the individual mind is hampered by restrictions on the exchange of ideas, so the prosperity of nations is impaired by the fetters which are placed on the production and exchange of material goods. Not until universal, free, and unrestricted commercial intercourse is established among the nations of the world will they reach the highest degree of material well-being.[25]

Universal and free trade was a desirable goal, List thought, but it was not what the other powers practiced. Germany was ''encircled by the custom barriers of England, France, and Holland,'' which kept German wares from entering those countries, while within Germany things were even worse.

> Thirty-eight customs boundaries cripple inland trade, and produce much the same effect as ligatures which prevent the free circulation of the blood. The merchant trading between Hamburg and Austria, or Berlin and Switzerland must traverse ten states, must learn ten custom-tariffs, must pay ten successive transit dues. Anyone who is so unfortunate as to live on the boundary-line between three or four states spends his days among hostile tax-gatherers and custom-house officials; he is a man without a country.[26]

While the German businessmen suffered this "miserable condition," things were quite different in France.

> From the Channel to the Mediterranean, from the Rhine to the Pyrenees, from the Dutch to the Italian borders, a great nation carries on its trade over free rivers and free roads without ever meeting a custom-house official. Customs and tolls, like war, can only be justified as a means of defense. But the smaller the country which imposes a duty, the greater is the loss, the more harmful the effect on national enterprise, the heavier the cost of collection; for small countries are all boundary. Hence our thirty-eight customs boundaries are incomparably more injurious than a line of custom-houses on the external boundary of Germany, even if in the latter case the imposts were three times as heavy. And so the power of the very nation which in the time of the Hansards carried on the world's trade under the protection of its own fleet, is now ruined by the thirty-eight lines of customs.[27]

It was the task of the German Confederation to defend Germany not only militarily but also economically, "through a tariff." Within Germany itself, the Germans had nothing to lose but their chains.

> We consider the internal dues of Germany (which fall as heavily on other German states as on the foreigner) to be fetters, and as long as they remain they will prevent all national prosperity or national patriotism.[28]

Those in power in Germany did not respond favorably to these appeals. Some considered the very idea of a *German* organization of merchants unacceptable; for example, the high official in the Prussian government was ready to deal with a Bavarian or a Saxon union, but not a "German" one. In Vienna, Metternich understood that unification of Germany had revolutionary implications, and his sentiment was shared by other government figures in Austria and elsewhere. When List realized a German customs union was not going to be founded under the sponsorship of the German Confederation, which had been his first preference, he supported a regional South German union—a "third Germany," i.e., other than Prussia and Austria. That too failed to materialize, however. When the case for German unification finally did take off, it was carried not by Listian liberals but by Prussian bureaucrats and diplomats. The German Customs Union or *Zollverein*, founded in 1834, was different from what List had proposed; for one, it was organized by Prussia, not by the German Confederation.[29] As Martin Kitchen has noted, Prussia "certainly did not see the *Zollverein* as a step towards the unification of Germany under Prussian leadership." Kitchen states that in those days, "German nationalism was still a suspect and a dangerous liberal cause," and that even later, in 1848, Frederick William turned down the German crown "not only because it was offered to him by liberals and Jews, but because he felt that his cousin in Vienna had a better claim."[30]

It is necessary to remember that nationalism was novel and revolutionary. It took time and considerable effort before the idea—as applied to the German case—became widely accepted that Königsberg and Baden, Hamburg and Munich could "naturally" live under one government.

Despite its failure, the Merchants Union that List helped to create is historically important. It propagated among the business classes a *German* national identity and consciousness, and it contributed to the dissemination of the idea that the existing states (some of which were relatively large, strong, and thus viable) were really parts of a "Germany" that needed to be united. Without doubt, the establishment of a united Germany was the work of generals and politicians. But the *idea* that such states as Bavaria and Prussia ought to be replaced by a "Germany" had been first formulated and argued by intellectuals like List, not by generals and diplomats, who were too practical for such fanciful notions. The importance of this work of List is recognized by scholars like Martin Kitchen who points out that despite the fact that "the association had little direct influence and was seriously divided . . . it was none the less extremely significant":

> It was the first important organisation of the middle class in Germany. Its activities had done much to heighten the political and economic awareness of the manufacturers and businessmen, many of whom for the first time became aware of the wider implications of their individual efforts. The association had brought the attention of the German governments to the problem of customs and trade, and although the initial reaction was negative, the arguments were not forgotten. A question had been raised which no longer could be ignored.[31]

James J. Sheehan reminds us of what that question was when he points out that "it is misleading to talk about a *German* economy in the 1830s, when local, regional, and transnational economic relationships almost certainly remained of much great importance for most central Europeans."[32] In other words, with their advocacy of a united Germany, List and his friends were *creating* a German economic entity.

Besides working for the Frankfurt-based Merchants Union, List retained an active role in Württemberg politics. He was elected in July 1819 to represent Reutlingen in the state's chamber of deputies. On a legal technicality, the election was invalidated (in July 1819 he was one month short of thirty years of age—the minimum age for election), but he was elected again in 1820. His political program emphasized the goal of German unity. He also spoke very strongly in favor of freedom of opinion as the precondition of a constitutional system and civil liberty. Soon after his election, List's political enemies, led by the king of Württemberg himself, brought charges of subversion against him. Under the king's pressure, he was expelled from the chamber of deputies and then tried in a criminal court on charges of "demagoguery." These resulted in a sentence of ten months' imprisonment. Rather than serve the sentence, List left Württemberg (1822). He moved to Strasbourg and then stayed for various periods of time in several German states and in Switzerland. In that time List met and won the support of the Marquis de Lafayette with whom he would remain in contact for many years. In 1824, he returned to Württemberg, hoping to win clemency, but he was jailed and forced to serve part of his sentence before being released on the condition that he would emigrate.

Accompanied by his wife and children, List moved to New York in June 1825.[33] He traveled to Philadelphia and then to Albany, New York, searching for General Lafayette, who was then touring the United States and who had earlier invited List to join him later on in America. To quote List's English biographer, W. O. Henderson:

> As a member of Lafayette's entourage he visited New England, Pennsylvania, and Virginia and was able to observe many aspects of the development of the United States. He met a number of prominent Americans such as President John Quincy Adams, Henry Clay, Daniel Webster, W. H. Harrison, and Chief Justice Marshall. . . . in Philadelphia . . . List was introduced to some of the leading members of the local business community, who established the Pennsylvania Society for the Promotion of Manufactures and the Mechanic Arts in December of the following year.[34]

The pace of his activity after these initial weeks did not slow down. List involved himself in a variety of projects and jobs. He entered business (mining and farming) and with a special enthusiasm promoted railroad construction. He became publisher and editor of the *Readinger Adler*, a German-language newspaper in Reading, Pennsylvania. This paper supported both the Greeks in their struggle for independence against Turkey and the Latin Americans fighting under Simon Bolívar against Spanish rule; List also wrote in support of the rights of North America's Indians. Moreover, in an article published in the *Readinger Adler* in 1828, List predicted that with their populations of 188 and 184 million respectively,

> Russia and the United States in one hundred years will be the two most populous empires on earth. Each will have as many inhabitants as currently all states of Europe combined. In their interests and constitutions they will oppose one another, each a giant of its kind, America a colossal republic, Russia a colossal monarchy.[34a]

List established particularly close contacts with the Pennsylvania Society for the Promotion of Manufactures and the Mechanic Arts, which,
as its name reveals, was a protectionist organization and was thus close
to his heart. He wrote a number of articles and pamphlets and delivered
many speeches on the subject of protection. As we see, this German
nationalist became transformed virtually overnight into an American one
(he even took U.S. citizenship).

While promoting various practical measures intended to benefit his new
country, List continued to formulate the main ideas that would later materialize in his book, *The National System of Political Economy*. His policy
recommendations included a national organization that was modeled on
the Pennsylvania Society and that was in fact the prototype of the future
National Association of Manufacturers. He also wanted an American national school of business modeled after the French *Ecole Polytechnique*.

The question of List's relationship to his American predecessors, contemporaries, and successors has been a subject of debate.[35] For our purposes, several simple points will be fully sufficient. First of all, even before
List's arrival, there existed in America an intellectual and political current
of thought called "the national school." The "national economists" criticized free trade as an instrument of England's policy to preserve its
industrial supremacy. They argued, as a modern scholar, Bernard Semmel,
has put it, that the "science" of political economy and the principle of
so-called "cosmopolitanism" had been "designed to keep the non-British
world in the humiliating and economically inferior position of serving as
suppliers of food and raw materials—mere hewers of wood and drawers
of water—to a British industrial metropolis."[36] The first of the national
economists was Alexander Hamilton, who as American Secretary of the
Treasury presented to Congress a "Report on Manufactures" in 1791.
"The labor of artificers," according to Hamilton, "being capable of greater
subdivision and simplicity of operation than that of cultivators," ought to
be improved in "its productive powers, whether to be derived from an
accession of skill or from the application of ingenious machines." Hamilton
further argued that preferring foreign manufactures over domestic ones
amounted to passing onto foreign nations "the advantages accruing from
the employment of machinery." Hamilton believed, according to Semmel,
that "the inherent nature of trade between an agricultural and a manufacturing country placed the former at a considerable disadvantage."[37] Accordingly, Hamilton asked Congress to enact protective and supportive
measures to "the degree in which the nature of the manufacturer admits
of a substitute for manual labor in machines." Hamilton did not want

America to depend on Europe for manufactures; it ought to possess "all the essentials of national supply."[38]

Other nationalist economists in America expressed similar opinions. They included, for example, Daniel Raymond and Matthew Carey. The editors of List's collected works thought that Raymond exercised a "positive influence" on the development of List's system and cited the following passage by Raymond to illustrate the closeness of their positions:

> A nation, it is true, is an artificial being, or a legal entity, composed of millions of natural beings; still it possesses all the properties and attributes of a being, which are as distinct and strongly marked, as the properties and attributes of any natural being, and this must be constantly borne in mind, if we would reason correctly on the interests or rights of this being. . . .
>
> The interests of a nation, and the interests of individuals, who are constituent parts of that nation, may be, it is true, and often are, in unison. They may be identical, but they are not necessarily so—so far is this from being the case, that they are often directly opposed. So national and individual wealth may be coincident; but they are not necessarily so.[39]

After his arrival in America, List expressed views that were very close to those of many native American economists. These economists, in turn, generally accepted him as someone who shared their views about what their country—List's new home—needed. Men like Henry Clay and James Madison praised List for his labors. Free traders, such as Thomas Cooper (1759–1839), on the other hand, opposed the views of List and other "national economists." Nevertheless, List was honored by the Pennsylvania Society, was widely recognized as an authority on fiscal matters, and was known as a leading protectionist.[40]

List's endorsement of and identification with the national cause of the Americans provides us with an extremely important insight into his conception of the nation. Had he been a nationalist of the German Romantic school, List would not have accepted the United States as a nation. Of what history could that society of immigrants and refugees boast? Where were *America's* medieval castles and legends? Where was its feeling of *Gemeinschaft*? Where was the common language, the folklore, the *Geist*?

Only someone whose concept of nation was closer to the Enlightenment (Erna Schulz seems to have been right after all) could accept as a bona fide nation an entity so recently formed. But List did more; he became an American himself, and this would make him a real *inter*-nationalist, especially compared with that world-historical individual, Marx (who remained a stranger and an exile throughout his decades in England).

In a short time, List became a major public figure in America. He involved himself in the debate on the "American System," whose proponents supported high tariffs and public works in order to stimulate industrial growth. (The System was opposed by the planters in the South.) According to Henderson, "List emerged from the obscurity of the editorial office of a local newspaper to become a powerful champion of the 'American System' in Pennsylvania."[41] He published widely read letters and articles, addressed meetings and conventions, spoke before the Pennsylvania legislature, and attended dinners in his own honor. The Pennsylvania Society for the Promotion of Manufactures and the Mechanic Arts invited him to prepare a popular textbook as well as "an elaborate treatise on political economy adopted particularly to the situation in the United States." List proudly informed Lafayette of this invitation.

> The Pennsylvania Society has engaged me to write a whole work on the American National Economy and I see now before me a life full of usefulness in this country.[42]

List did not write the proposed book. However, he formulated the essential ideas of his future system in a work that appeared in the form of letters to Charles J. Ingersoll, vice president of the Pennsylvania Society, and that was published in 1827 as *Outlines of American Political Economy.*[43] List looked back at those years in his preface to *The National System* and explained that his failure to produce a major work (*ein grösseres Werk*) was due to the distraction of his business activities.[44] (In passing, let us note that List was mostly unsuccessful in his entrepreneurial ventures. For example, his farm had to be sold at a considerable loss, and he also lost money in his industrial investments.) As List explained, literary work was poorly paid in America and he had no independent means to support himself.[45] In this respect, List was at a definite disadvantage compared to Marx, who for many years could count on his guardian Engels to pay his rent and the grocer's bill. Rather, List's situation resembled that of Engels, except that the cofounder of scientific communism was much better at extracting surplus value.

List's political involvements inevitably led to attacks on him. A defender of free trade said in the House of Representatives, "We appear to have imported a professor from Germany, in absolute violation of the doctrines of the American system, to lecture upon its lessons."[46] In the presidential campaign of 1828, List and his newspaper supported Andrew Jackson, and he was duly appointed for his services to a diplomatic post. Even though he had become an American citizen, List never lost his passionate concern for Germany's welfare. In the late 1820s, he closely followed such matters as railroad construction in his old country. He therefore welcomed the chance to return to his homeland with a diplomatic appointment that in turn would grant him immunity from the conditions of his release from prison in Württemberg in 1824. However, there were complications; the Free City of Hamburg (one of the thirty-eight German states) refused to accept List as American consul, and the U.S. Senate voted down his nomination as well.

But in November 1830, List did leave the United States for Paris on a special diplomatic mission (to negotiate a trade agreement) and stayed there until October 1831. He also used that time to write for the French press on railroad matters. Only in the summer of 1832 did he and his family leave America permanently. He managed to secure an appointment as American consul to Baden, but was rejected, and he was again turned down by Hamburg, too. In the end, List did assume a consular appointment in Leipzig (1834): The government of Saxony, unlike those of Baden and Hamburg, cared less about his political past. Still, as Henderson notes, List's enemies did not leave him in peace even then. Metternich considered him to be "one of the most active, crafty, and influential German revolutionaries" and pressured Saxony to reject his appointment. But the government of Saxony stood up firmly to the chancellor's appeals.[47]

In any case, List's consular duties took up very little of his time. He devoted himself with renewed energy to German politics. As a highly prolific writer and journalist, he promoted the cause of the German commercial union, which was being established at that time, and he also passionately advocated railroad construction. He founded and edited a journal devoted to railroads and entitled *Eisenbahn Journal und National Magazin*. He proposed the construction of a national railroad system radiating from Leipzig to major cities of Germany. He also served as a railway consultant, and one of his consulting engagements led to an agreement among several German states on a common railroad-construction policy. But just as his business operations had been usually unsuccessful, so as a rule were his consulting jobs: For the diplomatic achievement just mentioned, for example, he received a very modest payment and an honorary doctorate—"I get honors but no honoraria," he quipped—from the University of Jena (where Marx would earn his degree). He never received a government post in Germany, and his persistent attempts to be reinstalled in the Württemberg civil service were always rebuffed. (His criminal conviction was set aside, however, but not before 1841.)

List considered the railroad to be an essential precondition of Germany's economic unification.

> The railway system and the customs union are Siamese twins; born at
> the same time, physically attached to one another, *of one* mind and purpose.
> They mutually support one another, strive for one and the same great goal,
> for the unification of the German peoples into one great and cultured, one
> wealthy, powerful and inviolable nation. Without the customs union a Ger-
> man railway system would never have come up for discussion, let alone
> have been completed. Only with the help of the German railway system is
> the cooperative economy of the Germans able to soar to national greatness,
> and only as a result of this prosperity can the railway system attain its full
> importance.[48]

He also saw it as a major instrument for the national defense and for
the promotion of culture, and as a force ("a tonic for the national spirit")
that would eradicate the traditional divisions of Germany in economy,
politics, and culture—"the evils of provincialism and of provincial self-
conceit and prejudice."[49]

According to Edward Mead Earle, "the greatest single contribution
which List made to modern strategy was his elaborate discussion of the
influence of railways upon the shifting balance of military power."

> His understanding of the strategic implications to Germany of steam trans-
> portation is surprising and by any objective standards quite remarkable.
> Before the advent of the railway the strategic position of Germany was the
> weakest in Europe, with the result that she was the traditional battleground
> of the entire continent. List saw sooner than anyone else that the railway
> would make the geographical situation of Germany a source of great strength,
> instead of one of the primary causes of her military weakness.[50]

In the late 1830s, List tried his luck in France. He lived in Paris from
August 1837 to May 1840. There he wrote *The Natural System of Political
Economy*, in French, as an entry in a competition organized by the French
Academy of Moral and Political Sciences (1837). This was List's second
attempt, after his American essays, to put together a comprehensive statement of his economic and political views. Although the Academy did not
award a prize to anyone, List's essay was one of three that the jurors
termed *ouvrages rémarquables*. It remained unpublished until 1927, when
it appeared in the original French, accompanied by a German translation,
as volume 4 of his collected works.[51]

List was a Paris correspondent for the *Augsburger Allgemeine Zeitung*,
but he took a direct interest in French affairs as well. He submitted memoranda to King Louis-Philippe on matters of industrial development and
was received in an audience with the king. Just as he had done during his
previous stay in France (1831–1832), he wrote for French periodicals. He

published a pamphlet recommending the construction of railroad connections from Paris to Le Havre and to Strasbourg.

List's French period, next to his American phase, sheds another revealing light on his nationalism. As we saw, he wrote articles, pamphlets, and memoranda, including a major statement of his overall system—*The Natural System of Political Economy*—that were to help *the French* become a more modern and powerful nation via, among other means, railroad construction. This was not typical behavior for a German nationalist in the 1830s–1840s, or at any time, for that matter.

List's *French* "nationalist manifesto" represents a further development of the system he had begun to formulate in English in the 1820s. As he was developing his own position, List read relevant French literature. This fact, however, does not support Marx's charges that List plagiarized his ideas from Ferrier (see Chapter 3). Those charges were baseless, even though List had already read the French protectionists before 1825 and had cited some of them at various times.[52]

It was in Paris, in 1839–1840, that List finally found time, despite numerous distractions, to produce his big book. *The National System of Political Economy*, written in German, was published in Stuttgart by his friend, Johann von Cotta, in April 1841. Though only one volume (it was to be followed by others, but they never appeared, just as Marx himself published only *Capital*, volume 1), *The National System* is a comprehensive presentation of List's interpretation of history, of his concept of society and government, of his view of German politics in his own time, of his theory of international relations, and of his vision of world order. The book was an immediate success; the first edition sold out quickly, and there were several reprints before his death in 1846.

Back in Germany in May 1840, List divided his time between railroad affairs, journalism, and travel to promote his various causes (e.g., railway plans, economic negotiations between different governments, and so on). During one of his trips, he was received by his archenemy, Metternich; true to himself, List tried to sell Metternich on his railway projects. He was not successful. His visit to Hungary, however, was something of a triumph. He was fêted by the most prominent aristocrats, held discussions with political figures and journalists, was even elected a corresponding member of the Hungarian Academy of Sciences (1844). Lajos Kossuth, the future leader of the Hungarian Revolution of 1848–1849, welcomed List as the founder of the national system of political economy who also showed the Hungarians how to win independence.

In 1841, List had been offered (but declined for health reasons) the editorship of the *Rheinische Zeitung*—the post to which Moses Hess aspired. The owners thought Hess too radical, though, and so they gave the job to Karl Marx.[53] (The Russian Finance Minister, Kankrin, offered List a position in Russia, but he declined that, too.)

In his last years, there was one major cause that kept List fully involved: the movement for raising the *Zollverein* tariff in order to stimulate industrial growth. He edited a new periodical, *Zollvereinsblatt*, founded in January 1843. According to Henderson, List wrote most of its articles (about 650 in nearly four years). But his physical and mental powers were declining; he neglected his duties and the paper began to lose readers. He quarreled with people who had been close to him, such as his publisher, Johann von Cotta, and financial and professional disappointments were frequent. He suffered from a severe depression (caused by, among other things, his ever-precarious financial position) and from a persecution complex. On November 30, 1846, at Kufstein, in the Tyrol, while on a vacation to restore his health, List committed suicide.

# 8

# The National System: The World of Nations

Just as for Marx the division of human society into classes provided the key to human history, so for List the division of humanity into nations was the central truth. As List wrote in his *National System of Political Economy*:

> I would indicate, as the distinguishing characteristic of my system, NA-
> TIONALITY. On the nature of *nationality*, as the intermediate interest
> between those of *individualism* and of *entire humanity*, my whole structure
> is based.[1]

For List, it was an absolute axiom that "between each individual and entire humanity . . . stands the NATION." Every nation has its language and literature, its history and customs. It is through nation that "the individual chiefly obtains . . . mental culture, power of production, security, and prosperity," just as "civilization of the human race [is] only conceivable and possible by means of the civilization and development of the individual nations."[2]

List pronounced nations to be "eternal," to constitute a unity both in space and in time,[3] but his conception of nation was in fact historical. Admittedly, he recognized nations as features of human society at all times, but this was in an ethnographic or anthropological sense. Modern, that is, political (and not only linguistic), nations for List were a relatively recent phenomenon. Modern nations were characterized by overlapping and interrelated culturally, politically, and economically self-conscious communities that viewed the world around them through this prism of self-awareness. List's understanding of nation thus paralleled Marx's conception of class. The proletariat, Marx held, "constitutes itself as a class" only as it acquires a class consciousness and as it organizes itself. Accordingly, to use Hegelian terms in elucidating List's view, nation "in itself," i.e., one lacking a sense of its individuality and a corresponding structure, was a permanent fixture of human history, but nations "for themselves" were new. List strove to make the Germans a nation in that latter sense—a community with cultural, as well as political and economic forms of collective existence.

List's life was one of an activist; he was a man of practice, not of theory. He admitted this freely himself, as we saw in the preceding chapter. In his youth, he recalled, he did not want simply to teach young men the science of economics as it then existed; "I desired also to teach them by what economical policy the welfare, the culture, and the power of Germany might be promoted." The "prevailing theory," however, preached the principle of free trade. As early as 1818 or 1820, List said, he had begun to doubt "the truth of the prevailing theory of political economy, and endeavored to investigate (what appeared to me) its errors and their fundamental causes."[4] He had been aware of the benefits of free trade in France's and Britain's internal life, after provincial customs tariffs within those states had been removed. But he also acknowledged that a protectionist policy, specifically Napoleon's Continental System, had had a positive impact, while its abrogation had produced "destructive results." In the end, List resolved the apparent contradiction between free trade and protection: "The idea struck me that *the theory was quite true, but only so in case all nations would reciprocally follow the principles of free trade, just as those provinces have done.*"[5]

If List had at first believed that free trade, provided it was practiced by all, would be beneficial to everyone, he did not keep this opinion for long. The "popular theory," which was what List called Western political economy, ignored nations and paid attention to "the entire human race" on the one hand or to "single individuals" on the other. This became the basis for questioning the dominant theory. With nation as his point of reference, List was able also to notice that nations were different and that they differed from one another because they were at different stages of development.

> I saw clearly that free competition between two nations which are highly civilized can only be mutually beneficial in case both of them are in a nearly equal position of industrial development, and that any nation which owing to misfortunes is behind others in industry, commerce, and navigation, while she nevertheless possesses the mental and material means for developing

those acquisitions must first of all strengthen her own individual powers, in order to fit herself to enter into free competition with more advanced nations. In a word, I perceived the distinction between *cosmopolitical* and *political* economy. I felt that Germany must abolish her internal tariffs, and by the adoption of a common uniform commercial policy towards foreigners, strive to attain to the same degree of commercial and industrial development to which other nations have attained by means of their commercial policy.[6]

The passage above contains some of List's central ideas and at the same time is an early formulation of what is known in the twentieth century as the theory of uneven development. List asserted that a nation like Germany, because it was a "developing nation," required a policy of state intervention in order to survive as a competitive member of the international community.

It is a fundamental fact for List that nations existed—and *wanted* to exist and develop—and that they shared "the impulse of self-preservation" in a world of competing nations. The world of nations was diverse; it contained "giants and dwarfs, well-formed bodies and cripples, civilized, half-civilized, and barbarous nations." This fact defined the mission of politics and economics.

It is the task of politics to civilize the barbarous nationalities, to make the small and weak ones great and strong, but, above all, to secure to them existence and continuance. It is the task of national economy to accomplish the *economical development of the nation*, and to prepare it for admission into the universal society of the future.[7]

As we see, for List politics were supreme and economics ("national economy") a policy science, a discipline subordinated to politics.

What was the relation of politics understood as struggle, change, and competition to "the universal society of the future" that List mentioned in the passage just cited? There are passages in List's work where he seems to have believed that the ideal society, a world of harmony and peace, was already in sight. But they are declaratory statements, not "policy-relevant" or "operational" ones. For example, in one place List wrote that the process of a gradual unification of the world was already taking place. He purported to believe that "after a lapse of several decades the civilized nations of the earth will, by the perfection of the means of conveyance, be united as respects both material and mental interchanges in as close a manner as (or even closer than) that in which a century ago the various counties of England were connected."[8] He claimed to see evidence supporting this diagnosis around him, especially in the sciences, arts, industry, and inventions, which seemed to be pointing in that direction. Certain political and diplomatic trends also supported such a view. "The congresses of the great European powers," List said, may be "the embryo of a future congress of nations."[9]

Thus List readily granted that the "highest ultimate goal of rational politics is . . . the uniting of all nations under a common law of right," and he declared himself to be in support of that goal. However, he insisted that such a goal could be attained only under certain conditions, that is, "through the greatest possible equalization of the most important nations of the earth in civilization, prosperity, industry, and power, by the conversion of the antipathies and conflicts which now exist between them into sympathy and harmony."[10]

But he did not indicate how exactly he expected this prospect ever to become a reality. On the contrary, he appears to have assumed that the nations would compete indefinitely, for his concept of modernity itself was not one of a state that was achieved and retained forever. Rather, List's sense of the dynamics of history would make one expect that inventions and discoveries would follow in an unending succession and that therefore pioneers, i.e., leading nations, would always exist, as would those nations that remained (or slipped) behind. There are no grounds for supposing that List expected all nations, or even only the major nations, to achieve equality and thus the world to attain a state of equilibrium. There is no basis for discerning in List's overall world view the prospect of a "withering away" of national conflict and nations themselves—no analogy with Marx's vision of the end of classes and class conflict.

Throughout his argument, List clearly rejected the validity of the analogy that he had himself drawn between the economic integration of "the various counties of England" in the eighteenth century and the emerging economic ties linking the nations of the world. The nations were not to unite themselves under the aegis of the most advanced nation, but were to challenge it and aspire to (at least) an equal status with the leading power. This was not what had happened inside Britain where industrialization and urbanization of some parts of the country had as their corollary a relative decline—perhaps in some cases even absolute decline (including of population)—of other parts of the country. There was no protection against Manchester's or Glasgow's products in rural counties of England or Scotland. List's entire system was based on the idea that a fundamental difference existed between a nation's internal development and the international order. Clearly, what List said about the counties of England as a harbinger of things to come worldwide cannot be taken seriously as his own position.

List's real position was to stress the necessity for nations (by no means all nations, as we shall see) to attain a high level of economic development. To attain such a level, the nations whose economic and cultural development lagged behind England's would have to abandon free trade (which benefited mainly England) and employ a system of protection instead. "National economy" was a lesson in "how *every separate nation* can be raised to that stage of industrial development in which union with other nations equally well developed, and consequently freedom of trade, can become possible and useful to it."[11] List reasoned that one day freedom of trade would become a reality. But before this happened—or better, in order for it to happen—"the less advanced nations must first be raised by artificial measures to that stage of cultivation to which the English nation has been artificially elevated."[12]

List believed that if the world became unified under existing conditions, i.e., under England's leadership, the effect on the overwhelming majority of the world's population would be extremely negative. Rather than promote equality of all peoples, the economic unity of a world led by England would mean a world *dominated* by England. In such a unified world, should it be allowed to emerge, England would be the controlling power, the English would be the masters over all the nations on earth, and English culture would be superior. From such a unity, List thus anticipated increased inequality. (As we have seen, while List saw England as the dominant nation, Marx pointed at the bourgeoisie and saw the world becoming cosmopolitan.) A "universal republic," of which many dream, "can only be realized if a large number of nationalities attain to as nearly the same degree as possible of industry and civilization, political cultivation, and power."[13]

In List's conception of history, change and development were the dominant facts determining the relations among states, cities, empires, and nations, some of which were more advanced than others. To him, one nation's dominant role in the affairs of the human race was the rule of history. In his time, England was the most advanced nation on earth. To this particular German nationalist, England—not Prussia, as is all too often imagined—came nearest to fulfilling the ideal of a Great Society. List's testimonial for England can rightly be compared to Marx's assessment of the historical contribution of the bourgeoisie. List wrote:

> In all ages there have been cities or countries which have been pre-eminent above all others in industry, commerce, and navigation; but supremacy such as that which exists in our days, the world has never before witnessed. In all ages, nations and powers have striven to attain to the dominion of the world, but hitherto not one of them has erected its power on so broad a foundation.[14]

Just as Marx recognized that the bourgeoisie helped advance the progress of human society, so List acknowledged that *the world's* progress had been "immensely aided . . . by England." He recognized that England "has become an example and a pattern to all nations . . . Who can tell how far behind the world might yet remain if no England had ever existed? And if she now ceased to exist, who can estimate how far the human race might retrograde?"[15]

It did not follow from England's extraordinary contribution that English supremacy ought to go unchallenged, however. England had established "a universal dominion on the ruin of the other nationalities," which ought to both emulate and compete with England.[16] In any case, as List saw it, England was the world's first truly modern nation.

> The agricultural-manufacturing-commercial State is like a city which spreads over a whole kingdom, or a country district raised up to be a city. In the same proportion in which material production was promoted by this union, the mental powers must necessarily have been developed, the political institutions perfected, the State revenues, the national military power, and the population, increased. Hence we see at this day, the nation which first of all perfectly developed the agricultural, manufacturing, and commercial state, standing in these respects at the head of all other nations.[17]

List's depiction of the ways in which England had arrived at her dominant position reveals his view of the driving forces of history. The English understood both the importance of protection and of learning from others. They did this by transplanting "to their native soil the wealth, the talents, and the spirit of enterprise of the foreigners."[18] In addition, the English, in the seventeenth century, were the first to integrate nationality with political power and economic wealth in a single entity, the nation-state.

> At the period when great nationalities arose, owing to the union of entire peoples brought about by hereditary monarchy and by the centralization of public power, commerce and navigation, and hence wealth and naval power, existed for the most part . . . in republics of cities, or in leagues of such republics. The more, however, that the institutions of these great nationalities became developed, the more evident became the necessity of establishing on their own territories these main sources of power and of wealth.[19]

In continental Europe, List argued, liberty had traditionally resided in self-governing and economically developed cities. Fear of losing freedom made them unwilling to submerge themselves within newly rising monarchies. In fact, when those cities were incorporated into large kingdoms, their freedoms were abolished.[20]

In England, on the other hand, the rise of the state did not lead to the elimination of liberties enjoyed by the burghers: On the contrary, power of the state and the freedoms of its cities grew together. Royal power supported the cities (i.e., the urban middle class) and their liberties both in order to counteract the feudal aristocracy and to promote economic progress of the state. In this way, England met List's prerequisites for a modern nation: It was a large territorial state that extended over the entire land inhabited by one nationality, in this case, the English; it was powerful and wealthy; and it enjoyed political freedom.

List did not think that England's rise had been somehow preordained, however. It is revealing of List's overall nondeterministic view of politics, including implicitly his conception of what could be done by his contemporaries, that he considered some of the most momentous events of world history to have been decided by purely personal factors. Indeed, he appears to have thought that Germany, not England, might have become the first modern nation:

> Had Charles V cast away from him the crown of Spain as a man casts away a burdensome stone which threatens to drag him down a precipice, how different would have been the destiny of the Dutch and the German peoples! As Ruler of the United Netherlands, as Emperor of Germany, and as Head of the Reformation, Charles possessed all the requisite means, both material and intellectual, for establishing the mightiest industrial and commercial empire, the greatest military and naval power which had ever existed. . . .
>
> The conception of but one idea, the exercise of but one man's will, were all that were needed to have raised Germany to the position of the wealthiest and mightiest empire in the world, to have extended her manufacturing and commercial supremacy over every quarter of the globe, and probably to have maintained it thus for many centuries.[21]

Thus, if Charles V (1519–1556) of the Holy Roman Empire of the German Nation (this was the official designation of "Germany" in the sixteenth century) had chosen not to abdicate as Emperor in order to remain only King of Spain, which he did in 1556, he would have presided over a state that was at once large (it included the Netherlands, which to List were a German land), rich, and free. But on abdicating the imperial throne, Charles separated the Netherlands from Germany and placed them under Spain. This weakened Germany.

Instead of the Germans, therefore, the Dutch (who eventually freed themselves from Spain without rejoining Germany) grew to become a world power and remained ahead of the English in manufactures, navigation, and colonial possession until the middle of the seventeenth century. Whereas "the spirit of freedom [that] had become only a citizen spirit in

Holland'' sufficed for a time, a new age called for different qualities than those required in "mere mercantile aristocracies." The Dutch did not understand that in order to retain their "supremacy" they had to base it "on a great nationality" and support it by a "mighty national spirit." On the other hand, certain other states "developed their nationality . . . by means of monarchy." They were less developed in economy and commerce, and they envied and resented Holland's superiority in commerce, industry, and navigation. In their Revolution, the English carried out that major change that enabled them to surpass the Dutch: England's new national sentiment was reinforced by its "new-born Republic." The Navigation Laws were England's "challenge glove." The conflict between the Dutch and the English was ultimately resolved in England's favor because "the English nationality was of far larger calibre than that of the Dutch. The result could not remain doubtful." [22]

List thus recognized the diversity of circumstances that led to England's world supremacy, and while doing so he provided a description of what he understood a modern nation to be. He stressed "the people's innate love of liberty and of justice, the energy, the religious and moral character of the people," in explaining England's achievement. In addition, he recognized the importance of the nation's constitution, of its legal institutions, and of "the wisdom and power of the government and of the aristocracy." He thought that England's geographical location, "nay, even good luck," had helped too. When it came to bigger philosophical questions, he was of an uncertain mind "whether the material forces exert a greater influence over the moral forces, or whether the moral outweigh the material in their operation; whether the social forces act upon the individual forces the more powerfully, or whether the latter upon the former." However, he was sure that "there subsists an interchanging sequence of action and reaction" between them: "The increase of one set of forces promotes the increase of the other, and . . . the enfeeblement of the one ever involves the enfeeblement of the other." [23]

List expressly denied that England's rise was due to racial factors, such as "the blending of Anglo-Saxon with the Norman blood." It was not the Anglo-Saxon-Norman racial heritage that made England what it was, but "the germ from which all the English ideas of freedom and justice have sprung—the right of trial by jury." List also regarded England's "early banishment of the Latin language" from literature, culture, government, and law as a favorable development. In Germany, he insisted, the retention of Latin had had a negative effect. He also noted that England, rather than France or Germany, had taken advantage of scientific inventions and the discovery of new sea routes.[24] Finally, he allowed for chance and fortune. If Charles V and Henry VIII had changed places, and if the outcomes of some other events had been different, "Germany and the Netherlands might have become what England and Spain have become." If the English throne had been occupied not by Elizabeth I but by "a weak woman allying herself to a Philip II . . . the power, the civilization, and the liberties of Great Britain" would not have been the same.[25]

This subjectivist or indeterministic element in List's position, in contrast with Marx's view of history, could be projected also into the future. The message of this kind of history must have been that Germany's success or failure was in the hands of the Germans; there was no built-in guarantee that things would in the end turn out well.

Besides Germany and Holland, the also-rans or might-have-beens of List's history included Spain, among others.

While Spain, as List himself recognized, was a great power for a considerable length of time, it still, according to his terms, was a failure because it did not manage to harmonize power with freedom. List did not see the causes of Spain's decline as due to wrong economic or commercial policies alone:

> If Spain had not expelled the Moors and Jews, and had never had an Inquisition; if Charles V had permitted religious liberty in Spain; if the priests and monks had been changed into teachers of the people, and their immense property secularized, or at least reduced to what was actually necessary for their maintenance; if, in consequence of these measures, civil liberty had gained a firm footing, the feudal nobility had been reformed and the monarchy limited; if, in a word, Spain had politically developed herself in consequence of the Reformation, as England did, and if the same spirit had extended to her colonies, a prohibitive and protective policy would have had similar effects in Spain as it had in England. . . . [26]

To some readers, this may sound as though List was saying that if only Spain had been England, it would have been England. As the saying goes, "Why can't all men be like Englishmen?" Or as Spiegel puts it, "What List really wanted was to revise creation and turn everyone, as far as possible, into an Englishman."[27] Admittedly, List's most important "lesson of history," it appears, was to raise to the rank of universal model England's experience, or rather the outcome of that experience as he saw it in his time. But List did not want to "turn everyone . . . into an Englishman," and it is not true that "the nationality made little difference to List," which is Dorfman's opinion.[28] The following passage succinctly describes what List felt England had done so that others might learn from it:

> History . . . teaches us that such a degree of public well-being, namely a flourishing state of manufacturers and commerce, has been attained in only those countries whose political constitution (whether it bear the name of democratic or aristocratic republic, or limited monarchy) has secured to their inhabitants a high degree of personal liberty and of security of property, whose administration has guaranteed to them a high degree of activity and power successfully to strive for the attainment of their common objects, and of steady continuity in these endeavours.[29]

We shall soon turn to List's prescriptions for Germany's future, but before we do so, let us recapitulate a few points about his conception of history. We can see that for List, history contained no inevitability, no determinism; England's rise to supremacy was not a result of the workings of any objective forces. History might have turned out quite differently if certain leading figures had chosen to act differently. List recognized the role of ideas, values, and beliefs. In his view, religion, law, morality, intelligence, and inventiveness were not products of some single fundamental force or an underlying cause but could instead all be "independent variables" (to use a contemporary term). And to repeat, List recognized the role of the individual; history could not be reduced to any impersonal level: If Elizabeth I of England or Charles V of Germany and Spain had not existed, List believed that history would have been different. Unlike Marx, who promised the triumph of the proletariat, List did not promise the Germans anything; the lesson of *his* history was all that depended on them. But even so, there was an inner principle at work in List's history, a driving force that brought about change, for his history was the story of interactions between cities, states, empires, and nations. In his history, collective actors interacted with each other on a "horizontal" plane—in "space"—but also "in time," for they learned from history. While Marx's history was about classes placed one above another within a society, List's history was about diffusion of knowledge, broadly defined, from one city to another, from states to other states; it was the story of one nation's learning from another while striving for power. (Thus List's view bore a close resemblance to Herder's belief that the Germans' progress was due to their learning from other peoples.) A people's ability to learn was in turn conditional upon its freedom.

> History teaches that arts and trades migrated from city to city, from one country to another. Persecuted and oppressed at home, they took refuge in

cities and in countries where freedom, protection, and support were assured to them.[30]

Or as List said in the introduction to his book:

> International trade is one of the mightiest levers of civilization and prosperity, for by the awakening of new wants it incites men to activity and exertion and passes on new ideas, inventions, and faculties from one nation to another.[31]

While List as a German patriot was concerned with *his* native country's welfare, as a scholar he took a value-free, wholly unsentimental view of the world of nations. For example, he had no doubt that the Russian government's protectionist policies were beneficial to the country, and he advised his fellow Germans not to criticize them but to accept them as an example to follow. "Each nation, like each individual, has its own interests nearest at heart. Russia is not called upon to care for the welfare of Germany; Germany must care for Germany, and Russia for Russia."[32]

This comment reflected List's concept of world politics. Despite his declarations of support for the ideal of universal harmony and peace, he did not let this ideal influence his approach to the affairs of his time. As Edward Mead Earle has noted, "the primary concern of List's policies, both political and economic, was power, even though he linked power with welfare."[33] Nothing exemplifies List's power-centered approach more than his insistence that the essential requirements of normal nationality include a large population and territory.

> A nation restricted in the number of its population and in territory, especially if it has a separate language, can only possess a crippled literature, crippled institutions for promoting art and science. A small State can never bring to complete perfection within its territory the various branches of production.[34]

In defense of List, one could say that these were List's statements of fact, not declarations about what he thought desirable. However, as we shall see, List approved of a policy of expansion, and in this sense he may indeed be viewed as one of supporters of the *Lebensraum* doctrine.[35]

In List's analysis of the relations between the nations of the "temperate zone" (which included Europe and North America) and those of what he called "the torrid zone" of the globe, the idea of equality of nations was absent. He thought that an international division of labor, like the division of labor within a nation, was "chiefly determined by climate and by Nature itself."[36] Those "most favored by nature" were the nations of the temperate zone, because there, the manufacturing power especially prospers, by means of which the nation not merely attains to the highest degree of mental and social development and of political power, but is also enabled to make the countries of tropical climates and of inferior civilization tributary in a certain measure to itself. The countries of the temperate zone therefore are above all others called upon to bring their own national division of labor to the highest perfection, and to use the international division of labor for their enrichment.[37]

In accordance with this scenario for North-South relations, the North would produce and export manufacturing goods, and the South would forever remain the producer and exporter of agricultural produce and importer of industrial goods. It is true, though, that List did not attribute this unequal relationship (it was unequal on his own explicit terms) to any alleged inferiority (racial or otherwise) of the peoples of "the torrid zone," and he claimed to see that the decisive factor resided in the climate, that is, in "natural causes," which he thought would be effective "for all time."[38]

Upon this premise, List demanded that England stop trying to exclude the large nations of Europe from joining in the growing trade between the North and the South. Before those nations could join in, however, before they could "partake of the profitable business of cultivating waste territories and civilizing barbarous nations, or nations once civilized but which are again sunk in barbarism," they must develop their own industry, merchant marine, and naval power. If England were then to oppose them, they should unite to bring that nation to reason.[39]

List was of a divided mind on how "the nations of the second rank," i.e., states like France, Russia, or the United States, should go about persuading England to reduce her unreasonable pretensions. At times, he seemed to favor a confederation or federal union of major European nations, albeit one with an outstanding role for Germany. At other times, he thought Germany should secure for itself a place in the world by its own efforts. At all times, however, he was firm in his belief that the monopolistic position of England must be challenged in order to allow every "manufacturing nation . . . to establish direct intercourse with tropical countries," and so that "no nation will be permitted to maintain a predominant amount of colonial possessions in tropical countries." He also assumed that the tropical countries—the torrid zone—would indefinitely remain producers of colonial wares and importers of manufactured products.[40] In other words, he did not consider the possibility that a Listian nationalism could emerge in the torrid zone, which in our time is known as the Third World.

List was aware of the obstacles to a European alliance, although he did not clarify exactly why the other major nations of Europe should support German national ambitions. He thought that those nations shared a common interest with Germany in "the Eastern Question" and that a united Europe might be "taking the whole of Asia under her care and tutelage." Such a turn of events was possible, List thought, in light of his assessment of the impact of Europe on other parts of the world.

> Wherever the mouldering civilization of Asia comes into contact with the fresh atmosphere of Europe, it falls to atoms. . . . In this utter chaos of countries and peoples there exists no single nationality which is either worthy or capable of maintenance and regeneration. Hence the entire dissolution of the Asiatic nationalities appears to be inevitable, and a regeneration of Asia only possible by means of an infusion of European vital power, by the general introduction of the Christian religion and of European moral laws and order, by European immigration, and the introduction of European systems of government.[41]

List did not pursue the implications of the prospects he sketched out in the above statement, but the image of the "dissolution" of Asian nationalities under the impact of Europe bears clear resemblance to Marx's terms for the impact of British rule on India.

The Asian ambitions of the European nations, according to List, made for a conflict with England and at the same time, inasmuch as those ambitions required the freedom of the seas for their realization, they established a common interest between Europe and the United States. The earlier attempts to unify Europe, such as Napoleon's Continental System, List noted, brought about not only French continental supremacy but also "the humiliation, or destruction and dissolution" of the other nations of Europe.[42] A real Continental System would have to be based on an equality of all nations (read: *large* nations). Should such a system be established, the British might reconsider their hostility to Europe and join it in "a European coalition against the supremacy of America." The need for such a coalition would arise because "probably in the course of the next century," the United States "will surpass the position in which England stands, as far as at present England excells little Holland."[43]

Visions of this kind provide little basis for seeing List's system as a precursor of the post–1945 European Community, even though some authors—for example, Emmanuel N. Roussakis—have seen a model for the Common Market in List's program for a German economic and political unification. Roussakis has overlooked the crucial difference between a national cause, which List preached, and the supra- or international cause of a European unity. Roussakis has misunderstood List's campaign for Germany's inclusion of Belgium, the Netherlands, Denmark, and Switzerland and has presented it as a plan for an international union of those nations. But in fact List did not consider those four states to be nations at all, since they were small and had no right to exist, according to his criteria, and he proposed to liquidate them as independent entities.[44]

On the other hand, this prospect should not be viewed exclusively through the experience of Nazi theory and practice in the twentieth century. List's Germany was to be a liberal and constitutional state. In any case, a "Greater Germany" had been a radical ideal before 1848. In the 1840s, Friedrich Engels had expressed much more extreme views:

> Perhaps in opposition to many whose point of view I share in general, I am still of the opinion that the reconquest of the German-speaking left side of the Rhine is an affair of national honor: that the Germanization of Holland and Belgium, which have been wrenched away, is a political necessity for us. Shall we continue to let the German nationality be oppressed in those countries while in the East the Slavs are emerging ever stronger? . . . Without doubt it will come to another war between us and France, and we will then see who deserves to have the left bank of the Rhine . . . .[45]

Compared with those fiery words, let alone with the realities of Hitler's age, List's plans were moderate. There is no trace of racism in List's world view, and in this regard he was not only separated from the Nazis by an unbridgeable chasm, but he strikingly differed from his German nationalist contemporaries. Whatever List thought about this or that nationality, race played no role in his judgment. But what is one to make out of List's hostility toward and contempt for small nations and small cultures? Perhaps an exaggerated reaction to the particularly negative aspects of the notorious German *Kleinstaaterei* is partly responsible. (One may wonder if Marx's wholly negative view of the state, his treatment of it as a parasitical force, had not been also somehow related to that German form of "statehood.") But is the fact that many of those several hundred German states (reduced to a mere forty after Napoleon) had more vices than virtues sufficient reason to deny the right to exist to Denmark and the Netherlands? (Why not abolish also Sweden, Norway, or Portugal, the last being a perfect candidate for becoming Spanish?) Was the annexation by a large nation and state—a national euthanasia—the only proper course for them?

List's position is objectionable not only on moral but also on directly political grounds. List did not ask what should be done if a small nation selected by a major power for annexation *fights back*, especially if it finds a protector in another large power. Nor did he consider what should happen if that small nation refuses to accept its fate *after* having been annexed by a great power. He did not say what the large state should do if members of a previously independent nation organize political, cultural, perhaps even armed resistance, if they struggle for secession, for restoration of their old homeland. List often said he wanted his great nation-state to be free, liberal, and constitutional. Did his liberalism go far enough to tolerate a secessionist movement? Or was such a movement to be banned simply because it was "irrational," running against "historical inevitability," and therefore to be deposited in the "dustbin of history"?

List's preference for large states has raised serious questions about the extent to which such states would be liberal in their internal organization and about his understanding of international relations, international law, and international order. Edmund Silberner, who has subjected List's theory to a detailed analysis, believes it is "astonishing" that List "should have given to his doctrine the name of 'national system,' " for it was a system that applied only to the "great" nations, the ones List called "normal." "In other words," say Silberner, List's system is meant only for nations able to carry on a policy of expansion."[46]

The logic of List's argument, therefore, would lead to the legitimation of aggressive war against those weak states who refused to accept the decision of a great power to annex them. Silberner rightly concludes that List failed in his intentions to synthesize cosmopolitical economy with national economy; in other words, he failed to propose an international system under which all nations could live in peace. He also failed to show how exactly the raising of large nations to the levels attained by England would help to secure peace.[47]

List's world, we conclude, was to consist of a constellation of large, powerful states engaged in a perpetual rivalry that led at times to war, a virtual *bellum omnium contra omnes*. Admittedly, List at times spoke eloquently in favor of the alternative vision of a world of peaceful, co-operating nations, but this was not his central concern. Like Marx's class struggle, List's competition among nations was essentially a zero-sum game. But there was no promise in List's system that a nation would one day arise whose historic task would be to transcend and thus abolish nations. (If anyone's system contained that kind of promise, it was Marx's scenario in the "Hegel Critique," in which he envisioned a revolution that, while abolishing classes, would also turn "Germans" into "men.")

Perhaps a certain historical optimism would help explain why List did not seriously consider the internal threats to liberty that were posed by ethnic dissension or the disruptive international potential of his call for large states; he believed that *rationally* small states made no sense and that all concerned would sooner or later *see* it. Unlike the radicals of the Engels and Marx kind, List was also prepared to retain in a united Germany its distinct historic units and to respect their individuality. His large states were to be pluralistic. Similarly, he explicitly stated that the influence of the princes and aristocracy should be retained.[48] In class terms, List preached a "historic compromise" between the bourgeoisie and the intelligentsia on the one hand, and the traditional elites on the other. He did not, in other words, advocate a revolutionary upheaval that would lead to the destruction of the aristocracy. One may extrapolate from these points the acceptability, to List, of a broad autonomy within that "Greater Germany" and also within those parts that had been the independent states of Denmark and the Netherlands. This is said not to justify List's plan, but only to warn against parallels too close to Hitler.[49]

There is no denying, however, that in List's program, a powerful feeling of injured national pride is present. He strongly condemned those whom he blamed for Germany's humiliation: England most of all, but also France, and even the Netherlands, that "small maritime province formerly possessed by Germany and inhabited by Germans." But there was some satisfaction that things were getting better after all: The German Customs Union or *Zollverein*, in the few years of its operation, had already brought an improvement that List called a "miracle."[50]

But that was only a beginning, for Germany was uniquely qualified to become a major industrial power.

> If any nation whatever is qualified for the establishment of a national manufacturing power, it is Germany; by the high rank which she maintains in science and art, in literature and education, in public administration and in institutions of public utility; by her morality and religious character, her industry and domestic economy; by her perseverance and steadfastness in business occupations; as also by her spirit of invention, by the number and vigor of her population; by the extent and nature of her territory, and especially by her highly advanced agriculture, and her physical, social, and mental resources.[51]

For Germany to become this power, however, the free cities of Hamburg, Bremen, and Lubeck, which at the time of List's writing had not yet joined the *Zollverein*, and were therefore accused by him of "apostasy" ("the apostasy of these small maritime states"), would have to become part of the German nation. So would Holland, since List considered it to be both a part of the German nation and a state incapable of independent existence because of its smallness.[52]

Having settled those matters, Germany would turn its attention abroad, to the colonies. List opposed German colonization and economic penetration in North America, because he thought Germans would become rapidly assimilated to American nationality (he thought such an outcome normal).

Instead, the Germans should turn their eyes to Central and South America, including Texas (at that time not yet a part of the United States).[53]

The other area for a major German colonization effort was to be Southeastern Europe. List envisaged the territory of what is now Yugoslavia, Romania, and Bulgaria as areas for German industrial exports and agricultural settlement. He proposed that in this southeastern expansion the German *Zollverein* should be represented by Bavaria acting in cooperation with Austria, just as in German overseas expansion Prussia was to take a lead.[54]

List recognized the enormous advance England had made, but he felt its "manufacturing supremacy" should be challenged by Germany. A failure so to act, he feared, meant that the Germans would remain "far behind the French and North Americans, nay: far behind the Russians."[55]

List did not understand modernity as something that is once achieved. Germany's task was not simply to catch up with England, but to write a new chapter in the history of human progress.

> A future is approaching for manufactures, commerce, and navigation which will surpass the present as much as the present surpasses the past. Let us only have the courage to believe in a great national future, and in that belief to march onward. But above all things we must have enough national spirit at once to plant and protect the tree, which will yield its first richest fruits only to future generations.[56]

Modernization, as we see, was not a one-time affair for List. The only permanent feature of modernity was change, the impermanence of the status quo. In such a world, a nation that wanted to survive in independence had to keep abreast of the progress of science and technology and to set its goals and policies for generations to come. Who was to define those goals? Who was to implement those policies? What implications for a nation's political organization, for the role of the state, and for the role of the diverse elites—economic, intellectual, and political—did this vision of a changing world contain?

The following chapter will address some of these issues by taking as its point of departure, and its guiding theme, List's image of the planting and protecting of "the tree." The dialectic of "the tree" and "the forester," that chapter argues, concerns a central issue in List's political outlook.

# 9

# *The National System: Freedom Versus Organization*

When List spoke about peoples learning from other peoples, he invoked an image from the world of nature. He was reminded of how "the wind bears the seed from one region to another, and . . . thus waste moorlands have been transformed into dense forests." But the forester, List went on, does not wait for the wind to effect this transformation "in the course of ages."

> Is it unwise on his part if by sowing and planting he seeks to attain the same object within a few decades? History tells us that whole nations have successfully accomplished that which we see the forester do.

This is what the Germans ought to do as well, unless they prefer to "wait patiently until other nations are impolitic enough to drive out their industries and thus compel them to seek a refuge with us."[1]

List's metaphor is deceptively simple. It raises more questions about his conception of man, society, history, and politics than he himself was likely to have considered in any systematic manner. First of all, it is evident that List believed that man had the power to take charge over the course of social life, to determine the direction and outcome of development. He inspires questions about what kind of society he wanted Germany to become, about his concept of the national interest, and about the means by which it should be pursued. There is the question of national leadership. Who *is* "the forester"? (Who *hires* him?) Does the forester himself determine which plants out of the many should be planted? To whom is the forester responsible for his decisions?

It is easy to translate List's questions from the realm of forestry into questions about the relationship of the state to civil society or about the preferred form of government. What kind of government—republican or monarchist, absolutist or constitutional—was best suited to pursue a modernizing nation's interests and needs?

Some writers argue that nationalist theory does not allow for the separation of state and civil society but, on the contrary, subsumes the latter within the former.[2] Where did List stand on this issue? Who should rule in the state he wanted to create, and how much power should the government have over the population? These are central questions about List's politics. His metaphor of the forester is his own version of the age-old question first raised by Plato: Will the experts (''philosophers'') rule, or the rich, or the strong, or will the entire populace be rulers?

It would seem that in his own way List also posed the question that Marx would raise in his ''Theses on Feuerbach'':

> The materialist doctrine concerning the changing of circumstances and upbringing forgets that circumstances are changed by men and that it is essential to educate the educator himself. This doctrine must, therefore, divide society into two parts, one of which is superior to society.[3]

Marx's solution to the question of ''who shall educate the educator'' was contained in his concept of ''revolutionary practice'': ''The coincidence of the changing of circumstances and of human activity or self changing.''[4] (This means Marx expected that historical action would be that learning experience which would transform those engaged in it into persons capable of running their own affairs.)

As we survey the thoughts of List on the relations among the individual, the society as a whole, and the state, we shall also look for his answer to the question of ''who shall educate *the forester*?''

But List himself would probably have asked another question first. He would have reminded his readers that every nation lives in a larger world and that any decisions regarding the definition of a nation's interest, the setting of goals and methods of national policies, the choice of the form of government, and so forth, would have to take into account the world that directly influences the condition of every nation. Therefore, Bert F. Hoselitz is right when he comments that

> List is not interested in economic relations in an abstract, closed system, but as aspects of a system of nations. List believes that progress in human welfare is a function of association . . . the unit which List studies is the nation state, and his theory of economic stages must be understood as applying only to nation states.[5]

List's theory of stages is a device that enables one to compare any given nation with other nations, especially those with which it maintains economic, cultural, and political relations. According to List, all nations must pass the following stages in order to survive: "original barbarism"; pastoral; agricultural; agricultural-manufacturing; and agricultural-manu-facturing-commercial.[6] (Clearly, List assumed the existence of "nations" at all stages of history.)

He thought that a nation could pass from the savage or barbarian to the pastoral stage, from the pastoral to the agricultural, and from the agricultural to the first phase of manufacturing and navigation under a free trade with more advanced cities and countries. To attain the higher level of industrial development, however, it was necessary to employ the power of the state, that is, to modify or suspend the free-trade system.

List did not really care about the earlier stages and transitions. Hoselitz notes that the "crux of his [List's] theory of growth centers on a description of the conditions under which a mature agricultural state can exist, under which it may progress, and how an agricultural state can be transformed into one on a higher level by the introduction of manufactures."[7]

In Hoselitz's opinion, "basically, List recognizes only one dynamic element in the process of economic growth, the introduction of manufac-turing." However, List did not restrict the impact of manufacturing to the economic field: he saw the connection between agriculture and despotism and between manufacturing and liberty. This "non-economic dimension" of industrial growth, according to Hoselitz, was "a necessary ingredient of List's theory," and in this respect List was different from other advocates of industrial protectionism.

List was not concerned with comparing one industry with one branch of agricultural production, or industry with agriculture in general. He compared two different kinds of society. On the one hand, there was "a society based primarily upon agriculture, and inhabited by an indolent, tradition-oriented population with a narrow horizon and lack of a spirit of innovation." List contrasted that kind of society with "a society based upon manufacture and industry and the associated branches of production called forth by them, and peopled by a free, inventive, and forward-looking population." He saw "the basis for the superiority of industrial production over agriculture" not only in the industry's higher productivity, "but in the social and cultural features by which industrial and agricultural coun-tries differ."[8]

Bearing all these points in mind, it is easy to understand List's stand on the question of protection. He was not an advocate of protection in the early stages of a nation's development, as we have already noted, and he thought that, even during a nation's transition to an industrial society, protection should have a specific purpose and a restricted application: "Measures of protection are justifiable only for the purpose of furthering and protecting the internal manufacturing power." Moreover, List restricted this right to protection to a very limited number of cases.

> Only . . . nations which through an extensive and compact territory, large population, possession of natural resources, far advanced agriculture, a high degree of civilization and political development, are qualified to maintain an equal rank with the principal agricultural manufacturing commercial nations, with the greatest naval and military powers.[9]

List did not want to exclude foreign competition completely: Commercial restrictions were justified only when the required conditions and means for developing national industry were already present. Besides, protection should not extend uniformly to all branches of industry. In sum, List thought that "protection is only beneficial to the prosperity of the nation so far as it corresponds with the degree of the nation's industrial development. Every exaggeration of protection is detrimental: nations can only obtain a perfect manufacturing power by degrees."[10] At the same time, as Hoselitz has noted, List supported free competition within a country because he believed that competition "leads to optimum allocation of resources, and hence . . . to maximum stimulation of its productive forces." Clearly, List was not interested in theory for theory's sake. His goal was "to provide the theoretical underpinnings for . . . economic policies . . . for industrialization." Because of this, according to Hoselitz, "List's work resembles much of the present literature on economic growth, which is also elaborated with the aim of providing guidelines for planned economic development." Hoselitz finds it natural that "many of the ideas expressed by List are found again in contemporary literature on economic growth" and that "some passages in List's works have a thoroughly 'modern' flavor."[11]

If we bear in mind List's real concerns, we shall better understand his critique of Adam Smith and of the "School," meaning the followers of Smith.

Scholars generally agree that List's criticisms of Adam Smith are at best exaggerations, if not outright distortions, of the Scotsman's real views. It is not necessary to explore this question in depth here. It is enough to examine List's comments about Smith and/or the School mainly for what they reveal about List, not Smith. Often they reveal indirectly what List approved of. Let us take one example (and *The National System* is full of references to Smith and his disciples): Adam Smith's doctrine, according to List,

> ignores the very nature of nationalities, seeks almost entirely to exclude politics and the power of the State, presupposes the existence of a state of perpetual peace and of universal union, underrates the value of a national manufacturing power, and the means of obtaining it, and demands absolute freedom of trade.[12]

What List really says here is that he himself recognizes the nature of nationalities; includes politics and the power of the state in economic matters; presupposes a state of perpetual conflict among nations; recognizes the importance of a national economic power; and supports controls over trade for political reasons.

List's charge can be appreciated when it is quoted more fully:

> [Smith's] system at bottom is nothing else than a system of the *private economy of all the individual persons in a country, or of the individuals of the whole human race, as that economy would develop and shape itself, under a state of things in which there were no distinct nations, nationalities, or national interests—no distinctive political constitutions or degrees of civilisation—no wars or national animosities*; . . . it is nothing more than a theory of values; a mere shopkeeper's or individual merchant's theory—not a scientific doctrine, showing how the productive powers of an entire nation can be called into existence, increased, maintained, and preserved —for the special benefit of its civilisation, welfare, might, continuance, and independence.
>
> This system regards everything from the shopkeeper's point of view. . . .[13]

Smith was certainly innocent of the charge that he denied the role of the state and military power in securing a nation's well-being. Nor was he an absolute free trader; indeed, one scholar, Edward Mead Earle, finds elements of mercantilism in his views. Earle also shows that Smith expressly recognized defense as "the first duty of the sovereign."[14]

However, when List spoke about the mission of the state, he had in mind something other than just defense from foreign invasion or maintenance of internal order. He quoted with special disapproval the following passage from an early (1755) essay written by Adam Smith some twenty years before *The Wealth of Nations*:

> Man is generally considered by statesmen and projectors as the materials of a sort of political mechanics. Projectors disturb nature in the course of her operations in human affairs; and it requires no more than to let her alone,

and give her fair play in the pursuit of her ends, that she may establish her own designs. Little else is requisite to carry a state to the highest degree of opulence from the lowest barbarism, but peace, easy taxes, and a tolerable administration of justice; all the rest being brought about by the natural course of things. All governments which thwart this natural course, which force things into another channel, or which endeavour to arrest the progress of society at a particular point, are unnatural, and to support themselves are obliged to be oppressive and tyrannical.[15]

List thought that this statement denied those functions of the state that he, List, regarded as fundamental. What Smith really meant, according to List, was the following: "Statesmen who attempt to found a manufacturing power, to promote navigation, to extend foreign trade, to protect it by naval power, and to found or to acquire colonies, are in his [Smith's] opinion project makers who only hinder the progress of the community."[16]

List, on the other hand, wanted statesmen to *do* all those things. In the stand that he attributed to Smith, List saw a major flaw: It ignored the existence of *nation* as something distinct from and superior to the collectivity of individuals living under one government. Or as List put it, "For him [Smith] no *nation* exists, but merely a community, i.e., a number of individuals dwelling together. These individuals know best for themselves what branches of occupation are most to their advantage, and they can best select for themselves the means which promote their prosperity."[17]

It would have been natural for List to conclude his argument and explicitly state that he thought the opposite. To him, the nation should tell the individuals where to work and how to "promote their prosperity." But List did not make such a statement; indeed, as we shall see, he denied a desire to impose career choices on anyone.

But List did insist that politics—political considerations—should play a role in economic affairs. He made his point by attacking his one-time opponent in America, Thomas Cooper, who had called nation a "grammatical being" and a "grammatical contrivance," had denied that politics were an "ingredient" of political economy, and further had made fun of the idea that "national morality is a different thing from individual morality."[18] Against Cooper, List asked a series of rhetorical questions:

> Is the wisdom of private economy, also wisdom in national economy? Is it in the nature of individuals to take into consideration the wants of future centuries, as those concern the nature of the nation and the State? . . . Can the individual further take into consideration in promoting his private economy, the defense of the country, public security, and the thousand other objects which can only be attained by the aid of the whole community? Does not the State require individuals to limit their private liberty according to

> what these objects require? Does it not even require that they should sacrifice
> for these some part of their earnings, of their mental and bodily labor, nay,
> even their own life? We must first root out, as Cooper does, the very ideas
> of "State" and "nation" before this opinion can be entertained.
>
> No; that may be wisdom in national economy which would be folly in
> private economy, and *vice versa*; and owing to the very simple reason, that
> a tailor is no nation and a nation no tailor, that one family is something very
> different from a community of millions of families, that one house is some-
> thing very different from a large national territory.[19]

As a matter of fact, List continued, the state imposes many restrictions
and regulations on private industry. It bans slave trade, and regulates
shipbuilding, the sale of pharmaceutical products, and so on. The state is
likewise entitled to regulate matters that not only concern the welfare of
the individual, but that affect the nation as a whole. He further explained
that his support for protective duties did not mean he wanted the state to
tell an entrepreneur what to build or a young person what career to choose.[20]

List thought it self-evident that "only where the interest of individuals
has been subordinated to those of the nation, and where successive generations have striven for one and the same object, the nations have been
brought to harmonious development of their productive powers." But he
did not specify exactly *how* this subordination of the individual's interest
to the nation's interest was to be carried out. Nor did he state what kind
of body was competent to regulate such subordination. He limited himself
to stating that it was obvious to him that private industry could not prosper
"without the united efforts both of the individuals who are living at the
time, and of successive generations directed to one common object."[21]
Who was competent to coordinate the efforts of several generations under
one goal, List did not reveal. . . .

To List, the system of the School was really "a system of the private
economy of the human race" because it never addressed itself to the
question of how the advanced nations raised themselves to their power and
prosperity. One would not learn from the School "what means are to be
adopted . . . to bring the natural powers belonging to any individual nation
into activity and value, to raise a poor and weak nation to prosperity and
power." This was so because the School totally ignored politics, ignored
the nation's special conditions, "and concerns itself merely about . . . the
whole human race."[22] Most importantly, the School

> recognizes no distinction between nations which have attained a higher
> degree of economical development, and those which occupy a lower stage.
> Everywhere it seeks to exclude the action of the power of the State. . . .
> Statistics and history, however, teach, on the contrary, that the necessity

for the intervention of legislative power and administration is everywhere more apparent, the further the economy of the nation is developed.[23]

List insisted that contrary to the School's claims, a less advanced nation could never attain to "a perfectly developed manufacturing power of its own, nor to perfect national independence, without protective duties."[24] Industry could not arise in an agricultural country "in the natural course of things" (Smith's words). Just as a child could not defeat a strong man, so a newly born industry in one country could not compete with a developed one in another country.[25]

List thought that these ideas, which to him were self-evident truths, met with incomprehension and hostility in Germany because of the general backwardness of the nation. (This backwardness explained why the Germans fell for the ideas of English free traders.) It is interesting to note that List and Marx sounded very similar when they characterized the condition of Germany. When Marx wrote his own comments about Germany in the 'Hegel Critique,'' he may well have been influenced by the following words of List (whom he read shortly before writing his essay on Hegel):

> Germany developed herself in a totally different way from all other nations. Elsewhere high mental culture rather grew out of the evolution of the material powers of production, whilst in Germany the growth of material powers of production was the outcome chiefly of an antecedent intellectual development. Hence at the present day the whole culture of the Germans is theoretical. Hence also those many unpractical and odd traits in the German character which other nations notice in us.[26]

To List, the Germans as a nation resembled "an individual who, having been formerly deprived of the use of his limbs, first learned theoretically the arts of standing and walking, of eating and drinking, of laughing and weeping, and then only proceeded to put these in practice." This handicap explained the German "predilection for philosophic systems and cosmopolitan dreams." Lacking experience in the affairs of world, Germans turned their minds to speculation. For this reason, "nowhere has the doctrine of Adam Smith and of his disciples obtained a larger following than in Germany; nowhere else have people more thoroughly believed in the cosmopolitan magnanimity of Messrs. [George] Canning and [William] Huskisson."[27]

But when List wrote these words (which he did toward the end of his lifelong struggle to make the Germans change their ways), he was able to insert a more positive note, too. He recalled both the tribulations of German manufacturers and merchants and the formation of the unsuccessful Merchants Union in Frankfurt in 1819, but given the progress achieved by the gradual unification of German customs since then, he had reason to think that his work had not been wasted.

However, List's insistence on the role of the state in the economic relief of an emerging nation reflected more than a practical consideration for Germany at one particular moment. It was an essential element of List's argument, one that reflected his view of man and society, that the individual and the nation must think about and work for the future generations, just as they inherited from their predecessors "the mental capital of the present human race." Accusing the "popular School" of failing to see the reciprocal influence of "material wealth and political power," List proclaimed the subordination of the private interest to the public, that is, the supremacy of politics over economics. How else could the following prescription be realized?

> The nation must sacrifice and give up a measure of material property in order to gain culture, skill, and powers of united production; it must sacrifice some present advantages in order to insure to itself future ones.[28]

It is clear by now that the relationship between economic development and political leadership is central to List's entire argument. Is there a way of discovering whether List favored assigning leadership to one particular section of the nation?

We may move toward answering this question, and toward a better understanding of List's concept of politics, by focusing on what he considered his greatest theoretical achievement: the idea of productive power or the "power of producing wealth." Productive power, List said, was more important than wealth itself. He illustrated his meaning with a story about two farm-owning fathers. One father deposits his profits from the farm in order to earn interest at the bank and makes his sons perform "common hard work." The other father spends his profits on the education of his sons, who in due course become expert farmers or learn other specialized trades. The first father, according to List, acts in accord with the theory of values; the second follows the theory of productive powers,[29] which in fact was List's agenda for a nation.

> All expenditure in the instruction of youth, the promotion of justice, defense of nations, etc., is a consumption of present values for the behoof of the productive powers. The greatest portion of the consumption of a nation is used for the education of the future generation, for promotion and nourishment of the future national productive powers.[30]

While Adam Smith, according to List, thought that only "those who fatten pigs or prepare pills are productive," List thought that "instructors of youth and of adults, virtuosos, musicians, physicians, judges, and administrators, are productive in a much higher degree." List ridiculed the stand of the School, according to which makers of bagpipes and "the chemist's boy" are productive, but composers of music and physicians are not.[31]

Prominent among List's preferred professions or occupations was science. He understood that scientific discoveries were important for the development of industry and, less directly, of agriculture, and he recognized the important place of scientists in society.

> The necessity for education and instruction, through writings and lectures by a number of persons who have to bring into practice the results of scientific investigations, induces men of special talents to devote themselves to instruction and authorship. The competition of such talents, owing to the large demand for their efforts, creates both a division and cooperation of scientific activity . . . .[32]

Just as List's work is virtually a paean to urban life and industry, so his comments on village life strikingly resemble Marx's words in the *Manifesto* about "the idiocy of rural life." It is worth noting, however, that when List spoke about rural life he had in mind the farm worker or peasant, but when he extolled the joys and free spirit of urban life he spoke of the manager and the businessman—not the manual worker. Had he thought more of the worker, perhaps he would have admitted that industry, which in his era demanded a large portion of the worker's time, offered little intellectual or moral satisfaction, paid the worker poorly, and provided a life that was not much preferable to the farmer's plight. (But then perhaps List would have disagreed; perhaps he would have argued that some benefits of urban life did extend even to factory workers.)

Even when List spoke of a modernized or industrialized agriculture, which he thought a truly developed nation had to have, he saw the town-country relationship as being fundamentally uneven. To him, "the city" stimulated technological improvements in the country, and it generated political liberties that it then passed along to the country.

When List spoke of "the city," he did not simply mean the bourgeoisie, however. List was somewhat mistrustful of merchants, whom he accused of a virtually professional disinclination to follow the national interest in their commercial activity. So long as the merchants made money, they did not care how the goods they imported or exported affected the morality, prosperity, or power of the nation. The merchant, according to List, "imports poisons as readily as medicines. He enervates whole nations through opium and spiritual liquors." It is evident, List concluded, "that the interest of individual merchants and the interest of the commerce of a whole nation are widely different things.''[33] Clearly, List was not in favor of making the merchants a dominant force. He thought that no segment of the business class, left to itself, was capable of rising above its sectional concerns and interests.

List set high standards for establishing national goals and a nation's performance, and the demands he imposed on national leadership were likewise exacting.

> Every separate nation is productive only in the proportion in which it has known how to appropriate these attainments of former generations and to increase them by its own acquirements, in which the natural capabilities of its territory, its extent and geographical position, its population and political power, have been able to develop as completely and symmetrically as possible all sources of wealth within its boundaries, and to extend its moral, intellectual, commercial, and political influence over less advanced nations and especially over the affairs of the world.[34]

He did not explain how this kind of understanding and leadership could be attained in any country, let alone in a country that by definition was backward economically, culturally, and politically. Was it realistic to expect that such a country would both have a liberal constitutional order, which List explicitly favored (see Chapter 8 for his comments on what made England great), and pursue a policy that List felt was necessary to make it modern? Did List himself not say that Germany's backwardness lay behind the low level of its thinking about economy?

Although he clearly favored freedom, List admitted that he did not maintain "the absolute preferableness" of one government over another. In a country like Russia, he allowed, "people who are yet in a low degree of civilization are capable of making most remarkable progress in their national well-being under an absolute monarchy."[35] He thought that in the period of slavery and serfdom, the economic and intellectual progress of a nation like Russia would be advanced by absolute monarchy rather than by a limited or constitutional one.[36] But we must recall that he had earlier declared the Russia of his time ready for—and in need of— constitutional reforms. All in all, List was simply not sure which form of government was better for Russia.

But List was not even very clear about the right kind of leadership in a country like Germany, which was more advanced than Russia. Who should lead Germany? Certainly not the merchants. But the representatives of every discrete branch of industry and of every social group also had only their own, inevitably narrow, points of view. List did not say so explicitly, but if his prescriptions were to be put into practice, his theory would require a national authority, presumably some sort of intellectual dictatorship, capable of transcending or integrating all particular economic, professional, and other sectional interests. True, List affirmed his devotion to the principles of political freedom, constitutional government, and the rights of man. But his concept of national interest— if its prescriptions were to be acted upon—required a body, an institution, composed of persons who stood above all those particularistic interests. In this sense, it is legitimate to detect in List's outlook, along with his unquestionably sincere liberalism, certain antiliberal elements. It is certain that his doctrine did not call for bourgeois rule in the sense in which Marx's doctrine required the dictatorship of the proletariat for the realization of communism. Rather, List believed in a supraclass *national* authority, but he never defined its precise nature. This difficulty in List's system was noticed more than a hundred years ago by Eugen Dühring. He commented that List's plan did not make a provision for the establishment of a body that would define the interest of the whole nation while keeping the future in mind; under a liberal-constitutional state, Dühring added, all groups are concerned with their immediate advantage.[37]

Even if List's nationalism did not provide any explicit recommendations for giving power to the intelligentsia, his concept of a developed industrial society, a modern nation, did favor certain segments of society and thus implicitly assigned them a major role. We may elucidate this issue by reviewing Harry G. Johnson's comments on what he calls "economic nationalism" and by examining his attempt to identify those to whom that kind of nationalism is particularly advantageous and therefore attractive.

Johnson notes that "the intellectuals engaged in cultural activities and the owners and managers of communications media have an interest in nationalism."[38] The economic policy of nationalism, Johnson thinks, would support activities "selected for their symbolic value in terms of concepts of national identity." It would also promote activities "offering prestigious jobs for the middle class and/or the educated class," such as the bureaucracy in very backward countries, and the people in higher education and research in more advanced nations. Nationalism favors state control over (or direct state ownership of) economic enterprises and allocates preferential jobs to members of the nation.[39] Nationalism's economic policy produces "psychic income," i.e., "nationalistic satisfaction at the expense of material income," according to Johnson. Nationalism tends to "redistribute material income from the lower class toward the middle class, and particularly toward the educated middle class."[40] One-party regimes in new states tend to transfer real income from the mass of the population to the educated urban elements, for example, those working in the communications media. Thus economic nationalism means an economic loss for the population at large to benefit the middle class. However,

> this redistribution may perform a necessary function in the early stages of forming a nation, in the sense that the existence of a substantial middle class may be a prerequisite of a stable society and democratic government. In other words, an investment in the creation of a middle class financed by resources from the mass of the population by nationalistic policies, may be the essential preliminary to the construction of a viable national state. This problem, however, belongs in the spheres of history, sociology, and political science rather than economics.[41]

This is the kind of argument List would have understood (although it is unlikely he ever imagined one-party regimes of the kind that have proliferated in this century). Indeed, he advanced it himself in somewhat different terms. He would have followed Johnson up by adding that in the long run, all members of a nation would benefit from having in their own country an infrastructure of schools, publishing houses, newspapers, and libraries, and that owing to these, they would advance culturally, socially, and economically as members of their own independent nation. List might have argued that his story of the two fathers could be applied also to agrarian nations—one investing in research institutes, industrial facilities, schools of engineering, and libraries; the other spending its profits, derived from exports, on consumption —and remaining as backward as before.

But as Johnson points out, such choices do not belong to the domain of economics but are a matter of political values and preferences. List thought precisely the same. It is not especially fruitful to ask whether List's "national economy" was more "true" than the political economy of Adam Smith or of Karl Marx. George Lichtheim stresses in this connection that rather than ask whether an economic doctrine is "true" or "false," one should consider "the practical significance of theory: its relevance to the circumstances it sets out to explain." While Marx's labor theory of value was tautological, for example, it still performed an important task, because "it made possible a broadly accurate analysis of the manner in which the social product was distributed among various classes."[42]

Perhaps something like this can be said about List's theory of productive forces. Whether it was better or worse as economics than the labor theory, List's theory, as we noted earlier, recognized as productive those whom the labor theory considered unproductive: teachers, scientists, doctors, lawyers, judges, policemen, soldiers, officials, artists, and so forth.[43] Thus List in fact did establish certain guidelines or criteria for distributing national income and even assigned (at least implicitly) to certain groups a significant political role in the nation. What the proletariat—armed with the doctrine of "scientific socialism"— was to Marx, the modern intelligentsia—the intellectuals, technocrats, scientists, entrepreneurs, professionals, and white-collar workers—were to List.

On the other hand, List had little to say about the special social and economic interests and needs of the industrial workers. It is evident that he assigned to them a subordinate role. Even though he sympathized with their plight in purely human terms, he did not propose any political or social *programs* for improving the condition of labor.[44] Insofar as the peasants, craftsmen, and artisans were concerned (that is, the social strata Marx lumped together under the name of the "petty bourgeoisie"), List saw little future for them in his industrial civilization, just as Marx did not foresee a role for them under capitalism (let alone communism).[45] Thus both List and Marx viewed this social group in a fundamentally different manner than Herder, who saw it as the best representative of national character. We have to conclude that these different perceptions of the peasants, craftsmen, and artisans derived from the fact that Herder belonged to a preindustrial age while List and Marx responded to the industrial era.

It would be a grave mistake to see in List's system an implicit or explicit endorsement of the views and interests of a particular social class or stratum rather than a concern with the condition of a country as a whole. List advanced a program for building industrial society on a principle that was different from the dominant model of his time. For a better understanding of List's approach, it is helpful to refer to a discussion by Ralf Dahrendorf, who, in developing an argument first advanced by Max Weber, has suggested that two kinds of rationality were at work during the rise of capitalism: *market* rationality and *plan* rationality. The first, which Weber had spoken about, lay behind "entrepreneurial success, the origin of the profit motive and the motive force of a steady growth of needs." The plan rationality, according to Dahrendorf, was based on industrial discipline, the "discipline of rigid organization, the habit of subordination and obedience," which had been the principle behind "military training of the Prussian pattern." Dahrendorf concludes that these two "conditions of industrialism" were incompatible. On the one hand, says Dahrendorf, the market is rational in that it brings about an optimal result through the competition of the interests of all involved. But the plan is also rational in that available knowledge is used to determine in advance who has to do what and when. Market rationality involves rules of the game and referees; plan rationality involves a bureaucracy to design lines of action and to control their execution. In terms of market rationality, plan rationality is not rational; all plans may err, and reliance on them may lead to vast and expensive losses. In terms of plan rationality, market rationality is not rational; competition means a considerable waste of resources. Dahrendorf concludes that Adam Smith's theory of political economy is market rational and Friedrich List's theory of national economy is plan rational. The political theory and practice of liberalism imply an attitude of market rationality; the authoritarian and, more recently, the totalitarian state are based on an attitude of plan rationality. German society was not characterized simply by either rationality alone but by an institutionalized ambiguity of these two forms of rationality, by the mixture of free trade and state bureaucracy, private economy and interventionism, bourgeois and military order.[46]

Where Dahrendorf discovered institutionalized ambiguity in German society in the nineteenth century, a student of List's is inspired to detect a similar ambiguity in the Listian program. List favored market rationality in a nation's domestic affairs, and yet he insisted that a nation's economy, education, and culture should also be plan rational because of foreign-policy considerations. Using the title of Bertrand Russell's book cited in Chapter 1, let us say that List favored "freedom" at home but wanted "organization" to regulate his country's relations with the outside world.

There is no evidence that List was aware of this contradiction or dichotomy or of its political implications; he was a precursor and promoter of German industrialization, not its ex-post interpreter. But Dahrendorf's points help us understand why List's program for industrialization and, more generally, for national development could be given a more or less liberal form when it was imitated in other countries. Indeed, in some cases it was adopted by those who rejected flatly the liberal fixtures of his "package." Most notably, this happened to List's ideas in Russia when they were embraced by such authoritarian politicians as Sergei Witte. Witte liked List's call for industrialization because it would benefit Russia's might, but he rejected any linkage between economic development and political reform.

List's case thus anticipated the classic dilemma of liberal reformers in a developing country. On the one hand, they want political freedom, but on the other hand, they also realize that a Western-style constitutional regime, assuming it is possible in the first place, will not be able to raise their nation from the ranks of underdeveloped countries. The nation, would-be reformers soon discover, must organize, mobilize, and set goals for itself that are not necessarily acceptable to all social or economic groups within it. List wanted to see a political authority that worked for economic modernization, but he also asked for political liberty. As we saw, he did not explain how free trade at home would coexist with a state-controlled foreign trade. Nor did he identify those who would know what was good for the nation in the long run. Finally, List did not consider what would happen if any such optimum national plan (assuming that the right leadership had been found) were imposed on an unwilling, or at least uncomprehending, population—and how such a plan could be realized while retaining a liberal political regime.

These "failures" do not detract from List's achievement. He did not resolve the contradictions that his questions revealed, but those contradictions were not due to faulty logic. They reflected real contradictory trends and processes in the society of his time.

What, then, was List's historical achievement? Contemporary economists appear to be increasingly ready to recognize List as the first major critic of Adam Smith and David Ricardo from the point of view of "the later European developers," as John Gerard Ruggie put it.[47] What this critique involved is explained in an earlier work by Marcello de Cecco, *Money and Empire*. According to de Cecco, Smith and Ricardo assumed that nations participating in international trade would belong to "the civilized world," and they therefore ignored "problems resulting from differences in the stages of development reached by the exchanging countries." Ricardo believed that countries could invert their specializations in foreign trade, which was possible, says de Cecco, only between economies at the same stage of development. But Smith and Ricardo did not grasp the "important dynamic implications" of the specialization among countries finding themselves at different stages of development, e.g., England as a manufacturing nation and Portugal or Poland as nations that produce wine or wheat. Smith and Ricardo failed to see that such a division of labor implied "a faster rate of development for Britain than for those countries which do not specialize in the production of industrial commodities."[48]

In opposition to Ricardo, who "saw only quantitative differences between the producers of cloth and wine that free exchange would mutually reward," says Ruggie, "List stressed qualitative differences that free exchange would exacerbate and that the state, therefore, had to overcome."[49]

The linkage of economics with politics in List's system is stressed by de Cecco, who describes List as "the intellectual opposite of Smith and Ricardo." De Cecco writes:

> The latter try to establish political economy as an exercise in logic, a study of the internal consistency of abstractly formulated logical systems; the former attempts to immerse himself in the reality of economic history and to derive the most important lessons from it. His work, much more than

Smith's, is an inquiry into the real causes of the wealth of nations. For him, economics is one of the arts of statemanship. He does not care about discovering the immutable laws that govern the actions of *"homo oeconomicus"*—What he wants to understand is how to get Germany on to a path which might allow her to become an economically powerful state in the shortest possible time, since he is convinced that economic power is the necessary precondition of political power.[50]

It may well be that Eric J. Hobsbawm has defined the wider historical framework that is necessary for judging List's intellectual contribution. According to Hobsbawm, "of all the economic consequences of the age of dual revolution"—i.e., the Industrial and the French revolutions—the "division between the 'advanced' and the 'underdeveloped' countries proved to be the most profound and the most lasting."

> Until the Russians in the 1930s developed means of leaping this chasm between the "backward" and the "advanced," it [this division] would remain immovable, untraversed, and indeed growing wider, between the minority and the majority of the world's inhabitants. No fact has determined the history of the twentieth century more firmly than this.[51]

List, "the German economist," Hobsbawm writes, "as usual wearing the congenial costume of philosophic abstraction—rejected an international economy which in effect made Britain the chief or only industrial power and demanded protectionism, and so . . . minus the philosophy—did the Americans."[52]

What List's response amounted to is eloquently and competently described by de Cecco:

> The greatness of List's analysis lies . . . in his full utilisation of the classical method of reasoning in order to reach economic policy conclusions of a kind which are the perfect opposite to the classical ones. We can say that by adding dynamism and history to classical analysis, List obtains a strategy for fast economic growth that is perfectly suitable to the socio-economic conditions of his country as well as of many other countries which want to undergo a process of modernisation. If we read List in the light of recent historiography, we can clearly see—in his rejection of individual action as the basis for economic growth for countries other than Britain—his awareness of the impossibility of founding economic modernisation on a bourgeois revolution, i.e., on the English model, and of the ensuing need to find a different "national way," based on collective action, i.e., by grafting a modernisation process on to a social context that has not yet known the rise of a "liberated" bourgeoisie. List understands that in countries such as Germany modernisation must come as a "revolution from above," which will permit the country to jump, as it were, over one historical phase, i.e.,

the destruction of the ancient regime effected by the bourgeoisie, which characterised the modernisation process in England.[53]

Interestingly enough, Rosa Luxemburg (1871–1919) recognized in List a major advocate of the capitalist method of modernizing Germany, and she paid him a generous—by Marxist standards of polemic—tribute, especially considering her reputation as one of Marx's most orthodox disciples in matters of nationality. Favorably comparing List with Fichte, Luxemburg wrote in 1908:

> Friedrich List, with his trivial theory of "national economy," can be more justifiably considered the real messiah of the national unity of Germany than the idealist Fichte, mentioned usually as the first apostle of the German national rebirth. This "national" movement . . . basically represented only a medieval reaction against the seeds of the Revolution, which were brought to Germany by Napoleon, and against the elements of the modern bourgeois system . . . . By contrast, the gospel of that vulgar agent of German industry, List, in the thirties and forties based the "national rebirth" on the elements of bourgeois development, on industry and trade, on the theory of the "domestic market." The material basis for this patriotic movement, which in the thirties and forties of the nineteenth century aroused such strong political, educational, philosophical, and literary currents in Germany, was, above all, the need to unify all the German territories . . . into one great, integrated, capitalistic "fatherland," establishing a broad foundation for mechanized manufacturing and big industry.[54]

Since at the time Luxemburg was writing, Marx's critique of List was not known to have existed, she of course could not have known that Marx had in the 1840s vehemently denied what Luxemburg called "the need to unify all the German territories" into a *capitalist* Germany. (See Chapter 3.) For our purposes, however, Luxemburg's judgment is especially valuable. She recognized that there are different kinds of nationalism and that individual nationalist thinkers *do* make a difference. She saw that List, unlike his German nationalist predecessors or contemporaries, understood that the Industrial Revolution in Britain heralded more than economic change; he also grasped that it would exert a powerful political, and cultural economic impact on Germany and on the rest of the world. His nationalism recognized all this. Following the example of Marx and Engels, who had claimed that, in comparison with the utopian character of the teachings of their socialist predecessors, their doctrine was a "science," a student of nationalism might make a similar claim on behalf of List and might be encouraged to do so by Luxemburg's remarks. By incorporating the idea of developmental economics as a global process into nationalist thinking, one might argue, List transformed nationalism from a utopia into a "science."

Indeed, List's nationalism should be understood as "scientific" in the same sense in which one speaks of Marx's claim. Marx's and List's systems were "scientific" according to the peculiar, nineteenth-century definition of the term: They both saw in the progressive march of history, in the historical process itself, validation of their moral and political values. On this subject, a comment by Raymond Grew is especially illuminating:

> One of the things they [Marx and List] bequeathed to their followers was the assumption that these values did not need to be defended or even explicitly evoked, so that furthering a favorable historical process was its own justification and the dangers of proletarian dictatorships or the state as an instrument of justice did not need to be faced by Marx and the dangers of Realpolitik or economic growth directed by an elite did not need to be faced by List. Both men, then, speak to many of the liberal goals of their age while ignoring the liberal preoccupation with laws and representative government. Both appeal to democratic values while ignoring democracy.[55]

Grew helps us to understand why the authoritarian or totalitarian possibilities that we detected in Marx's and List's programs did not concern either of them. Both Marx and List expected the march of history to continue in the direction they thought had already been charted out. Marx anticipated an imminent collapse of capitalism and, along with this, a swift disappearance of nations and nationalism. List had a different global scenario, but for reasons that were very close to those of Marx, he expected an easy absorption of the small nations within the large ones. Marx and List did not anticipate the emergence of a serious challenge to that course, a challenge that would have to be met with repressive, large-scale countermeasures. Their "scientific" outlook had made no allowance for historical retrogression or for history's taking a prolonged detour from the highway of progress. Marx would live long enough to be surprised by history more than once. List died less than two years before his own scenario was to be challenged by a nationalism he had not even taken into consideration.

Borrowing a term from Teodor Shanin, who calls the List system the "first amendment" to the doctrines of Adam Smith and David Ricardo,[56] let us view Czech historian František Palacký's nationalist manifesto of 1848 as the first nationalist amendment to Friedrich List (see Chapter 10). Palacký proclaimed the right of all nations, large and small, rich and poor, strong and weak, to freedom. He denied that any reasons whatsoever justified one nation's rule over another.

Somewhat later, as nationalism spread to Asia and then to Africa, the

Listian assumption that political independence and industrialization should be the exclusive possession of the nations of the "temperate zone" was also challenged. And yet, while this Listian idea was being repudiated, List became the favorite theorist of those "torrid-zone" nations about whose future he had so little to say. (Marx's overwhelming success in Russia—a success that amazed him greatly, given that Russia was not one of his favorite countries—was strikingly similar.)

Both Marx and List shared certain assumptions about the prerequisites a society or a nation had to meet in order to qualify for participating in the future progress of history. Both Marx and List took for granted the existence of civil society, an economic, social, and cultural infrastructure that functioned side by side with the state. But their respective disciples, as we shall see, lived under different conditions— and worked out new programs. Let us begin by taking a look at nationalism in and after 1848.

# 10

# *Nationalism: The Unity of Theory and Practice*

Had List lived to see the events of 1848, he would have found much that he did not like. For, indeed, the outcome of the revolutions of 1848–1849 was a great failure from the point of view of not only Marx and communism, but also of German, Italian, Polish, and Hungarian nationalisms. Germany did not become a unified national state; neither did Italy. Hungary was reconquered by the Habsburgs. The Poles did not overthrow foreign rule.[1]

More importantly, in 1848 nationalism took a direction that List had not anticipated. In that year, the peoples of East Central Europe, for whom he had not foreseen any future in his *National System*, made themselves heard. These peoples—whom their enemies sometimes called "nonhistoric" or "peasant" nations—presented their own vision of the world and demanded the realization of their cultural, political, and socioeconomic aspirations. Their point of view was formulated by the Czech historian František Palacký, whom Engels would contemptuously call a "learned German run mad." (Obviously an educated Czech who did not *want* to be a German had to be insane.) Although Palacký spoke first of all for the Czechs as they asserted their desire to be a nation independent of Germany—Bohemia was considered a part of Germany by Germans of all persuasions, including List and Marx—his arguments had a wider significance and could be applied to other cases involving the nonhistoric nations.

Thus, besides having to fight the forces of reaction and absolutism and besides competing, more theoretically, with communism, the nationalist revolutionaries of Germany, Hungary, and Poland found themselves challenged in 1848–1849 by the Czechs, Slovenes, Slovaks, Croats, Romanians, and Ukrainians, who declared they did not wish to be members of the Polish, German, or Hungarian nations. The very myth of international solidarity of nations became a casualty of the revolutionary epoch: Germans and Poles fought over Poznania, and Germans and Danes over Schleswig; the Czechs and Germans clashed in Prague, as did the Poles and Ukrainians in Galicia; the Hungarians found themselves at war not only with Vienna but also with virtually all the peoples of their historic kingdom of St. Stephen.

We may suppose that List the German patriot would have been unhappy with developments such as Czech (or Slovene) nationalism, because they implied the diminishment of the Germany he wanted to build. Still, List the theorist and prophet of nationalism would have had every reason to feel gratified as even the peoples he had ignored, or in the case of the Asian and African nations, had written off, adopted one after another what in a very real sense was a Listian program for nation-building and modernization (to use anachronistic terms from our own times). Indeed, the peculiar Listian ways of looking at the world and dealing with its problems gradually became so widely adopted that they lost their original intellectual identity and ceased to be associated with List's own particular doctrine. As we shall argue, the doctrine of nationalism, including its Listian component, in the process of becoming realized in practice "abolished itself" as a distinct ideology. Even the Czechs in due course adopted a Listian method to fight the Germans, but of course they did not acknowledge this, let alone declare themselves followers of Listianism.

Two documents represent the nationalist philosophy of Palacký. The first was his letter of April 11, 1848 to the president of the Frankfurt Committee of the Fifty. The second, the "Manifesto of the First Slavonic Congress," was addressed to "the Nations of Europe" and was issued with Palacký's signature on June 12, 1848. (It appears that the only international meeting of consequence held during the revolutionary era was an international congress of nationalists.)

In his letter to Frankfurt, Palacký declined, for three reasons, to participate in the work of the Committee, whose task was to prepare the election to a German parliament. Two of his reasons were political and thus concern us less than his ideas about nationality, though they deserve to be noted as follows. Palacký believed that a unification of Germany, as understood by German nationalists of that time, implied the liquidation of the Habsburg monarchy. He considered the survival of the monarchy to be a necessity for the smaller peoples of East Central Europe in view of the alternative: the prospect of the rise of Russian hegemony—"a *universal monarchy*, that is to say, an infinite and inexpressible evil, a misfortune without measure or bound." Palacký explained that he was not an enemy of the Russians: "On the contrary, I observe with pleasure and sympathy every step forward which that great nation makes within its natural borders along the path of civilization." However, out of love for his own nation and even greater "respect for the good of humanity," he rejected "the bare possibility of a universal Russian monarchy... not because that monarchy would be Russian but because it would be universal."[2]

Secondly, Palacký believed that a German Republic was an unattainable goal and would be highly unstable were it to be realized. In any case, whatever the Germans would do, he opposed the introduction of the republican form of government in the lands of the Habsburgs: "Think of the Austrian Empire divided up into sundry republics, some considerable in size and others small—what a delightful basis for a universal Russian monarchy!"[3]

But these, as we noted, were secondary considerations. Palacký's first and main reason for not participating in the Frankfurt Committee's work was based on his theory of nationality. Looking back at the history of the relations between the Bohemian Crown and the German (Holy Roman) Empire, Palacký made the crucial distinction between a political relationship of rulers on the one hand and the rights and obligations of a nation (which he defined as something distinct from and independent of any such political arrangement) on the other.

> I am a Czech of Slavonic blood, and with all the little I possess and all the little I can do, I have devoted myself for all time to the service of my nation. That nation is a small one, it is true, but from time immemorial it has been a nation of itself and based upon its own strength. Its rulers were from olden times members of the federation of German princes, but the nation never regarded itself as pertaining to the German nation, nor throughout all the centuries was it regarded by others as so pertaining.... The entire connection of the Czech lands with the German Reich was regarded, and must be regarded, not as a bond between nation and nation but as one between ruler and ruler. If, however, anyone asks that, over and above this heretofore existing bond between princes, the Czech nation should now unite with the German nation, this is at least a new demand—devoid of any historical and juridical basis, a demand to which I for my person do not feel justified in acceding until I receive an express and authentic mandate for so doing.[4]

The rights of nations, Palacký continued, "are in truth the rights of Nature. No nation on earth has the right to demand that its neighbours should sacrifice themselves for its benefits, no nation is under an obligation to deny or sacrifice itself for the good of its neighbour. Nature knows neither dominant nor underyoked nations." He added that any state comprising diverse nations within its limits could be stable only on the condition that it granted and secured equality to them.[5]

These ideas were further developed in the "Manifesto of the First Slavonic Congress to the Nations of Europe." The "Manifesto" claimed that unlike the Slavs who were devoted to liberty more than to conquest and dominion, the Latin and Germanic nations had in the past centuries maintained independence of their own states mainly "by the might of the sword" while at the same time oppressing their own common people. The Slavic peoples had fallen victim to the power-drive of the Latin and Germanic peoples, but as the new era of freedom began, they were now demanding their freedom, too. The Congress welcomed the social and political changes taking place in the countries of Europe and stated that

> we Slavs reject and hold in abhorrence all dominion based on main force and evasion of the law; we reject all privileges and prerogatives as well as all political differentiation of classes; we demand unconditional equality before the law, an equal measure of rights and duties for all. Where a single slave is born among millions, true liberty does not exist in that place. Yes, *liberty, equality, fraternity* for all who live in the State is our watchword today, as it was a thousand years ago.[6]

At the same time, while endorsing the rights of the individual, the Congress asked that identical rights of nations be recognized: "No less sacred to us than man in the enjoyment of his natural rights is the *nation*, with its sum total of spiritual needs and interests."[7] The authors of the "Manifesto" were aware that profound differences existed among nations that were due to their different historical experience, but they insisted that

> the capacity of those other [less fortunate] nations for development is in no way limited. Nature in and for herself draws no distinction between nations as though some were noble and others ignoble; she has not called any one nation to dominate over others, nor set aside any nation to serve another as an instrument for that other's ends. An equal right on the part of all to the noblest attributes of humanity is a divine law which none can violate with impunity.[8]

Drawing inspiration from Herder and Rousseau, Palacký thus sought to provide a historical and philosophical basis for the emancipation of those peoples whose rights were not recognized by the German, Polish, or Hungarian nationalists. These nationalists supported the "historic" or "political" nations against absolutism and against foreign domination, but they defined those nations on the basis of such criteria as *political* history. In other words, according to German, Polish, or Hungarian nationalists, a nation was only a nation if it had a history as an independent state, a social structure that included the upper and middle classes and not just the common folk, a culture with higher education and a highly developed literary language, and a large size and population. On this criterion peasants speaking folk dialects would advance to a higher civilization by becoming literate in one of the already existing developed languages and by identifying with one of those political nations, not by creating new nations on the basis of village dialects or distant and vague historical legends.

Directly countering the political goals and cultural assumptions of the Poles, Germans, or Hungarians, the nationalisms of those "backward" peoples, who had formed cultural and academic movements before 1848, became politicized in that year and afterwards emerged as an increasingly potent force in Central and Eastern Europe. They, too, had been disappointed in 1848, but their subsequent development was facilitated by that year's one successful revolution—that is, the emancipation of the peasantry, the abolition of serfdom. The entry of the peasantry into "society," from which it had been excluded for centuries, created the necessary preconditions for transforming the heretofore "academic" and "cultural" endeavors of the intelligentsia into a cause with a popular, mass constituency. The nationalist revolutions of the World War I era, which resulted in the formation of several new sovereign states, were in a sense the final act of a political process inaugurated in 1848 and of cultural developments that went back even further—to the late eighteenth-early nineteenth century.

Since most of those emergent peoples were culturally, socially, and politically less developed than such historic nations as Poland and Germany, their first concern was to establish what the Poles and Germans already had: a standard language. In fact, historically, language as an element of a broadly defined culture became, after 1848, the primary concern in nation-building. Thus when the Polish freedom fighters were battling their conquerors militarily, politically, and diplomatically, the philologists of the emerging nationalities challenged the dominant order by creating new literary (that is, standard) languages. Recently, scholars have rightly called these individuals "language strategists," "language manipulators," and even "philological incendiaries."[9] The last epithet is especially apt because obsession with dialects, no less than a passion for the dialectic, fueled that *"fire in the minds of men"* about which James Billington writes in his book (see note 1 of this chapter). We might call them language revolutionaries, too, because their linguistic theories (and the practices inspired by them) "relativized," if not outright subverted, the existing religious, social, political, and economic hierarchies and divisions. "To publish Serbian songs in 1814–1815," Peter Burke says about the Serb cultural nationalist Vuk Karadžić (1787–1864), "was a political act." Karadžić, who believed that writing was the greatest human invention, also wrote a grammar of Serbian language and a spelling book, and composed a dictionary.[10] "The discovery of popular culture," Burke notes, "was closely associated with the rise of nationalism":

> Ironically enough, the idea of a "nation" came from the intellectuals and was imposed on the "people" with whom they desired to identify. In 1800 craftsmen and peasants usually had a regional rather than a national consciousness.[11]

The new historical ideas of the kind proffered by Palacký performed a similar political function. Palacký's celebrated dictum—"We were here before Austria, we shall be here after Austria"—was a revolutionary statement. It is in this sense that we can speak not only of linguistic but also of historical consciousness as a nation-forming factor and therefore may agree with the designation of Palacký as a "father of the Czech nation."[12]

What Palacký did, or more accurately, helped to do, was to establish a new national community from an ethnic group. If nations are "imagined communities" defined by "the style in which they are imagined," as argued by Anderson,[13] and if nationalism "invents nations where they do not exist," which is the view of Gellner,[14] then such figures as Palacký have been important historically as both thinkers and doers. Indeed, the very usefulness of a sharp contrast between intellectual history—the history of ideas—and social or political history—an account of "objectively" existing groups—is hard to maintain. This is especially so in view of the early stages of the rise of modern nationalities when intellectual history was *the* history of those national movements, that is, of nations in the making.

In support of this view, we may call on the contemporary Czech historian, Miroslav Hroch, who has proposed a three-stage periodization of national movements. The first is "academic," that is, it occurs when a small number of scholars begins to treat a certain ethnic group as a distinct entity from the point of view of philology, ethnography, history, etc. The second stage, which is cultural in scope, begins when a group so defined starts to function in the sphere of education, press and publishing, theater, and so on, gradually spreading the sense of a separate national identity to a wider public. The final stage is the political stage in which the masses become mobilized in political parties, participate in elections, etc.[15]

Thus, at an early stage, a small circle of intellectuals—students of language, history, and folklore—performs the crucial operation of *defining* a national category and thus takes the first step toward transforming that category into a nation. Like Hroch, W. J. Argyle also divides national movements into phases: "proposing the category, elaborating the category, making subsidiary corporations, mustering the people." Of these, the first two phases correspond to Hroch's academic stage, and the third and fourth to Hroch's cultural and political stages.[16]

While granting that stages and phases are helpful conceptual devices for identifying what one thinks is characteristic of a given historical situation, it is important to note that all those activities identified by Argyle and Hroch as typical of a particular stage in fact remained "on the agenda" during the entire epoch of nation-formation and state-building. This becomes clear when one places national movements in the framework of "modernization" theory. Some adherents of that school understand modernization as a process that leads to increased political "capacity," "equality," and "differentiation" and is attained by the resolution of crises of identity, legitimacy, participation, penetration, and distribution.[17] Writers on modernization as a rule assume that states are the agents in the process of "development" and that ethnic nationalities help or obstruct, as the case may be, the state-initiated and state-directed effort. But there is no reason to assume that this is invariably so. It is arguable that in the nineteenth century Polish nationalism was a modernizing force, while the states of Russia, Austria, and Prussia/Germany were at best alternative agents of modernization, if not always outright obstacles to it.[18] Might not something similar be said about Czech or Slovene nationalism contra Vienna or about Finnish or Latvian nationalism contra St. Petersburg? (Or German nationalism contra the thirty-eight governments of the thirty-eight German states?)

Nationalist movements by definition have their own solution for the crises of identity and legitimacy: They propose to establish a new state that corresponds to the nation for which they claim to speak. But their agenda is much broader; they have preferences about how their state should be governed (participation, penetration) and they usually take a stand on major economic and social questions (distribution).

This brings us back to List and economic nationalism. Nation-building, or state-formation, was a multidimensional undertaking. It included the standardization of language (that in many cases was based on a peasant dialect or group of dialects), the creation or reconstruction of the past, the establishment of a network and a hierarchy of educational and other cultural organizations, the formation of political parties, the creation or operation of governmental (local and central) agencies, and so on. It included, no less importantly, nation-building in the economic sphere. Economic development meant more than importing industrial machinery or hiring engineers and skilled workers from the advanced countries. In full accord with List's view of the role of ideas, science, and education, the industrial "late-comers" created, in the course of the nineteenth century, a hierarchy of technical schools. The creation of such schools, according to David Landes, was much more important in the long run than transmission of industrial skills on the jobs, which had been practiced in the earlier phase of industrialization. The French were the first to establish technical schools, but they were imitated in Austria, Prussia, Belgium, the Netherlands, Russia, and Sweden. According to Landes,

> the German system proved in the end stronger and more effective in training talent for industry, partly because German enterprise had more regard for the products of technical schools, partly because the German governments, especially that of Prussia, were convinced of the importance of education to the national economic effort and supported it more generously. Far more clearly than anyone else, the Germans understood the significance of formal training in overcoming the handicaps of backwardness. They reaped their harvest in the second half of the century, when technology became less empirical and when new industries resting directly on a foundation of applied science came to the fore.[19]

Ethnic nationalisms in Eastern Europe easily adopted the essentials of the List formula for economic modernization as a component of national emancipation (thus supporting Carlton J. H. Hayes' opinion, cited in Chapter 1, that the Industrial Revolution was itself neither nationalist nor internationalist). While doing so, they were not deterred by the thought that List himself would have denied them, had he been faithful to his original idea, the right to follow his program, for he believed that only peoples large in population and territory and only those of a sufficiently high level of cultural and social development were qualified. But List's program could be adopted by any nation whether it defined itself by one or another criterion or met this or that prerequisite. In other words, his was an implicitly *generic* nationalism. In fact, List had admirers and imitators not only in his native Germany, but also in Hungary and Ireland, Catalonia, Bulgaria, Italy, India, Japan, and Russia. As Rudolf Jaworski has noted in his important analysis of the economic component of nationalist theory and practice, among the nations of East Central Europe that lacked their own states there occurred an "ideologization of economic affairs" that extended to such areas as land ownership and the operation of cooperative savings and consumers associations. According to Jaworski, "national boycott and national self-help organizations functioned within multi-national economic systems like protective customs barriers of independent nation states."[20]

It would take another book to present a history of nationalism in Europe. It is enough to mention that the defeat of nationalism in 1848 proved to be temporary. Within two decades, Italy and Germany became united, although not within the territorial extension dreamed of by their respective nationalists. In 1867, Hungary gained virtual independence in domestic affairs within the Habsburg monarchy. After 1867, Austria's Poles also became a "nation of the state," enjoying wide autonomy in Galicia and exercising considerable influence in Vienna. At the same time, the national movements of the nonhistoric peoples were becoming stronger. As the Ottoman Empire declined, one Balkan people after another became independent; by 1914, Greece, Serbia, Montenegro, Bulgaria, Romania, and Albania were sovereign states. As early as the 1830s in the empire of the Romanovs, the dynastic state felt compelled to add "nationality" as one of the "principles" that had until then been confined to Orthodoxy and autocracy. This was the autocracy's tribute, however, insincere, to the new idea of nation, although the relationship between state and nation or society in Russia remained a complex and troubled one until the end of tsarism in 1917 (see Chapter 13). As to the other peoples of the Russian Empire, the Poles remained unreconciled to Russian rule, but as the century wore on they were joined in opposition by the Finns, Latvians, Armenians, Jews, Lithuanians, Ukrainians, Estonians, Tatars, and Georgians, all of whom demanded recognition as distinct cultural and political entities. These groups did not ask for separation from Russia (the Poles were an exception here), but they did protest discrimination and demanded respect for their national, religious, and cultural identity.

Nor is there room in this book for an account that would pay special attention to the economic programs of these nationalisms and to their relationship to List's ideas. In the absence of such a comprehensive examination, a few examples will suggest how broad the recognition was among nationalists of all kinds of the Listian program for nation-building.

The first foreign edition of List's *National System* appeared in Hungary, in 1843, that is, in his lifetime. (In the 1850s, there were also two editions of a French translation, by Henri Richelot, and one American edition, translated by G. A. Matile and published with the notes of the French translator.[21]) The Hungarian revolutionary leader, Lajos Kossuth, knew and claimed to accept List's teaching.[22] So did Count Szechenyi, the

"Hungarian List," who considered that economic modernization was an essential component in the making of a modern Hungarian nation. Also, after Hungary gained internal independence in the 1867 deal with the Emperor (the so-called "Hungarian Compromise"), the Budapest governments, in their effort to make all of the inhibitants of their kingdom "Hungarian" (Hungary included many peoples, such as Slovaks, Germans, Romanians, Serbs, Ruthenes, etc., who did not consider themselves members of the Hungarian nation), combined economic measures under state control or sponsorship with a comprehensive program of ethnic assimilation through the education system. At the same time, this "modernization" of Hungary was being carried out by a bureaucratic regime that in social terms represented the large landowners rather than a Listian intelligentsia or the bourgeoisie. This fact profoundly influenced the course and ultimate outcome of the undertaking, as it prevented the political and social modernization of Hungary from being realized in a way analogous to its economic progress.[23] Hungary was the first, but by no means the last, state to use List's ideas selectively.

The contemporary Hungarian economic historians, Ivan T. Berend and Gyorgy Ránki, have argued that economic issues, such as the question of Hungary's becoming a separate customs area (distinct from Austria), were used by the ruling nobility for political purposes. They see, in "the superficiality of the economic literature dealing with the subject and the neglect of the economic aspects of the issue when political compromises were made," a proof that the real reasons behind "the Hungarian desire for an independent customs area were of a political and nationalistic nature." "In Hungary, as in Germany, the idea of industrialization was connected from the very beginning with the theories of George [sic] Friedrich List. In other words, nationalist concepts were always championed in the guise of economic slogans."[24]

Although Romania was a very different country from Hungary, the idea that the state ought to be engaged in promoting national interests in the economic sphere found its supporters there, too. In 1887, a Listian, i.e., protectionist, law was adopted by Romania, and in the same year *The National System* was published in a Romanian translation. Interestingly enough, the leading Listians were Romanians from Transylvania, i.e., a region then belonging to Hungary.[25]

At the other end of Europe, in Catalonia, cultural nationalists and business leaders established an alliance, according to Pierre Vilar. Together, they sought "to organize practical arguments and the anxieties of the moment into a *body of doctrine*, to make protectionism the common denominator of the political aspirations of all classes." Vilar does not claim that the leaders of the Catalan movement were outstanding or original thinkers.

> They cited Carey, who exchanged long letters with Guell, because Carey liked to point to Spain as a victim of English free trade. They admired List spontaneously, whose influence on German nationalism, mystical and "historicist" as well as industrialist, paralleled, on many points, the links that were established between protectionism and the intellectual movement in Catalonia.[26]

Initially, in the period from approximately 1820 to 1885, according to Vilar, "the leaders of Catalan industry, having captured the mediocre Spanish national market, and struggling to protect it, aspired without success to lead not a Catalan state, but, indeed *the Spanish nation*." When they spoke of "national market," "national industry," or "national production," they meant "Spanish," not "Catalan." Vilar believes that only because (and after) it failed to secure "the state apparatus" and to identify its interests with those of "the whole of Spain" did the Catalan industrial bourgeoisie adopt Catalonia as its "national" focal point from which it pressed its class claims.[27]

Whether or not Vilar's facts and interpretations are sound is irrelevant. What matters most for our argument is not that Catalan nationalism won support of the local bourgeoisie, but that a Catalan nationalism, represented by the intelligentsia, already existed *before* the bourgeoisie could turn to it. Had there been no such preexisting nationalism, based on cultural, linguistic, and historical criteria, it is most unlikely that the bankers or industrialists of Barcelona would have proceeded to "invent" a Catalan nationalism and nation when it served their needs. One may suppose that at various times in the nineteenth century the local business interests of Manchester, Lyon, Milan, or Hamburg found themselves slighted or ignored by the ruling circles in London, Paris, Rome, or Berlin, but they did not become anti-English, anti-French, anti-Italian, or anti-German, and they did not quote List in support of their demands.

But the Irish nationalists—not the bourgeoisie of Dublin—did become anti-British. In Ireland, a generation after the period in Catalonia discussed by Vilar, Arthur Griffith (born in Dublin in 1871) found inspiration in his struggle against England in the example of the Hungarian leader, Francis Deak, who, owing to a masterly tactic of parliamentary boycott, managed to achieve the reestablishment of the Hungarian constitution by 1867. But Griffith found another source of inspiration, too: "This was the great German apostle of protection, Friedrich List," according to F. S. L.

Lyons. List's *National System*, Lyons says, "came to be Griffith's gospel, a book, as he himself wrote, that he would like to see in the hands of every Irishman."[28] According to Lyons, List impressed Griffith because "Bismarckian Germany could be regarded as a monument to his ideas; protectionism, in other words, was not just a beautiful dream, but could be, and had been, made to work."

> Perhaps even more importantly, List insisted that a protective tariff was as much a factor in emergent nationalism as a country's language, literature or history. Indeed, Griffith went so far as to adopt List's definition of a nation as his own.[29]

It did not disturb Griffith that List's definition of nation required that the nation should be large and populous, which Ireland certainly was not. What he found especially inspiring was List's insistence that manufacturing was the basis of a nation's independence. This ran counter to the view common in Ireland, where the Irish Question tended to be identified with the land-reform issue. Against the argument that in Ireland "it is not necessary . . . to pay attention to our manufacturing arm, since our agricultural arm is all-sufficient," Griffith responded in his book, *The Resurrection of Hungary*:

> With List I reply: A nation cannot promote and further its civilization, its prosperity and its social progress equally as well by exchanging agricultural products for manufactured goods as by establishing a manufacturing power of its own. A merely agricultural nation can never develop to any extent a home or a foreign commerce, with inland means of transport and foreign navigation, increase its population in due proportion to their well-being, or make notable progress in its moral, intellectual, social and political development, it will never acquire important political power or be placed in a position to influence the cultivation and progress of less advanced nations and to form colonies of its own.[30]

These words of an Irish nationalist were written already in this century. But we saw how the Czech nationalist Palacký answered the questions that were on the political agenda in 1848: reform or revolution, monarchy or republic? His reply was, "Bohemia!" In 1918, which was the year that Griffith's book was published and that Palacký's nation had just become a sovereign state, the Catalan nationalist Cambó delivered a speech in the Madrid parliament. Cambó repeated the questions that the parliament was debating and then gave his answer: "Monarchy? Republic? Catalonia!"[31]

But nationalism did not limit itself to providing only these few answers to such questions about monarchy or republic, reform or revolution. After Marx had formulated what *he* thought was *the* question of the age—

communism or capitalism?—the nationalists responded with several answers: "Poland!," "Ireland!," "Serbia!," "India!" . . . . This did not mean that they refused to recognize the issues raised by socialism, only that they made their stand on capitalism versus socialism dependent on which of the two was better for their nation in given circumstances.

Thus nationalism was not simply a program and a movement concerned with language, history, and folklore—or with politics and power. Nor was it just a program of economic development, whether in politically independent countries, such as Italy after its unification, or among those peoples lacking political independence. It was concerned with all three aspects together. Its adherents sought to develop economically while maintaining their distinct cultural identity and working for an eventual political independence as well. In essence, nationalism was a program and a movement for the establishment of new kinds of *communities*—nations.

We thus return to the previously cited conclusion of Ernest Gellner, according to whom nationalism "invents nations where they do not exist."[32] The same point, although made in more careful language, is reflected in Anderson's thought that nation can best be viewed as "an imagined political community—and imagined as both inherently limited and sovereign." He explains that imagined communities (this includes all communities larger than "primordial villages") are distinguished "not by their falsity/genuineness, but by the style in which they are imagined."[33]

But if this is so, it matters a lot *what* a nation imagines itself to be; in other words, the significance lies in the *content* of its nationalist self-image. It matters whether that image defines the nation as naturally peaceful or warrior-like, naturally democratic or authoritarian, sympathetic to new economic methods or traditionally agrarian, open to all who wish to join it or defined by racial (and therefore impenetrable) criteria, and so on. If Sewell is right that ideology is "constitutive of the social order,"[34] then for a nation to exist it is necessary that (at least some) individuals composing it should have a consciousness of their national identity based on history, race, political values, language, etc. They should also have some sense of their nation's place in the world, of its economic, political, and other interests and needs, of its "mission," and so forth.

Such understanding of what a nation is corresponds to Marx's concept of the proletariat. As he said in *The Communist Manifesto*, the proletariat constitutes itself as a class by developing its own class consciousness, that is, by forming its outlook on matters economic and political, by organizing itself accordingly, etc. In Lichtheim's interpretation, both the concept of the unity of theory and practice and the recognition of "the constitutive role of conscious activity" forms the "heart" of the doctrine of Marxism.[35]

Applying this thought to the history of nationalism and nations, we may say that because of a unique coincidence of political and intellectual circumstances, the Germans, Poles, Czechs, and others did for nationalism what the proletariat was supposed to do for Marx's "philosophy." The new idea of nationalism first found in the Poles a material force, just as the Poles found in that idea a justification for a claim that was more than a plea for the restoration of a status quo: The Poles had the right to a free life as a *nation* and not simply because they had been independent before. (The city of Venice and hundreds of German states had also been independent, but having lost their independence about the same time as Poland, they did not survive as national-independence movements.) Thus we may rightly say that the Polish case represented the original example of how it was possible for nationalism to achieve a union of theory and practice— something that Marxism has been much less successful in accomplishing, since to this day the proletariat has not become that universal and philosophical class Marx had expected it to become. After Poland, other nationalisms repeated the same kind of experience independently, each in accordance with its particular circumstances (including its own ideas about what it meant to be German, Czech, Hungarian, and so on).

In sum, the political nationalism in Germany had diverse causes. They included an acute resentment of the French cultural and political domination and a resultant sense of humiliation. Also important was the feeling that the political disunity of the nation, perceived as a negative phenomenon once ethnic community came to be seen as superior to the existing forms of political organization, made Germans a weak and contemptible member of the community of nations. Up until that time, a prenationalist German did not find cause for anxiety or resentment over the fact that Königsberg, Reutlingen, and Lübeck were not governed from the same place.

The Napoleonic wars contributed significantly to the destruction of the old order under which several hundred Germanies had existed. The Industrial Revolution exercised another kind of impact on Germany. As we noted, the question of the Industrial Revolution and of economic development in general produced a wide range of views among German's nationalist thinkers. It certainly *did* make a difference whether Adam Müller or Fichte or List ultimately succeeded in establishing his interpretation as *the* nationalist view of industrialization and its relation to the German Question.

Gradually the ideas of Herder, Burke, Rousseau—and List—and of their disciples won approval in many parts of Europe, notably first in Germany and Poland, but also in other areas, especially in the lands of the Austrian Empire and the Balkans. Under the impact of these ideas, increasing numbers of people questioned the status quo on the grounds that it did not recognize the principle of nationality.

Over time, the principle of nationalist thought, according to which the ethnic nation is "the community that legitimizes the state," was not limited to politics but became the organizing principle of scholarship.[36] The Czech historian František Graus has brilliantly summarized the linguistic and historical revolution that is associated with Herder's name. Graus has shown that this late-eighteenth-century revolution in scholarship resulted in, among other things, the "invention" of a "German" history, "German" law, and "German" folklore. The German example was soon imitated by eastern neighbors, who in turn invented (or "discovered") their "Slavic" counterparts. Needless to say, all this had profound and far-reaching political consequences as well.[37]

But it is important to remember that there had been a time when those consequences were still only a matter of conjecture, when Germany itself and German history had still to be created. As James J. Sheehan puts it:

> What then is German history in the eighteenth century? It is the history of these areal and linear institutions which gave shape and meaning to people's lives. It is the history of cultural richness and political diversity, of social fragmentation and economic isolation. It is also the history of the first faint stirrings toward national cohesion, the initial movement toward the creation of a *German* culture and society. But in writing the history of this movement, we must not confuse aspirations with accomplishments by positing the existence of some fictional entity we can call *Germany*. To do so obscures what may be the central fact about the era: German history, as a singular process, had not yet really begun.[38]

Eventually, the influence of nationalism, originally a novel and highly controversial way of looking at the world, became, in the words of Isaiah Berlin, "so pervasive, so familiar, that it is only by a conscious effort of the imagination that one can conceive a world in which it played no part."[39] Before Berlin, Carlton J. H. Hayes made the same point: "So much is nationalism a commonplace in the modes of thought and action of . . . the contemporary world that most men take nationalism for granted . . . . They imagine it to be the most natural thing in the universe and assume that it must always have existed."[40]

This extraordinary and unanticipated triumph of nationalist ideology— of what better proof can an ideology boast than that its propositions have become commonplace and taken for granted?—makes it easy to forget that nationalism once belonged to several clearly identifiable individuals. They deserve to be recognized. Or should we deny them originality because their ideas would one day appear self-evident and "natural"?

# Part Three

# 11

## *After 1848: Marx and Engels Face the Nation*

In 1848, the history of Europe took a turn that Marx had not anticipated and indeed did not think possible. The events in Germany, Austria, Hungary, Poland, France, and Britain ran counter to his assessment of the direction of historical development and, more immediately, signified the defeat of his practical program. For the author of the "List Critique" and *The Communist Manifesto*, the failures of the revolutionary years and the subsequent triumph of capitalism in Germany were not just a minor setback or disappointment; they represented nothing less than a catastrophe.

Marx had formulated his program in the 1840s. He then expected the overthrow of the capitalist system in the advanced countries to happen in the very near future. Certainly, this was going to happen before the bourgeoisie tried to seize power in Germany; Germany would be spared the experience of a bourgeois state. (Such was the basic view of the "List Critique.") In certain other works of the decade (for example, in the "Hegel Critique" and *The Communist Manifesto*), Marx conceded that the bourgeois revolution would occur in Germany. He was sure, however, that a revolution of the proletariat would follow immediately. That revolution, because of the very nature of the proletarian class, Marx believed, would be international in scope. Even toward the end of 1848, when things were clearly not turning out as he had expected just a year before, Marx was certain that Germany would not become a capitalist state. The only alternative to the communist revolution, he insisted, was the continuation of the old feudal-absolutist regime in Germany.

In light of these scenarios, Marx and Engels in their remaining years attempted to reconstitute a coherent program in the face of developments and trends for which they had not made any provisions in their original assessment of the direction of the historical process.

Marx lived for thirty-five years after 1848, and Engels for forty-seven. These men played a crucial role in the history of socialism as an intellectual and political force of their time. Although Marxism was not the only major socialist theory current among the working class and its sympathizers from other classes, it gradually established itself as the most powerful and influential of these theories. For many, Marxism became a synonym for socialism or communism.

By the time Engels died in 1895, the Second International, founded in 1889, had entered its golden age. (The First International, or to be precise, the International Workers Association, was founded in 1864 with Marx's direct participation, but it did not survive beyond the early 1870s.) The German Social Democratic Party, or social democracy, polled more votes than any other party in the German Empire founded by Bismarck. Marxism became a major intellectual and political force in Central Europe and in Russia. It would appear that the causes of the proletariat and of Marxism were moving from one victory to another. Despite the occasional defeats, such as the fiasco of the Paris Commune of 1871, the general trend seemed favorable to socialism.

However, Marx and Engels also witnessed the parallel rise of nationalism. The unification of Germany did not follow a Marxist scenario. The establishment of a united Italian state likewise strengthened rather than weakened the old forces. The national movements in Poland, Hungary, and Ireland were at best questionable allies of the communist cause. For the rise of the national movements of the Czechs, Croats, Slovenes, Slovaks, Romanians, and Ukrainians—or for the emergence of Zionism—the founders of scientific communism had no rational explanation. In countries where the proletariat was strong in numbers and influence, it did not define itself at all as the "universal class" Marx had expected. The social democracy in Germany was a *German* social democracy. The improvements in the material standard of living, social and political reforms (including extension of suffrage), universal education, and the rise of a mass culture all contributed to the "nationalization of the masses," to use George Mosse's phrase. In his late years, a bitter Engels, who had been observing the condition of the working class in England ever since the 1840s, described the British workers as "bourgeois" and thus contradicted one of the fundamental assumptions he and Marx had made about the necessary and inevitable connection between the proletariat's condition and its consciousness.

The first major modification of their original stand on nationalism occurred in 1848–1849, when Marx and Engels supported the national causes of the "historic" or "great" nations, such as the Hungarians, Poles, and of course, the Germans, all of whom wanted to establish large national states. The position taken by Marx in that period is commonly described as his first statement on nation and nationalism; we now know it was the second. In any case, Marx stated that the nationalists' goal was compatible with his "strategic" assessment of the prospects of the proletarian revolution: Large states would make it easier for the proletariat to advance its class goals.

However, Marx and Engels endorsed the German claims because Germans were superior to such "small" peoples as the Czechs and Danes, not because Germany happened to be on the eve of a communist revolution. Indeed, the 1848–1849 writings of Marx, and even more so those of Engels, contain many passages that might be interpreted as expressions of a rather extreme German nationalism. (Similarly, they supported the claims of Hungarian and Polish nationalism against those of other, smaller nationalities.) Both Marx and Engels took an unhesitatingly hostile stand toward the aspirations of the so-called "nonhistoric" nationalities, which for one reason or another stood in the way of German or Hungarian demands.

Engels especially expressed an anti-Slav sentiment during the 1848–1849 revolution itself, when his hopes in the revolutionary potential of Germany and Hungary had not yet been smashed. Those writings of the revolutionary period, published in the *Neue Rheinische Zeitung*, have been closely examined by Roman Rosdolsky in his highly regarded work, "Friedrich Engels and the Problem of the 'Nonhistorical' Peoples (The Nationality Question in the 1848–1849 Revolution in Light of the *Neue Rheinische Zeitung*)."[1]

Some of the statements made by Engels at that time remind one writer, Ian Cummins, of racism rather than of scientific socialism. Cummins cites, for example, Engels' remarks about how the Germans and Hungarians would "wipe out these petty hidebound nations, down to their very names," and he quotes Engels' forecast that

> the next world war will result in the disappearance from the face of the earth not only of reactionary classes and dynasties, but also of entire reactionary peoples. And that, too, is a step forward.[2]

As Cummins shows in his carefully documented study, both Marx and Engels expressed a strong preference for large centralized states, even when those states had been created by conquest. As Engels put it in an article on the Danish-German conflict in 1848,

By the same right under which France took Flanders, Lorraine and Alsace, and will sooner or later take Belgium—by that same right Germany takes over Schleswig; it is the right of civilisation as against barbarism, of progress as against stability . . . . This . . . is the right of historical evolution.[3]

Engels spoke with contempt about the "reactionary" Swiss. He welcomed the bourgeoisie's centralization of heretofore autonomous and isolated communes and expected that the proletariat would go even farther in that direction.[4] Speaking about the effects of industrialization on the Habsburg monarchy, Engels anticipated that the railroad would destroy "the granite walls behind which each province had maintained a separate nationality and a limited local existence."[5] As Cummins observes, Engels expected the steam engine to destroy the empire of the Habsburgs— something Napoleonic invasion and the French Revolution had not been able to do.[6] For example, Engels thought the Czechs would disappear as the consequence of the introduction of the steam engine. The Czechs and other Slavic peoples were the subject of Engels' special consideration in a series of articles that he wrote, but that were published under Marx's name in the *New York Daily Tribune* (1852) and that subsequently became known collectively as "Revolution and Counter-Revolution in Germany."

While the tone of the articles of the revolutionary era may have been colored by excitement over the events then taking place, "Revolution and Counter-Revolution in Germany" presents a more "detached" interpretation of the relations between the Germans and their eastern neighbors. That interpretation bears a striking resemblance to the conceptual formula List used in describing (and predicting the future of) the relations between Europe and Asia, although of course Engels used violent, vituperative language, of which there is no trace in List. Germany, according to Engels, represented "the city," the high culture, science, and industry, while the Slavs were associated with backwardness and their way of life was being dissolved by contact with a superior German culture. According to Engels, the Slavs, especially the Poles and Czechs, were "essentially an agricultural race: trade and manufactures never were in great favour with them." In their lands, the growth of population, of cities, and of the "production of all articles of manufacture" had accordingly been the work of the German immigrants. The exchange was the monopoly of Jews, who were closer to Germans than Slavs. The importance of the German element in the Slavic lands was further increased by the fact that it had been "found necessary to import almost every element of mental culture from Germany; after the German merchant and handicraftsman, the German clergyman, the German schoolmaster, the German savant came to establish himself upon Slavonic soil." Finally, "the iron tread of conquering armies, or the cautious, well-premeditated grasp of diplomacy, not only followed, but many times went ahead of the slow but sure advance of denationalisation by social developments."[7]

Engels condemned the use of force against Poland, and he expressly supported Polish independence; he even said that the Germans would have to give back to the Poles what they had gained in the "plunder" of Poland. But he also recalled that during the German Revolution of 1848 the question had been asked, "[should] whole tracts of land, inhabited chiefly by Germans, should large towns, entirely German, be given up to a people that as yet had never given any proofs of its capability of progressing beyond a state of feudalism based upon agricultural serfdom?"[8]

While Engels did not explicitly reject the legitimacy of asking such a question with reference to Poland, and while he endorsed Poland's right not only to independence but also to large territorial gains in "the East," he had no doubts whatsoever regarding the Czech Question. He conceded that Bohemia, "inhabited by two millions of Germans, and three millions of Slavs of the Czech tongue, had great historical recollections, almost all connected with the former supremacy of the Czechs." But he thought that the Czechs "had been broken ever since the wars of the Hussites in the fifteenth century." Their country was divided into the kingdom of Bohemia and the principality of Moravia, while the Slovaks formed part of Hungary. The Moravians and Slovaks lost "every vestige of national feeling and vitality, although mostly preserving their language, while Bohemia was not only surrounded by German countries but large numbers of Germans were settled in it, especially in Prague: "Everywhere capital, trade, industry, and mental culture were in the hands of the Germans."

> The chief champion of the Czech nationality, Professor Palacký, is himself nothing but a learned German run mad, who even now cannot speak the Czech language correctly and without foreign accent. But as it often happens, dying Czech nationality, dying according to every fact known in history for the last four hundred years, made in 1848 a last effort to regain its former vitality—an effort whose failure, independently of all revolutionary considerations, was to prove that Bohemia could only exist henceforth, as a portion of Germany, although part of her inhabitants might yet, for some centuries, continue to speak a non-German language.[9]

Czech (and Croat) nationalism, Engels thought, had been produced by "a few Slavonic dilettanti of historical science" who thus inspired "this ludicrous, this anti-historical movement" for the revival of the Slavic peoples. That movement "intended nothing less than to subjugate the civilised West under the barbarian East, the town under the country, trade, manufactures, intelligence, under the primitive agriculture of Slav serfs.''[10] The actual force behind that movement was the Russian Empire.[11]

In general, Engels denied that the Slavs of "Germany" (that "Germany" included the Czech lands) had the capacity for a national existence. Like the Welsh in England or the Bretons in France, they too were destined to be absorbed in a larger, civilized nation. Despite the obvious hopelessness of their cause, "these dying nationalities, the Bohemians, Carinthians, Dalmatians, etc., had tried to profit by the universal confusion of 1848, in order to restore their political *status quo* of A.D. 800. The history of a thousand years ought to have shown them that such a retrogression was impossible." They ought to have understood that "the natural and inevitable fate of these dying nations was to allow this process of dissolution and absorption by their strong neighbours to complete itself.''[12]

These statements were written by Engels, but Marx published them as his own, a fact that, along with other evidence, indicates that he thought exactly the way Engels did. Indeed, some years later, on October 8, 1858, Marx wrote Engels a letter in which he characterized the national movements of the Slavs, such as the Czechs, in strictly negative terms: "There are exceptionally big movements among the Slavs, especially in Bohemia, movements which are indeed counter-revolutionary but still add to the ferment of our movement.''[13]

It is necessary to conclude that the national movements of the East European peoples found no place in Marx's schema of historical progress. He believed that at best they contributed to the general "ferment" of the times, but there was nothing "progressive" in them, just as, to the Marx of 1845, there had been nothing worthy of approval in German nationalism. Marx was not dissuaded in his negative assessment by the fact, which he acknowledged, of the popular success—"big movements"—of those national causes.

A number of scholars, Marxist and non-Marxist, have shown that Marx and Engels had erred and that in fact they had not been good Marxists when they condemned the national causes of the small peoples. Excellent "Marxist" explanations have been produced that show why the Czech, Ukrainian, and other nationalist movements had been in fact "progressive" and how they can be explained in the overall Marxist scheme of history.[14] The fact remains, however, that neither Marx nor Engels cared to see any of this.

Following a different line of argument from that advanced here, Walker Connor has shown persuasively that the events of 1848 had a noticeable impact on Marx's, and especially Engels', treatment of nations and nationalities. In Engels' post–1848 writings, says Connor,

> socioeconomic classes were uncharacteristically slighted, their leading role as the principal vehicles of history expropriated by nations: class antagonisms were replaced by national antagonisms; warfare between nations now supplanted class warfare. Indeed, Engels's treatises on the events of 1848 read very much like a morality play, in which entire nations (more specifically, the Germans, Italians, Magyars, and Poles) had come to denote the forces of enlightenment and progress, a role previously reserved for the proletariat, while still other entire nations (particularly the non-Polish and non-Russian Slavic peoples), had now been substituted for the feudal aristocracy and the bourgeoisie in the role of darkness and reaction. The latter were described as unredeemable ethnic trash, the ruins of people, whose "chief mission . . . is to perish in the revolutionary holocaust."[15]

Citing the various comments of Engels on the *racial* qualities of different peoples, Connor observes: "The genetic determinism which permeates these and many other passages by Engels would probably appear extreme within any intellectual framework, but its appearance in the works of one of the two founders of a school described as 'scientific socialism' and predicated upon a theory of historical dialectical materialism borders on the bizarre."[16]

Throughout the 1850s, Marx and Engels expected the communist revolution to break out in the advanced countries in Europe at any given moment. "On the Continent," Marx wrote to Engels in the already quoted letter of October 8, 1858, "the revolution is imminent and will immediately assume a socialist character." He worried that it might be "crushed in this little corner" of the globe, considering that in the rest of the world the bourgeois society was still "in the ascendant."[17] Even though in that very same letter Marx spoke of the establishment of a world market and mentioned that production based upon that world market already existed, he obviously did not expect any longer that the non-European parts of the world would automatically follow the lead of the economically advanced West.

If one treated the world as a unit, which is what Marx usually did, then in this scenario the West would have been the center of the proletarian revolution, while the backward or peripheral parts of the globe would have been the seat of the bourgeois counterrevolution. In other words, Marx continued to assume that the West would be ahead, but he now feared that the unity of the world economy might be broken by a "secession," as it were, of the more backward nations, possibly even leading to their intervention *against* socialism at the center. Communist and Marxist thinking about this subject changed considerably after Marx, which is evident when comparing Marx's view with Lenin's scenario of 1923. As Ian Cummins has noted, Lenin viewed this problem ''from [an] almost precisely opposite angle'': He anticipated that the *source* of revolution would be the backward, peripheral colonial nations while the advanced nations still remained capitalist.[18]

Such a Leninist perspective obviously would not have made sense to Marx. Gradually, his expectation of an imminent revolution became less urgent, and he went instead to the British Museum to work on *Capital*.[19] This was an ironic turn for someone who in the 1840s had proudly declared in his ''Theses on Feuerbach'' that ''the philosophers have only interpreted the world, in different ways; the point is to *change* it.''[20]

When the first volume of *Capital* did appear in 1867, it did not predict an imminent communist revolution in England or in France, but instead assured readers that the victory of capitalism was inevitable where it had not yet taken place. England, Marx told his German readers (*Capital* was written in German), represented the image of Germany's future. Such a course was dictated by the laws of history ''working with iron necessity.''

> In this work I have to examine the capitalist mode of production, and the conditions of production and exchange corresponding to that mode. Up to the present time, their classic ground is England. That is the reason why England is used as the chief illustration in the development of my theoretical ideas. If, however, the German reader shrugs his shoulders at the condition of the English industrial and agricultural labourers, or in optimist fashion comforts himself with the thought that in Germany things are not nearly so bad; I must plainly tell him, ''*De te fabula narratur*! (The story is about you!)'' Intrinsically, it is not a question of the higher or lower degree of development of the social antagonisms that result from the natural laws of capitalist production. It is a question of these laws themselves, of these tendencies working with iron necessity towards inevitable results. The country that is more developed industrially only shows, to the less developed, the image of its own future.[21]

Thus, in 1867 Marx was presenting as inevitable what in 1845 he had considered impossible: the victory of capitalism in Germany. Marx did not admit this, and List was no longer around to see it, but in fact *Capital* was published at the time List's program was being realized (and would be completed several years later, when in 1871 a German Empire under the aegis of Prussia would be proclaimed). More importantly, Marx implicitly abandoned his position, stated as late as *The Communist Manifesto*, that capitalism would destroy national boundaries and create a single, global economic and political process. The preface to *Capital*, on the other hand, suggested that capitalism would affect individual countries as countries, which might be seen as an acceptance of the national roads to capitalism that Marx had ridiculed so mercilessly in his critique of List. It would appear that the Marx of *Capital* no longer saw historical stages as applicable to the history of human society as a whole and that he now adopted the view that individual nations were the entities undergoing such development through stages. If this indeed was the case, Marx unknowingly had adopted the view that nations (countries, peoples) had a history which transcended historical socioeconomic formations—in other words, that they existed above and beyond history understood as the history of *class* struggles. Such a conclusion would be reinforced by the following passage from the preface to *Capital*:

> One nation can and should learn from others. And even when a society has got upon the right track for the discovery of the natural laws of its movement—and it is the ultimate aim of this work, to lay bare the economic laws of motion of modern society—it can neither clear by bold leaps, nor remove by legal enactments, the obstacles offered by the successive phases of its normal development. But it can shorten and lessen the birthpangs.[22]

Jon Elster, who quotes this passage and contrasts it with Marx's earlier denial (in the "List Critique") that all nations have to go through the same development internally, sees in this later statement the expression of what he calls "the model of unique development, modified only by the possibility that the latecomers may spend less time in the successive stages than did the pioneers."[23] He then goes on to say that late in his life, "Marx abandoned this view and embraced explicitly [the Russian publicist Nikolai Gavrilovich] Chernyshevsky's idea that Russia could 'appropriate all the fruits of [the capitalist regime] without going through all its tortures.'"[24]

Scholars of Marx have exhibited a good deal of interest in Marx's last years, both from a biographical point of view (perhaps Marx's mind was declining, as some authors have argued, speaking of his "slow agony" over the years), and from the point of view of his contacts with the Russian revolutionaries and his reflections on Russia's position in the historical process and in the revolutionary movement. Not the least important is the fact that when a Russian Marxism did emerge, it was a post-*Capital* Marxism, that is, a doctrine that recognized individual countries as units of development and did so to a degree that had been lacking in the earlier Marx. The Marxism of *Capital*, but not the Marxism of *The Communist Manifesto* (or its predecessors), became an "ideology of industrialization" in *Russia*. It would appear that the Russian Marxists were drawing on the

Master to tell them how Russia as a country would fare in the broader
historical process to which Marx, they thought, had uncovered the key.
Marx, on the other hand, appears to have looked at Russia as a country
that did, indeed, display a rather unique combination of features, including
a nonproletarian, a nonbourgeois, but nevertheless an unquestionably revolutionary movement. He wondered if that revolutionary movement, which
was ''capitalizing'' (if one may say so) on the plight of the peasantry
(oppressed by the landlords and beginning to be affected by the inroads
of capitalist relations), might not at a certain historical conjuncture be
somehow connected with the outbreak of the proletarian revolution in the
West. Thus he began to think of linking Russia's peasant revolution with
the West's proletarian revolution. This was certainly a new step in Marx's
thought, considering that Ireland had first offered a similar combination,
but when he thought of it in the 1860s it did not inspire in him any idea
that Ireland might take a shortcut to socialism. On the contrary, in 1867,
the year of *Capital*'s publication, Marx wrote to Engels that while previously he had thought ''Ireland's separation from England impossible,''
he now thought it ''inevitable, although after separation there may come
*federation*.'' He wrote:

> What the Irish need is:
> (1) Self-government and independence from England.
> (2) An agrarian revolution . . . .
> (3) Protective tariffs from England . . . . Once the Irish are independent,
> necessity will turn them into protectionists, as it did Canada, Australia,
> etc. . . .[25]

Thus it is clear from the context of this passage that the ''agrarian
revolution'' Marx was referring to was to be a revolution that would help
to establish a capitalist economy—what else would it be in an Ireland that
was also to introduce protective tariffs from England? Marx allowed the
Ireland of the 1860s to take measures he had thought inadmissible in the
Germany of the 1840s. Was the Irish bourgeoisie more advanced than its
German sister had been twenty years earlier? The answer seems to lie in
Marx's conclusion that capitalism's life span would be longer than expected. (In a strange coincidence, this very Listian letter was dated No-
vember 30, 1867—an anniversary of List's death.)

According to Eric Hobsbawm, the Ireland of the nineteenth century
anticipated ''the revolutionary national movements of the underdeveloped
countries in the twentieth century,'' but its revolution was not fought under
socialist slogans: ''There was no socialism anywhere.''[26] Clearly, it did
not occur to the Irish—nor to Marx—that Irish nationalism might be some-

how fused or allied with a revolutionary socialism. This was precisely what later happened in Russia—and the late Marx, as we know, proved himself open to the possibilities this combination offered.

In his "Late Marx and the Russian 'Periphery of Capitalism,'" Teodor Shanin argues that at the end of his life Marx was moving toward abandoning (if he did not actually abandon) his 1867 prescription of "an evolutionary path for all countries." In connection with Russia, says Shanin, Marx raised problems that were "new to his generation but which would nowadays easily be recognized as those of 'developing societies,' 'modernization,' 'dependency,' or the uneven spread of global capitalism throughout the 'periphery.'" Although "Marx's new understanding" was never fully developed, its central component was the new notion of uneven development. Marx began to understand the peculiar structure of "backward capitalism."

> The idea of "dependent development" as we know it today is not there yet, but its foundation is laid. Marx had come to assume a multiplicity of roads of social transformation not only for precapitalist societies . . . but also for the capitalist epoch . . . . To sum it up bluntly, the industrially developed England that Marx knew did not any longer "show to the less developed" Russia the "image of its future."[27]

The existing evidence suggests that Shanin is right. In his letter to the editors of *Otechestvennye zapiski* (1877), Marx responded to the question of whether or not Russia had to pass through capitalism by saying that he had "arrived at this conclusion: if Russia continues to pursue the path she has followed since 1861, she will lose the finest chance ever offered by history to a people and undergo all the fatal vicissitudes of the capitalist regime."[28]

Marx explained that his "historical sketch" of primitive accumulation in Western Europe (this was in reference to a chapter in *Capital*) was just that, a sketch. It was applicable to Russia only in the sense that

> if Russia is tending to become a capitalist nation after the example of the West-European countries—and during the last few years she has been taking a lot of trouble in this direction—she will not succeed without having first transformed a good part of her peasants into proletarians; and after that, once taken to the bosom of the capitalist regime, she will experience its pitiless laws like other profane peoples. That is all.[29]

Marx explicitly refused to allow his critic Chernyshevsky to "metamorphose my historical sketch of the genesis of capitalism in Western Europe into an historico-philosophic theory of the general path every people is fated to tread, whatever the historical circumstances in which it finds itself" in order to achieve a communist social order.[30]

After referring to the fates of the proletarians in ancient Rome and of the poor whites in the American South, Marx made the following generalization, which he said stemmed from those examples:

> Thus events strikingly analogous but taking place in different historical surroundings led to totally different results. By studying each of these forms of evolution separately and then comparing them one can easily find the clue to this phenomenon, but one will never arrive there by using as one's master key a general historico-philosophical theory, the supreme virtue of which consists in being super-historical.[31]

Marx returned to the question of Russia's future in his letter to Vera Zasulich (1881), in one of the drafts of which (but not in the actual letter sent to her) he wrote: "To save the Russian commune, a Russian revolution is necessary."[32]

Marx addressed the same question for the last time in his preface to the Russian edition of *The Communist Manifesto* (dated January 21, 1882), which was his last published work before his death.

> The *Communist Manifesto* had as its object the proclamation of the inevitably impending dissolution of modern bourgeois property. But in Russia we find, face to face with the rapidly developing capitalist swindle and bourgeois landed property, just beginning to develop, more than half the land owned in common by the peasants. Now the question is: Can the Russian *obshchina* [village commune], though greatly undermined, yet a form of the primeval common ownership of land, pass directly to the higher form of communist common ownership? Or on the contrary, must it first pass through the same process of dissolution as constitutes the historical evolution of the West?
>
> The only answer to that possible today is this: If the Russian revolution becomes the signal for a proletarian revolution in the West, so that both complement each other, the present Russian common ownership of land may serve as the starting point for a communist development.[33]

On the one hand, this preface confirms a definite retreat from the position taken by Marx in *Capital* where he had said that all countries would follow a basically identical sequence of development (even though they would do so at a somewhat different rate and might learn from one another in the process). On the other hand, Marx now made the ability of the Russian revolution to use the village commune "as the starting point for a communist development" dependent on (or at least linked to) a subsequent proletarian revolution in the West. This might be seen as Marx's return to his earlier global view of history, especially now that his new formula worked in two directions: It also implied that the Russian revolution might become "the signal for," i.e., ignite or stimulate, a proletarian revolution in the West and no longer implied only that the progress of Russia would depend on what the West did.

The Russian problem clearly presented Marx with issues that posed fundamental challenges to his historical conception. He did not live long enough to address them directly or to show that he understood the implications of the admission that there could be *two kinds of revolution* occurring simultaneously in different parts of the world, each arising out of different circumstances and causes and yet ultimately compatible with one another. This was unlike the 1848 scenario in which one revolution (proletarian) followed another (bourgeois) as the latter's antagonist. Marx's admission of the possibility that a backward country might make up for its economic and social deficiencies by the use of political measures—revolution—in its march to communism brings to mind List's view that backward but developing countries could compensate for their relatively lower level of economic development by resorting to political measures, such as government tariff and customs policies, promotion of science and education, and so on. In any case, Marx was moving from a vertical vision of the world—class against class—to a horizontal one, with different parts of the world seen in relation to one another. This was the essence of List's vision.

The task of dealing with those questions fell to Marx's disciples in Russia and elsewhere. During the last decade of his life, Marx himself had to face nationalism in quite another, but even more unexpected, context: German socialism.

After 1871, German nationalists were concerned that the worker also be included in the national community, and for this reason they advocated appropriate social legislation, educational measures, and so forth. On their side, the workers—even those with quite radical views—were by no means unpatriotic. Had they been familiar with Marx's "List Critique," they would have been quite amazed by his statement that their nationality "is neither French, nor English, nor German, it is *labour, free slavery, self-huckstering*."[34]

Contemporary Marxist scholars freely acknowledge that workers *were* German, French or English. Eric Hobsbawm, a prominent Marxist of unimpeachable credentials, notes that both the Paris Commune in 1871 and the German socialism of Wilhelm Liebknecht and August Bebel drew on their respective nationalist traditions, the Commune on the Jacobin patriotism and the Germans on the radical nationalism of 1848. Accordingly, after 1871, German workers were not an exception when they ac-

cepted the new nation-state as the unit within which they would operate
and fight for their goals. Hobsbawm points out that German workers resented charges that they were unpatriotic; they were "not only workers
but good Germans." Hobsbawm then makes a point that is significant
generally, not only with reference to Germany:

> It was almost impossible for political consciousness not to be in some way
> or another nationally defined. *The proletariat, like the bourgeoisie, existed
> only conceptually as an international fact.* In reality it existed as an aggregate
> of groups defined by their national state or ethnic/linguistic difference: Brit-
> ish, French or, in multi-national states, German, Hungarian, or Slav. And,
> in so far as "state" and "nation" were supposed to coincide in the ideology
> of those who established institutions and dominated civil society, politics in
> terms of the state implied politics in terms of the nation.[35]

To make these admissions today is unremarkable, even for a Marxist.
We know that in the second half of the nineteenth century the socialist
parties, including those professing Marxism as their official philosophy,
gradually acquired a pronounced national character and outlook. This applied even to the German Social Democratic party, which for many years
was accused by the enemies of socialism as being an antinational force.
Indeed, for decades it operated outside the official national community as
represented by the state and its institutions, and even outside the official
"society." In this sense, German social democracy indeed formed a state
within a state, a nation within a nation, but its alternative state and nation
were nevertheless a German state and nation.

But we must not forget that *Marx* took a view of what was happening
in Germany that was quite different from that of his late-twentieth-century
disciples. He did not waver in his opposition to the infiltration or contam-
ination of the working class by nationalism. In 1875, before a congress,
which represented the two German socialist parties then in existence, met
in Gotha and formed a single German Social Democratic party, Marx wrote
a critique of the proposed party program and sent it to Wilhelm Liebknecht.
(These two parties were the Social Democratic Workers' Party, headed by
Liebknecht, and the General Workers Union, headed by Ferdinand Lassalle.) Marx's critique was not published until 1891, and the program was
adopted *despite* his criticism. However, his letter is important evidence
that he was concerned with the impact of nationalism on the thinking of
German socialists. He criticized the draft point by point on a wide variety
of issues, but for us the following item in the Gotha program is especially
noteworthy:

> The working class strives for its emancipation first of all *within the framework
> of the present-day national state*, conscious that the necessary results of its

efforts, which are common to the workers of all civilized countries, will be the international brotherhood of peoples.[36]

Citing this passage, Marx accused Lassalle of conceiving "the workers' movement from the narrowest national standpoint." Admittedly, Marx continued, "the working class must organize itself at home *as a class* and . . . its own country is the immediate arena of its struggle." He recalled the formulation in *The Communist Manifesto* about the working class's struggle being national "in form" but "not in content," and he continued:

> But the "framework of the present-day national state," e.g., the German empire, is itself in its turn economically "within the framework" of the world market, politically "within the framework" of the system of states. Every businessman knows that German trade is at the same time foreign trade, and the greatness of Herr Bismarck consists, to be sure, precisely in a kind of *international* policy.[37]

Marx further accused the German socialists of reducing their internationalism to phrases about "*the international brotherhood of peoples*," which he said had been borrowed from "the bourgeois League of Peace and Freedom." This was no substitute for the "international brotherhood of the working class in the joint struggle against the ruling classes and their governments. Not a word, therefore, *about the international functions* of the German working class!" Marx contrasted this nationalist stand of the socialists with that of the bourgeoisie, "which is already linked up in brotherhood against it [the proletariat] with the bourgeois of all other countries, and Herr Bismarck's international policy of conspiracy!"

> In fact the international consciousness expressed in the programme stands *even infinitely below* that of the Free Trade Party. The latter also asserts that the result of its efforts will be "the international brotherhood of peoples." But it also *does* something to make trade international and by no means contents itself with the consciousness—that all peoples are carrying on trade at home.[38]

Noting Marx's charges against the nationalism of the Gotha Program, Michael Löwy points out that Marx limited himself to criticizing others: He did not "put forward any perspective for the future by himself posing the question of the national State or 'national differences' at any level at all."[39] Löwy has no explanation for Marx's "silence"; he does not know if it had been caused by "tactical prudence," "political realism," "the conviction . . . that the fact of the nation was more tenacious than anticipated," or "the fear that the cosmopolitic idea would be used as a pretext for a 'leading State' to absorb other nations within itself."[40]

None of Löwy's guesses can be verified, of course. But there is evidence that at least Engels understood that the "internationalism" preached by socialists of a large and independent nation to socialists of a dependent nation tends to be a means to legitimize national oppression. When the English socialists proposed to include the Irish socialist groups in a single British organization, Engels protested:

> What would be said if this Council called upon Polish sections to ac-knowledge the supremacy of a Russian Federal Council in Petersburg, or upon Prussian, Polish, North Schleswig, and Alsatian sections to submit to a Federal Council in Berlin? Yet what was asked to do with regard to Irish sections was substantially the same thing. If members of a conquering nation called upon the nation they had conquered and continued to hold down to forget their specific nationality and position, to "sink national differences" and so forth, that was not Internationalism, it was nothing else but preaching to them submission to the yoke, and attempting to justify and to perpetuate the dominion of the conquerer under the cloak of Internationalism.[41]

Engels did not come up with any resolution of the problem either, except by concluding, as he did in a letter to the German socialist leader, Karl Kautsky (February 7, 1882), that "an international movement of the proletariat is in general only possible between independent nations . . . . To get rid of national oppression is the basic condition of all healthy and free development." This would amount to a major revision of his earlier stand had Engels also not said in the same letter that it is "historically impossible for a *large* people to discuss seriously any internal questions as long as its national independence is lacking."[42] This brings us back to square one: what about small nations? Can they discuss *their* internal questions when they lack their national independence? By 1882, Engels appears to have accepted the possibility that one day the smaller peoples of the Habsburg monarchy might establish their own states, but he was also sure that "six months of independence will suffice for most Austro-Hungarian Slavs to bring them to a point where they will beg to be readmitted."[43]

When he thought about Europe's relations with the world overseas, Engels managed to reconcile his disdain for the British proletariat ("the English workers think about colonial policy . . . the same as they think about politics in general: the same as the bourgeois think") with the continuing assumption that the European proletariat would show the way to the rest of the world. He expected the colonial countries inhabited by native populations (unlike those settled by European colonists, which were to become immediately independent) to be "taken over for the time being by the proletariat and led as rapidly as possible towards independence."

> Once Europe is reorganized, and North America, that will furnish such
> colossal power and such an example that the semi-civilized countries will
> of themselves follow in their wake; economic needs, if anything, will see
> to that. But as to what social and political phases these countries will then
> have to pass through before they likewise arrive at socialist organization, I
> think we today can advance only rather idle hypotheses. One thing alone is
> certain: the victorious proletariat can force no blessings of any kind upon
> any foreign nation without undermining its own victory by so doing. Which
> of course by no means excludes defensive wars of various kinds . . . .[44]

This statement clearly indicates that Engels continued to believe in a
unilinear historical process even when he admitted that some countries
outside Europe and North America might for some time lag behind the
pacesetters. What did Marx think about this subject? Marx's comments
about "Oriental despotism" are sometimes quoted in order to support the
argument that his history was not unilinear. In my view, Oriental despotism
was for Marx a historical detour. Although admittedly it affected huge
portions of mankind for very long spans of time, it was a detour or a blind
alley nonetheless. Sooner or later, the nations of the Orient would have
to get back on the main road of development, which was what the establishment of a world market was doing.

There may be more evidence to support those scholars who, like Teodor
Shanin, argue that toward the end of his life, as he faced the Russian
problem, Marx began to rethink some of the most basic premises of his
*schema* of historical development. In his thinking about Russia, Shanin
has argued, Marx was moving toward a recognition of a much greater
diversity in the historical paths of individual parts of the world than he
had admitted earlier. And yet, there is little reason to conclude from this
that Marx was about to downgrade the West European historical sequence
from the status of the *via regia* in humanity's development and to treat it
as one of several, equally significant variants. Just as in 1845 he had
asserted the universal significance of the English contribution to political
economy, the French to politics, and the German to philosophy, so in his
last years Marx must still have believed that the particular historical sequence that resulted in the rise of capitalism in Western Europe—and the
creation of Marxism—was of a universal import, too. There is no basis
for supposing that Marx anticipated for Russia a communism that was
different from that which he expected Europe would have.

What conclusion is one to draw from this account of Marx's confrontation with nation and nationalism?

In his original stand, formed in the 1840s, Marx treated nation and
nationalism as expressions of false consciousness—"ideology"—that fell

into the same category as religion, law, state, and other mystifications. Nation was to disappear, along with religion and the rest, as people became "world-historical individuals" under communism. Later, Marx reluctantly recognized a role for German nationalism and for other nationalisms of large nations. His approach to these, however, was purely instrumental; he judged them by the test of whether or not they could help the revolutionary cause of the proletariat.

Marx appears never to have grasped—or to have acknowledged openly—that there was simply no way for the working class to function outside and above the national identities within which its segments lived. When in the decade of the 1870s German socialists accepted the framework of the nation-state, the German nation had only recently undergone a fundamental transformation. Once a nationalist program becomes realized (as happened in Germany in 1864–1871), Geoff Eley says, the "conditions of existence for nationalist movements and ideas" are transformed.

> The nation comes to represent an ideological and institutional structure of immense power, which begins to set limits on the possible forms of political action and belief. Almost imperceptibly nationalism loses its character as a sectional creed articulating the aspirations of liberal and other tendencies within the bourgeoisie, and passes into the common heritage of a political culture—becoming, as Tom Nairn puts it, "a name for the general condition of the modern body politic, more like the climate of political and social thought than just another doctrine."[45]

With the unification of Germany, German nationalism achieved a unity of theory and practice and thus transformed both itself and the Germans, who by realizing their national identity became another people. That transformation, as Eley says in quoting Nairn, changed "the general condition" of the nation. There was no way in which German socialists could have escaped or "seceded" from the entity into which the formation of a united Germany had thrust them. There was simply no way anyone could become a member of an international community without being first a German, an Italian, and so on. (Engels sensed this when he discussed Irish-English relations and said that a renunciation of nationalism by the Irish implied not a move toward internationalism but a concession to English nationalism.) To quote Hobsbawm again:

> The alternative to a "national" political consciousness was not, in practice, "working-class internationalism" but a sub-political consciousness which still operated on a scale much smaller than, or irrelevant to, that of the nation-state. The men and women on the political left who chose clearly between national and supranational loyalties, such as the cause of the in-

ternational proletariat, were few. The "internationalism" of the left in practice meant solidarity and support for those who fought the same cause in
other nations and, in the case of political refugees, the readiness to participate
in the struggle wherever they found themselves. But, as the examples of
Garibaldi, Cluseret of the Paris Commune (who helped the Fenians in America) and numerous Polish fighters prove, this was not incompatible with
passionately nationalist beliefs.[46]

There is no evidence that what a contemporary Marxist now regards
as virtually self-evident had ever been accepted by Marx. Indeed, many
later disciples of Marx, including some who proved to be influential, also
failed to modify the "classic" Marxist position on the question of nation.
Among them, the record of Rosa Luxemburg, the brilliant socialist thinker
and activist of the late-nineteenth–early-twentieth centuries, is especially
instructive. Her biographer, J. P. Nettl, has subjected the question of
nationalism and internationalism in Luxemburg's politics to a close and
subtle scrutiny. He points out that internationalism "is usually a negative,
not a positive quality, a revolt against national disappointment rather than
an embrace of a wider, more diffuse unity. Most rebels of this sort seek
a fervent new nationalism, some a millenarian (or other) religion, a few
became citizens of the world—but always in negation." In such cases, the
"emotions that usually find fulfillment in patriotism become stunted," but
"many of the patriotic characteristics and attitudes remain" nevertheless.[47]
In contrast to this, says Nettl, Luxemburg's "onslaught on national self-
determination was a positive substitution of one fatherland for another.
Why, after all, should the notion of patriotism be confined to arbitrary
political and ethnic frontiers, and be based on the artifact of a nation
state?"[48]

Nettl cites the following representative statement of Luxemburg's
position:

> In a society based on classes, the nation as a uniform social-political whole
> simply does not exist. Instead, there exist within each nation classes with
> antagonistic interests and "rights." There is literally no social arena—from
> the strongest material relationship to the most subtle moral one—in which
> the possessing classes and a self-conscious proletariat could take one and
> the same position and figure as one undifferentiated national whole.[49]

Nettl stresses that the "notion of a national fatherland, even of a special
cultural home, was entirely alien" to Luxemburg and that her struggle
against Polish national self-determination "cannot be understood merely
in terms of a negation, but by the superimposition of nationalist sentiment
on to political and class ideology." In opposition to nation and nationalism,

Luxemburg attempted to "make operational the Marxist concept of class as the primary social referent, and to break once and for all *the old alternative stranglehold of nation*. In this respect her contribution is second to none."[50]

Writing in the 1960s, Nettl sensibly enough questioned whether it was possible to "be a Marxist without achieving not only a substitution of class consciousness for patriotic consciousness, but an immersion in class *instead* of nation." He doubted whether the leaders of Soviet Russia or Communist China had achieved that substitution and pointed out that they retained the national unit as "fact and concept." Even Lenin, according to Nettl, reconciled his hatred of Russian chauvinism "with full acceptance and manifestation of Russian culture and attitudes; was he an internationalist?"[51] At any rate, he was sure that of all the major Marxists, Luxemburg had been truly faithful to Marx's position.

But how successful was Luxemburg really in breaking "once and for all the . . . stranglehold of nation"? Nettl's answer is far from reassuring. The only fatherland Luxemburg knew, he says, was "the proletariat in general and German Social Democracy in particular."[52] "German Social Democracy," indeed!

As we know, Luxemburg did not have to face the problem that every universal ideology faces when it becomes, to use Hobsbawm's words, "the possession of one state among others." Such a turn of events infuses a national or nationalist element in that ideology, which happened, according to Hobsbawm, with "Americanism"—"originally a universal programme . . . an invitation to all men to become Americans if they so chose."[53] That problem confronted the Russian Bolsheviks when they established themselves in control of what had been the Russian Empire, and in later years it also confronted other Communists once they won power.

Luxemburg was not among them, but mindful of Lenin's experience and of Hobsbawm's observation, let us imagine that Luxemburg had chaired the Council of People's Commissars of the German Socialist Republic, instead of being murdered, in 1919. Would that state's territorial claims, in the eventuality of the German Revolution's failure to become international, have been any different from what List had claimed for his Germany (and from what Marx and Engels claimed after List)? Would a Soviet Germany have dealt with the Poles or Czechs any differently than Lenin treated the Georgians and Ukrainians?

We shall never know what a German government headed by Luxemburg would have done. Would it have presided over the formation of a German Soviet "official nationalism" akin to what emerged in Russia after the revolution? (See Chapters 13 and 14, in which the post–1917 ideological developments in Russia are discussed.) We do know that in the Weimar Republic, German Communists—more broadly, German Marxists—established a certain style of "proletarian" politics that treated the proletarian cause in isolation from the nonproletarian classes and strata of the nation: The left (Communists and socialists alike) remained in and maintained what Geoff Eley has aptly called "the class-political ghetto." While under attack by the radical right, the socialists and Communists faced the issue of "how to win popular support for socialism by electoral means" after it had become clear that the proletariat would not form a numerical majority of the population—thus refuting a Marxist prediction—and that "a reformist practice had ceased to show tangible returns." In this situation, says Eley, "it became imperative for the left to break out of the class-political ghetto for which its entire previous history had prepared it." This could have been done by recognizing the concerns and needs of (and by building political alliances with) small owners, pensioners, students, professionals, and other groups.

> Most of all, it was imperative to conceive of other-than-class collectivities rallying the people as consumers, as women, as tax-payers, as citizens, even as Germans . . . as the coherent basis for the broadest possible democratic unity. Yet it was in this democratic project that the politics of the left proved lamentably deficient.[54]

It is not essential for our argument to ask whether the socialists and Communists could have agreed at that time in their understanding of "socialism" or "democracy." (For the Communists, the USSR was *the* democracy; not so for the socialists.) But Eley is right in noting the self-exclusion, so to say, of the left from broader national issues, its unwillingness to "reach out" and to project a *left* model of the nation. This political attitude sharply contrasted with the tactic of the Nazis, who, owing to what Eley calls the "promiscuous adaptability" of the Nazi propaganda, extended their influence far beyond those elements that sympathized with their ideological positions. In Italy, the Fascists also managed to gain "access to the suppressed Mazzinian tradition of unfulfilled radical-nationalist expectations."[55]

"Consciously or not," Isaiah Berlin writes, "Marx all his life systematically underestimated nationalism as an independent force." This "illusion," he continues, "led his followers in the twentieth century to a faulty analysis of Fascism and National Socialism, for which many of them paid with their own lives, and which led to a good deal of false diagnosis and prediction of the course of history in our own time."

> Despite the depth and originality of his major theses, Marx failed to give
> an adequate account of the sources and nature of nationalism, and under-
> estimated it, as he underestimated the force of religion, as an independent
> factor in society. This is one of the major weaknesses of his great synthesis.[56]

It is evident that the failure of the left to appreciate the Nazi challenge
and threat corresponded to Luxemburg's and ultimately Marx's approach
to the question of nation. The disorientation of the left was further com-
pounded by the split between the socialists and the Communists and by
the latter's insistence, until as late as 1932, that their "real fatherland"
was the Soviet Union—which Germany in due course would join as its
constituent republic. (Thus the "nationalization" of communism within
Russia produced a side effect abroad: It further reduced the Communists'
capacity to act as a bona fide national force in Germany, France, or Poland.)

The impact of Marx's ideas in the twentieth century aside, let us return
to Marx himself. As we saw, neither Marx nor Engels reconsidered his
view of the origins or significance of Slavic and other nationalism in East
Europe. Their undisguised contempt for "the village" as a representative
of barbarism (the "idiocy of village life") must have predisposed them to
treat with hostility any movement that took a favorable view of—let alone
idealized—the peasant life, culture, and language, which nationalism did.
Similarly, having identified Judaism with certain economic practices and
having denied any independent cultural value to Jewish life in modern
history, Marx and Engels alike were insensitive to many aspects of the
nineteenth-century world, such as the ethnic awareness, that would lead
someone like Moses Hess, Marx's erstwhile friend and mentor, to embrace
Zionism while remaining a socialist. (The same awareness compelled another prominent contemporary of Jewish descent, Benjamin Disraeli, to
try to reconcile, however confusedly, his religious and national Jewish
origins with his career in British politics.) But a view of the world embraced
by a Hess (or the view of a Disraeli) made no sense to Marx.[57]

Marx was not prepared to admit that there might be something in the
national character, national traditions, or national community that would
call for a response not related to the class point of view and that yet might
deserve being supported through political means. (This did not preclude
his calling individuals or their behavior "typically German," etc., as long
as such epithets carried no political implications.)[58] Most notably, Marx
failed to acknowledge that even if a future world communist civilization
would have no nations as working entities, the historic, that is, established,
nations would survive in that civilization—at least as a memory and legacy
from the precommunist era— while the underdogs, the nonhistoric peoples,
having failed to win independence before the coming of communism,

would disappear from history altogether. This particular prospect offered no comfort to socialists of the nonhistoric nations, for whom communism was otherwise convincing. In the Marxist scenario, the Czechs would forever be under the Germans.[59]

Marx's old friend, Moses Hess, asked the same question with reference to the Jews. According to Shlomo Avineri, Hess asked, "In the name of what principle of liberty or socialism would the Jews then be asked to forgo their own collective identity in a world where all other similar [larger] entities would be able to maintain their national existence?" Hess's solution—"the creation of a Jewish commonwealth in Palestine"—was "an integral part of his general *Weltanschauung*." Hess believed that it did not conflict with his socialism, but was rather "the realization of the emancipatory principle of socialism as applied to the specific context of Jewish existence."[60]

Marx was not prepared to accept such reasoning or the analogous approaches advanced by Czech, Slovak, Ukrainian, Romanian, and all other Marxists, for that matter. But neither did he leave a legacy that could be interpreted only in one way. On the contrary, according to Walker Connor, instead of a clear-cut message, the Marx-Engels legacy contained "three strains" in its treatment of the nationality problem. The first of these strains, that of "classical Marxism," insisted on "the primacy of class struggle and was therefore irreconcilable with nationalism." The second strain formally recognized the right of national self-determination and selectively supported national movements in practical politics. These two strains, says Connor, were not naturally harmonious, but they could be reconciled if one remembered "that nationalism was a bourgeois and therefore ephemeral ideology whose progressiveness... dwindled as society progressed from feudalism through capitalism to socialism." Finally, there was the third strain, "national Marxism." Connor sees it "in references to national characteristics that transcend epochs" and in recognition of "the role of nations as the principal instrumentality of historical forces." (This strain was noticeable especially in Engels.) Connor thinks that national Marxism was "irreconcilable with classical Marxism's emphasis upon classes and class warfare."[61]

These contradictions in the Marxist position were a reflection of the fact that nation and nationalism proved themselves much more influential, tenacious, and complex than Marx and Engels had imagined in the 1840s. As Samir Amin puts it, "European history during the decades 1850–1914 was in fact primarily the history of national struggles . . . . Marx and Engels considered classes to be more important than nations. Thus they adopted a pragmatic attitude toward national struggles . . . ."[62]

The three strains about which Connor speaks form, in a sense, a chronological sequence. Marx and Engels had begun with a wholly negative view of the prospects of nation and nationalism. Then they modified it somewhat in practice. Still later, they came close to recognizing that the phenomenon of nationality contained something that could not be wholly "decoded" or exposed in class terms. But the founders of Marxism, even at that later date, did not reexamine their general theoretical stand. They failed to develop any comprehensive theory of nation and nationalism—unless we say, not at all frivolously, that the Marxist theory of nation is that nation requires no theory.

# 12

## *After 1848: Nationalists Face the Social Problem*

In the second part of the nineteenth century, nationalism took new directions. This was due to several causes, among them the challenge of socialism, to which the nationalists felt they had to respond. In some cases, nationalism turned to the traditional right and defined itself as a fundamental opponent of socialism. In other cases, nationalists recognized the importance of the issues raised by socialism and argued that "in its real nature" the "social question" was simply an aspect of, and therefore should be solved within, the more fundamental "national question." They sought to integrate the working classes in a national community by persuading them to reject Marxist philosophy, revolutionary class politics, and proletarian internationalism. The workers were to pursue their class aspirations within a national community, in a democratic framework.

It is important at this point to make explicit what has been implicit in our argument so far. The doctrine of List responded to the Industrial Revolution in a way that accepted the ideals of the French Revolution while seeking their realization in a world of nations that were unequal economically and politically. List wanted his Germany not only to be strong economically but also to be liberal and constitutional, with freedom for the individual. Although the pursuit of some of List's goals made the implementation of some of those other ideals difficult, if not impossible in practice, it should be borne in mind that List stood for 1789. But of course there had always been other currents of nationalism that took a sharply negative view of 1789. They did not disappear after List had presented his model of nation and nationalism. Indeed, Hitler's "national socialism," a current that had various intellectual and political sources, was an offshoot (however deformed), if not a specimen, of nationalism, but it represented a complete repudiation of the ideals of 1789 (and of List's). More directly, it was opposed to those democratic versions of "national socialism" that preached social reform and national emancipation in a constitutional system.[1]

Also, in those parts of the world where Listian nationalism might have found its natural habitat because they were less developed and in need of political, economic, and cultural modernization, nationalism began to take positions that departed from the classical European model. Because they lived under conditions that were profoundly different and because they were aware of socialism, whose ideas also began to spread around them, non-European nationalists created new versions of nationalism. These versions incorporated certain Marxist notions and socialist goals into the nationalist ideology. Those nationalists concluded that to overcome economic backwardness and to preserve (or to win) their nation's independence, they should draw on Marxism as a guide. One might say that they were drawing on Marx to modify an outlook that had been inspired by List.

Let us start with post-Listian, post-1848 Germany, where as we recall, nationalism had preceded socialism, especially Marxism. Nationalism, as represented by List, had adopted a strong proindustrialization stand in its overall program for a unified national state. Early German nationalism was liberal politically (indeed, in 1848–1849, it even was radical); early German socialists were patriotic. The opposition to nationalism, on the other hand, had initially come from the forces of reaction on the right, such as the feudal nobility and the princes. The national cause created a common "national" framework that brought together the bourgeoisie, the petty bourgeoisie, and even the proletariat, and as nationalism gained in popularity and influence its initial opponents on the right also became "national."

German nationalism itself changed as it was adopted and co-opted by the Prussian state and the noble class. The establishment of the Second German Reich in 1871 was only partially the realization of the List program. List had not looked to Prussia when he sought ways to bring about German unity, and the forces that eventually created and dominated the new Germany—the military, the bureaucracy, the monarchy, the landed interests— were not the ones that List had wanted to play the leading role. This does not of course mean that after 1871 the German bourgeoisie did not attain a satisfactory legal and political arrangement for the pursuit of its ambitions and interests; List's liberal doctrine was not the only available program in nineteenth-century Germany. Granting this, we must nevertheless admit that, on balance, Germany—and Europe—after 1870 conformed more closely to List's 1841 vision than to anything Marx had expected to happen when in 1845 he attacked List.

Certain recent writers, for example, Robert M. Berdahl, have called for a reappraisal of the traditional emphasis on the role of ideas in German unification. Bismarck's Reich, Berdahl wrote in 1972, "was not 'pre-determined,' it was 'self-determined,' not by popular sovereignty or the Volk, but by its leading statesmen." He pointed out that German unification was not complete because some German-speaking areas were left out of the Reich while others, where non-German languages prevailed, were included. This led Berdahl to conclude that thus "culture did not 'form' the German national state, it legitimized it."[2]

However, to show that a certain ideal was not realized completely and perfectly does not prove that the ideal had not been instrumental in bringing about what *was* accomplished. The nationalist ideas supplied that underlying premise that made comments like Berdahl's possible. One first had to draw a mental map with a "Germany" as an "imagined community" on it, so that politicians, generals, and business leaders could pursue policies whose goal was to put a Germany on the political map of Europe.

To recognize the role of nationalist ideas in creating the very possibility of a "German unification problem" does not oblige us, however, to claim that List's specific recommendations had a direct influence on the German economic policies before or after 1870. In the pre-1870 era, protectionism had not been a dominant or even a particularly popular slogan. After 1870, a return to protectionism ensued that extended even to agriculture, but this was something List had opposed. True, List's books were coming out in new editions, and Bismarck himself claimed to be an admirer of List. But the economic policies of imperial Germany that resulted in the agricultural tariff of 1879, or in those that followed, were not compatible with List's recommendations. List had opposed agricultural protectionism as a matter of principle and had recommended industrial tariffs only in a developing country. The Germany of the 1880s was no longer the developing country it had been in List's time.[3] It is impossible, therefore, to agree with Hayes' comment that "by 1880 the German national state, under Bismarck's nominal guidance, was actually treading the economic path which had been blazed by Friedrich List."[4] Rather, Henderson is right when he says that "List would . . . certainly have criticized Bismarck's tariff of 1879 since it protected farmers as well as industrialists and was not designed to help 'infant industries.'"[5]

Such economic policies were not limited to Germany; elsewhere in Europe a revival of protectionism and a corresponding retreat from free trade also took place.[6] Along with them, there emerged social Darwinism, social imperialism, and integral nationalism, while liberalism declined. In those circumstances, the economic nationalists changed their stand. More openly than before, they subordinated economic considerations to national interest, while the earlier position tended to assume a measure of natural compatibility between the two. Using an American example, one might say that the earlier formula, "American Motors is better for the United States than British Motors and therefore deserves support," was replaced with a new slogan, "What is good for the United States is good for American Motors" (that is, "ought to be good" for American Motors).[7]

In Germany, the so-called Historical School in economics represented the new nationalist approach. Its leading figure was Gustav von Schmoller (1838–1917). Schmoller thought that "all protective movements are closely connected with national sentiments, strivings after international authority, [and] efforts toward the balance of power." He expected such protectionist efforts to continue because along with developed states there existed those states that aspired to achieve economic development and because all kinds of "weapons" could be used for economic purposes.[8] Schmoller and the other leading representative of the German protectionist school, Adolph Wagner, admitted (as noted by Arcadius Kahan) that national interests and national policy did not always agree with the requirements of economic rationality, and they therefore subordinated the latter to the former.[9] Thus Wagner argued that not only such national needs as defense, civil administration, justice, education, and welfare, but "also the maintenance of the permanent economic and numerical strength of the nation through an adequate and sturdy agrarian population [requires] sacrifices."[10]

George Lichtheim, in his book *Imperialism*, points out that Schmoller's "main theme throughout his career was that economic life depended on political decision-making." In this connection, Lichtheim approvingly quotes Charles Wilson, who defined mercantilism as "state-making—not state-making in a narrow sense, but state-making and national economy-making at the same time."[11]

This new approach became dominant in international relations. Imperial Germany, as a late-comer, "was trying to make up for lost time." Schmoller and his friends (who "were leaders of opinion in the Germany of Bismarck and William II") helped to form the German imperialist outlook by laying "the theoretical basis for German policy in the new age of empire-building." In this situation, their political conservatism left them with nothing more entrancing . . . than self-aggrandizement as a national goal. German imperialism thus got under way *without a universal idea to sustain it*, and this circumstance in the end proved to be its ruin.[12]

The Historical School was also concerned with domestic politics. It recognized the importance of the social question and recommended special measures, including legislative enactments, to improve the position of the working classes. By advancing a program of "social policy," the economists of the Historical School wanted to compete with socialism for the allegiance of the masses. Bismarck identified with the "antisocialist social policy of the historical economists."[13]

Schmoller and his associates did not restrict themselves to writing and teaching; they founded the Association for Social Policy (*Verein für Sozialpolitik*) to promote their cause among the wider public. (Schmoller was also influential abroad, in such countries as Britain and the United States.)[14]

The antisocialist campaigns did not succeed in destroying German socialism. Rather, the socialists survived government repression and emerged, after the repeal of antisocialist laws, as a mass party. By 1913, they appeared to be facing the prospect of winning an electoral majority in the Reichstag. However, the sustained antisocialist campaigns did succeed in alienating the socialist movement and its extensive institutional structures from the state and the official "society" in Germany. German socialism was closely identified with the industrial proletariat and made no preparations for the eventuality that if it seized power it would have to constitute itself as the leader of the whole society. A certain "ghetto mentality" thus developed in the socialist ranks. This became even stronger in the Weimar Republic, when the Communists openly defined themselves as "international," or outside the nation. Their stand precluded interclass "cohabitation" (to borrow anachronistically a French concept from the 1980s) and represented instead a form of ideological celibacy, especially as contrasted with the "promiscuous adaptability" of the Nazis (see Eley's comments about this in Chapter 11). Thus the German left, having been solidly national as early as 1848, abandoned the national agenda to the Nazis. (This happened, ironically enough, when the German left itself was split into socialism and communism, with the latter preaching its allegiance to another power.)

But let us return to German nationalism after 1870. Among its concerns at the time were those issues that cannot be classified as either purely domestic or foreign. The Second Reich was a multinational state. It ruled over a strong, vocal, and well-organized Polish minority in the Poznan region and Silesia and was becoming intensely nationalistic during the Bismarck era.

The Polish Question, however, was not simply an internal German problem: Many Poles lived in the Habsburg monarchy as well (not to mention the Russian Empire). There, the Germans were numerous, but after 1871 they found themselves in an unclear position. On the one hand, they were unquestionably the leading element. From a nationalist point of view, on the other hand, the unification of Germany had left them out (*"Germania irredenta"*). The German Empire was the mightiest power in Europe—but German nationalism remained unfulfilled so long as millions of its conationals lived "abroad." The Germans of the Habsburg lands (Austria proper, Bohemia, Moravia, the Austrian portion of Silesia) faced competing claims for their allegiance. From one perspective, dynastic loyalty, the principle of *Kaisertreue*, demanded that they continue to serve the Emperor in Vienna. Yet German nationalism postulated either the incorporation of all Germans in a single state, to be ruled from Berlin, or, as a second-best choice, the transformation of the monarchy into a second German state.[15]

The position of the Germans in the Austrian half of the Habsburg monarchy, unsolved as it remained from a strictly national standpoint, was made even more awkward by the rise of the ethnic nationalisms of the Czechs, Poles, Slovenes, Ukrainians, Romanians, and others. During the late 1800s and early 1900s, currents that in some respects anticipated Nazism emerged among the Germans of the Czech-German borderlands: They used socialist slogans when addressing workers and calling upon them to join the nation. This amounted to an admission that these German nationalists no longer expected the German problem to be solved in the framework of heretofore "normal" political processes.

During those rising ethnic tensions, one might have expected the social democratic movement, professing adherence to the principles of Marx, to provide a counterweight to nationalism and thus to function as an integrating force in the Empire. This was not the case, however. At first, when the socialists formed a single, centralized party in Austria, the non-Germans viewed it as a Germanizing, not an internationalist, force. By the end of the nineteenth century, the Austrian Social Democratic party succumbed to nationalism and openly transformed itself into a federation of national parties. This outcome may have contributed to further lowering the national standing of social democracy in the eyes of the German bourgeois. Also, by 1914, the trade union movement, originally united, consisted of distinct, nationally defined, and autonomous units.[16]

As mentioned earlier (Chapter 11), it was within the Austrian socialist movement that a current emerged to revise the classical Marxist stand on the nationality question. That current has passed into history under a name—"Austro-Marxism"—that would have hardly pleased Marx: He had considered Austria an anomaly and had preached its dissolution as early as 1848, while the Austro-Marxists sought ways of maintaining Austria as a multinational state.

Otto Bauer may have been the most original of the Austro-Marxists writing on the nationality question. In his book, *Die Nationalitätenfrage und die Sozialdemokratie* (The Nationality Question and the Social Democracy), Bauer argued that nation was a culture-based community that had a history going as far back as the primitive society. In the course of history, the national community evolved under the impact of its experiences, and the national character itself changed. By asserting the continued existence of the nation across different socioeconomic formations, Bauer explicitly rejected the orthodox Marxist view that nation was a product of capitalism and would disappear after the overthrow of capitalism. Bauer claimed that capitalism transformed nations by including into a conscious and active national life those social elements that had heretofore been excluded from such participation. On the other hand, capitalism further isolated the working classes from their class counterparts in foreign countries: "Modern capitalism slowly demarcates more sharply the lower classes of the various nations from each other, for they, too, gain a share in national education, national cultural life, and the national standard language." Bauer prophesied that socialism, "through the differences in national education . . . will mark off the entire peoples so sharply from each other, as today only the educated strata of the different nations are separated from each other."[17] He clearly disagreed with Marx and most Marxists, who expected nations to dissolve under socialism.

Bauer stated openly what was being tacitly recognized by the socialists in Western, Central, and Eastern Europe—to wit, that nation was a stable, enduring community based on a common character, which in turn was the product of a common past (*Schicksalgemeinschaft*).

Whatever intellectual merit (or long-range impact on European socialism) those Austro-Marxist searches may have had, the Austrian socialists did not utilize their new insights to their political advantage. Social democracy in Austria transformed itself into a loose federation of ethnic parties, thus basically replicating the process occurring in European socialism as a whole. The Second International, founded in 1889, remained to the end an association of sovereign socialist parties that were built along state or national lines. Representatives of those parties met from time to time at international congresses, but the International resembled the future

League of Nations and the United Nations in that it lacked an effective central machinery. It certainly was not the agency to realize Marx's call: "Workers of all lands, unite!"

In order to defuse the challenge of ethnic nationalisms in the 1900s, the Austrian prime minister, Ernst Koerber, conceived an ambitious plan of modernization, including industrialization, based on Austrian patriotism. Koerber tried to unite the peoples of the state through their common economic interest. According to Gerschenkron (who wrote a book on Koerber's attempt), Koerber adopted a more reconciliatory policy toward the socialists because he expected that they, for reasons of their own, would support industrialization, with its concomitant rise of the proletariat. However, the socialists did not grasp the broader importance of the Koerber program and refused to give him their support. This may have been an occasion when social democracy had an opportunity to assume leadership in advancing a cause with an "above-class" appeal, but it failed to rise above its narrowly conceived *class* standpoint. Koerber also failed to win over the general public, despite having as an advisor no less an expert than Theodor Herzl (who helped Koerber write some of his speeches).[18]

Thus, as we see, neither socialism nor a nonethnic "patriotism" proved capable of challenging nationalism in the struggle to replace a declining dynastic loyalty. The peoples of Austria increasingly identified themselves with their respective ethnic communities instead. Although the monarchy collapsed only in 1918, after a long war, the emotional and political bonds that tied its subjects had been dissolved much earlier.

The interaction of nationalism with socialism in a country that faced the problem of economic modernization took another turn in Italy. After the unification, some Italians became aware of their country's economic underdevelopment, or in Luigi de Rosa's words, of the "contrast between a political Italy which now existed virtually in its final and complete form, and an economic Italy which was still entirely to be created."[19] These Italians believed that nation-building did not stop with becoming an independent *state*—they criticized the dominant free trade ideas and demanded protection. While the free traders were organized in "Adam Smith Societies," the protectionists, who considered themselves followers of German economic theories, created their own Association for the Advancement of Economic Studies. The Association recognized Friedrich List as an authority and found List's views on Germany applicable to the Italian situation.[20] One Italian disciple of List, Alessandro Rossi, argued in 1878 that England and America owed their economic advancement to protectionism and that the same was also true of France and Germany.

Rossi claimed that free trade was "a total negation of the much desired moral emancipation of our laboring classes."[21]

Rossi did not think that protectionism was the only means to raise Italy as an industrial power. He believed, just as List did, that the principle of protectionism was not equally valid for all times and circumstances. Moreover, each nation should have an economic system reflective of its particular history and needs. And the economic life of a nation, he argued, ought to be guided by moral forces. According to de Rosa, Rossi held that the state as "the organ of public order" should ensure the proper balance between production and distribution. It should also guarantee to national industries a position of equality against foreign competition.[22]

A generation later, in 1914, Alfredo Rocco, an economist and an active member of the Italian Nationalist Association, referred to the ideas of List when proposing new economic policies for Italy. According to Rocco, it was owing to List that the Germans had grown aware of their national needs in the economic sphere and become "the feared and often victorious rival of England in terms of industry and trade."[23]

The followers of List did not determine the economic policies in post-unification Italy, however, and they failed to create a strong popular movement in favor of industrialization. Italy lacked an intellectual and political counterpart to the industrialization ideologies that emerged at comparable stages of development in England, France, Germany, and Russia. According to Gerschenkron, Italy failed to produce "any strong ideological stimulus to industrialization." Protectionism in Italy served vested interests and "failed to develop into a strong intellectual movement."

It may be significant, in view of Italy's subsequent political experience, that although Marxism already enjoyed popularity in the 1890s among the Italian intelligentsia (thus bringing to mind analogous developments in Russia at the same time), "unlike the Russians, the Italian Marxists showed, if at all, a very restrained interest in the problems of industrial evolution of the country." The leaders of the Italian labor movement supported the then existing industrial-tariff structure, and neither they nor the general public were concerned "to speed up the change that was afoot in the land."[24]

This would suggest that neither Italian Marxism nor the labor movement, as broadly defined, concerned itself with the question of *Italy's* national economic development. In the early twentieth century, the nationalist movement, a precursor of fascism, took up Italy's economic backwardness as its own ideological issue. It presented the condition of Italy in the framework of relations between developed and developing nations, that is, in a Listian way. It also quite openly employed concepts taken from Marxism. One of its leading spokesmen, Enrico Corradini, said at the First Nationalist Congress held in Florence in 1910, that what socialism had done for the workers—and the Italian nationalists acknowledged that socialism did help to improve the workers' material and spiritual well-being—nationalism would do for Italy. Corradini borrowed the Marxist dichotomy of "proletariat—bourgeoisie" and superimposed it on the relations between states. Quite unconsciously, we suppose, Corradini copied the language of Russian populists of the 1870s (see Chapter 13)—not only the ideas of List—when he declared:

> We must start by recognizing the fact that there are proletarian nations as well as proletarian classes; that is to say, there are nations whose living conditions are subject, to their great disadvantage, to the way of life of other nations, just as classes are. Once this is realized, nationalism must, above all, insist firmly on this truth: Italy is, materially and morally, a proletarian nation. What is more, she is proletarian at a period before her recovery. That is to say, before she is organized, at a period when she is still groping and weak. And being subjected to other nations, she is weak not in the strength of her people but in her strength as a nation. Exactly like the proletariat before socialism came to its aid.[25]

According to A. James Gregor, the Italian Fascists, in their treatment of Italy's backwardness and industrialization, drew on List's ideas.[26]

In Bulgaria, the Marxists and Listians developed their positions along parallel lines. Under the influence of Russian Marxism, the Bulgarian Marxists insisted on the "inevitability of capitalist development" and assumed that "the course of industrialization, as described by Marx, would essentially repeat itself in Bulgaria." They saw this as a necessary precondition for the eventual victory of socialism in their country. According to Gerschenkron, in this favorable "attitude toward industrialization, Bulgarian Marxians stood close to those relatively small groups of Bulgarian intelligentsia which, influenced by List, thought in terms of 'national production' and 'development of the nation's productive forces.'" That group published a journal named *Promishlenost* (Industry) in the late 1880s. Later on, it supported I. E. Geshov's policy of industrial promotion.[27]

The socialist Dimitr Blagoev, says Gerschenkron, surpassed the nationalist minister Geshov in his advocacy of industrial protectionism and severely criticized Geshov for not going far enough in protectionism. Blagoev wanted him to support large-scale industrial enterprises in Bulgaria, instead of being concerned with "the economic conditions of the Bulgarian peasantry." While Geshov acted like a practical capitalist businessman, the socialist Blagoev "was a product of the revolutionary movements among Russian university students and a disciple of Plekhanov.'' Russian Marxism of the 1890s taught him to accept ''an unpopular and burdensome industrialization in a very backward country.'' Gerschenkron comments, ''Few things are more apt to enhance men's willingness to promote a certain course of events than the firm belief in its inevitability.'' Blagoev was highly optimistic when assessing the chances of, and discussing the prerequisites for, modern industrial development in Bulgaria.[28]

However, despite Blagoev's belief that Bulgaria had all the prerequisites for ''an impetuous industrial development,'' such development did not in fact occur.[29] This is an interesting outcome, but even more interesting is the fact that the late-nineteenth-century Bulgarian Marxists, like the Listians, clearly thought in terms of ''capitalism in one country'' even when that country was as small as Bulgaria. In the Marxists' assessment, a socialist transformation of Bulgaria would depend on *Bulgaria's* becoming an industrialized, capitalist country first. This view of economic development appears to have had more in common with List than with Marx. (For Marx's view, see Chapter 3.)

Already in the nineteenth century, Listian nationalism was spreading not only in Europe, but also in China, Japan, Korea, and other countries.[30] In Japan after 1885, according to Chitoshi Yanaga, students of political economy, as well as the policymakers, were interested in German political ideas. They especially liked List's advocacy of free trade in the early stages preceding industrialization and of protectionism for a developing industry, so that it might compete successfully in the world market.[31]

Listian nationalism also found followers and imitators in a British-dominated India. As early as the 1890s, leaders of the Indian National Congress spoke in unmistakably Listian tones. Thomas Balogh, in a recent book that deals primarily with contemporary issues (*The Irrelevance of Conventional Economics*), refers to List's *National System*, which, Balogh says, ''demonstrated the evil impact on the weaker partners in any trading exchange.'' Balogh quotes Lala Murlidhar, whose speech at the 1891 meeting of the Indian National Congress bears a close resemblance to List's points.

> Of course, I know that it was pure philanthropy which flooded India with English-made goods, and surely, if slowly, killed out every indigenous industry—pure philanthropy which, to facilitate this, repealed the import duties and flung away three crores a year of revenue which the rich paid, and to balance this wicked sacrifice raised the Salt tax, which the poor pay ....Free Trade, fair play between nations, how I hate the sham! What fair play in trade can there be between impoverished India and the bloated capitalist England? As well as talk of a fair fight between an infant and a

strong man—a rabbit and a boa-constrictor. No doubt it is all in accordance with high economic science, but, my friends, remember this— this, too, is starving your brethren.[32]

M. G. Ranade, whom Heinz Wolfgang Arndt calls "the Indian disciple of List," argued for industrialization of India not only because it would bring material benefits, but because "manufactures are, if possible, more vital in their bearing on education of the intelligence and enterprise of the nation."[33]

The Indian and Japanese nationalists before World War I shared List's commitment to political liberalism and his belief that an underdeveloped country should use political means to advance its economic development. (In so doing, they were not deterred by List's Eurocentrism.)[34] The later generations of Asian (or African or Latin American) nationalists differed from those early Listians in Asia in that they no longer shared List's political beliefs, such as his preference for constitutional government. Their nationalism was more radical. It thus reflected not only the specific intellectual provenance of their ideas and the greater economic and political backwardness, including social conflict, of their respective countries, but it also recognized the impact of the Soviet Union.

Thus, if the "national-liberation" movements since the Second World War—that is, the revolutionaries in Asia, Africa, and Latin America—have invoked Marx and Lenin as their inspiration, there are historical reasons for their having done so. For several decades after 1945, after the defeat of nazism and fascism, the Soviet experience served as the most impressive political influence in the colonial or post-colonial world. (This may have begun to change more recently.) It was in Russia that the first "nationalization" of communism took place. It was in Russia that Marxism, having found itself in power, was transformed from a theory advocating the withering away of the state in highly developed countries into a program to modernize a backward society under the direction of a strong state. That was the Marxism that impressed the Third World. It is proper, therefore, that we should next explore Russia's encounters with Marx and List.

# 13

## *List and Marx in Russia*

Russian political thought and, more broadly, a modern national conscious-ness developed during, and was a response to, Russia's opening up to the West. Ever since the time of Peter the Great (1689–1725) and especially since the reign of Catherine II (1762–1796), Russians discussed their prob-lems by comparing themselves with the West, by formulating them in terms of "Russia and Europe" or "Russia and the West."

The preoccupation of Russian thinkers with the "fate" of Russia, Andrzej Walicki stresses,

> had nothing in common with narrow provincialism. On the contrary: all nineteenth-century Russian thinkers, independently of their attitude towards the West, were deeply "westernized" in the sense of being acquainted with and interested in the intellectual life of Europe; they saw Russia within the context of European problems and in their cogitations about Russia's destiny utilized the instruments of thought devised by the best minds of the more developed Western countries. One of the peculiar advantages of backward-ness was that Russia could learn from the experience and use the achieve-ments of Europe, that the intellectual and cultural impact of the West served as a powerful catalyst in the emergence and development of Russian social thought. It was the deepened and intensified process of cultural contact which raised Russia to the level of self-awareness, called into being the Russian intelligentsia, and posed in all its various aspects the problem of the meaning of Russia's history and the possible path of her further development.[1]

This being the case, Russia would appear ideally suited for a Listian view of the world, which regarded as central the relations between nations, especially between advanced and backward nations. Did not List so define Germany's condition when he presented his homeland as a developing country, except that what the Russians called "the West" was, for List, called England?

And yet, as we turn to the Russian case and remember the Gerschenkron thesis on ideologies of industrialization (Saint-Simon in France, List in Germany, Marx in Russia), the question arises: Why did nationalism *not* become the ideology of industrialization in Russia? Why did Marxism win out instead?

In an effort to understand the interaction of nationalism and Marxism in Russia, it is necessary to begin, however briefly, with certain essential facts of modern Russian history.

First, Russia became a multinational empire before a modern Russian national identity was formed. In the West, empire-building came after nation-building. Moreover, there was a clear territorial separation of the metropolis, where the nation-state was built, from that state's colonial possessions overseas. According to Richard Pipes, the two phenomena were blurred in Russia. The Muscovite state gradually expanded into non-Russian territories contiguous to lands inhabited by the Russians. In effect, the Russians had an empire before completing their nation-building. Because of this "reversal" of stages, the Russians found it difficult to distinguish between "Russia proper," that is, their national homeland, and their tsar's imperial possessions that were not Russian in the same sense. This confusion, in turn, made the Russians more suspicious of their subject nationalities and their demands, which they treated as a threat to the state's integrity.[2]

The second, and perhaps more important factor influencing Russia's political and intellectual history, was the role of the state. Beginning in the Middle Ages and continuing over the course of centuries, a distinction between state and society emerged in Western Europe. This development was made possible by the separation of the status of the monarch as a ruler in terms of public law and his standing as an owner of private property, which was regulated by civil law. As a medieval jurist put it, the emperor was "lord in the political sense, but not in the sense of an owner" in his country.[3]

In Russia, sovereignty included "the attributes of patrimonial or dominial power, i.e., full ownership of the land and its inhabitants." This meant that the concept of the state, and its corollary, society, was unknown. According to Pipes, these concepts remained "imperfectly assimilated" after their introduction in the seventeenth century.[4]

Even after Russia had established relations with the West, tsarism refused to introduce political and legal reforms and thus held back the formation of a modern Russian nation, which was unthinkable without recognizing society as something separate from the state. The government could not prevent the formation of political ideas among the educated elements of the population, however. Those educated and politically thinking Russians debated the question of what the Russian nation should be like: The famous Slavophile-Westernizer controversy was clearly one such debate on the "content" of Russian nationality. The ideologists of autocracy, in an effort to counteract the formation of a Russian nation that would have a life of its own apart from the state, responded with their own solution. This was the celebrated theory of "Official Nationality" that proclaimed Orthodoxy, autocracy, and *narodnost* (or "nationality") as the distinguishing characteristics of the Russian people. In other words, tsarism defined the Russian nation by its subjection to autocracy, which was a form of government in which society played no role and was not represented. This was to deny the Russian nation a separate identity.[5]

The following statement by a Russian aristocrat, Prince Vladimir Odoevsky (1835), illustrates if not the full realities of Russian life (for tsarist autocracy was not *that* perfect), then at least the official ideal:

> Service here in Russia is *the only way to be useful to the Fatherland....* [In Russia] there is no inborn . . . aspiration for enlightenment. Tell me, who among us builds schools? The government. Who builds factories and machines? The government. Who makes discoveries possible? The government. Who supports companies? The government and only the government. All these things do not—and will not in the future—occur to private individuals. [But] the government needs people for its undertakings. Dissociating oneself from it means dissociating oneself from that which moves all of Russia forward and gives her life and air to breathe.[6]

Even if Odoevsky's description was overdrawn, there can be little doubt that nineteenth-century Russia was very different from the Germany of List's youth. Though Russia was a unified state (unlike List's Germany), autocracy did not allow the "society" even that limited freedom which the industrialists and merchants enjoyed in Metternich's Germany, when in 1819, for example, they formed a voluntary association to promote the economic and political unity of German states. Indeed, the Russian society had less civic freedom, including freedom of association and opinion, than the Indians did under British rule: A Russian "National Congress," analogous to the Indian National Congress, in which one, as early as the 1890s, could criticize British rule in India from a Listian perspective, would not have been tolerated in the tsarist empire.

Literature and journalism were the only areas where an educated Russian could work openly for the people in accordance with his own ideals without being a part of the official state apparatus. Those Russians who engaged in such activities without becoming members of the state bureaucratic machine came to be known as the intelligentsia. That category, however, did not include all educated people, for government employed many more of those: To be an *intelligent*, you had also to be separated from the state, by outlook if not always by the source of your income. "The rise of the intelligentsia," Tibor Szamuely has noted, "coincided with the great flowering of Russian literature and literary criticism."[7]

For those whose inclinations were wholly political, the only alternative to state service was the revolutionary underground. The first Russian revolutionaries—the members of the so-called Decembrist movement (1825)—had been liberals and democrats, but their successors in conspiratorial politics were socialist. These activists rejected the idea that a nation was comprised of different social classes including the bourgeoisie, that is, they rejected the concept of nation that had been established in the West and was being formed in a country like Germany. Their program for Russia was different.

The Russian "society" could openly debate national affairs only after the emancipation of the peasantry (1861) and under the related reforms in administration, local self-government, and the judiciary system, as well as under the liberalization of censorship. By 1881, Russia had reached a phase of development when it seemed that the society would be admitted to participation in governing the country. The so-called constitutional plan of the tsarist minister Loris-Melikov envisaged a reform of the Council of State, an exclusively bureaucratic agency, by adding to it elected representatives of "society." That plan was shelved after Alexander II's assassination (1881).

The reception of List's teaching offers a very revealing insight into the "state-society" interaction in Russia. As we recall, List paid attention to Russia when he reviewed the condition of individual states of Europe. He was convinced that Russia had all the necessary material prerequisites for becoming a major industrial power. He approved of protectionist measures being taken by the government (even when they hurt German commercial interests), but he stressed that Russia's problems were not solely economic. He decried the "want of civilization and political institutions" in the country. He thought that Russia's political conditions could be "harmonized" with the requirements of industry

> by the introduction of efficient municipal and provincial constitutions, by the gradual limitation and final abolition of serfdom, [and] by the formation of an educated middle class and a free peasant class.[8]

List's program, which amounted to the formation of a modern Russian nation, appears in retrospect to have provided a very solid basis for building Russia's future. Indeed, there were people in Russia who did pay attention to List. For example, Count E. F. Kankrin, Nicholas I's Minister of Finance, was the first major government official who knew of List's teachings.[9]

Even before List, some Russians understood that their country was industrially underdeveloped in comparison with the West, and they thought that its industry required government support. The most prominent among them was Count S. N. Mordvinov (1754–1845). Mordvinov, according to Alec Nove, put forward "ideas of national economic development" long before List. He argued for protection of Russian industry against British competition. He wanted Russia to penetrate Asia economically, strongly supported education, and favored the abolition of serfdom, although he counseled caution in the process.[10]

Mordvinov's plans were not realized, however. Only in the late 1880s, when Sergei Iu. Witte became Minister of Finance, did a declared follower of List assume a powerful post in the government of Russia. In 1889, just as he began his tenure at the finance ministry, Witte published a short book under the title *National Economy and Friedrich List*. According to Theodore H. Von Laue, that work "showed the direction in which he and Russia were travelling." In List's work, Witte "found a basis for a Russian system of economic development; it remained the foundation for his thought and action thereafter."[11]

However, as Von Laue acknowledges, "there was one profound catch to the application of Friedrich List's theory to Russian conditions." List had recommended legal and political reforms (not only economic measures) and thought that constitutional government was a precondition of progress in industry and commerce. Witte, in his presentation of List, left out references to List's liberalism and ignored the social and political implications of List's program. Witte did not tell his Russian readers that List not only believed that industrialization would benefit them, but he also thought that "industrialization carried with it, in tiny seeds, the ideals of constitutional government and liberty." Witte wanted to isolate "the economic factors of industrial growth" from "the surrounding social and political tissues" in order "to succor autocracy."[12]

Thus Witte's program suffered from profound and insoluble contradictions. On the one hand, he "was determined to weld industrialism onto the existing system of autocracy."[13] On the other hand, his policy was not really acceptable to autocracy, for it required major structural transformations of the government machine. It also required a release of the subjects' initiative and, at the same time, their acceptance of the values that were promoted and of a discipline that was imposed by an industrializing state.[14] But as a spokesman for autocracy, Witte was not prepared to allow the Russian bourgeoisie (whose interests his program benefited) to act independently and thus to learn from its own mistakes. Witte thought that the Russian imperial government, because it was responsible for Russia's sovereignty, "could never become a mere mouthpiece of the bourgeoisie."[15] Witte's program was undemocratic and could not count on the support of the Russian population whose outlook remained premodern. The realization of his program therefore depended on the preservation of autocracy (or better still, Von Laue implies, on the establishment of a modern state machine committed to industrialization).[16]

A student of Russian intellectual history can easily categorize the Witte system as an Official Nationality form of economic nationalism. It is clear that it negated List's view that Russia was ready for a constitutional and liberal government and that society should be emancipated from the autocratic state.

In the 1890s, there finally emerged a liberal version of Russian Listianism that was more compatible with List's original ideas.[17] It was symptomatic of the Russian situation, however, that the most articulate and prominent spokesman for that Listian nationalism, Peter Struve, was a Marxist before he became a nationalist. In his *Critical Remarks on the Question of Russia's Economic Development* (1894), Struve sought to demonstrate, in the words of his biographer Richard Pipes, that "the transition to a money economy occurring in Russia is inevitable and progressive." Struve thus challenged "the anticapitalist spirit deeply rooted among the Russian left and right alike." While it was a Marxist tract, Struve's book was "first and foremost a treatise extolling the historic mission of capitalism, especially its role in organizing production in the most efficient manner known." Pipes points out that in this respect Struve's book resembled Friedrich List's *National System*. In fact, Struve frequently quoted List and described *The National System* as "the victory hymn of triumphant commodity production, proclaiming to all its historical-cultural power and its relentless advance." In Pipes' view, the same words "with equal justice can be applied to *Critical Remarks*."[18]

When Witte and Struve preached their Listian doctrines, the educated Russian public had been familiar with the ideas of Marx for several decades. Marxism was safely entrenched as the intelligentsia's mode of discourse; even Struve had begun as a Marxist. List's *National System* came out in Russian only in 1891, but *Capital* had appeared already in 1872. (This edition was the first translation of *Capital* anywhere. The original German edition was in 1867.) Marxism, not Listian nationalism, created the conceptual framework for the intelligentsia to debate Russia's condition and plan its future. The adoption of Marxist concepts did not guarantee a unanimity of views among those who used them, but it did contribute to reinforcing the traditional neglect of political and legal, especially constitutional, issues that was characteristic of both the left and right in Russia. Marx taught his Russian disciples that violent social revolution, not piecemeal political reform, offered the solution to Russia's problems.

With the moderate middle-class "nation-builders" silenced during the crucial decades of Russia's economic and social change, socialism presented the only effective alternative to tsarism. However, Russian socialism opposed not only tsarism. It also rejected a Western-style alternative to tsarism, the constitutional state and capitalist economy. In the West, too, the socialists were critics of the liberal state, but they accepted its historical role in their society's evolution. In Russia, socialists sought to prevent the establishment of a constitutional form of government and opted for transition to socialism directly from the then existing old social order. This transition to socialism would take place under the leadership of the revolutionary intelligentsia in a brief, violent upheaval. They believed that a strong dictatorial state was capable of determining whether Russia would go capitalist or socialist. If they, the intellectuals, seized power, socialism would win.[19]

Thus, unconsciously, but perhaps not paradoxically from an outsider's point of view, Russian socialists adopted the fundamental premise of the traditional Russian outlook regarding the creative role of the state— even though they wanted to have that state led by the intelligentsia, not by a hereditary monarchy and its bureaucracy.

As they reflected on the condition of Russia, the early Russian socialists, known as populists, asked if in order to attain socialism their country would have to pass through the same stage of capitalism, bourgeois rule, and industrialization that had taken place in Western Europe. They read the early Western socialist critiques of capitalism and concluded that because of its special characteristics, Russia would not become a Western-style capitalist country, even if the government or the bourgeoisie tried to make it one. Despite its backwardness, Russia would pass from "feudalism" and autocracy directly to socialism.

As Gavin Kitching has noted, the Western socialist critiques of capitalist industrialization based themselves on ethical and social arguments and stressed the human costs of the process.[20] However, unlike the Western "populist" critics who lived under capitalism, Russian populism opposed a system that did not yet exist in Russia. In order to justify their rejection of capitalism, and in spite of capitalism's evident superiority over the system prevailing in Russia, the populists argued that Russia had the preconditions for socialism—that is, a civilization superior to capitalism. Those preconditions, they said, were rooted in rural Russia's still surviving institutions and values. Thus the populist Alexander Herzen (1812–1870) argued that Russia's supposed "backwardness" was in fact its advantage, and that owing to it, Russia might avoid the stage of capitalism. Even when, in the 1880–1890s, capitalism made inroads in Russia's economy, socialists continued to oppose it. Such populists as V. P. Vorontsov and N. Danielson, for example, admitted the fact of capitalist industrialization in Russia, but insisted that it would fail to change Russia in the way that it had changed the West. According to Danielson, Russia could industrialize only by carrying out a socialist revolution. Vorontsov did not think that a socialist revolution was necessary, but believed that the tsarist state might enact major economic and legal reforms in Russia and thus prevent the country from becoming capitalist.[21]

By viewing capitalism as an external threat, the populists were led to the conclusion that capitalism made Russia, and not just the working people, one of its victims. Thus Russian socialists adopted an essentially nationalist stand, even though their "nation" comprised the "people" (*narod*) and excluded the "privileged" classes. Kitching points out that by advocating socialism in Russia, Herzen produced the concept (although not the term) of "proletarian nation." "All this added up," says Kitching, "to a muted but persistent nationalism."[22]

This nationalism became more explicit after Herzen. When Vorontsov expected that the tsarist state would nationalize industry in order to safeguard Russia's interests, he clearly assumed that the state would place the welfare of Russia as a country above the interests of any classes or groups. Vorontsov hoped that tsarist Russia "could embark on the socialist road" because "industrialization was an objective necessity for the Russian state and . . . could not be achieved by means of capitalist methods." In Andrzej Walicki's view, Vorontsov thought that a "non-capitalist industrialization under the auspices of the State" would liquidate Russia's backwardness, and that in this way, Russia would set an example for the workers in the West. Russia's mission was to realize equality and fraternity, but Vorontsov conceded that "she is not destined to fight for freedom."[23]

Danielson (who considered himself a Marxist and had been the translator of *Capital*) also believed that the state could play a major role in directing the course of economic development toward socialism. Such a view appeared quite absurd to the orthodox Marxist Georgi Plekhanov. In a letter to Engels, Plekhanov commented:

Let us suppose that the peasant commune is really our anchor of salvation. But who will carry out the reforms postulated by Nikolai-on [Danielson]? [The] Tsarist government? Pestilence is better than such reformers and their reforms! Socialism being introduced by Russian policemen—what a chimera![24]

As we see, a socialist like Danielson and the tsarist official Witte agreed that the state would carry out fundamental economic and social changes in Russia and that no corresponding political reforms restricting that state were necessary. Noting that the populists also thought it essential to maintain Russia's position in the world, Walicki characterizes Russian populism as "the first ideological reflection" of the situation of the "late-comers"— that is, "backward agrarian countries carrying out the process of modernization in conditions created by coexistence with highly industrialized nations." The populists believed that capitalism posed an external threat to the whole Russian nation. They wanted to prevent not only the "proletarianization" of the Russian peasants, but also "the proletarianization of Russia as a nation, . . . to prevent her from being exploited by more advanced countries."[25]

These concerns and attitudes were carried over into Leninism. Lenin considered himself an orthodox Marxist and believed that the laws of history discovered by Marx in *Capital* applied to Russia, too. In this, Lenin differed from the populists, who hoped that Russia would be able to escape capitalism. Lenin accepted the inevitability of capitalism and insisted that capitalist relations of production had firmly established themselves in Russia, particularly in agriculture. However, he thought that under Russian conditions it would be possible to speed up the transition from capitalism to socialism. The acceptance of historical inevitability, instead of making Russian Marxists like Lenin fatalistic or passive, inspired them intellectually and emotionally.[26]

Their intellectual independence was not stifled by any supranational Marxist program or leadership. *Capital* itself had implicitly granted autonomy to national Marxists when it recognized individual countries as distinct units of historical development. (Note Marx's warning to Germany: *"De te fabula narratur!"*) The Second International, which the Russians duly joined, was not a centralized organization and did not set policies for its constituent parties, and thus no international body could guide or monitor the socialists in their respective countries. After the death of Engels (1895), no Marxist thinker or leader exercised an unquestioned personal authority in the international movement.

Insofar as the question of revolution in Russia was concerned—Lenin's Marxist credentials have been questioned since his seizure of power in

1917—there were two traditions in Marx and Engels regarding this issue. At one time, "the classics" approved of a revolution that would launch Russia toward communism, provided that revolution was linked to a proletarian revolution in the West (according to Marx's 1882 preface to the Russian edition of *The Communist Manifesto*).[27] On other occasions, the classics approved of any revolutionary seizure of power in Russia (according to Engels' letter to Vera Zasulich, April 23, 1885). As Tibor Szamuely stresses, Engels accepted such revolutionary takeover unconditionally, and not because it would be somehow related to anything taking place elsewhere. Szamuely concludes that "it is difficult to sustain the view that the Bolshevik revolution of 1917 was carried out in breach of the principles of Marxism."[28]

It is another question whether Lenin's goals after the seizure of power and whether his methods in pursuing those goals were derived from (or compatible with) Marx. As Alfred G. Meyer has noted, Lenin was no exception among those Russians who, in their concern for Russia's conditions, compared their own country with the nations of the West. They all agreed that Russia was behind the West, but they did not agree about the ways in which its backwardness should be overcome. Some, including the Mensheviks, thought that Russia should duplicate the West's capitalist industrialization and liberal and democratic politics. For the Mensheviks and for "bourgeois" liberals and democrats, the October revolution accordingly signified an interruption of Russia's gradual and, they believed, basically successful, Western evolution.[29]

Lenin drew opposite conclusions from Russia's backward conditions. When the liberals cited 1789 as their goal for Russia, Lenin replied that 1789 had been good enough for the eighteenth century, but its repetition in a twentieth-century Russia would not be enough; only new and more radical means could overcome Russia's backwardness. Lenin concluded that countries like Russia could survive as independent entities only if they industrialized without "duplicating the superstructure of Western capitalist property relations." Although in the West modern industry had been built by capitalism, Lenin said, it did not follow that backward countries like Russia had to follow the same path. Besides, Lenin thought that capitalism was not "essential to the industrial way of life."[30]

The aim of the "proletarian" revolution as Lenin understood it was "economic construction for the sake of national emancipation." This was to be achieved through "political, ideological, in short, 'superstructural,' means." Nations not prepared for industrialization by their internal economic evolution could still adopt it as a political goal, and Lenin assigned the task of realizing this goal to the state. Leninism, Meyer states, may therefore be considered a "theory of the state." "Here all the supposed laws of Marxist historical materialism are overthrown. Political action determines economic development; consciousness is stronger than social relations. Causes turn into effects, and effects into causes."[31]

Lenin's concept of the party and its relation to the proletariat, a concept which he developed as early as the beginning of the century, anticipated his future treatment of the state. Lenin held the view that "the party" expresses and articulates the objective interests of the proletariat and that it does so because it has a stratum or cadre of professional revolutionaries. That element makes it possible for the party to carry out policies compatible with the laws of history and society. Lenin expressly did not include the industrial workers as a class among this element. Indeed, he stressed that the workers by themselves were capable of rising merely to a "trade-union" consciousness that accepted the capitalist system. Lenin went even further in 1917–1918, when he held that the Bolsheviks also "represented" the peasantry, in addition to being the proletariat's spokesmen and leaders. George Lichtheim has commented in this connection that Lenin should have admitted (but did not do so) that the party could play this role only if it "represented an independent force, namely the 'classless' intelligentsia, which alone could staff the cadres of a ruling political elite."[32]

Lenin's stand implied a departure from the Marxist treatment of class struggle. While classical Marxism, and moderate Marxian thinkers later on, "identified Marxism with the working-class movement" and insisted that "without labor there would be no Marxist movement," Leninism separated them. According to Meyer, Leninism's

> point of departure is not the conditions of the working class, but the conditions of society as a whole, which are unfailingly viewed critically. The Leninist endeavors to detect within society forces of disintegration and construction, and give them consciousness and organization, no matter what the forces are.[33]

Thus it would appear that in his concept of the party, Lenin imitated the tsarist doctrine of the state as a supraclass force. At the same time, his claim to provide a "scientific leadership" appears to have reflected a concern close to List's search for a national elite. More directly, Lenin's politics can be placed in the Russian revolutionary tradition, with its characteristic faith in a selfless and educated leadership that guides the masses toward a just society.

But Lenin's stand was not totally alien to that of Marx. Meyer points out that Lenin's position was compatible with the Marxist sociology of knowledge, with its thesis that "the underdog is always readier and better equipped to criticize and transcend evil and outdated features of a ruling group."[34]

However, Marx did not consider backward nations to be that kind of an "underdog"; he meant social classes. Because Lenin viewed the conflict between backward and advanced nations as central, he produced "an entirely new theory of development." That theory divided the existing societies into two types: the industrially advanced countries and those countries that were not advanced. Lenin thought that advanced countries would support the status quo, because they benefited from the backwardness of the others. The backward countries, on the other hand, would be "revisionist or rebellious in fact and in thought" and would "strive to attain the achievements of the leading societies and to improve on them."[35]

This Leninist typology, and Lenin's program as a whole, were obviously Listian, not Marxist. As Meyer points out, Lenin's dialectics of international relations were derived from Friedrich List and Alexander Hamilton.[36] Like List, Lenin thought that developing nations ought to learn from—but not copy—the leading industrial nations, but there was also a fundamental contrast between Lenin and List in their respective concepts of the nation. Lenin refused to accept the membership of the proletariat in the Russian nation. Indeed, his view of the party implied, to quote from the title of A. J. Polan's recent book on Lenin, "the end of politics." Lenin did not recognize political conflict as something normal: Those who disagreed with him and had to be suppressed were either bourgeois or agents of the bourgeoisie inside the working class.[37]

This approach carried certain implications not only for the Russian nation per se, but also for the non-Russian peoples of the Empire. When Lenin and the Bolsheviks refused to join the national society of Russia—that nascent "society" we discussed when speaking of its alienation from the state—they of course repudiated the Russian nationalism preached by Struve. Thus they were a national outsider and in this way resembled the "secession" of German social democracy from the German society and state before 1914. But they went further.

To express their hostility to bourgeois nationalism, the Social Democrats, including the Bolsheviks, adopted a political and territorial designation for their party (*rossiiskaia*) that was coextensive with the whole of the Russian Empire and that therefore implicitly retained its integrity. They did not, in other words, identify themselves ethnically (*russkaia*), which would have limited their party to "Russia proper."

One might argue, though, that Lenin recognized the right of all nations to separation. Indeed he did. However, he qualified his position in two ways. First, he insisted that "international" interests of the proletariat should take precedence over national rights and that those international interests would be better served in large states—such as Russia—than in small ones. Second, by making his party operate in the whole empire, Lenin denied to the non-Russian nationalities the right to form a socialist party that could actually exercise the right of a nation to independence without being accused of "bourgeois nationalism."

Before 1914, these issues were largely academic; by 1917, they had acquired practical importance. In certain parts of the Russian Empire, such as the Ukraine, Communists remained subordinate to the central party in Moscow even though their republics were formally sovereign states. When the Ukrainian Communists applied to join the Communist International as a party independent of Lenin's party, they were rebuffed.[38] Stalin stated with absolute frankness what had been implicit in Lenin: The right of self-determination ought to be understood "not as a right for the bourgeoisie, but for the working masses of the nation concerned" and therefore "must be subordinated to the principles of socialism." On these terms, any demand for secession could be condemned as bourgeois, and a minority that, within a nation, supported union with Russia could be recognized as a representative of the masses.[39]

As Lenin rejected long before the revolution a "national" approach to the question of nationalities in the Russian Empire, he had no choice in 1917 and thereafter but to fall back in practice on the only available alternative—that is, an "imperial" or "statist" definition of Russia. This "imperial" perspective produced a clash between the Bolsheviks and the national-liberation movements in the "borderlands," notably in Central Asia and the Caucasus, but it also enabled many *Russian* opponents of Lenin to recognize the Soviet state as a national force.

Indeed, literally weeks after the October coup, certain Russians concluded that 1917 was a major event in the *national* development of Russia. Admittedly, a majority of the liberal and democratic politicians who had been concerned with "nation-building" before 1914 continued to oppose communism on philosophical, ideological, and political grounds after 1917. Notable among them was Peter Struve. However, some figures in politics, academia, letters, and journalism, including members of Struve's own constitutional democratic party (the *Kadety*, as they were popularly called), drew different conclusions from Lenin's victory. Lenin's regime, they argued, served certain fundamental interests of Russia as a nation. Thus there emerged a current of opinion that came to be known as *smenovekhovstvo* (after the title of its publication, *Smena vekh*, that is, "Change of Landmarks") or "national bolshevism."

The National Bolsheviks called upon the Russian "patriots" to accept the Bolshevik takeover as a Russian *national* revolution. They recognized Lenin as the restorer of Russian "statehood" and as the only leader capable of bringing the non-Russian areas of the former Empire back under Russian control. It did not matter to them that this was being done in the name of proletarian solidarity of all nations and a world revolution, so long as all those peoples and areas were ruled from Moscow.[40]

The leading spokesman for this position, Nikolai V. Ustrialov (1890–1938), put it in this way: "The first and most important thing is . . . the restoration of Russia as a great and united state. All else will follow."[41] Ustrialov thought that the "pygmy states" created in the formerly Russian borderlands (this was his name for nations like Latvia, Armenia, and Georgia) would sooner or later be reincorporated in Russia. The Soviet government, he wrote, would seek to recover them in the name of world revolution; Russian patriots would "fight for the same thing—in the name of a great and united Russia." Despite the profound ideological difference between the Russian patriots and the Soviet regime, Ustrialov concluded, "their practical course is the same."[42]

Many years later, Stalin's biographer Isaac Deutscher agreed that indeed the actions of the Bolshevik regime in relation to the borderlands realized the program of Russian nationalists such as Ustrialov.

> The Leninists still believed that socialism demanded equality between nations; but they also felt that the reunion of most, if not all, of the Tsar's dominions under the Soviet flag served the interests of socialism. At this point the line of division between Leninism and Ustrialovism became blurred.[43]

The convergence of Leninist and Ustrialovist positions was a matter of more than intellectual interest. After October 1917, many thousands of tsarist officers, officials, managers, and other members of the old establishment served the Bolsheviks. (Deutscher speaks of half a million former tsarist officials entering Soviet government service after the civil war.) They did this because they thought like Ustrialov, not because they were converted to Marxism or Leninism. To quote Deutscher again:

> Nothing was more natural for the old civil servants than to promote, directly and indirectly, the idea of "great and indivisible" Russia in their new environment. In this they found justification before their own conservative consciences for their submission to the revolution. Acts like the invasion of Georgia and the reunion of other outlying provinces with Russia they acclaimed as *their* ideological triumph. The authentic Leninists, on the other hand, approved those acts as conquests for the revolution, not for Russia. In their eyes Russia herself was merely the first domain, the first rampart,

of international revolution: her interests were to be subordinated to the supernational strategy of militant socialism. For the time being, however, the boundaries of both Russia and victorious socialism were the same.[44]

A mass-scale entry of officials began immediately after October 1917. According to William G. Rosenberg and Moshe Lewin, from the very beginning the Bolsheviks undertook the work of "state-building." In that work, they received the support of many opponents of a liberal or democratic form of government for Russia—in other words, of men from the extreme right.[45]

Lewin notes that as early as 1918 "the industrial workers—the mainstay of the revolution in ideological terms—showed signs of faltering" and that the rescue came "from quite unexpected quarters": members of the tsarist bureaucracy, "considerable numbers of former tsarist officers," and "numerous former members of other parties." This leads Lewin to observe that "the ideological and political realities of the social basis of the revolution did not exactly match."

> The ideological mainstays at times wavered or gave in, ideological enemies or groups considered shaky often gave important political support to a system whose final aim and many current practices were not acceptable to them.[46]

The Bolshevik success in that "impressive state-building activity" was thus due also to their receiving "help from a cross section of [old] elites and non-elites."[47] Thus, clearly, the ultimate victory of the Bolshevik side in the civil war was the result of a "historic compromise" between the Leninists and Ustrialovists. That unspoken "compromise" accepted the preservation of old Russia's territorial unity as the supreme goal and was directed against the nationalists of Russian "borderlands," including non-Russian nationalists of socialist or communist persuasion.[48] The Bolsheviks' right-wing allies sacrificed their class interests for the national cause as they understood it.

After 1917, the Bolsheviks appreciated the contribution of their former class enemies. They encouraged Ustrialovist ideas within the Soviet state so that they could use tsarist and capitalist cadres for their own purposes. (Stalin was especially eager to promote such uses.) The Bolsheviks were also aware of the danger this alignment posed. Lenin and certain other Communists voiced misgivings on the ideological and political consequences of such saturation of the Soviet apparatus with alien elements. Nikolai Bukharin was also openly suspicious of Ustrialovism. Trotsky, however, not only condoned such views, but he himself resorted to "Red nationalist" arguments.[49]

The Bolsheviks were less suspicious of the engineering and managerial

cadres, which had their own ideological reasons for cooperating with the
Bolsheviks. The "technical intelligentsia" (we might also call them
"technocrats," at least in aspiration), were concerned with modernizing
Russia through scientific and industrial development. Intellectually, they
drew on Dmitrii I. Mendeleev, the great scientist of the prerevolutionary
era who had advanced grand plans for a scientific and technological transformation of Russia.[50] It is possible to view those "bourgeois" specialists
as Russian disciples of List, although their ideas and projects were directly
inspired by scientists like Mendeleev and public figures like Witte, rather
than by List himself.[51]

Some Communists distrusted those "technocrats," however. Mikhail
Pokrovsky, for example, saw them as potential aspirants to political power
and thus as challengers to the proletarian dictatorship. Even Bukharin saw
a potential danger coming from that milieu.[52] Stalin had no intention of
tolerating any institutional or intellectual autonomy of the intelligentsia,
and after 1928, when he was firmly in power, many of those ex-bourgeois
"*spetsy*" fell victim to terror.[53]

Before the Stalinist purges, however, the Bolsheviks maintained a
number of agencies in which Russian Listians could work for the Soviet
state while remaining loyal to their ideals. One such agency was the State
Planning Commission, or *Gosplan*. The *Gosplan* and similar agencies were
a locus for cooperation between technocrats and Communists, because the
ideas of both parties were recognized therein. According to E. H. Carr,
Lenin's approach to industrial management and planning closely resembled
the German industrial-military system of the First World War; in terms of
intellectual pedigree, his approach reflected List's rather than Marx's
ideals. Carr stresses that, historically, List had preceded Marx as "the
father of the theory of planning," just as Rathenau, the organizer of "the
first planned economy" (in Germany during World War I), preceded Lenin,
who drew on those German models in Soviet economic planning.[54]

Theodore H. Von Laue has reached a conclusion similar to that of
Carr. In his book on Witte, Von Laue declares that List's "views . . . are
basic for an understanding of Witte and even of Soviet industrialization.
. . . List fused nationalism and industrialization in an ironbound combination more fitting to the twentieth than to the nineteenth century."[55]

Even if List's ideas on industrialization influenced the Soviet regime,
the institutional structure that the Soviets erected bore a closer resemblance
to its tsarist predecessor than to what we may suppose List would have
preferred. The Bolsheviks, according to Galia Golan, chose "the 'etatist'
interpretation of socialism" and introduced accordingly institutions connected with the autocratic tsarist state.[56]

In this connection, one is reminded of Marx's comment on how, in the history of Western nations, successive social classes at certain stages of their respective histories, in the process of establishing their power, identified themselves with society as a whole. In the Russian experience, the failure of the "bourgeoisie" so to unify the society (as shown by its record before October 1917) was followed by an identical failure of "the proletariat": Instead of "constituting itself" as a "nation" (in the sense suggested by Marx in *The Communist Manifesto*), the proletariat—or the party speaking for it—constituted itself as the state or, to be more precise, was taken over by the state. The result of this process was best described by Joseph Stalin, one of the men most responsible for its having occurred, when he defined the Soviet state apparatus "in the profound meaning of the term":

> The Soviet state apparatus does not consist solely of the Soviets. The Soviet state apparatus, in the profound meaning of the term, consists of the Soviets, plus all the diverse non-party and Party organizations, which embrace millions, which unite the Soviets with the "rank and file," which *merge* the state apparatus with the vast masses and, step by step, destroy everything that serves as a barrier between the state apparatus and the people.[57]

While Marx wanted "society" to abolish "the state," Stalin abolished or dissolved society in the state. Stalin's interpretation acquired the status of a "classic" Marxist-Leninist formula on the subject, but the historian of Russia has no difficulty in discovering behind Stalin's "Soviet" or "Marxist" language the old tsarist idea that society has no existence except in the state. Stalin's position was also consistent with Lenin's denial to the working class of the right to be independent of the party. If the institutions of the Soviet state "greatly resemble" those of tsarist Russia, as Galia Golan asserts, this may be due to several causes. The first was because the Communist party identified itself with the working class, and then the state founded by the party submerged society in itself. The second was because the Soviet state ultimately identified itself with its tsarist predecessor geographically and historically—in other words, because it became a multinational empire itself. (The ex-tsarist generals and bureaucrats could feel that they got their part of the deal with the Bolsheviks.) And the third cause was due to the fact that modernizing nationalism, represented by politicians like the liberal Struve, proved to be very weak in Russia. It lost, it would seem, for two reasons. Most obviously, it lost because the educated middle-class society failed to establish its leadership over the popular masses that remained a world apart from it culturally and socially.

Communism and Nationalism

The other reason may be found in the relationship between the state and civil society.

In this regard, Hans Rogger's comparison of the Russian experience with that of the West is especially illuminating. Rogger argues that in the West "the transition from the dynastic to the national state, the dissolution of old loyalties and allegiances had, by the nineteenth century, made nationalism a major factor of political loyalty and social integration."[58] In the West, nationalism drew together members of different classes and religious groups and "reconciled society . . . to the state."

> As the state had become more national, nationalism had become more state-minded and had transformed itself from a romantic vision or a millennial hope into a harsher and hardier phenomenon. It had come not only to accept but to affirm the state.
> This did not happen in Russia. Modern Russia did not develop a nationalism that was capable of reconciling important segments of Russian society to one another and to the state.[59]

The tragedy of men like Struve lay in the fact that even middle-class liberals and conservatives remained alienated from the state. The gulf between them and the world of an autocracy that refused to compromise with "society" was never closed. The state, says Rogger, ought to have acted as "the instrument of modernization and reform." It also needed to respect "the civil and political liberties" it granted after 1905. (In Japan, tsarism's counterparts avoided the tsar's mistake and enacted political reforms to accompany the economic changes.) Such steps might have helped to diminish "society's" hostility to the state and might perhaps have brought them together. After 1905, however, nationalism "failed . . . to find a wide public resonance because of the stumbling block of the state and the diversity in interests and outlook between the various sectors of Russian society."[60]

In light of these comparisons, we can appreciate the following assessment of the political condition of Russia. Writing early in 1918—that is, almost immediately after the Bolshevik takeover—Thomas G. Masaryk, the distinguished expert in the theory and practice of nationalism, stated that "the Russians themselves have not developed to the point of national consciousness; the masses of the people have their religious viewpoint, and the *intelligentsia*, as far as it is socialistic, does not feel nationally." Masaryk attributed this political underdevelopment to the continuing impact of tsarism on the outlook of the Russian masses: "The tsarism of the Romanoffs was without culture and brutal. . . . The tsarism of the Russian masses and revolutionaries is worse; they rid themselves of the Tsar, but they have not yet ridden themselves of tsarism'' (that is, a view of politics under which the government is not legally limited by free institutions).[61]

This was Masaryk's way of saying what we have argued here: By 1917, Russian nationalism had failed to integrate the diverse groups and strata of Russia's population into a national community. Instead, the masses remained ''sub'' or ''prepolitical,'' while the intelligentsia—or at least its major segment—was ''socialistic'' and thus did not ''feel nationally.'' And finally, some of the educated elements that had served tsarism opted for Lenin against the democrats and liberals.

Nationalism's failure to win what Rogger calls ''a wide public resonance'' may be explained by its lateness in comparison with the emergence of socialism in Russia. It must be significant that in Russia the first political organization of the middle class was founded after such an organization of the proletariat had been in existence for some time.[62] In Germany, the ''nationalist manifesto'' of List and the formation of the bourgeoisie's first political organization had preceded *The Communist Manifesto*.

This observation brings us back to the Gerschenkron thesis on ideologies of industrialization (see Chapter 1). The linkage between nation-building and industrialization, noted by Gerschenkron in the sphere of ideology, produced three outcomes.

First, in France, a modern nation had already been formed (in the revolution of 1789 and during its aftermath) when industrialization began. Accordingly, when the strains of the Industrial Revolution made themselves felt, France's national identity had already been settled. Saint-Simon could take the existence of a French nation for granted when he considered the impact of industrialization and drew up his plans for European unity.

Second, in Germany, the making of a nation (the question of unification) coincided with the beginning of industrialization. Owing to figures like List, the problem of the Industrial Revolution became integrated within the German ''national question'' as one of the aspects of cultural, political, and economic unity and power.

Third, in Russia, the Industrial Revolution made itself felt *before* the processes of nation-building (along the lines first developed in the West) had been properly inaugurated. Marxism had taken hold before nationalism. In the end, the liberal nationalists failed both to work out a compromise with the premodern and non-national state and to win over for their cause the broader masses of the population. The masses had in the meantime been exposed to socialism, whether populist or Marxist-Leninist, or remained prepolitical. (Was it only a coincidence that both Japan and India, Western-style democracies as they now are, had progressed further than Russia in building a liberal civil society—and thus a modern nation—

*before* industrialization and *before* the socialist and nationalist revolutions unleashed in World War I?)

According to Adam Ulam, "the ideal society for revolutionary Marxism is the one that is 'arrested' in its response to industrialization."[63] Russia, as we have seen, was "arrested" not only economically and socially, but also politically, and thus proved receptive to Lenin's revolutionary Marxism. However, by becoming "Marxist," Russia did not escape the problems that had been the central concerns of List. Lenin translated List into a Marxist language and adapted him to the Russian political tradition, but, as we shall see, he did not transcend or abolish the Listian dialectic of a world of nations.

# 14

## Conclusion

The world in which Karl Marx and Friedrich List lived, which they interpreted, and which they worked to transform was destroyed at a historical juncture whose central event was the Russian Revolution of 1917.

The events of that period marked a turning point in the history of socialism, Marxism, and the international labor movement, and were equally important for Russia, Russian nationalism, and indeed for nationalism everywhere. It is therefore appropriate to close this examination of the ideas of Marx and List and of their impact by focusing on that period. Both Marxism and nationalism were transformed then, and so was their relation to one another. The ideas of Marx and List remained powerful—indeed, they gained in influence after 1917. But their respective doctrines lost their former intellectual and political unity and coherence. Marxism, or to be more precise, Marxism-Leninism, became a variant of nationalism.

Since this book's theme is Marx and List, certain other consequences of the Russian Revolution, momentous though they have been, are left out. (The break-up of the international socialist movement into communism and democratic socialism, or the rise of fascism in Italy and national socialism in Germany as a nationalist reaction to communism are some of the issues not examined in this volume.)

The revolutionary ideology of Marxism had already been formed in the 1840s, but it was only in 1917, that is, seventy years later, that a revolution aiming to establish the dictatorship of the proletariat as a step toward communism first took place. There had been outbreaks of labor unrest before, to be sure, and there was at least one major workers' insurrection, the Paris Commune of 1871, but none had professed Marxism as its guiding doctrine. The Bolsheviks thus seemed to have at last inaugurated an era of the proletarian revolution, a historical epoch in which Marx's theory would at last be "realized" in revolutionary practice, while the proletariat would "abolish itself" in the process of its self-liberation. Lenin and his comrades wanted not only to overthrow the rule of the bourgeoisie in existing states but, as the next step, proposed to abolish the state as such.

The communist revolution, said Lenin, Trotsky, and other Bolshevik leaders, was inevitably a worldwide process because the proletariat was by its very nature an international (and internationalist) force. The Russian Revolution was a product of that worldwide struggle between the proletariat and the bourgeoisie, they said, and it would survive in Russia only if the proletariat established itself in power in at least a few of the other major nations of Europe. Its victory would mark not only the defeat of capitalism but also the destruction of that pernicious bourgeois ideology, nationalism. Once again, just as in 1848–1849, the aims of communism were diametrically opposed to those of nationalism.

Lenin's revolution took place at a critical moment in the history of nationalism as well. It coincided with a new upsurge of nationalism that was released by the Great War and that aimed at the establishment or expansion of states. Even since 1848, nationalism had enjoyed a long series of successes, exemplified in the formation of new nation-states and in the ever-widening and deepening process of the "nationalization of the masses" within the already existing states. In 1914, at the onset of the Great War, nationalist politics reached a new stage. The belligerent nations were swept by a wave of chauvinist emotion to which even the workers proved to be susceptible. The Second International collapsed. And just as Lenin and the other revolutionary Marxists, in Russia and elsewhere, were calling for a new International that would at last make Marx's "Workers of All Lands, Unite!" a material force, nationalism stepped forward with its own alternative revolutionary program. Thomas Masaryk, Józef Piłsudski, and other nationalists issued a call for the transformation of the Great War of states into a revolutionary war for the liberation of nations.[1]

After 1914, Palacký's, and indirectly List's, disciple and successor, Masaryk, clashed with Marx's disciple and successor, Lenin. The intellectual confrontation of communism with nationalism that had taken place in the 1840s, with Marx and Engels on one side, and List and Palacký on the other, was thus replayed on the political stage in 1917–1918. The two "great waves" of the modern age, about which Friedrich Meinecke spoke in his *German Catastrophe*, crisscrossed over themselves once again, and out of their confrontation a new nationalism and a new Marxism emerged.

There is no need to recount in detail the events after 1917. Lenin's revolution did not become international. In some countries, such as Germany, Austria, and Hungary, the "bourgeoisie" proved to be stronger either on its own or because it received help from abroad. The concluding moments of the Great War and its aftermath witnessed the failure of socialism and communism in Central Europe. The socialists came to power in Vienna and Berlin, to be sure, and in Budapest a socialist government was rapidly succeeded by a Communist regime. But that regime was overthrown by Allied intervention before it could follow Lenin's example by assuming the role of defender of Hungary's territorial integrity. The contemporary Hungarian historian, Tibor Hajdu, notes that the leader of the Soviet Hungarian Republic, Bela Kun (and thus the exact counterpart to Soviet Russia's Lenin), "once in power found himself preaching war—in theory for World Revolution, but in practice for the parts of Hungary annexed by Czechoslovakia and Rumania." However, this decision to fight for historic Hungary's unity (when the Allies were supporting the cause of Czechoslovakia and Romania), says Hajdu, "gave Paris all too good an excuse to stamp out Hungarian Bolshevism."[2]

In Germany and Austria, the socialist ascendancy coincided with a war lost and with the refusal of the Allies to let the German nation become united in a single state. (The Union of German Austria with Germany was a "left" slogan in 1919, as was the incorporation of the Sudetenland in German Austria and/or a Greater Germany—exactly as they had been in 1848–1849.) But neither socialists nor Communists proved capable of uniting all German lands or of preventing the disintegration of Central and Eastern Europe into mutually antagonistic and highly nationalistic states. Instead, the heretofore stateless nations, including those Marx and Engels had called "nonhistorical," carried out their nationalist revolutions against Germany and Hungary and established their independent states. In this sense, too, 1918 appears in a direct causal connection with 1848.[3]

After the war, Masaryk published an account of his activities in a book titled *World Revolution*. What that revolution was about was made explicit in the title of the English-language edition of that book, *The Making of a State*.[4] Both titles proved to be prophetic about the subsequent history of the twentieth century, when a wave of anticolonial, nationalist revolutions would sweep Asia and Africa. All those revolutions, like Masaryk's earlier revolution, pursued one central goal: the making of a state. (Political science after World War II would say "nation-building.")

Having established themselves in power, the leaders of the new (or expanded older) Eastern and Central European states made the same discovery some Italians had made in the 1860s, after the unification: Political sovereignty did not prevent the new state from lagging behind the advanced nations, such as Germany, France, or Britain, in economic development. The new states adopted the program of economic nationalism with a strong emphasis on industrialization in order to deal with this problem. These new policies in planning and control restricted the political, social, and legal rights of citizens, especially those belonging to ethnic minorities. East European nationalisms were thus becoming "statist" (or "etatist")— although not to the degree reached by the "etatization" of communism in Russia under Lenin and Stalin.

As Arcadius Kahan notes, with the intensification of nationalism in the post–1918 period, "the link between nationalism and industrialization became much stronger":

> the commitment to industrialize gained in seriousness and strength because nationalism in the post-World War I period achieved a more durable fusion with radicalism than it had achieved previously. It is the infusion of radicalism that drives nationalism not only to the extreme of autarky vis-à-vis the outside world but also to the subordination of all group interests to the national interests, however defined.[5]

It was an economic nationalism of this new, more radical kind that dominated the outlook of the new states of Eastern Europe. The break-up of the Habsburg monarchy and the establishment of the successor states, Harry G. Johnson observes, had lent "a strongly nationalistic tone to discussions of economic policy and development problems in these countries." Those discussions were influenced by how the East Europeans perceived German economic policy and what they learned from their study of German economists. Furthermore, the leading participants in those discussions had studied in Germany.[6]

The Hungarian Marxist economic historian Ivan T. Berend has described this nationalism as an "ideology of retrograde revolt." However, Berend concedes that there was a " 'rationality' of irrationality" in that "revolt." This may be his way of admitting that all those countries (including Italy) had become aware of, and tried to do something about, their backwardness from a nationalist point of reference. Since their condition in the twentieth century resembled that of nineteenth-century Germany, they adopted ideologies, as Berend notes, akin to those of Fichte and List.[7]

According to Berend, this "revolt of the periphery" assumed various forms, not all of them necessarily fascist. The Turkish national movement after World War I, for example, developed a "theory of the 'Third World' type." Each of these movements, however, drew on the original German notion that opposed class conflict within the nation and placed the conflict in the sphere of relations between nations.[8]

Relations between nations, and not just classes, played a vital role in determining the outcome of the Bolshevik Revolution, as we noted (in Chapter 13). Virtually within weeks after October 1917, certain Russian opponents of communism perceived the Bolshevik takeover as a positive, desirable event from a national point of view, even though the Bolsheviks destroyed their former class position. The Bolsheviks, some enemies of communism concluded, would best be able to preserve the territorial unity of Russia against the separatism of its non-Russian nationalities. Their calculations proved to be basically sound. Only Finland and Poland managed to secede from Russia, despite the assistance "their" Communists received from the Red Army. (Latvia, Lithuania, and Estonia remained separate for twenty years.) But the Bolsheviks defeated the nationalists in the Ukraine, Georgia, Armenia, Russian Central Asia, and certain other borderlands of the Russian Empire.

Before long, it became clear that the Bolshevik revolution had failed to spread abroad and yet, despite its failure to do so, retained power in Russia. As this fact contradicted Marxist-Leninist assumptions, some Communists began to ask whether the revolution had any national, Russian historical roots besides being a product of a worldwide class conflict, which was the official Marxist-Leninist view. Where was 1917 in the *Russian* revolutionary calendar?

Lenin himself provided a basis for a "national" interpretation. In an article commemorating Herzen and written five years *before* the October coup, Lenin included the nobility among the successive classes in the history of the Russian Revolution.[9]

This inclusion raised certain potentially awkward questions regarding the national, as opposed to class, character of the Russian revolutionary movement. If nobles had been at one time revolutionary in a state that, according to Lenin, was ruled by the nobility, their revolutionary engagement must have been concerned with the welfare of Russia, not with that of their own class. After 1917, Lenin stated openly what had been implicit in his 1912 article: He referred to "Russia's national awakening" in the October revolution and spoke of Russia's "rise anew out of servitude to independence" under the Bolsheviks. At the same time, however, Lenin insisted that the revolution's "salvation" would come only "through the international revolution on which we have embarked." Thus while Alfred

G. Meyer is no doubt right when he says that Lenin assigned to Russia "a central place in the history of human progress,"[10] it is important to remember that Lenin treated Russia as one of a whole group of dependent nations. Lenin implied that once India, China, and other nations had also carried out their "October revolutions," all of them would form together with Russia some sort of international community of "underdog" nations. "In the last analysis," Lenin wrote in 1923, "the outcome of the struggle will be determined by the fact that Russia, India, China etc. account for the overwhelming majority of the population of the globe." Only owing to this would "the complete victory of socialism" be "fully and absolutely assured" in Russia.[11] (However, certain writers question Lenin's commitment to international revolution. Karl Dietrich Bracher, for example, argues that Lenin, "as a realist in power politics, had opposed the ideology of world revolution ever since 1917–18 by concentrating on safeguarding his Russian dictatorship, as socialism in one country.")[12]

Lenin's successor as leader of both the Soviet state and the international communist movement, Stalin, went further than Lenin had ever gone in "Russifying" Soviet communism. Already in 1922–1923, Stalin began to find some positive qualities in the tsarist multinational state,[13] and by 1931 he was presenting tsarist Russia as a perennial victim of external aggression (from the West and the East alike). Russia, he said, had been ceaselessly "beaten by all—for her backwardness. For military backwardness, for cultural backwardness, for political backwardness, for industrial backwardness, for agricultural backwardness." Stalin also drew a topical conclusion: "We are fifty or a hundred years behind the advanced countries. We must make good this lag in ten years. Either we do it or they crush us."[14]

Of course, Stalin's depiction of Russia's plight bore little resemblance to historical reality and contradicted the stand of Marx and Lenin. In Stalin's version, tsarism—depicted by pre-1917 Marxists as a cruel exploiter of the working masses of the Russian Empire and as an oppressor of the non-Russian peoples at home and abroad—disappeared. Instead, "Russia," a classless "Russia," emerged at the center of the scene, and Stalin fully identified the Soviet state with its predecessor.

Thus, crudely in Stalin, more subtly in Lenin, Marxism-Leninism was openly reformulated as a doctrine of national liberation. From this perspective, the revolution of 1917 was treated as the emancipation of Russia from dependence on the Western powers. The Soviet regime's greatest domestic achievement became industrialization, not a new social and political order. Marxism won in Russia, it would seem, but it did so only by becoming a nationalism. In that doctrine, Marx had to share room with List.

This new nationalism was an amalgam of three rather diverse components: Marxism, Listianism, and an indigenous Russian political tradition that recognized, as we saw, the superiority of the state over society and attributed to the state a creative role in all areas of human endeavor.

It was an uneasy, insincere nationalism. Not only did the Russian nation lose its political rights, but the official ideology refused to acknowledge that the political entity the Bolsheviks were ruling was Russia, a country dominated by the Russians. In 1922, the Soviet republics of Russia, the Ukraine, Belorussia, and the Caucasus (Georgia, Armenia, Azerbaidjan), heretofore formally independent, established a new entity, the Union of Soviet Socialist Republics. Within it, Russia was to be the formal equal of the other republics. The organization of the Soviet Union was a tribute both communism and the Russian center paid to the nationalism of those who had failed to win independence in their national revolutions. It legitimized the inclusion of non-Russian areas under Moscow's government in an era of national self-determination.

But the new designation of the state also declared a continuing allegiance to proletarian internationalism: By proclaiming the Soviet state as a multinational structure of a new type, the Communists created a model to be presented all over the world for a future organization of the globe under socialism. In due course, the communist line asserted, other peoples would join the USSR as its constituent republics, or they would form some other ties with the USSR. Before this happened, workers of all lands already had in the USSR their "real fatherland," as distinct from their bourgeois-ruled countries. The Communists thus claimed to have resolved what appeared to be a paradoxical situation—or a "dialectical contradiction"—when a dictatorship of the proletariat (i.e., of a class that by its very nature was international) was confined to the boundaries of a nation-state that was, to boot, the legal heir of the Empire. (This was so, at least in the eyes of international law, to which the Soviets had to pay lip service.) Not so, the Communists replied: The USSR *was* a world state in the making, even if temporarily it happened to be confined to a fraction of the globe.

The Communist International served a more practical function, but it too had an ideological significance. Founded in 1919, the Communist or Third International was, according to its rules, a world workers' party. All the national parties, including the Russian, were merely territorial, regional branches of the International, to which they were formally subordinated. The task of the International was to work for a revolution worldwide, and its existence formally acknowledged the perception of the proletariat as a transnational force, just as the proletariat's chief enemy, capitalism, was perceived as a worldwide phenomenon.

Inevitably, a dialectical tension arose between the Soviet state and party on the one hand and the International on the other. It surprised few that the former emerged victorious and that the International became the Soviet government's instrument.

If there had ever been a moment when the International might conceivably have transcended its role as a dependent of the Soviet government and become instead a genuinely international body, that moment occurred in the final stage of the Second World War. It was becoming increasingly evident that East European Communists would be installed in power by the Red Army. Might not the International have acquired a life of its own if it had included other ruling parties besides the Soviets? Stalin dissolved the International in 1943. He clearly preferred to maintain direct, bilateral relations with East European parties and regimes, and he also vetoed a plan put forward by East European Communists after the war for a confederation of communist-ruled states of Yugoslavia, Bulgaria, Albania, and Romania. Stalin professed the principle of "national sovereignty" for all states—and practiced Great-Power domination over weaker nations.

This practice was challenged in 1948: Yugoslavia made it clear to Stalin that it would no longer obey his orders nor tolerate his interference in its domestic affairs. Stalin accused Tito, Yugoslavia's leader (and in many ways Stalin's double) of nationalism and a betrayal of Marxism-Leninism. Tito responded with his version of what Marx and Lenin "really meant." Lenin had shown that it was possible to win and keep power and build socialism in one country, said Tito. The Yugoslavs followed Lenin's example by building socialism in *another* country. What was nationalistic about their doing exactly what Lenin had done (and Stalin was still doing)? To be sure, one day all socialist states would unite. But that would happen in a distant future and then only by their free accord. In the meantime, all of them were sovereign and *equal*.[15]

What would become known as "national communism" was thus formally born. In reality, it had been born much earlier, when the Russian Communists had identified themselves with the interests of Russia. Properly speaking, Lenin had been the first National Communist, but this had not been clear until Tito had become the second. The 1948 conflict between Moscow and Belgrade, therefore, was not a clash of an international Marxism or communism with nationalism; it was a conflict between two states, two communist nationalisms in power, one big and one small.

The Russian Revolution did not ignite a proletarian insurrection in the advanced countries of the West, nor did it establish a new international order, as the story of Soviet-Yugoslav, Soviet-Chinese, Chinese-Vietnamese, Vietnamese-Laotian, and other intercommunist relations shows.

To Benedict Anderson, the Soviet Union stands out, along with the United Kingdom, as an entity that refuses to place nationality in its name, that is, to define itself clearly as a nation-state. This, says Anderson, may suggest that the USSR is "the legatee of the prenational dynastic states" of the nineteeenth century rather than the "the precursor of a twenty-first century internationalist order."[16] Domestically, it has failed to resolve those issues that had occupied Russian public opinion before 1917: the relations between state and society, and the relations of the Russians to the non-Russians.

The Soviet Union's real ideological impact has been to provide an example to the dependent peoples of Asia and Africa, and possibly also to underdeveloped nations of Latin America, of how a national liberation occurs as social revolution.

The contemporary ideology of national liberation, according to S. Neil MacFarlane, differs from older forms of nationalism in that national liberation includes social transformation of an anticapitalist kind. In that doctrine, now current in the Third World, says MacFarlane, "social revolution is an *integral* part of the very concept of national liberation." MacFarlane attributes this stand (correctly in my view) to Marxist-Leninist influence. He also notes that the doctrine of national liberation is characterized by a "statist approach to the problems of economic, social and cultural development" and consequently leads to concentration of power. MacFarlane recognizes that this Third World ideology shares List's belief in national economic independence, but he thinks it is anti-Listian in its opposition to capitalism. He also acknowledges that the national liberation doctrine is "distinct from Marxism in its fundamental commitment to national identity. One might say that the national liberation revolution is national not only in form but also in essence."[17]

While national liberation's commitment to national independence is clearly contrary to Marx's stand, it is less obvious that the anticapitalist bias of the doctrine is anti-Listian in all respects. True, List favored capitalism or, better still, took capitalism for granted; he expected that within the national state free trade would be the rule. But List also allowed that in certain less developed countries the political factor might exercise stronger control over the economic sphere. In some situations, he said, absolutist or dictatorial government might be the only force capable of inaugurating the necessary measures for a country's economic modernization. List stood for nation, not the bourgeoisie. We are therefore inclined to agree with Theodore H. Von Laue when he characterizes List as the "great-grandfather of all present [i.e., post-colonial] industrial planners throughout the world" and includes among List's disciples Sukarno, Nkrumah, and even Mao. (Von Laue suggests that those national leaders received their Listian message via tsarist and Soviet intermediaries.)[18]

We thus arrive at a conclusion that parallels and completes our initial argument in this book: Nationalism stubbornly refuses to be pigeonholed in the capitalism-or-communism compartment.

On the other hand, the nationalization of communism is a fact. Successful communist revolutions, Benedict Anderson says, have defined themselves in "national terms" and are grounded "in a territorial and social space inherited from the prerevolutionary past."[19] National communism, according to Peter Zwick, has established itself as "the dominant mode of the Marxist movements."[20] All Marxist movement and states, Eric Hobsbawm concurs, have become "national not only in form but in substance, i.e., nationalist."[21]

This unquestionably signifies a break with a central idea of Marx and classical Marxism. However, national communism or communist nationalism has not become procapitalist by virtue of its breaking with internationalism. As Alfred G. Meyer puts it, in the post–1945 era "ethnicity— the tribal, racial, religious, cultural, traditional, irrational, and disruptive— has gained in strength and influence all over the globe." But it is "a principle of social organization (or production relations) fundamentally at odds with global production processes." Nationalism (Meyer speaks of "ethnicity" where we use "nationalism") "inspires and mobilizes the nations of the world to rebel against the universal, all-pervasive dominance of global capitalism." Meyer recognizes that political developments in the newly independent states have stood on their head certain axioms of theory and history as previously known. For example, the national state now appears to have "taken over the role and function which the property-owning entrepreneur played within the Marxist model of capitalism." The revolutions that were to abolish the contradictions of capitalism have reproduced them, "though in novel form."[22]

The conclusion reached by George Lichtheim in the early 1970s is close to these 1981 comments of Meyer. In today's Third World, according to Lichtheim,

> the burden of revolution is cast upon the peasantries of Asia, Africa, and Latin America, who are to take up where the industrial working class—now supposedly integrated into the system—left off. Thus nationalism is identified with socialism, the peasantry with the proletariat, anti-imperialism with anti-

capitalism, until all the distinctions painfully elaborated in Marxist literature for a century are cast overboard in favor of a simple dichotomy: Western imperialism versus the starving masses of the Third World.[23]

In such a situation, it is best to accept as fact that the original doctrines of communism and nationalism, of Marx and List, no longer function in contemporary politics.

The same may be said about academic research and ideological discourse. Current writing on "dependency" and "underdevelopment," for example, is generally considered to be part of the Marxist intellectual orientation. In fact, "dependency theorists," who have included such well-known figures as Paul Baran, Andre Gunder Frank, Samir Amin, Arghiri Emmanuel, and others, while they generally identify themselves with the Marxist traditions, may be more correctly viewed as "the heirs of Flerovsky, Vorontsov, [and] Danielson," i.e., of Russian populists. Gavin Kitching, who makes this point, states that those contemporary thinkers have abandoned the position of Marx and the later classical Marxist writing that "never broke with Marx's conviction of the long-term 'progressiveness' of imperialism." In modern dependency theories, Kitching detects certain "close parallels to Russian populist positions." He speaks about "pessimism" regarding the prospects of native capitalism, about "hostility to free trade and a certainty that it leads to national exploitation," and about support for "national" industrialization under state leadership, industrialization that takes place either in socialist or capitalist form.[24]

The intellectual ties of these views to Russian populism are easy to see, but they are linked to List as well.

According to Harry G. Johnson, the ideas of economic nationalism, originally formulated in Germany and then developed further in Central and Eastern Europe, entered Anglo-Saxon economic literature after the emigration to Britain or America of such figures as K. Mandelbaum, Nicholas Kaldor, Paul Rosenstein-Rodan, and Thomas Balogh. Johnson illustrates his thesis with the teachings of Balogh:

> Balogh's intellectual history and writings are particularly interesting in this respect: a fairly simple conceptual framework, translating into economic language the power politics of the 1930s relationship between Hungary and Germany, is turned successively to the war and post-war relationship of the United Kingdom (and Europe in general) to the United Sattes, then (briefly) to the rivalry between Britain and Germany in post-war Europe, and subsequently to the relationship between the less developed and the advanced countries.[25]

Those Central European economists like Balogh implanted in the Western world "the habit of thinking in nationalist rather than cosmopolitan terms,'' and they established ''the fictional concept of a nation as an economic entity endowed with consistent objectives and a consensus in favor of realizing them by national economic policy.'' Johnson considers these economists specifically responsible ''for the strong emphasis on the need for industrialization, and the potency of protectionist policies as a means of achieving it.''[26] He argues that

> in spite of the dominance in the mainstream of economic thought of the liberal and cosmopolitan ideas of the English classical economists, the nationalist and interventionist ideas of the German economist Friedrich List have been transmitted indirectly through Germany's Central European emulators to become the dominant ideas of Anglo-Saxon economics on questions relating to the promotion of economic development in the new nations.[27]

The original concern of these writers had been to design ''policies for developing the Balkan states on the German model,'' but they presented their ideas as ''universals'' after their move to the West. Later on, according to Johnson, those ideas ''proved equally congenial to the psychological attitudes of the new nations in their relations with the developed countries and in their conception of their development problems.''[28]

Whether or not Johnson's argument is historically correct—namely, that there was an ''infiltration of ideas from Central Europe into the Anglo-Saxon tradition,''[29] which in turn influenced Third World thinking—a link definitely exists between the contemporary ''Marxist'' thought on the problems of development and underdevelopment and the classical Listian nationalism. Some contemporary figures may be unaware of the fact that they hold a Listian view and indeed may imagine that theirs is a Marxist perspective on the problems of underdeveloped countries. But in actuality, they have at least as much in common with the German nationalist List as with the author of *The Communist Manifesto*. Giorgio Mori, in his introduction to the Italian edition of *The National System*, points out some similarities and parallels in the ideas of writers like Arghiri Emmanuel and those of List. Mori asks ''how is it possible,'' when speaking of intellectual precursors of current thought, ''not to add, at least to add, to the name of the founder of scientific socialism that of his contemporary?''[30]

Economists have tried to determine whether those nationalist approaches to industrialization, including the fascist variant, are the most rational from the economic point of view.[31] Yet one may doubt whether it is at all possible to evaluate such questions in academic terms. It appears the nationalists simply believe that political considerations should override economic criteria when conflict arises between the two. Their outlook may be summarized in several simple propositions. First, they take a territorially bound state, not the world, as their basic geographic and political unit of reference. Second, they treat the state as a nation-state that needs to be built economically, politically, and culturally, not as one that already exists and is fully developed. Third, they assign a leading role in nation-building to the intelligentsia, that social stratum which claims to rise above sectional economic or occupational interests. (List never developed this theme of leadership, but some of the current ideas on national leadership are implicit in List's argument.) Fourth, and very important, dependency theories see the world as consisting of three kinds of interrelated nations: developed, developing, and underdeveloped. This is List's own classification, although his precise words were different.

This perspective is different from the Marxist or Marxist-Leninist theories of capitalism in the era of imperialism as well as from the related concepts of uneven development of capitalism, the relations between the metropole and the colonies, and so on. All those Marxist views, even when they recognized the anti-imperialist direction of nationalism in colonial countries, also assumed that this nationalism would be an ally of the proletarian revolution and would in fact form part of a unified revolutionary force. (Lenin's 1923 text cited earlier in this chapter illustrated this conception of nationalism as an ally of, and a subordinate force to, an international communist revolutionary movement.)

In reality, however, nationalism has established itself—in the *Third World*—as a third force that is sometimes an ally, sometimes a rival, of communism and capitalism alike. Its refusal to be subsumed under the East-West dichotomy is expressed politically in the idea of "nonalignment"—i.e., the belief that it is possible to avoid the choice between East and West. Third World thinking treats the North-South division of the globe as central—which is pure List, of course. Some Marxists may be openly adopting a Listian perspective on global relations. Andre Gunder Frank, for example, in a contribution to the recently published volume *Socialism on the Threshold of the Twenty-first Century*, suggests that "much of the East-West conflict, especially between Washington and Moscow, is a smokescreen for North-South conflicts."[32]

While it is indeed true that the Third World today is Listian in its outlook and that even Marxism has become "Listianized," it would be inaccurate to restrict this phenomenon to Asia, Africa, and Latin America. We have already spoken about national communism in Yugoslavia and in the Soviet Union itself. We might add a note—rather ironic—about List's and Marx's own homeland. The German Democratic Republic, ruled by Marx's followers, honors List as one of Germany's illustrious and progressive figures. The German Academy of Sciences (East Berlin) recently published a new edition of his *National System of Political Economy* (of which there have been several earlier editions in East Germany since 1945). The East Germans of course published Marx's critique of List soon after its Russian translation appeared in Moscow in 1971. But they also noted that Marx's criticism had been "one-sided" because List's program for Germany contained progressive elements, too.[33]

The East German editors did not specifically mention the idea of German unity as one of those progressive elements in List's program. But one may wonder about the timing of Moscow's choice, in 1971, to publish Marx's attack on German nationalism. For it so happens that after the 1970 opening of a new phase in the relations between West and East Germany, talk was revived about German reunification. The publication of the 1845 Marxian text, with its emphatic denial that the bourgeoisie and the proletariat of Germany had anything whatsoever in common, may have been a warning to the East German comrades: As Marx said, a single German nation embracing the proletariat and the capitalists is a bourgeois idea.

Whether this Kremlinological guess has merit or not, it is clear that the world of our time is ruled not by the state of reason but by the reason of state (*raison d'état*). Marx had believed that the "Cunning of Reason" would ultimately prevail against men's schemes. But it is possible that in the confrontation of communism with nationalism, the Cunning of Reason—*die List der Vernunft*—has been overcome by *die Vernunft des List*— "the reason of List."[34] Or that, alternatively, reason itself has chosen to play a trick on Marxism by turning that ideology of global unification into an instrument for national self-assertion against one single model of social, political, and cultural development. There is no country today about which a latter-day Marx would confidently say what he had said in 1867 about England: "*De te fabula narratur!*" Nationalism, whether Listian or Marxist, represents a revolt against historical inevitability espoused by classical Marxism. It also celebrates cultural and linguistic diversity as a normal and desirable condition of mankind—instead of deploring it as a form of alienation, which is what Marx did.

But if modern nationalism has so obviously won, its triumph has been problematic and "ironic." As Meyer noted, the governments of the newly liberated nations have inherited, as it were, the exploitative function of the former ruling power. Von Laue has observed that the nationalist plans, the Listian and Leninist "schemes of industrialization," have "turned sour."[35]

In their pursuit of national independence and power, nationalist leaders have apparently forgotten what their spiritual great-grandfather List had considered to be an essential prerequisite of true progress: freedom. It was freedom, intellectual and political, that List stressed in his program for Germany. He recognized limitations on freedom in certain particularly backward and therefore difficult situations, but even these he considered only temporary. Bertrand Russell spoke of freedom and organization as among the world's central problems created by the French Revolution and modern industry. When the contemporary national liberation regimes or more conventional Marxist-Leninist ones find it so difficult (if not impossible) to generate scientific, technological, and industrial progress, their excessive preoccupation with organization and their corresponding neglect of freedom may be to blame.

Modern nationalists also ignore or underestimate another precondition of progress that List had recognized: an openness to the outside world. That national isolation prevents intellectual and material progress had been clear to Herder as early as 1772.

There is also a "Marxist" reason for the current problems of Marxist-Leninist or national liberation regimes. Marx and the Marxists believed that the abolition of private property in the means of production would by itself create the preconditions for (indeed, provide a stimulus to) an advance in productivity based on scientific progress. But is nationalization a panacea? Does science depend on property relations or on economic conditions in general?

Though formulated over fifty years ago, Russell's criticism of Marx's view of history may well identify a source of current Marxist-Leninist and nationalist difficulties. Russell wrote:

> Much the most necessary correction in Marx's theory is as to the causes of changes in methods of production. Methods of production appear in Marx as prime causes, and the reasons for which they change from time to time are left completely unexplained. As a matter of fact, methods of production change, in the main, owing to intellectual causes, owing, that is to say, to scientific discoveries and inventions. Marx thinks that discoveries and inventions are made when the economic situation calls for them. This, however, is a quite unhistorical view. Why was there practically no experimental science from the time of Archimedes to the time of Leonardo? For six centuries after Archimedes the economic conditions were such as should have made scientific work easy. It was the growth of science after the Renaissance that led to modern industry. This intellectual causation of economic processes is not adequately recognized by Marx.[36]

However, Marx's failure to recognize "intellectual causation of economic processes" was consistent with his view of "human beings as above all tool-making and [tool-] using animals" (to quote Anthony Giddens' summary of Marx's conception of human nature). While Marx treated this quality as "the single most important criterion distinguishing the 'species being' of humanity from that of animals," Giddens prefers Lewis Mumford's view of man as "a mind-making, self-mastering, and self-designing animal."[37] List's view of human nature was of course identical with that of Mumford and Giddens. Accordingly, List regarded intellectual causation of economic processes as a cornerstone of his conception of history and of his program for national development. His position in this regard was expressed in the view that "productive powers" (or "forces") were much more important for a nation's progress than "material wealth."

The contemporary Marxist-Leninists and national liberation ideologues have thus taken over from Marxism a belief in industrialization, but they have rejected Marx's cosmopolitanism and his commitment to the liberation of the human being. National independence, national character, and national self-expression are, in their outlook, a legacy of classical nationalism, but their outlook does not also contain the earlier nationalists' belief that nationality is ultimately a step toward humanity.

While we recognize the historical impact and present power of Marxism and nationalism, we note that the world has fundamentally changed in recent decades under the impact of science (and especially its military applications). Science is international: The scientists, more than any other group—certainly more than industrial factory workers—satisfy Marx's requirements for "world-historical individuals." For that matter, the current problems that science has created for mankind are "world-historical" as well. That nationality and class are recognized now as essential components of individual identity and political legitimacy is a proof of how profoundly our modern outlook has been shaped by the ideologies of nationalism and Marxism. Without denying what these two world views have contributed, it is now necessary to affirm as fundamental values the rights of the individual and humanity's community of fate.

# Notes

## Chapter 1

1. "Karl Marks o knige F. Lista 'Natsional'naia sistema politicheskoi ekonomii,' " *Voprosy istorii KPSS*, no. 12 (1971):3–27. The original German version appeared as K. Marx, "Über Friedrich Lists Buch 'Das nationale System der politischen Ökonomie,'" *Beiträge zur Geschichte der Arbeiterbewegung*, no. 3 (1972). It was reprinted as an appendix in Friedrich List, *Das nationale System der politischen Ökonomie*, ed. Günter Fabiunke (Berlin: Akademie-Verlag, 1982), pp. 441–477. The English translation, Karl Marx, "Draft of an Article on Friedrich List's Book *Das nationale System der politischen Ökonomie*," is in Karl Marx and Frederick Engels, *Collected Works*, vol. 4 (New York: International Publishers, 1975), pp. 265–293. It will be cited here as the "List Critique."

2. Gavin Kitching, "Nationalism: The Instrumental Passion," *Capital and Class*, no. 25 (Spring 1985):115.

3. Karl Marx and Frederick Engels, *Collected Works*, vol. 38, p. 28. (See also pp. 11 and 79). Emphasis in the original.

4. Frederick Engels, "Speeches at Elberfeld," *Collected Works*, vol. 4, p. 256. (See pp. 258–259 for specific references to List.) Emphasis in the original. Material from this volume, as well as from volumes 6 and 8 of Marx and Engels' *Collected Works* (New York: International Publishers), is quoted by permission of the publisher.

5. "Speeches at Elberfeld," pp. 261–262. Emphasis in the original.

6. "Speeches at Elberfeld," p. 263.

7. George Lichtheim, *Marxism: An Historical and Critical Study* (New York: Praeger, 1962), pp. xiii, 24–25.

8. Lichtheim, *Marxism*, pp. xiv–xv, xvii–xviii.

9. The linkage between the two revolutions—the idea of a "dual revolution"—provides the organizing principle of E. J. Hobsbawm's *The Age of Revolution 1789–1848* (New York: New American Library, 1962.

10. Trygve R. Tholfsen, *Ideology and Revolution in Modern Europe: An Essay on the Role of Ideas in History* (New York: Columbia University Press, 1984), p. 76.

11. J. L. Talmon, "The Age of Revolution," *Encounter* 21 (September 1963):15, quoted in Trygve R. Tholfsen, *Ideology and Revolution*, p. 76.

12. François Furet, *Interpreting the French Revolution* (Cambridge: Cambridge University Press, 1971), pp. 46 and 23, as quoted by Tholfsen, *Ideology and Revolution*, p. 35.

13. Furet, *Interpreting the French Revolution*, p. 25, quoted by Tholfsen, *Ideology and Revolution*, p. 36.

14. The following passage in Tholfsen, in which he further cites Furet, is important enough to justify extensive quotation, if only in a footnote:

> "As Marx realized in his early writings, the Revolution was the very incarnation of the *illusion of politics*: It transformed mere experience into conscious acts. It inaugurated a world that attributes every social change to known, classified and living forces." The classic form of revolutionary consciousness, expressed in Jacobinism, was founded "on immanence in history, on the realization of values in and by political action, so that those values were at stake in every conflict, were embodied by the actors, and were as discoverable and knowable as truth itself."

(Tholfsen, *Ideology and Revolution*, p. 36, quoting Furet, *Interpreting the French Revolution*, pp. 25 and 29.)

15. Tholfsen, *Ideology and Revolution*, pp. 36–37.

16. Carlton, J. H. Hayes, *The Historical Evolution of Modern Nationalism* (New York: Macmillan, 1950), p. 237.

17. Hayes, *The Historical Evolution*, pp. 232–233.

18. Hayes, *The Historical Evolution*, p. 249.

19. Hayes, *The Historical Evolution*, p. 262.

20. Bertrand Russell, *Freedom versus Organization, 1814–1914* (London: George Allen and Unwin, 1949 [first ed. 1934]), p. 8.

21. Alexander Gerschenkron, "Economic Backwardness in Historical Perspective," in a collection of essays titled *Economic Backwardness in Historical Perspective* (Cambridge, MA: Harvard University Press, 1966, reprinted 1979), p. 24.

22. Gerschenkron, "Economic Backwardness," p. 25.

23. David Blackbourn and Geoff Eley, *The Peculiarities of German History: Bourgeois Society and Politics in Nineteenth-Century Germany* (Oxford and New York: Oxford University Press, 1984).

24. This is the point Eley rightly stresses in Blackbourn and Eley, *The Peculiarities of German History*, p. 86.

25. Alfred Meusel, *List und Marx. Eine vergleichende Betrachtung* (Jena: Gustav Fischer, 1928).

26. Friedrich Lenz, *Friedrich List, die "Vulgärökonomie" und Karl Marx* (Jena: Gustav Fischer, 1930).

27. Karl Löwith, *From Hegel to Nietzsche: The Revolution in Nineteenth-Century Thought*, tr. David E. Green (Garden City, NY: Anchor Books, 1967; original Swiss edition published in 1941), p. 133.

28. Eduard Heimann, *History of Economic Doctrines. An Introduction to Economic Theory* (New York: Oxford University Press, 1964), pp. 130–131.

29. Heimann, *History of Economic Doctrines*, p. 131.

30. Hans Gehrig, *Friedrich List, Wegbereiter einer neuen Wirtschaft* (Berlin: Erich Schmidt, 1966), p. 19.

31. Franz Schnabel, *Deutsche Geschichte im neunzehnten Jahrhundert*, vol. 3, *Erfahrungswissenschaften und Technik* (Freiburg: Verlag Herder, 1954), p. 368.

32. Edgar Salin, "Ein Nachwort zur List-Ausgabe als Vorwort für künftige List-Leser," *Mitteilungen der Friedrich-List Gesellschaft* 3, no. 11/12 (December 31, 1962):347.

33. Friedrich Meinecke, *The German Catastrophe: Reflections and Recollections*, trans. Sidney B. Fay (Boston: Beacon Press, 1963), p. 3.

34. Meinecke, *The German Catastrophe*, p. 5.

35. Meinecke, *The German Catastrophe*, p. 3.

36. Salo Wittmayer Baron, *Modern Nationalism and Religion* (New York: Meridian Books; Philadelphia: The Jewish Publication Society of America, 1960), p. 1.

## Chapter 2

1. Frederick Engels, "Preface," in Karl Marx and Frederick Engels, *Manifesto of the Communist Party*, ed. and annotated by Friedrich Engels (New York: International Publishers, 1948; reprinted 1966), p. 6. This edition will be cited here and in other chapters, especially Chapter 5, as *The Communist Manifesto*. Engels added:

> The proposition, which, in my opinion, is destined to do for history what Darwin's theory has done for biology we, both of us, had been gradually approaching for some years before 1845. How far I had independently progressed towards it, is best shown by my *Condition of the Working Class in England*. But when I again met Marx at Brussels, in spring 1845, he had it already worked out, and put it before me, in terms almost as clear as those in which I have stated it here. (Ibid.)

2. Frederick Engels, "On the History of the Communist League," *Selected Works*, vol. 3 (Moscow: Foreign Languages Publishing House, 1969), p. 178, as quoted in Gareth Stedman Jones, "Engels and the Genesis of Marxism," *New Left Review*, no. 106 (1977):97.

3. See the quotation from Marx's letter to Ruge (September 1843) in Leszek Kolakowski, *Main Currents of Marxism. Its Origin, Growth, and Dissolution*, vol. 1 (Oxford: Oxford University Press, 1978), p. 128.

4. Kolakowski, *Main Currents of Marxism*, p. 130.

5. Michael Evans, "Karl Marx's First Confrontation with Political Economy: The 1844 Manuscripts," *Economy and Society* 13, no. 2 (1984):116. Also see Allen Oakley, *Marx's Critique of Political Economy. Intellectual Sources and Evolution*, Vol. 1, *1844 to 1860* (London: Routledge and Kegan Paul, 1984), pp. 29, 74–79, for Marx's study of List in the course of developing his own critique of capitalism. Marx's notes from his reading of List are in Karl Marx and Frederick Engels, *Gesamtausgabe, vierte Abteilung, Exzerpte, Notizen, Marginalien*, Band 2 (Berlin: Dietz Verlag, 1981), pp. 506–546.

6. Jones, "Engels and the Genesis of Marxism," p. 98.

7. Robert C. Tucker, ed., *The Marx-Engels Reader*, 2nd ed. (New York: Norton, 1978), contains selections from "Contribution to the Critique of Hegel's *Philosophy of Right*" on pp. 16–25, and "A Contribution to the Critique of Hegel's *Philosophy of Right:* Introduction," (i.e., the "Hegel Critique" in our usage), on pp. 53–65. Both texts are available in full in Karl Marx, *Critique of Hegel's 'Philosophy of Right,'* ed. Joseph O'Malley (Cambridge: Cambridge University Press, 1978), and in Marx and Engels, *Collected Works*, vol. 3.

8. Maximilien Rubel and Margaret Manale, *Marx without Myth: A Chronological Study of His Life and Work* (Oxford: Blackwell, 1975), p. 40.

9. Rubel and Manale, *Marx without Myth*, p. 40.

10. Rubel and Manale, *Marx without Myth*, p. 41.

11. "Hegel Critique," in Tucker, *The Marx-Engels Reader*, pp. 53–54. Selections from this work are quoted by permission of W. W. Norton & Co., Inc.

12. "Hegel Critique," p. 54. (All emphases in this and the subsequent quotations from the "Hegel Critique" are Marx's.)

13. "Hegel Critique," p. 54.

14. "Hegel Critique," pp. 54–55.

15. "Hegel Critique," p. 57.

16. "Hegel Critique," pp. 57–58.

17. "Hegel Critique," p. 58.

18. "Hegel Critique," p. 58.

19. "Hegel Critique," p. 59.

20. "Hegel Critique," pp. 59–60.

21. "Hegel Critique," p. 60.

22. "Hegel Critique," p. 62.

23. "Hegel Critique," p. 62.

24. "Hegel Critique," p. 62.

25. "Hegel Critique," p. 63.

26. "Hegel Critique," p. 63.

27. "Hegel Critique," p. 63.

28. "Hegel Critique," p. 64.

29. "Hegel Critique," p. 64. For the treatment in the literature of the 1830s–1840s of the condition of industrial workers in terms of pauperism and "social question," see Wolfram Fischer, "Social Tensions at Early Stages of Industrialization," *Comparative Studies in Society and History* 9 (1966): 64–83, and Friedrich Lenz, "Vom Pauperismus zum Proletariat: Friedrich List, die Arbeiterfrage und Karl Marx," in *Beiträge zur Wirtschafts—und Gesellschaftsgestaltung. Festschrift für Bruno Gleitze zum 65. Geburtstag,* ed. Friedrich Lenz (Berlin: Duncker und Humblot, 1968), pp. 15–43.

30. "Hegel Critique," p. 65.

31. "Hegel Critique," p. 65. The third sentence in this quotation appears as: "*The emancipation of Germany* will be an *emancipation of man.*" Also, O'Malley renders it, without italicizing any words, as: "The emancipation of Germany is the emancipation of man." In *Collected Works*, vol. 3, p. 187, the sentence in question is rendered in conformity with Marx's own meaning. Marx wrote: "*Die Emancipation des Deutschen* ist die *Emancipation des Menschen.*" (See Karl Marx, "Zur Kritik der Hegelschen Rechtsphilosophie. Einleitung." In Karl Marx and Friedrich Engels, *Gesamtausgabe*, 1st series, vol. 2 [Berlin: Dietz Verlag, 1982], p. 183.) By speaking of "the German's," not "Germany's," emancipation, Marx made clear his lack of nationalist concerns.

32. The editor's note in Tucker, *The Marx-Engels Reader*, p. 65.

## Chapter 3

1. Karl Marx, "Draft of an Article on Friedrich List's Book *Das nationale System der politischen Ökonomie*," *Collected Works*, vol. 4, p. 265. This work will be cited below as the "List Critique." (See Ibid., pp. 698–699, for an editorial note on the condition of the Marx manuscript, the nature of editorial work preceding its publication, etc.) Unless otherwise indicated, all emphases in the quotations are Marx's own.

2. "List Critique," p. 274.

3. "List Critique," p. 281.

4. "List Critique," p. 283.

5. "List Critique," p. 267.

6. "List Critique," p. 280.

7. "List Critique," p. 280.

8. "List Critique," p. 280.

9. "List Critique," p. 275.

10. "List Critique," p. 281.

11. "List Critique," p. 280.

12. "List Critique," p. 275.

13. "List Critique," p. 275.

14. "List Critique," p. 274.

15. "List Critique," p. 274. The square brackets in this and preceding quotations are by the editors of the volume.

16. "List Critique," p. 266.

17. "List Critique," p. 267.

18. "List Critique," p. 266.

19. "List Critique," p. 275.

20. "List Critique," p. 282.

21. "List Critique," p. 282. The expression "industrial education," as editors of the Marx work point out, was often used by List.

22. "List Critique," p. 281.

23. "List Critique," p. 281.

24. "List Critique," p. 281.

25. "List Critique," p. 282.

26. "List Critique," pp. 273–274.

27. "List Critique," p. 290. As a matter of curiosity, let us note that Marx's casual remark, in a later work (*Theories of Surplus Value*), on Ferrier as the main source of List's economic doctrine led one author, E. Ladenthin, to undertake a special study of the otherwise forgotten Frenchman (1912). As reported by W. O. Henderson, "Friedrich List and the French Protectionists," *Zeitschrift für die gesamte Staatswissenschaft* 138 (1982):272, Ladenthin "provided no satisfactory evidence that List was in any way indebted to Ferrier." Mindful of what Marx himself has often been accused of having done, one might have properly responded, if the results of that search had been different, with "So what?"

28. "List Critique," p. 293.

29. Karl Marx, "The Protectionists, the Free Traders and the Working Class," *Collected Works*, vol. 6, p. 279. (This work was first published in *Zwei Reden über die Freihandels- und Schutzzollfrage von Karl Marx* (Hamm, 1848). Published in English for the first time in the cited edition.)

30. "The Protectionists, the Free Traders and the Working Class," p. 280.

31. "The Protectionists, the Free Traders and the Working Class," p. 281.

32. Marx's (undelivered) speech, as summarized in Frederick Engels, "The Free Trade Congress at Brussels," *Collected Works*, vol. 6, p. 290. This account by Engels was first published in *The Northern Star*, no. 520 (October 9, 1847) and signed "From Our German Correspondent."

33. Karl Marx, "Speech on the Question of Free Trade," *Collected Works*, vol. 6, pp. 463–464.

34. "Speech on the Question of Free Trade," p. 464.

35. "Speech on the Question of Free Trade," p. 465.

36. In the 1880–1890s, German socialists would cite Marx's speech on free trade — especially his remark that it was possible for "one nation to grow rich at the expense of another" — in order to justify their support of protective tariffs adopted by the imperial

government. On this topic, see the book by the socialist deputy to the Reichstag, Max Schippel, *Grundzüge der Handelspolitik. Zur Orientierung in den wirtschaftlichen Kämpfen* (Berlin and Bern: Akademischer Verlag für sociale Wissenschaften, 1902), pp. 89–90 and 346–347. For other socialist attempts in that period to interpret Marx and especially late Engels as Listians, see Meusel, *List und Marx*, pp. 90–95, and Schippel, *Grundzüge*, especially pp. 89–111 and 344–352.

37. "Speech on the Question of Free Trade," p. 465.

## Chapter 4

1. Karl Marx and Frederick Engels, *The German Ideology*, ed. C. J. Arthur (New York: International Publishers, 1978), p. 78. All quotations from this work are by permission of the publisher.

2. *The German Ideology*, p. 78.

3. *The German Ideology*, p. 94.

4. Frederick Engels, "The Festival of Nations in London," *Collected Works*, vol. 6, p. 6. (This article was written at the end of 1845 and published in the journal *Rheinische Jahrbücher zur gesellschaftlichen Reform*, Bd. 2 (1846). It was published in full in English for the first time in this edition of *Collected Works*.)

5. This is the quoted passage in the original:

> Die Proletarier aber haben in allen Ländern ein und dasselbe Interesse, einen und denselben Feind, einen und denselben Kampf vor sich; die Proletarier sind der groben Masse nach schon von Natur ohne Nationalvorurteile, und ihre ganze Bildung und Bewegung ist wesentlich humanitarisch, *antinational*. Die Proletarier allein können die Nationalität vernichten, das erwachende Proletariat allein kann die verschiedenen Nationen fraternisieren lassen. (Emphasis added.)

See Karl Marx and Friedrich Engels, *Historisch-kritische Gesamtausgabe*, vol. 4, ed. V. Adoratskii (Glashütten im Taunus: Detlev Auvermann, 1970), p. 460. (This is a reprint of the 1932 edition.)

6. Karl Marx and Frederick Engels, "[On Poland]," *Collected Works,* vol. 6, p. 388. (First published in the *Deutsche-Brüsseler-Zeitung*, no. 98 (December 9, 1847). Printed according to the newspaper. Published in English for the first time in this edition of *Collected Works*.)

7. "[On Poland]," p. 388.

8. Frederick Engels, "Extraordinary Revelations.-Abd-el-Kader.- Guizot's Foreign Policy," *Collected Works*, vol. 6, p. 471.

9. "Extraordinary Revelations," pp. 471–472.

10. Frederick Engels, "[The Anniversary of the Polish Revolution of 1830]," *Collected Works*, vol. 6, pp. 391–392. (Written on November 30, 1847. First published in *La Reforme*, December 5, 1847. Published in English for the first time in this edition of *Collected Works*.)

11. "[The Anniversary of The Polish Revolution of 1830,]" pp. 391–392.

12. Marx and Engels, "[On Poland]," p. 389.

13. "[On Poland]," pp. 389–390.

14. "[On Poland]," p. 390.

15. Frederick Engels, "Principles of Communism," *Collected Works*, vol. 6, pp. 351–352.

16. "Principles of Communism," pp. 356–357.

17. Karl Marx, "The Revolutionary Movement," *Collected Works*, vol. 8, p. 215.

18. "The Revolutionary Movement," pp. 214–215.

19. "The Revolutionary Movement," p. 215.

20. Karl Marx, "The Bourgeoisie and the Counter-Revolution," *Collected Works*, vol. 8, p. 161. Emphases in the original.

21. "The Bourgeoisie and the Counter-Revolution," pp. 161–162.

22. "The Bourgeoisie and the Counter-Revolution," p. 162.

23. Marx and Engels, *The German Ideology*, p. 57.

24. *The German Ideology*, p. 52.

25. *The German Ideology*, p. 55.

26. *The German Ideology*, p. 55.

27. Frederick Engels, "Draft of a Communist Confession of Faith," *Collected Works*, vol. 6, p. 103. First published in the book *Gründungsdokumente des Bundes der Kommunisten (Juni bis September 1847)*, Hamburg, 1969.

28. "Draft of a Communist Confession of Faith," p. 103. Engels reaffirmed his stand in October 1847. (See Engels, "Principles of Communism," p. 354.)

29. See David McLellan, *Marx before Marxism*, 2nd ed. (London: Macmillan, 1980), pp. 134, 138. "On the Jewish Question" is available in Tucker, *The Marx-Engels Reader*, pp. 26–51.

30. McLellan, *Marx before Marxism*, p. 139.

31. Marx, "On the Jewish Question," in Tucker, *The Marx-Engels Reader*, p. 32. Quotations from this work are by permission of W. W. Norton & Co.

32. "On the Jewish Question," p. 47.

33. "On the Jewish Question," p. 51.

34. Engels, "Principles of Communism," p. 350. In "The Festival of Nations," Engels stated that *"Democracy nowadays is communism"* (italics in the original), and explained that after the French Revolution "a purely political democracy became a complete absurdity," which implied that communism would be a more complete democracy. Even if "the masses" do not have a very precise idea of democracy, they "all have at least an obscure feeling that social equality of rights is implicit in democracy." Therefore, the Communists should be able to count on the support of the masses in their struggle. (See "The Festival of Nations," p. 5.)

35. "Draft Plan for a Work on the Modern State," *Collected Works*, vol. 4, p. 666. (Hal Draper, *Karl Marx's Theory of Revolution*, vol. 1 [New York and London: Monthly Review Press, 1977], pp. 187 n–188 n, reproduces a version slightly different from the source, although he claims to be quoting it.)

36. Eric J. Hobsbawm, "Marx, Engels and Politics," in *The History of Marxism*, vol. 1, *Marxism in Marx's Day*, ed. Eric J. Hobsbawm (Bloomington, IN: Indiana University Press, 1982), pp. 230, 260 n.

37. Anthony Giddens, *A Contemporary Critique of Historical Materialism*, vol. 1, *Power, Property and the State* (Berkeley and Los Angeles: University of California Press, 1981), p. 189.

38. Giddens, *A Contemporary Critique*, vol. 1, p. 198.

39. Claudia von Braunmühl, "On the Analysis of the Bourgeois Nation State within the World Market Context, " in *State and Capital. A Marxist Debate*, ed. John Holloway and Sol Picciotto (Austin, TX: University of Texas Press, 1978), p. 171.

40. Braunmühl, "On the Analysis of the Bourgeois Nation State," p. 171.

41. Z. A. Pelczynski, "Nation, Civil Society, State: Hegelian Sources of the Marxian Non-theory of Nationality," in *The State and Civil Society: Studies in Hegel's Political Philosophy*, ed. Z. A. Pelczynski (Cambridge: Cambridge University Press, 1984), p. 277.

42. Pelczynski, "Nation, Civil Society, State," p. 278.

43. Pelczynski, "Nation, Civil Society, State," p. 262.

44. Pelczynski, "Nation, Civil Society, State," pp. 265–266.

45. Pelczynski, "Nation, Civil Society, State," p. 273.

46. Pelczynski, "Nation, Civil Society, State," p. 275.

47. Pelczynski, "Nation, Civil Society, State," p. 277.

48. Pelczynski, "Nation, Civil Society, State," p. 277.

49. Kolakowski, *Main Currents of Marxism,* p. 131.

50. Kolakowski, *Main Currents of Marxism*, p. 410. In this connection, it may be worth adding that this Marxist stand, as Steven Lukes, *Marxism and Morality* (Oxford: Clarendon Press, 1985), p. 35, puts it, "has virtually nothing to say about any bases of conflict, whether social or psychological, other than class. It is virtually innocent (and totally so at the level of theory) of any serious consideration of all the inter–personal and intra–personal sources of conflict and frustration that cannot, or can no longer, plausibly be traced, even remotely, to class divisions." (For some of the basic questions that Marx and Marxism leave unanswered, see ibid., pp. 98–99.) It is evident that Marx's approach toward legal rights was consistent with his stand on religion, nationality, and politics.

51. Michael Löwy, "Marx and Engels: Cosmopolites," *Critique* 14 (1981):11.

## Chapter 5

1. Since two names appeared on the title page, the question of Engels' contribution arises. According to David McLellan, *Karl Marx: His Life and Thought* (New York: Harper and Row, 1973), p. 180, "the actual writing of the *Communist Manifesto* was done exclusively by Marx." This appears to be the general consensus today.

2. *The Communist Manifesto* (New York: International Publishers, 1948; reprinted 1966), p. 23.

3. "Theses on Feuerbach," in *Karl Marx: Selected Writings*, ed. David McLellan (Oxford: Oxford University Press, 1978), p. 158.

4. Pierre Vilar, "Marx and the Concept of History," in Hobsbawm, *The History of Marxism*, p. 68.

5. Isaiah Berlin, "Socialism," *Chambers's Encyclopaedia*, rev. ed., vol. 12, (Oxford: Pergamon, 1967), p. 646.

6. Here is a sampling of recent journal articles indicating the continuing interest of scholars in that Marxian text: Y. Wagner and M. Strauss, "The Programme of the Communist Manifesto and Its Theoretical Foundations," *Political Studies* 17, no. 4 (December 1969):470–484; Horace B. Davis, "Nations, Colonies and Social Classes: The Position of Marx and Engels," *Science and Society* 29, no. 1 (1965): 26–43; John Cunliffe, "Marx's Politics—The Tensions in the *Communist Manifesto,*" *Political Studies* 30, no. 4 (December 1982):569–574; Roman Rosdolsky, "Worker and Fatherland: A Note on a Passage in the *Communist Manifesto*," *Science and Society* 29, no. 3 (Summer 1965):330–337; J. M. Blaut, "Nationalism as an Autonomous Force," *Science and Society* 46, no. 1 (Spring 1982):1–23; Paul N. Sigel, "The Style of the *Communist Manifesto*," *Science and Society* 46, no. 2 (Summer 1982):222–229; and Michael Levin, "Deutschmarx: Marx, Engels, and the German Question," *Political Studies* 29, no. 4 (December, 1981):537–554.

7. Harold J. Laski, "An Introduction," in Karl Marx and Friedrich Engels, *The Communist Manifesto* (New York: New American Library, 1982), pp. 50–51.

8. *The Communist Manifesto* (New York: International Publishers, 1948; reprinted 1966), p. 9.

9. *The Communist Manifesto*, p. 29.

10. *The Communist Manifesto*, p. 9.

11. *The Communist Manifesto*, p. 9.

12. *The Communist Manifesto*, p. 17.

13. *The Communist Manifesto*, p. 23.

14. *The Communist Manifesto*, p. 19. The passage continues:

> If by chance they are revolutionary, they are so only in view of their impending transfer into the proletariat; they thus defend not their present, but their future interests; they desert their own standpoint to adopt that of the proletariat. (Ibid.)

Thus Marx did not admit the possibility that any of these groups might per se be revolutionary. There was no "third force", no "third way."

15. *The Communist Manifesto*, p. 10.

16. *The Communist Manifesto*, p. 12.

17. *The Communist Manifesto*, p. 11.

18. *The Communist Manifesto*, p. 14.

19. *The Communist Manifesto*, p. 13.

20. *The Communist Manifesto*, p. 13. (Emphasis added.)

21. *The Communist Manifesto*, p. 12. He thus restated the position he took in 1846:

> Generally speaking, big industry created everywhere the same relations between the classes of society, and thus destroyed the peculiar individuality of the various nationalities. And finally, while the bourgeoisie of each nation still retained separate national interests, big industry created a class, which in all nations has the same interest and with which nationality is already dead. (*The German Ideology*, p. 78.)

22. *The Communist Manifesto*, p. 28.

23. *The Communist Manifesto*, pp. 12–13.

24. *The Communist Manifesto*, pp. 18–19.

25. *The Communist Manifesto*, p. 20.

26. *The Communist Manifesto*, p. 20.

27. *The Communist Manifesto*, p. 28. (Emphasis in the original.)

28. Benedict Anderson, *Imagined Communities: Reflections on the Origin and Spread of Nationalism* (London: Verso and NLB, 1983), p. 13. (Emphasis in the original.)

29. *The Communist Manifesto*, p. 13.

30. *The Communist Manifesto*, p. 28.

31. *The Communist Manifesto*, p. 28.

32. *The Communist Manifesto*, p. 21.

33. *The Communist Manifesto*, p. 21.

34. *The Communist Manifesto*, p. 20.

35. Alfred G. Meyer, "Review of *A Dictionary of Marxist Thought*" (ed. Tom Bottomore et al. [Cambridge: Harvard University Press, 1983]), *Political Theory* 12, no. 3 (August 1984):448.

36. *The Communist Manifesto*, p. 21.

37. *The Communist Manifesto*, p. 18.

38. *The Communist Manifesto*, p. 18. The adoption of a law, in *capitalist* England, that restricted the maximum length of a working day, i.e., benefited *workers*, was a major proof that political struggle could be effective.

39. *The Communist Manifesto*, p. 19.

40. *The Communist Manifesto*, p. 19.

41. *The Communist Manifesto*, p. 19.

42. *The Communist Manifesto*, p. 22.

43. *The Communist Manifesto*, p. 43.

44. *The Communist Manifesto*, p. 43.

45. *The Communist Manifesto*, pp. 43–44.

46. *The Communist Manifesto*, p. 44.

47. *The Communist Manifesto*, p. 35.

48. *The Communist Manifesto*, p. 36.

49. *The Communist Manifesto*, pp. 36–37.

50. *The Communist Manifesto*, p. 37.

51. *The Communist Manifesto*, p. 37.

52. *The Communist Manifesto*, p. 38.

53. Friedrich Engels, "The Festival of Nations," as translated from the German original by Dirk J. Struik, *Birth of the Communist Manifesto* (New York: International Publishers, 1975), p. 77. See *Collected Works*, vol. 6 (London, 1976), p. 3, for a slightly different, "official" translation of this passage.

54. Lichtheim, *Marxism*, pp. 24–26. See also James H. Billington, *Fire in the Minds of Men: Origins of the Revolutionary Faith* (New York: Basic Books, 1980).

55. Isaiah Berlin, "Nationalism," in Berlin, *Against the Current: Essays in the History of Ideas* (New York: Viking, 1979), p. 337.

## Chapter 6

1. Hugh Seton-Watson, *Nations and States* (Boulder, CO: Westview Press, 1977), p. 445.

2. Ernest Gellner, *Nations and Nationalism* (Ithaca, NY, and London, England: Cornell University Press, 1983), p. 124.

3. Anderson, *Imagined Communities*, pp. 14–15.

4. William H. Sewell, Jr., "Ideologies and Social Revolutions: Reflections on the French Case," *Journal of Modern History* 57, no. 1 (March 1985):60–61.

5. Sewell, "Ideologies and Social Revolutions," pp. 83–84.

6. *Moniteur*, January 28, 1794, pp. 519–520, quoted in Hayes, *The Historical Evolution*, p. 65.

7. Hayes, *The Historical Evolution*, pp. 77–78.

8. *Moniteur*, March 13, 1794, pp. 699–700, quoted in Hayes, *The Historical Evolution*, p. 79.

9. Bernard Crick, *In Defence of Politics* (Harmondsworth, England: Penguin, 1966), pp. 78–79. "Nationalism . . . represented a system of authority which poured into the vacuum left by the failure of the French revolution and . . . the double failure of Autocratic Legitimacy." (Crick, p. 79.)

10. Jean-Jacques Rousseau, "Constitutional Project for Corsica," in *Rousseau: Political Writings*, ed. and tr. Frederick Watkins (Edinburgh: Nelson, 1953), p. 293. Compare this with Rousseau's remarks on pp. 277–278 on the proper relationship between the government and the people.

11. Rousseau, "Considerations on the Government of Poland," Watkins, *Rousseau*, p. 168.

12. Alfred Cobban, *Rousseau and the Modern State* (Hamden, CT: Archon Books, 1961), pp. 166–167.

13. Eric Hobsbawm, "Some Reflections on Nationalism," in *Imagination and Precision in the Social Sciences: Essays in Memory of Peter Nettl*, ed. T. J. Nossiter, A. H. Hanson and Stein Rokkan (London: Faber and Faber, 1972), pp. 391–392.

14. Cobban, *Rousseau*, p. 176.

15. Hayes, *The Historical Evolution*, pp. 88–95, and Cobban, *Rousseau*, pp. 158–159. See also Cobban, *Edmund Burke and the Revolt Against the Eighteenth Century* (New York: Barnes and Noble, 1960).

16. Andrzej Walicki, *Philosophy and Romantic Nationalism: The Case of Poland* (Oxford: Oxford University Press, 1982) is a superb study of the Polish problem after the partitions. Piotr S. Wandycz, *The Lands of Partitioned Poland, 1795–1918* (Seattle: University of Washington Press, 1974) is the standard history of the period.

17. John Emerich Edward Dalberg Acton, First Baron Acton, *Essays on Freedom and Power* (London: Thames and Hudson, 1956), pp. 146–147.

18. Benedict Anderson, *Imagined Communities*, pp. 20–24. The quotation from Erich Auerbach, *Mimesis. The Representation of Reality in Western Literature*, tr. Willard Task (Garden City, NY: Doubleday Anchor, 1957), p. 282.

19. Anderson, *Imagined Communities*, pp. 46–48. Elizabeth L. Eisenstein, *The Printing Press as an Agent of Change*, 2 vols. (Cambridge: Cambridge University Press, 1979) considers the impact of printing on religious and scientific developments in early modern Europe.

20. A. J. Polan, *Lenin and the End of Politics* (Berkeley and Los Angeles: University of California Press, 1984), pp. 212 and 214. Paul Hirst and Penny Woolley have spoken of "the socially explosive nature" of Luther's "concept of the person as the steward of his own soul," in *Social Relations and Human Attributes* (London: 1982), p. 137, as quoted in Polan, *Lenin*, p. 213.

21. Anderson, *Imagined Communities*, pp. 26–28, notes a connection between the evolution of the state and cultural developments.

22. See Polan, *Lenin*.

23. Gale Stokes, "Cognition and the Function of Nationalism," *Journal of Interdisciplinary History* 4, no. 4 (Spring 1974):530, 532–533, 537. Although Stokes attributes the rise of "operational" persons to the effect of "economic systems," it is evident from his overall argument that school, not factory bench, creates "operational individuals." He points out that in isolated societies children learn the skills and attitudes they need by participating in activities where those skills and attitudes are used, and thus they fail to attain "operationalism." On the other hand, "in societies in which industrial development has occurred, it is impossible to pass on all the skills an adult will need in the direct, palpable way. . . . The universal solution to this difficult problem . . . has been the school." In school, the child learns "through the use of abstractions" (Stokes, "Cognition," p. 533). This means, however, that the printing revolution, not the much later Industrial Revolution, was the crucial event in the creation of individuals capable of thinking "nationalistically."

24. James J. Sheehan, "What is German History? Reflections on the Role of the *Nation* in German History and Historiography," *Journal of Modern History* 53, no. 1 (March 1981):10. The argument on "linear" and "areal" (i.e., limited to a single town or a handful of villages) relationships was advanced by Edward Whiting Fox, *History in Geographic Perspective. The Other France* (New York: Norton, 1971), especially pp. 37–39 and 36, cited by Sheehan, "What is German History?" pp. 9–10.

25. Polan, *Lenin*, p. 213, speaks of countries of "classical capitalism . . . wherein individuals, groups and institutions—disparate, autonomous, localized, spontaneous—produce in economy, polity, culture, technology and civil society that which elsewhere must *ab initio* be sponsored and directed by the state." This dichotomy leaves out the intermediate situation wherein individuals approximating the above description either live in a state that needs to be persuaded to favor reform, such as tsarist Russia, or belong to stateless "nations," i.e.,

groups whose agenda of reform includes most prominently the goal of *establishing* a state of one's own.

26. J. G. Herder, *Sämliche Werke*, vol. 13, ed. B. Suphan (Berlin, 1877–1913), pp. 110, 146–147, as quoted in F. M. Barnard, tr. and ed., *J. G. Herder on Social and Political Culture* (Cambridge: Cambridge University Press, 1969), p. 20.

27. Barnard, *Herder on Culture*, p. 20.

28. Isaiah Berlin, "The Counter-Enlightenment," in his *Against the Current*, p. 12.

29. Berlin, "The Counter-Enlightenment," in *Against the Current*, pp. 18–19. This position, in the words of Berlin, "looks upon every human activity as a form of individual self-expression." Creative activity by men, according to this view, involves "stamping" of their unique personalities, "individual or collective, conscious or unconscious," upon external objects and realizing "values which are themselves not given but generated by the process of creation itself." See also Roger Hausheer, "Introduction," in Berlin, *Against the Current*, p. xxxv, and Charles Taylor's enlightening and important discussion in *Hegel* (Cambridge: Cambridge University Press, 1983), pp. 13–29.

30. Isaiah Berlin, *Vico and Herder. Two Studies in the History of Ideas* (New York: Viking, 1976), p. 204. Berlin gives the following references to Herder: J. G. Herder, *Sämliche Werke*, vol. 8, pp. 33 and 252. For man's being created by his world, the reference is to vol. 2, p. 61.

31. Berlin, "The Counter-Enlightenment," in *Against the Current*, p. 18.

32. Alfred Cobban, *Rousseau*, p. 156.

33. Berlin, "The Counter-Enlightenment," in *Against The Current*, p. 20.

34. Berlin, "The Counter-Enlightenment," in *Against The Current*, p. 10.

35. In this connection, see John Breuilly, *Nationalism and the State* (Chicago: University of Chicago Press, 1985), p. 337: "If language is thought, and can be learned only in a community . . . each community has its own mode of thought."

36. Berlin, "The Counter-Enlightenment," in *Against the Current*, pp. 11–12. Anthony Giddens, *Contemporary Critique of Historical Materialism*, vol. 2, *The Nation-State and Violence* (Berkeley and Los Angeles: University of California Press, 1985), p. 217, sees in Herder's ideas an implied claim to an "intrinsic superiority" of one culture and state over others. This seems to be a misunderstanding of Herder's real stand, although not necessarily of that of some of Herder's successors.

37. Herder, "Essay on the Origin of Language" (1772), in Barnard, *Herder on Culture*, pp. 167–168.

38. Herder, "Essay on the Origin of Language" (1772), in Barnard, *Herder on Culture*, pp. 173–174. Herder's emphasis.

39. Berlin, *Vico and Herder*, p. 204 n.

40. Anthony D. Smith, *Theories of Nationalism* (New York: Harper and Row, 1973), p. 21.

41. Anthony D. Smith, *Theories of Nationalism*, pp. 23–24. (Emphasis added.)

42. Anthony D. Smith, *Theories of Nationalism*, p. 20.

43. Anthony D. Smith, *Nationalism in the Twentieth Century* (New York: New York University Press, 1979), p. 13.

44. Anthony D. Smith, *Theories of Nationalism*, p. 21.

45. Anthony D. Smith, *Nationalism in the Twentieth Century*, p. 186.

46. Perhaps it bears repeating that *modern* nations, not ethnic communities per se, are meant here. The history of the latter goes much further back, as John A. Armstrong, *Nations before Nationalism* (Chapel Hill, NC: University of North Carolina Press, 1982), and Anthony D. Smith, *The Ethnic Origins of Nations* (Oxford: Basil Blackwell, 1987), remind us.

## Chapter 7

1. The fullest biographical account of List in English is William Otto Henderson, *Friedrich List: Economist and Visionary 1789–1846* (London: Frank Cass, 1983), pp. 1–89. Besides a general chronological narrative, Henderson's book contains separate chapters on List's public activities ("The Champion of Economic Unity" and "The Railway Pioneer") and one long chapter on his economic views, beginning with his memoranda of 1819–1820 and ending with *The National System of Political Economy*. Henderson's book contains a selective bibliography in the main languages. There are numerous biographic studies of List in German, but none as recent as Henderson's, which has also just appeared in a German translation. For a brief overview of List's life, times, and ideas, see Louis L. Snyder, "Economic Nationalism: Friedrich List, Germany's Handicapped Colbert," in his book *Roots of German Nationalism* (Bloomington, IN: Indiana University Press, 1978). Snyder's chapter contains certain bibliographic items that are not included in Henderson's bibliography. Margaret E. Hirst, *Life of Friedrich List and Selections from His Writings* (New York: Charles Scribner and Sons, 1909), remains useful, too. The fullest biography (up to 1825) in German is Paul Gehring, *Friedrich List. Jugend und Reifejahre, 1789–1825* (Tübingen; J. C. B. Mohr Verlag, 1964). There is a very helpful chronology of List's life and work in Günter Fabiunke, *Zur historischen Rolle des deutschen Nationalökonomen Friedrich List (1789–1846)* (Berlin: Verlag Die Wirtschaft, 1955, pp. 231–295. I have used it in this chapter.

2. Henderson, *Friedrich List*, p. 17.

3. "Vorrede," in Friedrich List, *Das nationale System der politischen Ökonomie*, ed. Arthur Sommer (Basel: Kyklos-Verlag 1959), p. 1. (Omitted from the English edition.)

4. Friedrich List, *The National System of Political Economy*, tr. Sampson S. Lloyd (New York: Augustus M. Kelley, 1966, a reprint of the 1885 edition), pp. xxvi–xxvii. (Hereafter cited as *The National System*.)

5. Henry William Spiegel, *The Growth of Economic Thought*, rev. ed. (Durham, NC: Duke University Press, 1983), p. 417. (Spiegel's comments on Burke are on pp. 415–416.) For a more detailed discussion of Adam Müller's views, see Alexander Gray, *The Development of Economic Doctrine*, 2nd ed. (New York and London: Longman, 1980), pp. 202–212. For Müller, also see Desider Vikor, *Economic Romanticism in the Twentieth Century* (New Delhi: New Book Society of India, 1964), pp. 23–33.

6. Spiegel, *The Growth of Economic Thought*, p. 417.

7. Gray, *The Development of Economic Doctrine*, p. 212:

> Müller's claim to consideration rests on the fact that his point of view is so largely reflected in Friedrich List. . . . List was no visionary dreamer. He played a very practical part in the affairs of his day; and though the world broke him, he was yet a man of the world. But, to a large extent, the substance of his views is in line with Müller's thought. What Müller saw darkly through a haze of mysticism and symbolism, and expressed in a cloud of words, List wrote and expounded in the spirit of a political pamphleteer.

8. Charles Gide and Charles Rist, *A History of Economic Doctrines from the Time of the Physiocrats to the Present Day* (Boston: D. C. Heath, 1948), pp. 286–287.

9. Joseph Finkelstein and Alfred L. Thimm, *Economists and Society: The Development of Economic Thought from Aquinas to Keynes*, 2nd ed. (Schenectady, NY: Union College Press, 1981), pp. 118–119.

10. Arcadius Kahan, "Nineteenth-Century European Experience with Policies of Economic Nationalism," in *Economic Nationalism in Old and New States*, ed. Harry G. Johnson (Chicago: University of Chicago Press, 1967), p. 20. Kahan quotes a very revealing summary

of the Müller position given in a work of an earlier German scholar, Hans Freyer, *Die Bewertung der Wirtschaft im philosophischen Denken des 19. Jahrhunderts* (Leipzig, 1921), pp. 52, 53:

> Müller viewed the economy not necessarily as the commercial struggle of atomized interests . . . but as an aspect of the activity of a commonwealth, as a supra-individual relationship (superseding individuals) that does not follow mechanistic laws: a market, according to Müller, is not exclusively a meeting place for the exchange of commodities into money-equivalents, but also is an outlet for relations between humans. . . . [Economic activity] is also a part of the totality of *physical and spiritual forces of the nation* in the change and continuity of generations. . . . [While for Adam Smith] the human being was essentially an individual, [for Müller] he is basically a citizen; therefore, in one concept of the economy the creative activity originates with the individual and spreads within the economy . . . while in the second case the movement is a reciprocal process . . . every individual produces the society, while society produces also the individual citizen. (Quoted in Kahan, "Nineteenth-Century European Experience," pp. 20–21.)

11. Kahan, "Nineteenth-Century European Experience," p. 22.

12. See Hayes, *The Historical Evolution*, pp. 263–266, for a summary of Fichte's doctrine. Hayes thought that certain measures of the Soviet government after the revolution were "curiously reminiscent" of Fichte's recommendations. There is a chapter on Fichte ("Fichte's Blueprint for Autarky") in Michael H. Heilperin, *Studies in Economic Nationalism* (Geneva: Droz; Paris: Minard, 1960), pp. 82–96.

13. Spiegel, *The Growth of Economic Thought*, pp. 410–433, discusses a whole group of authors, including Fichte, Müller, and List, as well as the Historical School, in a chapter titled "The Hegelian Variant of Historical Economics." Similarly, Edmund Whittaker, *Schools and Streams of Economic Thought* (Chicago: Rand McNally, 1960), in a chapter called "Romanticism and Historical Economics," begins his discussion with a section on "Hegelianism" (see pp. 191–194).

14. See Friedrich Lenz, *Friedrich List's Staats- und Gesellschaftslehre: Eine Studie zur politischen Soziologie* (Neuwied and Berlin: Luchterhand, 1967), pp. 9–13.

15. See Ghita Ionescu, "Introduction," in *The Political Thought of Saint-Simon*, ed. Ghita Ionescu (Oxford: Oxford University Press, 1976), pp. 42–43. Cf. Saint-Simon's memorandum, "On the Reorganization of European Society," ibid., pp. 83–98.

16. Erna Schulz, "Friedrich Lists Geschichtsauffassung. Ihre Gestalt und ihre Bedeutung für Lists Wirtschaftslehre," *Zeitschrift für die gesamte Staatswissenschaft* 97, no. 2 (1937):333 (see also pp. 291, 296–298).

17. Schulz, "Friedrich Lists Geschichtsauffassung," p. 292.

18. *The National System*, p. xxv.

19. *The National System*, p. xxvi.

20. "Vorrede," *Das nationale System* (1959), p. 2.

21. *The National System*, p. xxvi.

22. "Petition on Behalf of the Handelsverein to the Federal Assembly, April, 1819, " in Hirst, *Life of Friedrich List*, p. 137.

23. "Petition," in Hirst, *Life of Friedrich List*, p. 140.

24. "Petition," in Hirst, *Life of Friedrich List*, p. 138.

25. "Petition," in Hirst, *Life of Friedrich List*, p. 138. As reproduced in E. K. Bramsted and K. J. Melhuish, eds., *Western Liberalism: A History in Documents from Locke to Croce* (London and New York: Longman, 1978), p. 331, this document is "corrected." Instead of "Rational," the editors put "National": "National freedom is the first condition of all

human development, whether physical or mental." However, in the original German we read about *Vernünftige Freiheit*, which is what Hirst correctly rendered as "Rational freedom." (See Friedrich List, *Schriften. Reden. Briefe*, vol. 1, pt. 2 [Berlin: Verlag von Reimar Hobbing, 1933], p. 491).

26. "Petition," in Hirst, *Life of Friedrich List*, p. 139.

27. "Petition," in Hirst, *Life of Friedrich List*, p. 140.

28. "Petition," in Hirst, *Life of Friedrich List*, p. 142.

29. "Henderson, *Friedrich List*, pp. 18, 44, 46–47, 50–51, and Martin Kitchen, *The Political Economy of Germany 1815–1914* (Montreal: McGill Queen's University Press, 1978), pp. 35–38.

30. Kitchen, *The Political Economy of Germany*, p. 43.

31. Kitchen, *The Political Economy of Germany*, p. 37.

32. James J. Sheehan, "What is German History?" p. 12. In his stimulating essay, Sheehan discusses, among others, the works of Frank B. Tipton, "The National Consensus in German Economic History," *Central European History* 7, no. 3 (1974):195–224; Richard Hugh Tilly, "Los von England; Probleme des Nationalismus in der deutschen Wirtschaftsgeschichte," *Zeitschrift für die gesamte Staatswissenschaft* 124, no. 1 (1968):179–196; and W. O. Henderson, *The Zollverein*, 2nd ed. (Chicago: Quadrangle Books, 1959).

33. List's wife, Karoline Neidhard (1789–1866), was the daughter of a professor of classics at Tübingen, David Christoph Seybold. Her first husband, Johann Friedrich Neidhard, died in 1816. She had one son, Karl, by that first marriage. Karoline and Friedrich were married in 1818 and were the parents of three daughters—Emilie (1818–1902), Elise (1822–1893), and Karoline (1829–1911)—and one son, Oskar (1820–1839). Oskar died of typhus while serving in the French Foreign Legion in Algeria. Karl Neidhard was the only member of the family to remain in the United States permanently. He became a physician and died in Philadelphia in 1895. (Eugen Wendler, *Friedrich List: Leben and Wirken in Dokumenten* [Reutlingen: Verlagshaus Reutlingen Oertel und Spörer, 1976], pp. 12–13.)

34. Henderson, *Friedrich List*, p. 68.

34a. Quoted in William Notz, *Friedrich List in Amerika* (Hamburg: Broschek, 1925), p. 227. (This work was an offprint of a study originally published in *Weltwirtschaftliches Archiv* 21 and 22, 1925.) List's prediction reminded Georg Weippert of the celebrated passage in *Democracy in America* (1835), in which Alexis de Tocqueville spoke about the Russians and the Anglo-Americans as the "two great nations in the world which, starting from different points, seem to be advancing toward the same goal":

> The American fights against natural obstacles; the Russian is at grips with men. The former combats the wilderness and barbarism; the latter, civilization with all its arms. America's conquests are made with the plowshare, Russia's with the sword.
>
> To attain their aims, the former relies on personal interest and gives free scope to the unguided strength and common sense of individuals.
>
> The latter in a sense concentrates the whole power of society in one man.
>
> One has freedom as the principal means of action; the other has servitude.
>
> Their point of departure is different and their paths diverse; nevertheless, each seems called by some secret design of Providence one day to hold in its hands the destinies of half the world.

[See Georg Weippert, *Der späte List. Ein Beitrag zur Grundlegung der Wissenschaft von der Politik und zur politischen Ökonomie als Gestaltungslehre der Wirtschaft* (Erlangen: Universitätsbund Erlangen, 1956), pp. 85–86. The English translation used here is taken from Alexis de Tocqueville, *Democracy in America*, tr. George Lawrence (Garden City, NY: Anchor Books, 1969), pp. 412–413.]

35. Snyder, "Economic Nationalism: Friedrich List, Germany's Handicapped Colbert," in Snyder, *Roots of German Nationalism,* pp. 24–30, shows how nationalist pride became involved in academic discussions about List's American connection. Also see Charles Patrick Neill, *Daniel Raymond: An Early Chapter in the History of Economic Theory in the United States,* John Hopkins University Studies in Historical and Political Science, vol. 6, no. 15 (Baltimore: Johns Hopkins University Press, June 1897), pp. 46–63 (series pages 256–273.) There is a useful discussion in Hirst, *Life of Friedrich List,* chapter 6; in Gide and Rist, *A History of Economic Doctrines,* esp. pp. 286–287; and Henderson, *Friedrich List,* pp. 154–155.

36. Bernard Semmel, *The Rise of Free Trade Imperialism, Classical Political Economy, the Empire of Free Trade and Imperialism 1750–1850* (Cambridge: Cambridge University Press, 1970), p. 177.

37. Semmel, *The Rise of Free Trade Imperialism,* p. 177. The quotations of Alexander Hamilton are from "Report on Manufactures," in *Papers on Public Credit, Commerce, and Finance* (New York: Columbia University Press, 1934), pp. 182–192, 200–201.

38. Semmel, *The Rise of Free Trade Imperialism,* p. 178. Quotations are from Hamilton, "Report on Manufactures," pp. 234–235, 249, 227.

39. Daniel Raymond, *The Elements of Political Economy,* vol. 1, 2nd ed. (Baltimore, 1823), p. 35 f., as quoted in List, *Schriften. Reden. Briefe,* vol. 6, p. 575.

40. Henderson, *Friedrich List,* p. 154.

41. Henderson, *Friedrich List,* p. 70.

42. These two quotations are in Henderson, *Friedrich List,* p. 71, who cites them from "The Resolution of the Committee of the Pennsylvania Society for the Promotion of Manufactures and the Mechanic Arts, November 21, 1827," in List, *Schriften. Reden. Briefe,* vol. 2, p. 26, and from List's letter to Lafayette, November 29, 1827, in *Schriften. Reden. Briefe,* vol. 8, p. 352, respectively.

43. Its full title was *Outlines of American Political Economy in a Series of Letters addressed by Frederick List, Esq. to Charles J. Ingersoll, Esq.* (Philadelphia: Samuel Parker, 1827). It was reprinted in Hirst, *Life of Friedrich List,* pp. 145–272.

44. Henderson, *Friedrich List,* p. 71, referring to *Schriften. Reden. Briefe,* vol. 6, p. 15. See "Vorrede," *Das nationale System* (1959), p. 8.

45. "Vorrede," *Das nationale System* (1959), p. 8.

46. Joseph Dorfman, *The Economic Mind in American Civilization, 1606–1865,* vol. 2 (New York: Viking, 1946), p. 582.

47. Henderson, *Friedrich List,* pp. 73–74.

48. Friedrich List, "Das deutsche Eisenbahnsystem," *Schriften. Reden. Briefe,* vol. 3, pt. 1 (1929), p. 347, translated by Adrian del Caro as "On the Use of the Railway," in *The German Mind of the Nineteenth Century,* ed. Hermann Glaser (New York: Continuum, 1981), p. 183.

49. List, "Das deutsche Eisenbahnsystem," p. 348, and "On the Use of the Railway," p. 184.

50. Edward Mead Earle, "Adam Smith, Alexander Hamilton, Friedrich List: The Economic Foundations of Military Power," in *Makers of Modern Strategy: Military Thought from Machiavelli to Hitler,* ed. Edward Mead Earle (New York: Atheneum, 1966), p. 149. But there were more lyrical moments in List's (and his friends') fascination with the railroad, too. List's Paris acquaintance in 1830–1831, the German writer Ludwig Börne, commented in a letter that if List's railroad plans were realized,

> one could travel to Strasbourg from the French capital in 12 hours and on to Frankfurt am Main in 18 hours. . . . But Heine said that it is an awful thought that one could

be in Germany again in 12 hours! List and I are really keen on railways because of their immense political potentialities. Every despotism would have its neck broken and wars would be quite impossible in the future. (Henderson, *Friedrich List*, p. 131, quoting from Ludwig Börne, *Gesammelte Schriften* vol. 9, p. 149f., and Fabiunke, *Zur historischen Rolle*, pp. 253–254.)

51. List's biographer W. O. Henderson has translated and edited the volume. See the "Editor's Introduction," in Friedrich List, *The Natural System of Political Economy 1837* (London: Frank Cass, 1983), pp. 1–14. The French original together with a German translation first appeared in *Schriften. Reden. Briefe,* vol. 4 (1927).

52. The best source for this is Henderson, "Friedrich List and the French Protectionists," pp. 262–275. Also see Gide and Rist, *A History of Economic Doctrines,* pp. 286, 297.

53. Henderson, *Friedrich List*, pp. 85–89, and McLellan, *Marx before Marxism*, p. 81.

# Chapter 8

1. List, *The National System,* pp. xxix-xxx. Emphasis in the original in this and other quotations.

2. *The National System*, pp. 174–175.

3. "Die Staatskunde und Staatspraxis Württembergs im Grundriss," in List, *Schriften. Reden. Briefe*, vol. 1, p. 314, quoted in Schulz, "Friedrich Lists Geschichtsauffassung," p. 311.

4. *The National System*, p. xxv.

5. *The National System*, p. xxvi.

6. *The National System*, p. xxvi

7. *The National System*, p. 175.

8. *The National System*, p. 124.

9. *The National System*, p. 125.

10. *The National System*, p. 410.

11. *The National System*, p. 127.

12. *The National System*, p. 131.

13. *The National System*, pp. 126–127.

14. *The National System*, p. 365.

15. *The National System*, pp. 365–366.

16. *The National System*, p. 366.

17. *The National System*, p. 339.

18. *The National System*, p. 111.

19. *The National System*, p. 337.

20. *The National System*, p. 337.

21. *The National System*, p. 31.

22. *The National System*, p. 32.

23. *The National System*, pp. 49–50.

24. *The National System*, pp. 50–51.

25. *The National System*, pp. 51–52.

26. *The National System*, p. 322. (For what Poland would have been had it not been Poland, see pp. 186, 388.)

27. Spiegel, *The Growth of Economic Thought*, p. 419.

28. Dorfman, *The Economic Mind in American Civilization,* vol. 2, p. 583.

29. *The National System*, p. 334.

30. *The National System*, pp. 109–110.

31. "Introduction to the National System, 1841," in Hirst, *Life of Friedrich List*, pp. 301–302.

32. *The National System*, p. 93.

33. Earle, "Smith, Hamilton, List," p. 142.

34. *The National System*, p. 176.

35. Earle, "Smith, Hamilton, List," p. 144. Woodruff D. Smith, *The Ideological Origins of Nazi Imperialism* (Oxford: Oxford University Press, 1986) likewise takes this view, but if one is to ignore the fundamental difference between Listian and Nazi ideas of expansion, then one must also consider that Marx and Engels have an even stronger claim as Hitler's forerunners insofar as Germany's relations with East Europe were concerned.

36. *The National System*, p. 161.

37. *The National System*, p. 162.

38. *The National System*, p. 270.

39. *The National System*, p. 270.

40. *The National System*, pp. 415–416 (see also pp. 190–191).

41. *The National System*, p. 419.

42. *The National System*, pp. 421–422.

43. *The National System*, p. 423.

44. Emmanuel N. Roussakis, *Friedrich List, the Zollverein, and the Uniting of Europe* (Bruges, Belgium: College of Europe, 1968), pp. 110–111. It is therefore a mistake to speak, as Roussakis does, of a union of "six nations" envisioned by List that was to consist of France, Belgium, Switzerland, the Netherlands, Denmark, and Germany; all of them except France were to become part of Germany first.

45. Friedrich Engels, "Ernst Moritz Arndt," in *Marx-Engels Gesamtausgabe*, 1st Series, vol. 2 (Berlin: 1930), p. 108, quoted in Horace B. Davis, *Nationalism and Socialism: Marxist and Labor Theories of Nationalism to 1917* (New York and London: Monthly Review Press, 1967), p. 3.

46. Edmund Silberner, *The Problem of War in Nineteenth Century Economic Thought*, tr. Alexander H. Krappe (Princeton: Princeton University Press, 1946), p. 160.

47. Silberner, *The Problem of War*, pp. 161–162, 170.

48. See List's preface, "Vorrede," *Das nationale System* (1959), pp. 28–29. Furthermore, List said that for the Germans to establish any other than a a "constitutional-monarchist" government would be as harmful as for the United States to adopt a monarchist—or for Russia, a constitutional—form of government.

49. See Earle, "Smith, Hamilton, List," pp. 144–145, 153, and Woodruff D. Smith, *The Ideological Origins*, passim.

50. *The National System*, p. 389.

51. *The National System*, p. 425.

52. *The National System*, pp. 404–405.

53. *The National System*, pp. 429–432.

54. *The National System*, pp. 433–434.

55. To appreciate List's comments on the Russians, let us add that toward the end of his life he modified his 1828 prediction that Russia would become one of the two great powers in the twentieth century. (See Chapter 7.) He wrote in 1845 that in the middle of the twentieth century there would be only two superpowers—England and the United States—and three or four other independent nations—France, Germany, Russia, and Spain. All other nations and states would be dependent and tied by alliances or other "external circumstances" to some of those large states. List was not sure about Russia's prospects as a first-class power: Russia's great-power status—"however powerful it might be in the present"—was not se-

cured by its internal cultural, constitutional, legal, or administrative conditions, but was based instead on military power that ruled over that "undeveloped nation and a number of barbarian hordes." See "Die politisch-ökonomische Nationaleinheit der Deutschen," in List, *Schriften. Reden. Briefe*, vol. 7, pp. 482–483. For discussion of this issue, see Weippert, *Der späte List*, p. 47.

56. *The National System*, p. 194.

## Chapter 9

1. *The National System*, p. 110.

2. John Breuilly, *Nationalism and the State*, pp. 335–338.

3. Karl Marx, "Theses on Feuerbach," in McLellan, *Karl Marx: Selected Writings*, p. 156.

4. "Theses on Feuerbach," in McLellan, *Karl Marx: Selected Writings*, p. 156.

5. Bert F. Hoselitz, "Theories of Stages," in *Theories of Economic Growth*, ed. Bert F. Hoselitz (New York: The Free Press, 1960), pp. 196–197.

6. *The National System*, p. 177.

7. Hoselitz, "Theories of Stages," p. 199–200.

8. Hoselitz, "Theories of Stages," pp. 201–202.

9. *The National System*, p. 309.

10. *The National System*, p. 324.

11. Hoselitz, "Theories of Stages," p. 196.

12. *The National System*, p. 347.

13. *The National System*, p. 350. (Emphasis in the original.)

14. Earle, "Smith, Hamilton, List," pp. 347–348.

15. Adam Smith is quoted here from the original English text as it appeared in the editorial notes in List, *Schriften. Reden. Briefe*, vol. 6, p. 600. It is cited there from Dugald Stewart's introduction to Adam Smith, *Essays on Philosophical Subjects* (Basel, 1799), p. xcviii, which I have not seen. The essay in question was never published; its text was lost, and only a fragment remains (as quoted by Stewart). The English edition of *The National System*, pp. 347–348, quotes Smith in a translation back into English from the German translation by List (who cited no source for the Smith fragment).

16. *The National System*, p. 348.

17. *The National System*, pp. 348–349.

18. Thomas Cooper, *Lectures on the Elements of Political Economy*, 2nd ed. (Columbia, South Carolina, 1829), p. 28, quoted in List, *Schriften. Reden. Briefe*, vol. 6, p. 560.

19. *The National System*, p. 165.

20. *The National System*, pp. 166–167.

21. *The National System*, p. 163.

22. *The National System*, pp. 170–171.

23. *The National System*, pp. 171–172.

24. *The National System*, p. 316.

25. *The National System*, pp. 299–300.

26. *The National System*, p. 82.

27. *The National System*, p. 82.

28. *The National System*, p. 144.

29. *The National System*, p. 138.

30. *The National System*, p. 139.

31. *The National System*, p. 142.

32. *The National System*, p. 201.

33. *The National System*, p. 260.

34. *The National System*, p. 140.

35. *The National System*, p. 334.

36. *The National System*, pp. 334–335.

37. Eugen Karl Dühring, *Kritische Geschichte der Nationalökonomie und des Sozialismus* (Leipzig: Fues Verlag, 1879), p. 353.

38. Harry G. Johnson, "A Theoretical Model of Economic Nationalism in New and Developing States," in Johnson, *Economic Nationalism*, p. 9.

39. Johnson, "A Theoretical Model," p. 14.

40. Johnson, "A Theoretical Model," p. 14.

41. Johnson, "A Theoretical Model," pp. 15–16.

42. Lichtheim, *Marxism*, p. xvii.

43. Johannes Burkhardt, "Das Verhaltensleitbild 'Produktivität' und seine historisch-anthropologische Voraussetzung," *Saeculum* 25, no. 2–3 (1974):277–289, examines the concept of productivity and productive labor in various economic doctrines, including those of the Physiocrats, Adam Smith, Karl Marx, and Friedrich List, and suggests that they reflect philosophical as well as political assumptions of their authors, rather than being scientifically neutral economic categories. Burkhardt links the idea of productive forces in List to his view of Germany as a developing country (see especially pp. 281–283). Burkhardt also refers to Jakob Baxa, "Der Ursprung von Friedrich Lists Theorie der produktiven Kräfte," *Zeitschrift für Volkswirtschaft and Sozialpolitik* (1923), pp. 123 ff., for the sources of List's doctrine of productive forces.

44. Friedrich Seidel, *Das Armutsproblem im deutschen Vormärz bei Friedrich List* (Cologne: Forschungsinstitut für Sozial- und Wirtschaftsgeschichte an der Universität Köln, 1971), pp. 32, 50–51, passim, observes, in a comprehensive review of List's statements on the problem of poverty in modern society, that while List expressed sympathy for the poor, he did not think in terms of fighting poverty through legal and social reform, nor did he think of workers as a social *class* with its distinct group interests.

45. W. O. Henderson, "Friedrich List and the Social Question," *Journal of European Economic History* 10, no. 1 (1981): 697–708, especially pp. 707–708. For a discussion of this question along both biographic and topical lines, see Lenz, "Vom Pauperismus zum Proletariat," pp. 15–43.

46. Ralf Dahrendorf, *Society and Democracy in Germany* (Garden City, NY: Doubleday, 1969), pp. 54–55.

47. John Gerard Ruggie, "Introduction: International Interdependence and National Welfare," in *The Antinomies of Interdependence: National Welfare and the International Division of Labor*, ed. John Gerard Ruggie (New York: Columbia University Press, 1983), p. 6.

48. Marcello de Cecco, *Money and Empire: The International Gold Standard, 1890–1914* (Oxford: Basil Blackwell, 1974), pp. 5–6. See also Ruggie,"Introduction: International Interdependence," pp. 4–6.

49. Ruggie, "Introduction: International Interdependence," p. 7.

50. De Cecco, *Money and Empire*, p. 9.

51. E. J. Hobsbawm, *The Age of Revolution*, p. 217. From the perspective of the late 1980s, Hobsbawm's view that in the 1930s the Russians "developed means of leaping this chasm" appears less self-evident. Gorbachev certainly does not share it.

52. Hobsbawm, *The Age of Revolution*, p. 216.

53. De Cecco, *Money and Empire*, p. 11. When de Cecco refers to "recent historiog-

raphy," he cites Barrington Moore, Jr., *The Social Origins of Dictatorship and Democracy* (Cambridge, MA: Beacon Press, 1964.)

54. Rosa Luxemburg, *The National Question*, ed. Horace B. Davis (New York and London: Monthly Review Press, 1976), pp. 160–161.

55. Raymond Grew, unpublished comments on an earlier version of my book.

56. Teodor Shanin, *Russia as a 'Developing Society': The Roots of Otherness: Russia's Turn of the Century*, vol. 2, *Russia, 1905–1907: Revolution as Moment of Truth* (New Haven and London: Yale University Press, 1986), p. 248: While Smith and Ricardo "reflected and explored the first capitalist surge in Europe," List's "first amendment" came to define "the policies of 'the second wave' of industrialization in Germany and Japan" (and the policies of Sergei Witte in Russia).

## Chapter 10

1. Arnošt Klíma, "The Bourgeois Revolution of 1848–1849 in Central Europe," in *Revolution in History*, ed. Roy Porter and Mikuláš Teich (Cambridge: Cambridge University Press, 1986), pp. 74–100, views the events of those years in terms of the aspirations and actions of social classes (the proletariat, the liberal and radical bourgeoisie, the peasantry). Klíma treats the problem of nationality as a diversion from class conflict, but he admits at the same time that it was "one of the central issues of the revolution." "It was one which neither the liberal nor radical bourgeoisie was able to resolve." (Ibid., p. 86.) (Klíma does not say how "the proletariat" would have solved that problem.) For a less ideological treatment, see Leonard Krieger, "Nationalism and the Nation-State System, 1789–1870," in *Chapters in Western Civilization*, vol. 2, 3rd ed., ed. the Contemporary Civilization Staff of Columbia College, Columbia University (New York: Columbia University Press, 1962), pp. 103–139, and Otto Pflanze, "Nationalism in Europe, 1848–1871," *Review of Politics* 23, no. 2 (April 1966):129–143. Billington, *Fire in the Minds of Men*, pp. 146–172, shows Europe's nationalist generation of 1830–1848 focusing on its preoccupation with music, opera, and revolutionary violence.

2. "Letter sent by František Palacký to Frankfurt," *Slavonic and East European Review* 26, no. 67 (April 1948):305.

3. "Letter by Palacký," p. 308.

4. "Letter by Palacký," p. 304.

5. "Letter by Palacký," p. 306.

6. "Manifesto of the First Slavonic Congress to the Nations of Europe," *Slavonic and East European Review* 26, no. 67 (April, 1948):310.

7. "Manifesto of the First Slavonic Congress," p. 310.

8. "Manifesto of the First Slavonic Congress," p. 310.

9. Brian Weinstein, "Language Strategists: Redefining Political Frontiers on the Basis of Linguistic Choices," *World Politics* 31, no. 3 (April 1979): 345–364; Seton-Watson, *Nations and States*, pp. 429–433; and Anderson, *Imagined Communities*, p. 81. The reader who believes that the story told here (in Chapter 10 and earlier in Chapter 6), with its accent on the linkage between linguistic and political components of nationalism, is parochially European or "Germanic," may wish to consult David D. Laitin, "Linguistic Dissociation: A Strategy for Africa," in *The Antinomies of Interdependence: National Welfare and the International Division of Labor*, ed. John Gerard Ruggie (New York: Columbia University Press, 1983), pp. 317–368. Laitin's late-twentieth century Africa strikingly resembles the mid-nineteenth century Central and Eastern Europe discussed here.

10. Peter Burke, *Popular Culture in Early Modern Europe* (New York: Harper and Row, 1978), p. 13.

11. Burke, *Popular Culture*, p. 12. Burke's use of "imposed" in describing what the intellectuals did suggests coercion. This was not the case: Intellectuals like Herder, Karadžić, or Palacký were themselves powerless critics of the then dominant regimes.

12. Józef Chlebowczyk, "Świadomość historyczna jako element procesów narodotwórczych we wschodniej Europie Środkowej" [Historical Consciousness as an Element of Nation-Forming Processes in East-Central Europe], in *Polska, czeska i słowacka świadomość historyczna XIX wieku* [Polish, Czech and Slovak Historical Consciousness in the 19th Century], ed. Roman Heck (Wrocław: Ossolineum, 1979), pp. 9–24. For Palacký, see Josef F. Zacek, *Palacký. The Historian as Scholar and Nationalist* (The Hague and Paris: Mouton, 1970).

13. Anderson, *Imagined Communities*, pp. 14–15.

14. Ernest Gellner, *Thought and Change* (London: Weidenfeld and Nicolson, 1964), p. 168. Gellner's most recent *Nations and Nationalism* restates this point (see pp. 48–49, 50, 55, 123–125, and so on).

15. Miroslav Hroch, *Die Vorkämpfer der nationalen Bewegung bei den kleinen Völkern Europas* (Acta Universitatis Carolinae Philosophica et Historica, monographia 24, Prague, 1968), p. 24. This work is now available in English as *Social Preconditions of National Revival in Europe. A Comparative Analysis of the Social Composition of Patriotic Groups among the Smaller European Nations*, tr. Ben Fowkes (Cambridge: Cambridge University Press, 1985). For the question of phases, see pp. 22–24.

16. W. J. Argyle, "Size and Scale as Factors in the Development of Nationalist Movements," in *Nationalist Movements* ed. Anthony D. Smith (London: Macmillan, 1976), pp. 31–33.

17. Raymond Grew, "The Crises and Their Sequences," in *Crises of Political Development in Europe and the United States*, ed. Raymond Grew (Princeton: Princeton University Press, 1978), pp. 6–7; and Leonard Binder et al., *Crises and Sequences in Political Development* (Princeton: Princeton University Press, 1971).

18. See Roman Szporluk, "Poland," in Grew, *Crises of Political Development*, pp. 383–416.

19. David Landes, "The Industrial Revolution: 1750–1850," in *Chapters in Western Civilization*, p. 172.

20. Rudolf Jaworski, "Nationalismus und Ökonomie als Problem der Geschichte Ost-mitteleuropas im 19. und zu Beginn des 20. Jahrhunderts," *Geschichte und Gesellschaft* 8, no. 2 (1982):184–204, especially pp. 199–200.

21. Henderson, *Friedrich List*, p. 260.

22. Henderson, *Friedrich List*, p. 243.

23. Andrew C. Janos, *The Politics of Backwardness in Hungary 1825–1945* (Princeton: Princeton University Press, 1982).

24. Ivan T. Berend and Gyorgy Ránki, "Economic Factors in Nationalism: A Case Study of Hungary at the Turn of the Twentieth Century," in *Underdevelopment and Economic Growth: Studies in Hungarian Social and Economic History*, ed. Ivan T. Berend and Gyorgy Ránki (Budapest: Akademiai Kiado, 1979) p. 85.

25. Pamfil Seicaru, *Istoria partidelor national, taranist si national taranist* [History of the National, Peasantist, and National-Peasantist Parties] (Madrid: Editura Carpatii Traian Popescu, 1963), pp. 81–83. (I thank Irina Livezeanu for this reference.)

26. Pierre Vilar, "Spain and Catalonia," *Review* 3, no. 4 (Spring 1980):552–553.

27. Vilar, "Spain and Catalonia," pp. 550–551.

28. F. S. L. Lyons, *Ireland since the Famine* (London: Collins Fontana, 1973), pp. 251–252.

29. Lyons, *Ireland*, p. 253. Lyons points out that "Griffith was also to some extent influenced by the American protectionist, Henry Carey, but List's work, which he read in translation, was much the most important formative element in his economic policy." (Lyons, *Ireland*, p. 793).

30. Arthur Griffith, *The Resurrection of Hungary* (Dublin, 1918), p. 144, as quoted in Lyons, *Ireland*, p. 254.

31. Vilar, "Spain and Catalonia," p. 543.

32. Gellner, *Thought and Change*, p. 168. It is only fair to remember that Gellner often sounds more extreme than he is. For example, while his recent *Nations and Nationalism* reiterates that "nationalism engenders nations, and not the other way round," he is careful to add that "nationalism uses the pre-existing, historically inherited proliferation of cultures or cultural wealth" and that nations, treated by him as "new units," in fact use "as their raw material the cultural, historical and other inheritances from the pre-nationalist world." (*Nations and Nationalism*, pp. 55 and 49.)

33. Anderson, *Imagined Communities*, pp. 14–15.

34. Sewell, "Ideologies and Social Revolutions," p. 61.

35. Lichtheim, *Marxism*, p. 252.

36. See David M. Potter, "The Historian's Use of Nationalism and Vice Versa," in *Generalizations in Historical Writing*, ed. Alexander Riasanovsky and Barnes Reznik (Philadelphia: University of Pennsylvania Press, 1963), pp. 125–27.

37. František Graus, "Slavs and Germans," in *Eastern and Western Europe in the Middle Ages*, ed. Geoffrey Barraclough (New York: Harcourt Brace Jovanovich, 1970), pp. 15–42.

38. James J. Sheehan, "What is German History?" p. 10.

39. Isaiah Berlin, "Nationalism, Past Neglect and Present Power," in *Against the Current*, p. 337.

40. Hayes, *The Historical Evolution*, p. 289.

## Chapter 11

1. Roman Rosdolsky, "Friedrich Engels und das Problem der 'geschichtslosen' Völker (die Nationalitätenfrage in der Revolution 1848–1849 im Lichte der 'Neuen Rheinischen Zeitung')," *Archiv für Sozialgeschichte*, 5 (1964):87–282.

2. Friedrich Engels, "The Magyar Struggle," *Collected Works*, vol. 8, p. 238, as quoted by Ian Cummins, *Marx, Engels, and National Movements* (London: Croom Helm, 1980), pp. 40–41.

3. Friedrich Engels, "The Danish-Prussian Armistice," *Neue Rheinische Zeitung*, no. 99 (9 September 1848); *Collected Works* vol. 7, pp. 421, 422, 423, as quoted in Cummins, *Marx, Engels, and National Movements*, p. 46.

4. Engels, "The Civil War in Switzerland," *Deutsche-Brüsseler- Zeitung*, no. 91 (14 November 1847); *Collected Works*, vol. 6, p. 372, as quoted in Cummins, *Marx, Engels, and National Movements*, p. 32.

5. Engels, "The Beginning of the End in Austria," *Deutsche-Brüsseler-Zeitung*, no. 8 (27 January 1848); *Collected Works*, vol. 6, p. 531, quoted in Cummins, *Marx, Engels, and National Movements*, p. 40.

6. Cummins, *Marx, Engels, and National Movements*, p. 40.

7. Friedrich Engels, "Revolution and Counter-Revolution in Germany," in *The German Revolutions*, ed. Leonard Krieger (Chicago: University of Chicago Press, 1967), pp. 174–175. In this and subsequent quotations from Engels, I have replaced Engels' terms, "Slavonian" and "Tschech," with "Slav" and "Czech."

8. "Revolution and Counter-Revolution in Germany," p. 175.

9. "Revolution and Counter-Revolution in Germany," pp. 176–177.

10. "Revolution and Counter-Revolution in Germany," p. 178.

11. "Revolution and Counter-Revolution in Germany," p. 178.

12. "Revolution and Counter-Revolution in Germany," p. 210.

13. Marx to Engels, October 8, 1958, in *Karl Marx on Colonialism and Modernization*, ed. Shlomo Avineri (Garden City, NY: Doubleday, 1969), pp. 463–464.

14. On this matter, see especially the pathbreaking work of Rosdolsky, "Friedrich Engels und das Problem." In contemporary Marxist scholar Michael Löwy's "Marxists and the National Question," *New Left Review* no. 96 (March-April 1976):84, he argues that because Engels "failed to grasp the true *class* reasons for the failure of 1848–9, Engels tried to explain it with a metaphysical ideology: the theory of inherently counter-revolutionary 'non-historic nations.' " Löwy stresses that this theory owed much to Hegel and the conservative German historical school. (This is to be distinguished from the Historical School in economics in the second half of the nineteenth century.)

15. Walker Connor, *The National Question in Marxist-Leninist Theory and Strategy* (Princeton: Princeton University Press, 1984), p. 15. The quotation within quotation is from Engels' "Hungary and Panslavism," in *The Russian Menace to Europe*, ed. P. Blackstock and B. Hoselitz (Glencoe, IL: Free Press, 1952), p. 59.

16. Connor, *The National Question*, p. 16.

17. Cummins, *Marx, Engels, and National Movements*, p. 23. Cummins quotes Marx from Marx and Engels, *Selected Correspondence* (Moscow: Foreign Languages Publishing House, n.d.), p. 134. See also note 13 in this chapter.

18. Cummins, *Marx, Engels, and National Movements*, p. 27. Cummins cites V. I. Lenin, "Better Fewer but Better" (1923), in V. I. Lenin, *The National Liberation Movement in the East* (Moscow: Foreign Languages Publishing House, 1957), p. 315, in support of his interpretation.

19. Cummins, *Marx, Engels, and National Movement*, p. 23.

20. Tucker, *The Marx-Engels Reader*, p. 145.

21. Karl Marx, "Preface," *Capital*, vol. 1, in *Karl Marx: Selected Writings*, ed., David McLellan (Oxford: Oxford University Press, 1978), p. 416.

22. "Preface," *Capital*, vol. 1, in McLellan, *Karl Marx: Selected Writings*, p. 417.

23. Jon Elster, "Historical materialism and economic backwardness," in *After Marx*, ed. Terence Ball and James Farr (Cambridge: Cambridge University Press, 1984), p. 44.

24. Elster, "Historical Materialism" in Ball and Farr, *After Marx*, p. 44. The quotation within quotation comes from Marx's letter to the editors of *Otechestvennye zapiski*, as translated by Elster from *Marx-Engels Werke*, vol. 19. Marx's letter may be found in Avineri, *Karl Marx on Colonialism*, pp. 467–470, and in McLellan, *Karl Marx: Selected Writings*, pp. 571–572 (selections).

25. Karl Marx's letter to Engels, November 30, 1867, in McLellan, *Karl Marx; Selected Writings*, p. 590. See also Karl Marx and Friedrich Engels, *Ireland and the Irish Question* (New York: International Publishers, 1972), p. 143, quoted in Connor, *The National Question*, p. 27.

26. E. J. Hobsbawm, *The Age of Capital 1845–1875* (New York: New American Library, 1979), p. 99.

27. Teodor Shanin, "Late Marx and the Russian 'Periphery of Capitalism,' " *Monthly Review* 35, no. 2 (June 1983):19–20. Shanin ends this passage as follows: "By one of history's ironies, a century later we are still trying to shed the opposite claim: the assumption that Russia is to show to all of the Englands of our time the image of their socialist future." (Ibid., p. 20.)

28. "Marx to the Editors," in Avineri, *Karl Marx on Colonialism*, p. 468.

29. "Marx to the Editors," p. 469.

30. "Marx to the Editors," p. 469.

31. "Marx to the Editors," p. 470.

32. "Letter to Vera Sassoulitch [sic]," in McLellan, *Karl Marx: Selected Writings*, p. 580.

33. "Preface to the Russian Edition of the *Communist Manifesto*," in McLellan, *Karl Marx: Selected Writings*, pp. 583–584.

34. Marx, "List Critique," p. 280.

35. Hobsbawm, *The Age of Capital*, p. 101. (Emphasis added.)

36. Karl Marx, *Critique of the Gotha Programme*, with appendices by Marx, Engels, and Lenin (New York: International Publishers, 1938), p. 12. (For the text of the Gotha program, see Marx, *Critique*, pp. 89–91.)

37. *Critique of the Gotha Programme*, p. 13. There are selections from this work in McLellan, *Karl Marx: Selected Writings*, pp. 564–570, and in Tucker, *Marx-Engels Reader*, pp. 525–541.

38. *Critique of the Gotha Programme*, p. 13.

39. Löwy, "Marx and Engels: Cosmopolites," p. 12.

40. Löwy, "Marx and Engels: Cosmopolites," p. 12.

41. Marx and Engels, *Ireland and the Irish Question*, p. 303, as quoted in Walicki, *Philosophy and Romantic Nationalism*, p. 375.

42. Friedrich Engels to Karl Kautsky, February 7, 1882, in *Friedrich Engels' Briefwechsel mit Karl Kautsky*, ed. Benedikt Kautsky (Vienna, 1955), pp. 50–53, as quoted in Davis, *Nationalism and Socialism*, p. 17. (Emphasis added by R.S.)

43. Friedrich Engels, "Nationalism, Internationalism and the Polish Question," in Blackstock and Hoselitz, *Russian Menace to Europe*, p. 119, as quoted in Connor, *The National Question*, p. 27.

44. Engels to Kautsky, September 12, 1882, in Avineri, *Karl Marx on Colonialism*, p. 473. In the same letter, Engels said: "the [English] workers gaily share the feast of England's monopoly of the world market and the colonies." List would not have said it better.

45. Geoff Eley, "State Formation, Nationalism and Political Culture in Nineteenth-Century Germany," in *Culture, Ideology and Politics*, ed. Raphael Samuel and Gareth Stedman Jones (London: Routledge and Kegan Paul, 1983), p. 288. The quotation within quotation is from Tom Nairn, *The Break-Up of Britain: Crisis and Neo-Colonialism* (London: New Left Books, 1977), p. 94.

46. Hobsbawm, *The Age of Capital*, p. 100. There is an interesting discussion of the phantom of "internationalism" in the Marxist movement in Tom Nairn, "Internationalism: a Critique," *Bulletin of Scottish Politics* 1, no. 1 (August 1980):101–125.

47. J. P. Nettl, *Rosa Luxemburg*, vol. 2 (London, New York, and Toronto: Oxford University Press, 1966), p. 861.

48. Nettl, *Rosa Luxemburg*, vol. 1, p. 33.

49. "Kwestia narodowościowa i autonomia" [The nationality question and autonomy], in Róża Luksemburg [Rosa Luxemburg], *Wybór Pism* [Selected writings], vol. 2 (Warsaw: Książka i Wiedza, 1959), pp. 147–148, as translated and quoted in Nettl, *Rosa Luxemburg*, vol. 2, p. 849. (This article originally appeared in 1908.)

50. Nettl, *Rosa Luxemburg*, vol. 2, pp. 860, 862; vol. 1, pp. 32–33. (Emphasis added.)

51. Nettl, *Rosa Luxemburg*, vol. 2, pp. 861–862.

52. Nettl, *Rosa Luxemburg*, vol. 1, p. 33.

53. Eric J. Hobsbawm, "Some Reflections on Nationalism," p. 395.

54. Geoff Eley, "What Produces Fascism: Preindustrial Traditions or a Crisis of a Capitalist State," in Geoff Eley, *From Unification to Nazism: Reinterpreting the German Past* (Boston, London, and Sydney: Allen and Unwin, 1986), p. 269.

55. Eley, *From Unification to Nazism*, pp. 269–270. The NSDAP (the National Socialist German Workers Party, i.e., the Nazis), says Eley, besides controlling the right, "united a broadly based coalition of the subordinate classes, centered on the peasantry and petty-bourgeoisie, but stretching deep into the wage-earning population." Those impressed and taken in by Nazi and Fascist "national" claims included no less a figure abroad than the president of Czechoslovakia, Edvard Beneš, who in an article published in 1936 viewed the Fascist regime in Italy as "the latest stage in the Italian Risorgimento" and added that "the same is true about Hitlerism in the centralizing evolution of Germany today." (Edvard Beneš, "Naš největší úkol národní" [Our greatest national task], in *Idea Československého Státu*, vol. 2, [Prague, 1936], p. 224, quoted in Roman Szporluk, *The Political Thought of Thomas G. Masaryk* [Boulder, CO: East European Monographs, 1981], p. 162.)

56. Isaiah Berlin, "Benjamin Disraeli, Karl Marx, and the Search for Identity," in *Against the Current*, p. 280.

57. See the essays of Berlin, "Disraeli, Marx," and "The Life and Opinions of Moses Hess," in *Against the Current*, pp. 252–286 and 213–251, respectively. According to Berlin, both Marx and Disraeli, having become alienated from their roots, searched in vain for an alternative idealized (and imaginary) identity. In Marx's case, that imaginary alternative was "the great class of the disinherited workers, in whose name he could thunder his anathemas. . . . Marx had as little affinity with individual proletarians . . . as Disraeli with the inner core of the British upper class. . . . The proletariat remains an abstract category in Marx." (Berlin, *Against the Current*, p. 281.) (See also pp. 282–283 for Marx and the proletariat.)

58. Bruce Mazlish, *The Meaning of Karl Marx* (New York: Oxford University Press, 1984), pp. 148–149, speaks of Marx as a "German nationalist" in that sense, for example, by quoting Marx's remark that his *Capital* was "a triumph of German science, something an individual German can avow since it is in no way *his* merit, but belongs more to the nation." While not a nationalist in the sense understood in this book, Marx was indeed open to charges advanced, among others, by Moses Hess or the Czech nationalists that under his internationalism the large nations like Germany would still stand above the nonhistoric underdogs.

59. See on this Józef Chlebowczyk, "Ruch robotniczy a kwestia narodowa w monarchii Habsburgów" [The workers movement and the national question in the Habsburg monarchy], *Z pola walki* [From the battle field], 11, no. 1 (1968), p. 103.

60. See the chapter on "Moses Hess: Socialism and Nationalism as a Critique of Bourgeois Society," in Shlomo Avineri, *The Making of Modern Zionism: The Intellectual Origins of the Jewish State* (New York: Basic Books, 1981), p. 46.

61. Connor, *The National Question*, pp. 19–20.

62. Samir Amin, *Class and Nation. Historically and in the Current Crisis*, tr. Susan Kaplow (New York and London: Monthly Review Press, 1980), p. 106.

## Chapter 12

1. The precise relationship of nationalism to national socialism of the Hitlerian type is a complex issue that cannot be adequately treated here. Whether one sees fascism and nazism as challengers to nationalism (which is the view of Anthony D. Smith, *Nationalism in the Twentieth Century*, especially Chapter 3), or argues that there were affinities between them, which in opposition to Smith has been argued by John Breuilly, *Nationalism and the State*, there can be no question that List has nothing to do with Hitler. (When Anthony D. Smith, *Nationalism in the Twentieth Century*, p. 211 n., refers to George Mosse, "The Mystical Origins of National Socialism," *Journal of the History of Ideas* 22 (1961):81–96, as being "on List, Schuler, and Tarnhari," he does not make it clear that the List in question was Guido von List [born 1849], not Friedrich List [deceased 1846]). In any case, Hitler's "national socialism" must be distinguished from, say, that of the Czech National Socialist Party, formed in the 1890s, which advocated democratic reforms, social legislation, and national emancipation of the Czechs. (See Bruce M. Garver, *The Young Czech Party 1874– 1901 and the Emergence of a Multi-Party System* [New Haven, CT: Yale University Press, 1978], pp. 295–298, and passim.)

2. Robert M. Berdahl, "New Thoughts on German Nationalism," *American Historical Review* 77, no. 1 (February 1972):70.

3. Henderson, *Friedrich List*, pp. 214–215, quotes the following comments of I. W. Lambi, *Free Trade and Protection in Germany, 1868–1879* (n.p., 1965):

> List's arguments were no longer fully applicable to the conditions of a more advanced economy. It was difficult to demand protection for German industry on the ground that it was underdeveloped and to justify the damage caused to the consumer public. It was also useless politically to subordinate the interests of agriculture to those of industry, for not only were the agrarians clamorous in the representation of their interests, but agriculture was no longer such a primitive occupation as viewed by List.

4. Hayes, *Historical Evolution*, p. 272.

5. Henderson, *Friedrich List*, p. 215.

6. See Kahan, "Nineteenth-Century European Experience," pp. 24–25, for specific circumstances of Germany's turn to protectionism.

7. Kahan, "Nineteenth-Century European Experience," p. 20 (and p. 28).

8. Gustav von Schmoller, "Verhandlungen des Vereins für Socialpolitik," *Schriften des Vereins für Socialpolitik* (1902), pp. 264–271, as quoted in Kahan, "Nineteenth-Century European Experience," p. 23. For a recent account of the Historical School, its predecessors (including Friedrich List), and successors, see Spiegel, *The Growth of Economic Thought*, pp. 411–433. (Spiegel also has an excellent bibliography.)

9. Kahan, "Nineteenth-Century European Experience," pp. 18–19.

10. Adolph Wagner, *Agrar- und Industriestaat* (Jena: G. Fischer, 1901), p. 25, quoted by Kahan, "Nineteenth-Century European Experience," p. 18.

11. George Lichtheim, *Imperialism* (London: Allen Lane/Penguin, 1971), p. 63, quoting Charles Wilson, *Mercantilism* (London: Routledge and Kegan Paul, 1958), p. 6.

12. Lichtheim, *Imperialism*, pp. 68–69. (Emphasis in the original.) However, Lichtheim stresses that "imperialism" was not the exclusive property of the Germans: Even during the era of free trade and liberalism, it had never disappeared completely, and it was again adopted by the Great Powers during the 1880s. (See Lichtheim, *Imperialism*, pp. 76–77, who quotes, on this matter, from E. J. Hobsbawm, *Industry and Empire* [London: Weidenfeld and Nicolson; New York: Pantheon, 1968], pp. 123–124.)

13. Spiegel, *Growth of Economic Thought*, p. 425.

14. Spiegel, *Growth of Economic Thought*, pp. 426, 431–433; Lichtheim, *Imperialism*, p. 64.

15. Henry Cord Meyer, *Mitteleuropa in German Thought and Action 1815–1945* (The Hague: Martinus Nijhoff, 1955) is a useful guide to the problematics, economic and otherwise, of German relations with East Central Europe.

16. On Marxism and nationalism in the Habsburg monarchy, see Hans Mommsen, *Die Sozialdemokratie und die Nationalitätenfrage im Habsburgischen Vielvölkerstaat* vol. 1, *Das Ringen um das supranationale Integration der zisleithanischen Arbeiterbewegung, 1867–1907* (Vienna: Europa-Verlag, 1963), and *Arbeiterbewegung und nationale Frage* (Göttingen: Vandenhoeck and Ruprecht, 1979).

17. Otto Bauer, *Die Nationalitätenfrage und die Sozialdemokratie*, 2nd ed. (Vienna: Volksbuchhandlung, 1924), p. 135, as quoted by Karl W. Deutsch, *Nationalism and Social Communication. An Inquiry into the Foundations of Nationality*, 2nd ed. (Cambridge, MA: M.I.T. Press, 1966), pp. 286 n–287 n. For the most recent edition in the original, see Otto Bauer, *Werkausgabe,* vol. 1 (Vienna: Europa-Verlag, 1975), where the passage cited above appears on p. 194. Bauer follows in the next paragraph with his definition of nation: "Nation is the collectivity of people united by a community of fate into a community of character." ("*Die Nation ist die Gesamtheit der durch Schicksalgemeinschaft zu einer Charaktergemeinschaft verknüpften Menschen.*") Bauer's book, first published in 1907, remains unavailable in English. For brief selections, see Tom Bottomore and Patrick Goode, eds. *Readings in Marxist Sociology* (Oxford: Clarendon Press, 1983), pp. 194–199, and Tom Bottomore and Patrick Goode, eds., *Austro-Marxism* (Oxford Clarendon Press, 1978), pp. 102–117. The latter volume contains an analysis, representative selections from the Austro-Marxist texts, and a fine bibliography.

18. Alexander Gerschenkron, *An Economic Spurt That Failed* (Princeton: Princeton University Press, 1977), pp. 58, 62–68, 70, 78, passim.

19. Luigi de Rosa, "Economics and Nationalism in Italy," *Journal of European Economic History* 11, no. 3 (Winter 1982):537–574.

20. de Rosa, "Economics and Nationalism," pp. 547–550.

21. Alessandro Rossi, "Le transformazioni dell'industria e i loro effetti in Inghilterra ed America," *Nuova Antologia* (April 15, 1878), p. 681, as quoted in de Rosa, "Economics and Nationalism," p. 552.

22. de Rosa, "Economics and Nationalism," p. 552.

23. de Rosa, "Economics and Nationalism," p. 572, quoting from Alfredo Rocco, "Economia liberale, economia socialista ed economia nazionale," *Rivista delle Societá commerziali* (April 30, 1914), p. 299.

24. Gerschenkron, *Economic Backwardness,* pp. 86–87.

25. Enrico Corradini, "The Principles of Nationalism," in *Italian Fascism: From Pareto to Gentile,* ed. Adrian Lyttelton (New York: Harper and Row, 1975), p. 146.

26. A. James Gregor, *Italian Fascism and Developmental Dictatorship* (Princeton: Princeton University Press, 1979), p. 138.

27. Gerschenkron, *Economic Backwardness,* pp. 217–218.

28. Gerschenkron, *Economic Backwardness,* pp. 218–219.

29. Gerschenkron, *Economic Backwardness,* p. 221.

30. See Henderson, *Friedrich List*, p. 261, for List's influence in Japan, Korea, China, and other countries. In the 1920s, List's *National System* was translated into Chinese (Henderson, *Friedrich List*, p. 217).

31. Chitoshi Yanaga, *Japan Since Perry* (New York: McGraw-Hill, 1949), pp. 73–74.

For the influence of German economists, including List, in Japan, also see Kenneth B. Pyle, "Advantages of Followership: German Economics and Japanese Bureaucrats, 1890–1925," *Journal of Japanese Studies* 1 (Autumn 1974):127–137.

32. As quoted in Thomas Balogh, *The Irrelevance of Conventional Economics* (London: Weidenfeld and Nicolson, 1982), p. 250. Balogh adds after this quotation the following comment of his own:

> The need for discrimination in favour of the "less developed" areas ("infant industries") has in the last decade or so been accepted. The advance made in this respect has been largely nullified by the special protection against low-wage competition and the international impact of wage inflation in the industrial sphere. The rise in the price of oil engineered by the OPEC countries has been a unique phenomenon.

Furthermore, according to Balogh, the "free trade doctrine was, perhaps, even more pernicious in its influence on policy in weaker countries than was its twin in the domestic sphere, Say's Law of the Markets." Balogh argues that under "the 'free' play of international market forces," "inequality between nations has increased" in modern times. (Balogh, *The Irrelevance*, p. 183.)

33. M. G. Ranade, "Indian Political Economy" (1892), in *Essays on Indian Economics* (Bombay: Thacker, 1899), p.20, as quoted in Heinz Wolfgang Arndt, *Economic Development: The History of An Idea* (Chicago: The University of Chicago Press, 1987), p.19.

34. Also after the First World War Indians continued to draw inspiration from List in dealing with their own problems, as indicated by the title of a book by Bhasker Anand Saletore, *Der Wert der Listschen Lehren für die Lösung der indischen Frage* [The value of the List teaching for the solution of the Indian question] (Leipzig: Universitätsverlag von Robert Noske, 1933). Saletore pointed out similarities between Germany in List's time and India in the first half of the twentieth century, and he also identified the main differences, such as, for example, the fact that India had already become to some extent an industrial state and that it had a publicly owned railroad network. (Ibid., pp. 35–42.) However, just as in List's Germany some nationalists had opposed industrialization, so in twentieth-century India the prominent fighter for India's independence, Mahatma Gandhi, called machinery "a great sin," while another, Jawaharlal Nehru, advocated in the 1930s a socialist industrialization for India. (Arndt, *Economic Development*, pp. 19–20.)

## Chapter 13

1. Andrzej Walicki, "Russian Social Thought: An Introduction to the Intellectual History of Nineteenth-Century Russia," *Russian Review* 36, no. 1 (January 1977):1–2. This essay summarizes Walicki's major books: *A History of Russian Thought (From the Enlightenment to Marxism)*, tr. Hilda Andrews-Rusiecka (Stanford: Stanford University Press, 1979); and *The Slavophile Controversy*, tr. Hilda Andrews-Rusiecka (Oxford: Oxford University Press, 1975). Many stimulating ideas on the problem discussed here are also in E. H. Carr, " 'Russia and Europe' as a Theme of Russian History," in *Essays Presented to Sir Lewis Namier*, ed. Richard Pares and A. J. P. Taylor (London: Macmillan; New York: St. Martin's Press, 1956), pp. 357–393.

2. Richard Pipes, "Introduction: The Nationality Problem," in *Handbook of Major Soviet Nationalities*, ed. Zev Katz (New York: Free Press; London: Macmillan, 1975), p. 1.

3. Paul Vinogradoff, *Roman Law in Medieval Europe* (Oxford, 1929), p. 62, as quoted in Richard Pipes, *Russia Under the Old Regime* (New York: Scribners, 1974), p. 65.

4. Pipes, *Russia Under the Old Regime*, pp. 64–65, 70. Cf. Marc Raeff, *Understanding Imperial Russia: State and Society in the Old Regime*, tr. Arthur Goldhammer, New York: Columbia University Press, 1984.

5. Nicholas V. Riasanovsky, *Nicholas I and Official Nationality in Russia, 1825–1855* (Berkeley and Los Angeles: University of California Press, 1967).

6. P. N. Sakulin, *Iz istorii russkago idealizma: Kniaz' V. Odoevskii, myslitel' pisatel'* [From the history of Russian idealism: Prince V. Odoevskii, a thinker and a writer], vol. 1, pt. 2 (Moscow: Sabashnikov, 1913), p. 174, quoted in Edward C. Thaden, *Conservative Nationalism in Nineteenth-Century Russia* (Seattle: University of Washington Press, 1964), p. 10. (Emphasis in the source.)

7. Tibor Szamuely, *The Russian Tradition*, ed. Robert Conquest (London: Secker and Warburg, 1974), p. 147.

8. List, *The National System*, p. 93.

9. William L. Blackwell, *The Beginnings of Russian Industrialization, 1800–1860* (Princeton: Princeton University Press, 1968), pp. 140–141.

10. Alec Nove, *Political Economy and Soviet Socialism* (London: George Allen and Unwin, 1979), p. 33.

11. Theodore H. Von Laue, *Sergei Witte and the Industrialization of Russia* (New York: Columbia University Press, 1963), p. 56. Witte's short book was titled *Po povodu natsionalizma. Natsional'naia ekonomiia i Fridrikh List*. I have had access to the second edition published by Brokhaus-Efron in St. Petersburg in 1912, with a new preface by Witte. (The text appears to be the same as in the 1889 edition, which preceded a Russian edition of List by two years.) (See *Po povodu*, p. 10.)

12. Von Laue, *Sergei Witte*, pp. 62–63.

13. Von Laue, *Sergei Witte*, p. 64.

14. Von Laue, *Sergei Witte*, p. 306.

15. Von Laue, *Sergei Witte*, pp. 304–305.

16. Von Laue, *Sergei Witte*, p. 305.

17. Sergio Amato, "The Debate Between Marxists and Legal Populists on the Problems of Market and Industrialization in Russia (1882–1899) and Its Classical Foundations," *Journal of European Economic History* 12, no. 1 (Spring 1983):139, refers to several works that note the influence of List in Russian debates on industrial and commercial development, especially V. Zheleznov, *Ocherki politicheskoi ekonomii*, 3rd ed. (Moscow: Biblioteka dlia samoobrazovaniia, 1912), pp. 188–191, 792–814, 847–850. (That work was not available to me.)

18. Richard Pipes, *Struve: Liberal on the Left 1870–1905* (Cambridge, MA: Harvard University Press, 1970), p. 104. The quotation within quotation is from P. Struve, *Kriticheskiia zametki k voprosu ob ekonomicheskom razvitii Rossii*, vol. 1 (St. Petersburg: Skorokhodov, 1894), p. 124. For references to List, see Struve, *Kriticheskiia zametki*, pp. 116, 121–124, 181–182, 211.

19. Szamuely, *The Russian Tradition*, p. 415.

20. Kitching, *Development and Underdevelopment*, p. 21.

21. Kitching, *Development and Underdevelopment*, pp. 35, 37–38.

22. Kitching, *Development and Underdevelopment*, pp. 147–148.

23. Andrzej Walicki, *The Controversy over Capitalism: Studies in the Social Philosophy of the Russian Populists* (Oxford: Oxford University Press, 1969), pp. 120–121. Walicki quoted from V. V.[orontsov], *Sud'by kapitalizma v Rossii* (St. Petersburg, 1882), p. 63, and p. 124.

24. Walicki, *The Controversy*, p. 127, quoting from *Perepiska K. Marksa i F. Engel'sa*

*s russkimi politicheskimi deiateliami* [Correspondence of K. Marx and F. Engels with Russian political figures], 2nd ed. (Moscow, 1951), p. 334.

25. Walicki, *The Controversy*, p. 129. (Kitching, *Development and Underdevelopment*, pp. 151–152, quotes Walicki more extensively.)

26. Albert Resis, "*Das Kapital* Comes to Russia," *Slavic Review* 29, no. 2 (June 1970):237, 224. The same point is made by Gerschenkron, *Economic Backwardness*, p. 221.

27. Karl Marx, "Preface to the Russian Edition of the *Communist Manifesto*," in McLellan, *Karl Marx: Selected Writings,* p. 584.

28. Szamuely, *The Russian Tradition*, p. 404.

29. Alfred G. Meyer, *Leninism* (New York: Praeger, 1965), p. 262.

30. Meyer, *Leninism*, pp. 262–263.

31. Meyer, *Leninism*, p. 272.

32. Lichtheim, *Marxism*, p. 348.

33. Meyer, *Leninism*, pp. 270–271.

34. Meyer, *Leninism*, pp. 264–265 n. Meyer draws support from the following passage from *The German Ideology*:

> It is understood that big industry does not attain equal levels of development in every locality of a country. This does not, however, retard the class movement of the proletariat, because the proletarians begotten by big industry assume leadership over this movement and carry the entire mass with them [here Marx and Engels express Lenin's principle of proletarian leadership over the petty bourgeois masses] and because the workers who are excluded from big industry are placed by this big industry into an even more miserable condition of life than the workers of big industry itself [a very curious departure from stereotyped conceptions of the theory of maturity!]. Furthermore, the countries in which big industry has developed have an impact on the *plus ou moins* nonindustrial countries, *in the measure in which world traffic has dragged them into the universal struggle of competition.* ("Die deutsche Ideologie," in Karl Marx and Friedrich Engels, *Gesamtausgabe*, vol. 5, pt. 1, p. 50 [emphasis added], as quoted in Meyer, *Leninism*, p. 265 n. The text in square brackets is Meyer's.)

35. Meyer, *Leninism*, p. 264.

36. Meyer, *Leninism*, p. 261. Those who find the suggestion of an intellectual link between Lenin and List (and Hamilton) somewhat hyperbolic will be no less perturbed by the idea that Trotsky's theory of "combined and uneven development" may have combined Listianism in its recognition of facts with Marxism in the conclusions he drew from those facts. First, he acknowledged that the world was not becoming more like England or the West and that in fact the economically advanced countries tended to favor the status quo (instead of spearheading revolution) while the backward countries, whose backwardness was being reinforced by their relations with the West, were developing a revolutionary consciousness against the status quo. This was the Listian part of Trotsky's theory. However, Trotsky also held that this unevenness of development would work to promote the unification of the proletariat on a global scale as a function of the unification of the world economy in a single world market. Trotsky expected that, in the conflict between the world economy and the nation-state, the economy would win. He refused to draw a Listian conclusion that the revolutionary movement would be nationalist. Here, Trotsky followed the Marx of the *Manifesto*, even though the facts on which he claimed to base his analysis were quite unlike those on which Marx had based his scenario. It is not clear if Trotsky knew List, but Alexander Helphand, better known as Parvus, certainly did. This is important because Parvus preceded

Trotsky in formulating the theory of uneven development. In one of many articles on the problems of foreign trade, protectionism, and socialist policy, Parvus expressed regret that the founders of scientific socialism had died too soon, before they had worked out a proper stand on those matters. (See Parvus, "Die Handelspolitik und die Doktrin," *Die Neue Zeit* 19 [1900–1901]:580–589. See also Meusel, *List und Marx*, pp. 90–95, for interest in List among late-nineteenth-century German socialists with whom Parvus worked.) For a detailed treatment of Trotsky's combined and uneven theory, see Baruch Knei-Paz, *The Social and Political Thought of Leon Trotsky* (Oxford: Clarendon Press, 1978), Michael Löwy, *The Politics of Combined and Uneven Development: The Theory of Permanent Revolution* (London: Verso, 1981), and Ernest Mandel, *Trotsky: A Study in the Dynamic of His Thought* (London: NLB, 1979).

37. A. J. Polan, *Lenin and the End of Politics*.

38. Richard Pipes, *The Formation of the Soviet Union: Communism and Nationalism, 1917–1923* (New York: Atheneum, 1968); and Connor, *The National Question*. There are well-taken points in Tom Nairn, "Internationalism: A Critique," pp. 116–119.

39. Nettl, *Rosa Luxemburg*, vol. 2, p. 858. Nettl quotes Stalin from "Report on the National Question (1918)," *Sochineniia*, vol. 4 (Moscow: Gospolitizdat, 1947), pp. 31–32.

40. The most important work on the subject is Mikhail Agursky, *Ideologiia natsional-bol'shevizma* (Paris: YMCA Press, 1980). This work has appeared as *The Third Rome. Ideology of National Bolshevism* (Boulder, CO: Westview Press, 1987).

41. N. V. Ustrialov, *Bor'ba za Rossiiu* (Kharbin: "Okno," 1920), p. 5, as quoted by Darrell P. Hammer, "N.V. Ustrialov and the Origins of National Bolshevism" (Paper presented to the Third World Congress of Soviet and East European Studies, Washington, DC, October 31–November 4, 1985), p. 11. Also see Jane Burbank, *Intelligentsia and Revolution: Russian Views of Bolshevism, 1917–1922* (New York: Oxford University Press, 1986).

42. Ustrialov, *Bor'ba za Rossiiu*, p. 11, as quoted in Hammer, "N.V. Ustrialov," pp. 11–12.

43. Isaac Deutscher, *Stalin: A Political Biography*, 2nd ed. (New York: Oxford University Press, 1967), p. 243.

44. Deutscher, *Stalin*, pp. 242–243. Agursky, *Ideologiia natsional-bol'shevizma*, p. 55, says that approximately one half of the 130,000 commanders of the Red Army had been tsarist officers or generals.

45. See William G. Rosenberg, "Russian Labor and Bolshevik Power After October," *Slavic Review* 44, no. 2 (Summer 1985):213–238; Moshe Lewin, "More Than One Piece is Missing in the Puzzle," ibid., pp. 239–243; and Rosenberg's "Reply," ibid., pp. 251–256.

46. Lewin, "More Than One Piece," p. 242. See also Rosenberg, "Reply," p. 252.

47. Lewin, "More Than One Piece," p. 242.

48. Alexandre A. Bennigsen and S. Enders Wimbush, *Muslim National Communism in the Soviet Union: A Revolutionary Strategy for the Colonial World* (Chicago and London: University of Chicago Press, 1980).

49. Deutscher, *Stalin*, pp. 240–242; Hammer, "N.V. Ustrialov," pp. 16–17; and Agursky, *Ideologiia natsional-bol'shevizma*, pt. 4 ("Socialism in One Country"), where he examines in detail Stalin's stand on Ustrialovism. Agursky also stresses Trotsky's use of National Bolshevik arguments. (*Ideologiia*, pp. 144–146.)

50. Jeremy R. Azrael, *Managerial Power and Soviet Politics* (Cambridge, MA: Harvard University Press, 1966), Chapter 3, deals with the relations between the bourgeois specialists and the Bolsheviks after 1917. (For the linkage between the technocrats of the 1920s and the ideas of Mendeleev, see pp. 35–36.)

51. This point was suggested by Professor Loren Graham, Cambridge, MA, September 1985.

52. See Roman Szporluk, "Pokrovskii's View of the Russian Revolution," *Slavic Review* 26, no. 1 (March 1967):83–84, for references to the relevant comments of Pokrovsky and Bukharin.

53. Azrael, *Managerial Power*, pp. 56–64.

54. E. H. Carr, *The Bolshevik Revolution, 1917–1923*, vol. 2 (Baltimore, MD: Penguin, 1966), p. 360.

55. Theodore H. Von Laue, *Sergei Witte*, p. 59.

56. Galia Golan, "Elements of Russian Traditions in Soviet Socialism," in *Socialism and Tradition*, ed. S. N. Eisenstadt and Yael Azmon (Atlantic Highlands, NJ: Humanities Press, 1975), p. 21.

57. J. V. Stalin, *Works*, vol. 7 (Moscow: Foreign Languages Publishing House, 1954), p. 164. In another work, Stalin defined the "system of the dictatorship of the proletariat" as a structure in which the party constitutes "the main directing force," while all the remaining organizations—the Soviets, the trade unions, the cooperative, women's, youth and other organizations "link" the party with "the masses." (Stalin, *Works*, vol. 8, pp. 37–38.)

58. Hans Rogger, "Nationalism and the State: A Russian Dilemma," *Comparative Studies in Society and History* 4 (1962):253.

59. Rogger, "Nationalism and the State," p. 253.

60. Rogger, "Nationalism and the State," p. 263.

61. Thomas G. Masaryk, *The New Europe (The Slav Standpoint)*, rev. ed. (Lewisburg: Bucknell University Press, 1972), pp. 118, 123.

62. For "political backwardness" of the Russian bourgeoisie, see M N. Pokrovskii, "Bourgeoisie in Russia," in *Russia in World History*, ed. Roman Szporluk, tr. Roman and Mary Ann Szporluk (Ann Arbor, MI: University of Michigan Press, 1970), pp. 78–82.

63. Adam B. Ulam, *The Unfinished Revolution: An Essay on the Sources of Influence of Marxism and Communism* (New York: Vintage Books, 1964), p. 153.

# Chapter 14

1. I discuss the World War's role in launching the socialist and nationalist revolutions in my book, *The Political Thought of Thomas G. Masaryk*.

2. Tibor Hajdu, "Socialist Revolution in Central Europe, 1917–1921," in *Revolution in History*, ed. Roy Porter and Mikuláš Teich (Cambridge: Cambridge University Press, 1986), p. 115.

3. Sir Lewis Namier, in his famous essay, "1848: Seed-plot of History," argued that "every idea put forward by the nationalities of the Habsburg Empire in 1848 was realized at some juncture, in one form or another," during the following century, and that 1918 was an especially important event in this regard. (See his *Vanished Supremacies; Essays on European History 1812–1918* [New York: Harper and Row, 1963], p. 28.)

4. Thomas G. Masaryk, *Světová revoluce za války a ve válce, 1914–1918* (Prague: Čin and Orbis, 1925) and *The Making of a State*, ed. Henry Wickham-Steed (London: F. A. Stokes, 1927).

5. Kahan, "Nineteenth-Century European Experience," p. 30.

6. Harry G. Johnson, "The Ideology of Economic Policy in the New States," in Johnson, *Economic Nationalism*, p. 131.

7. Ivan T. Berend, "Alternatives to Class Revolution: Central and Eastern Europe after

the First World War," in *The Power of the Past: Essays for Eric Hobsbawm*, ed. Pat Thane, Geoffrey Crossick, and Roderick Floud (Cambridge: Cambridge University Press; Paris: Editions de la Maison des Sciences de l'Homme, 1984), pp. 251–282. (See especially pp. 273–281.)

8. Berend, "Alternatives to Class Revolution," pp. 279–280. In his recent book, *The Crisis Zone of Europe: An Interpretation of East-Central European History in the First Half of the Twentieth Century*, tr. Adrienne Makkay-Chambers (Cambridge: Cambridge University Press, 1986), pp. 50–51, 66, Berend recognizes that the national revolution should be distinguished from "the right-wing radicalist attempt" such as fascism.

9. "In Memory of Herzen," in V. I. Lenin, *Selected Works*, vol. 1 (New York: International Publishers, 1967), p. 597. In a conversation with this author, Professor Mikhail Agursky emphasized the importance in Lenin's outlook of "In Memory of Herzen" (November 1985).

10. Meyer, *Leninism*, pp. 259–260, 263.

11. V. I. Lenin, "Better Fewer but Better" (1923), quoted in Cummins, *Marx, Engels and National Movements*, p. 27. (Cummins contrasts Lenin's view with that of Marx.)

12. Karl Dietrich Bracher, *The Age of Ideologies: A History of Political Thought in the Twentieth Century*, tr. Ewald Osers (New York: St. Martin's Press, 1982), p. 61 n. Bracher cites the work of Piero Melograni, "Lenin e la revoluzione mondiale," *Mondoperaio*, no. 7/8 (July–August 1981):111 ff., in support of this interpretation.

13. J. V. Stalin, "The Immediate Tasks of the Party in the National Question," in Stalin, *Works*, vol. 5, pp. 16–17.

14. Deutscher, *Stalin*, p. 328.

15. Josip Broz-Tito, "The National Question, Nationalism, and Internationalism," in Tito, *The National Question* (Beograd: Socialist Theory and Practice, 1983), pp. 92–94.

16. Anderson, *Imagined Communities*, p. 12. For a comprehensive critique of the Soviet record in terms of its links with the tsarist policy, see Ivan Dzyuba, *Internationalism or Russification? A Study in the Soviet Nationalities Problem* (London: Weidenfeld and Nicolson, 1968).

17. S. Neil MacFarlane, *Superpower Rivalry and Third World Radicalism: The Idea of National Liberation* (Baltimore, MD: Johns Hopkins University Press, 1985), pp. 7, 14, 210–211.

18. Theodore H. Von Laue, *The Global City: Freedom, Power and Necessity in the Age of World Revolutions* (Philadelphia and New York: Lippincott, 1969), pp. 147 n–148 n. For curiosity's sake, let us also add that List has been referred to at least once as "an early Maoist." (See Dieter Senghaas, "Friedrich List und die Neue internationale ökonomische Ordnung," *Leviathan* 3 [1975]:297.)

19. Anderson, *Imagined Communities*, p. 12.

20. Peter Zwick, *National Communism* (Boulder, CO: Westview Press, 1983), p. 145.

21. Eric Hobsbawm, "Some Reflections of 'The Break-up of Britain,'" *New Left Review*, no. 105 (September–October 1977):13, quoted in Anderson, *Imagined Communities*, p. 12.

22. Alfred G. Meyer, "Eastern Europe: Marxism and Nationalism," in *The Politics of Ethnicity in Eastern Europe*, ed. George Klein and Milan J. Reban (Boulder, CO: East European Monographs, 1981), p. 11.

23. Lichtheim, *Imperialism*, p. 147.

24. Kitching, *Development and Underdevelopment*, pp. 152, 160.

25. Johnson, "The Ideology of Economic Policy," p. 131.

26. Johnson, "The Ideology of Economic Policy," pp. 131–132.

27. Johnson, "The Ideology of Economic Policy," p. 132.

28. Johnson, "The Ideology of Economic Policy," p. 131.

29. Johnson, "The Ideology of Economic Policy," p. 131. For more on the pre-1945 origins of modern development theory, see Arndt, *Economic Development*.

30. Giorgio Mori, "Introduzione," in Friedrich List, *Il sistema nazionale di economia politica*, ed. Giorgio Mori, tr. Helmut Ari and Paolo Tinto (Milan: ISEDI, 1972), p. xiii. For List as the major intellectual precursor of contemporary thought on development, see the forceful argument of Dieter Senghaas, *The European Experience: A Historical Critique of Development Theory*, tr. K. H. Kimmig (Leamington Spa/Dover, New Hampshire: Berg Publishers, 1985), passim. Also see Dudley Sears, *The Political Economy of Nationalism* (Oxford: Oxford University Press, 1983), and Gavin Kitching, *Development and Underdevelopment in Historical Perspective: Populism, Nationalism and Industrialization* (London: Methuen, 1982).

31. Kahan, "Nineteenth-Century European Experience," p. 28.

32. Andre Gunder Frank, "The Political Challenges to Socialism and Social Movements," in *Socialism on the Threshold of the Twenty-first Century*, ed. Miloš Nicolić (London: Verso, 1985), p. 64.

33. Carl-Erich Vollgraf, "Karl Marx über die Ökonomische Theorien von Friedrich List," *Wirtschaftswissenschaft* 25, no. 7 (July 1977):991–1010 (see especially pp. 1009–1010); Friedrich List, *Das Natürliche System der politischen Ökonomie*, tr. (from the French) and ed. Günter Fabiunke (Berlin: Akademie-Verlag, 1961). For earlier East German interest in List, see Noboru Kobayashi, "Die List-Forschung in Ostdeutschland," Economic Series, no. 29 (Tokyo: The Science Council of Japan, Division of Economics, Commerce and Business Administration, 1962). The post-1945 German Marxist stand is represented in Jürgen Kuczynski, "Friedrich List. Vorkämpfer der deutschen Einheit," *Der Aufbau* 3 (1947):418–423.

34. This "Listian" pun was inspired by Ian Cummins: "Where Hegel had seen the Cunning of Reason (*das List der Vernunft*) as the agent of historical change, Engels, for his part, was cunning enough to consider the ideas of Friedrich List as having a part to play in preparing the national arena for revolution." (Cummins, *Marx, Engels, and National Movements*, p. 178.)

35. Von Laue, *The Global City*, p. 148 n.

36. Russell, *Freedom versus Organization*, pp. 229–230.

37. Anthony Giddens, *A Contemporary Critique of Historical Materialism*, vol. 1, *Power, Property and the State* (Berkeley and Los Angeles: University of California Press, 1981), pp. 155–156, quoting from Lewis Mumford, *The Myth of the Machine* (London: Secker and Warburg, 1967), p. 9. Giddens also quotes Viktor E. Frankel's view of "search for meaning" as a key to human existence and concludes that Mumford and Frankel "are closer to supplying the basis for a philosophical anthropology of human culture than Marx was." Giddens, *A Contemporary Critique*, pp. 155–156, quoting Viktor E. Frankel, *Man's Search for Meaning* (New York: Washington Square Press, 1963).

# Bibliography

Acton, John Emerich Edward Dalberg, First Baron Acton. *Essays on Freedom and Power*. London: Thames and Hudson, 1956.

Agursky, Mikhail. *Ideologiia natsional-bol'shevizma*. Paris: YMCA Press, 1980.

Amato, Sergio. "The Debate Between Marxists and Legal Populists on the Problems of Market and Industrialization in Russia (1882–1899) and Its Classical Foundations." *Journal of European Economic History* 12 (Spring 1983):119–143.

Amin, Samir. *Class and Nation: Historically and in the Current Crisis*. Translated by Susan Kaplow. New York and London: Monthly Review Press, 1980.

Anderson, Benedict. *Imagined Communities: Reflections on the Origin and Spread of Nationalism*. London: Verso and NLB, 1983.

Argyle, W. J. "Size and Scale as Factors in the Development of Nationalist Movements." In *Nationalist Movements*. Edited by Anthony D. Smith. London: Macmillan, 1976.

Armstrong, John A. *Nations Before Nationalism*. Chapel Hill, NC: University of North Carolina Press, 1982.

Arndt, Heinz Wolfgang. *Economic Development: The History of An Idea*. Chicago: The University of Chicago Press, 1987.

Avineri, Shlomo, ed. *Karl Marx on Colonialism and Modernization*. Garden City, NY: Doubleday, 1969.

———. *The Making of Modern Zionism: The Intellectual Origins of the Jewish State*. New York: Basic Books, 1981.

Azrael, Jeremy R. *Managerial Power and Soviet Politics*. Cambridge, MA: Harvard University Press, 1966.

Bagchi, Amiya Kumar. *The Political Economy of Underdevelopment*. Cambridge: Cambridge University Press, 1982.

Baldwin, David A. *Economic Statecraft*. Princeton: Princeton University Press, 1980.

Balogh, Thomas. *The Irrelevance of Conventional Economics*. London: Weidenfeld and Nicolson, 1982.

Barnard, F. M. *Herder's Social and Political Thought: From Enlightenment to Nationalism*. Oxford: Oxford University Press, 1965, 1967.

————, tr. and ed. *J. G. Herder on Social and Political Culture*. Cambridge: Cambridge University Press, 1969.

Baron, Salo W. *Modern Nationalism and Religion*. New York: Meridian Books; Philadelphia: The Jewish Society of America, 1960.

Bauer, Otto. *Werkausgabe*. Vol. 1. Vienna: Europa-Verlag, 1975.

Beneš, Edvard. "Naš největší úkol národní." In *Idea Československého Státu*. Prague: Národní Rada Československá, 1936.

Bennigsen, Alexandre A., and S. Enders Wimbush. *Muslim National Communism in the Soviet Union: A Revolutionary Strategy for the Colonial World*. Chicago and London: University of Chicago Press, 1980.

Berdahl, Robert M. "New Thoughts on German Nationalism." *American Historical Review* 77 (February 1972):65–80.

Berend, Ivan T. "Alternatives to Class Revolution: Central and Eastern Europe after the First World War." In *The Power of the Past: Essays for Eric Hobsbawm*. Edited by Pat Thane, Geoffrey Crossick, and Roderick Floud. Cambridge: Cambridge University Press; Paris: Editions de la Maison des Sciences de L'Homme, 1984.

————. *The Crisis Zone of Europe: An Interpretation of East-Central European History in the First Half of the Twentieth Century*. Translated by Adrienne Makkay-Chambers. Cambridge: Cambridge University Press, 1986.

Berend, Ivan T., and Gyorgy Ránki, eds. *Underdevelopment and Economic Growth. Studies in Hungarian Social and Economic History*. Budapest: Akademiai Kiado, 1979.

Berlin, Isaiah. *Against the Current: Essays in the History of Ideas*. New York: Viking, 1979.

————. "Socialism." *Chambers's Encyclopaedia*. Vol. 12. Rev. ed. Oxford: Pergamon Press, 1967.

————. *Vico and Herder. Two Studies in the History of Ideas*. New York: Viking, 1976.

Bertier de Sauvigny, G. de. "Liberalism, Nationalism and Socialism: The Birth of Three Words." *Review of Politics* 32 (1970):147–166.

Billington, James H. *Fire in the Minds of Men: Origins of the Revolutionary Faith*. New York: Basic Books, 1980.

Binder, Leonard, James S. Coleman, Joseph LaPalombara, Lucian W. Pye, Sidney Verba, and Myron Weiner. *Crises and Sequences in Political Development*. Princeton: Princeton University Press, 1971.

Blackbourn, David, and Geoff Eley. *The Peculiarities of German History: Bour-*

*geois Society and Politics in Nineteenth-Century Germany.* Oxford and New York: Oxford University Press, 1984.

Blackstock, Paul W., and Bert F. Hoselitz, eds. *The Russian Menace to Europe.* Glencoe, IL: Free Press, 1952.

Blackwell, William L. *The Beginnings of Russian Industrialization, 1800–1860.* Princeton: Princeton University Press, 1968.

Blaut, J. M. "Nationalism as an Autonomous Force." *Science and Society* 46 (Spring 1982):1–23.

Bloom, Solomon Frank. *The World of Nations. A Study of the National Implications in the Work of Karl Marx.* New York: Columbia University Press, 1941.

Bottomore, Tom, and Patrick Goode, eds. *Austro-Marxism.* Oxford: Clarendon Press, 1978.

———, eds. *Readings in Marxist Sociology.* Oxford: Clarendon Press, 1983.

Bracher, Karl Dietrich. *The Age of Ideologies: A History of Political Thought in the Twentieth Century.* Translated by Ewald Osers. New York: St. Martin's Press, 1982.

Bramsted, E. K., and K. J. Melhuish, eds. *Western Liberalism. A History in Documents from Locke to Croce.* London and New York: Longman, 1978.

Braunmühl, Claudia von. "On the Analysis of the Bourgeois Nation State within the World Market Context." In *State and Capital. A Marxist Debate.* Edited by John Holloway and Sol Picciotto. Austin, TX: University of Texas Press, 1978.

Breuilly, John. *Nationalism and the State.* Chicago: University of Chicago Press, 1985.

Brinkmann, Carl. *Friedrich List.* Berlin: Duncker und Humblot, 1949.

Burke, Peter. *Popular Culture in Early Modern Europe.* New York: Harper and Row, 1978.

Burkhardt, Johannes. "Das Verhaltensleitbild 'Produktivität' und seine historisch-anthropologische Voraussetzung." *Saeculum* 25 (1974):277–289.

Carr, E. H. *The Bolshevik Revolution, 1917–1923.* Baltimore, MD: Penguin, 1966.

———. " 'Russia and Europe' as a Theme of Russian History." In *Essays Presented to Sir Louis Namier.* Edited by Richard Pares and A. J. P. Taylor. London: Macmillan; New York: St. Martin's Press, 1956.

Cecco, Marcello de. *Money and Empire: The International Gold Standard, 1890–1914.* Oxford: Basil Blackwell, 1974.

Chlebowczyk, Józef. "Ruch robotniczy a kwestia narodowa w monarchii Habsburgów." *Z pola walki* 11 (1968):97–105.

———. "Świadomość historyczna jako element procesów narodotwórczych we wschodniej Europie Środkowej." In *Polska, czeska i słowacka świadomość historyczna XIX wieku.* Edited by Roman Heck. Wrocław: Ossolineum, 1979.

Clairmonte, Frederick. *Economic Liberalism and Underdevelopment.* New York: Asia Publishing House, 1960.

————. "Friedrich List and the Historical Concept of Balanced Growth." *The Indian Economic Review* 4 (February 1959):24–44.

Cobban, Alfred. *Edmund Burke and the Revolt Against the Eighteenth Century.* New York: Barnes and Noble, 1960.

————. *Rousseau and the Modern State.* Hamden, CT: Archon Books, 1961.

Cole, G. D. H. *What Marx Really Meant.* New York: Knopf, 1934.

Connor, Walker. *The National Question in Marxist-Leninist Theory and Strategy.* Princeton: Princeton University Press, 1984.

Cooper, Thomas. *Lectures on the Elements of Political Economy.* 2nd ed. Columbia, South Carolina, 1829.

Corradini, Enrico. "The Principles of Nationalism." In *Italian Fascism: From Pareto to Gentile.* Edited by Adrian Lyttelton. New York: Harper and Row, 1975.

Crick, Bernard. *In Defence of Politics.* Harmondsworth, England: Penguin, 1966.

Cummins, Ian. *Marx, Engels, and National Movements.* London: Croom Helm, 1980.

Cunliffe, John, "Marx's Politics—The Tensions in the *Communist Manifesto.*" Political Studies 30 (December 1982):569–574.

Dahrendorf, Ralf. *Society and Democracy in Germany.* Garden City, NY: Doubleday, 1969.

Dann, Otto. *Nationalismus und sozialer Wandel.* Hamburg: Hoffman und Campe, 1978.

Davis, Horace B. *Nationalism and Socialism: Marxist and Labor Theories of Nationalism to 1917.* New York and London: Monthly Review Press, 1967.

————. "Nations, Colonies and Social Classes: The Position of Marx and Engels." *Science and Society* 29 (1965):26–43.

Deutsch, Karl W. *Nationalism and Social Communication. An Inquiry into the Foundations of Nationality.* 2nd ed. Cambridge, MA: M.I.T. Press, 1966.

Deutscher, Isaac. *Stalin: A Political Biography.* 2nd ed. New York: Oxford University Press, 1967.

Dorfman, Joseph. *The Economic Mind in American Civilization, 1606–1865.* 2 vols. New York: Viking, 1946.

Draper, Hal. *Karl Marx's Theory of Revolution.* New York and London: Monthly Review Press, 1977.

Dühring, Eugen Karl. *Kritische Geschichte der Nationalökonomie und des Sozialismus.* Leipzig: Fues Verlag, 1879.

Durkheim, Emile. *Socialism and Saint-Simon.* Yellow Springs, OH: Antioch Press, 1958.

Dzyuba, Ivan. *Internationalism or Russification? A Study in the Soviet Nationalities Problem.* London: Weidenfeld and Nicolson, 1968.

Earle, Edward Mead. "Adam Smith, Alexander Hamilton, Friedrich List: The Economic Foundations of Military Power." In *Makers of Modern Strategy: Military Thought from Machiavelli to Hitler.* Edited by Edward Mead Earle.

New York: Atheneum, 1966. This essay is also included in the revised edition of *Makers of Modern Strategy*. Edited by Peter Paret. Princeton: Princeton University Press, 1986.

Eisenstein, Elizabeth L. *The Printing Press as an Agent of Change*. 2 vols. Cambridge: Cambridge University Press, 1979.

Eley, Geoff. *From Unification to Nazism: Reinterpreting the German Past*. Boston, London, and Sydney: Allen and Unwin, 1986.

————. "Nationalism and Social History." *Social History* 6 (1981): 83–107.

————. "State Formation, Nationalism and Political Culture in Nineteenth-Century Germany." In *Culture, Ideology and Politics*. Edited By Raphael Samuel and Gareth Stedman Jones. London: Routledge and Kegan Paul, 1983.

Elster, Jon. "Historical materialism and economic backwardness." In *After Marx*. Edited by Terence Ball and James Farr. Cambridge: Cambridge University Press, 1984.

Engels, Friedrich. "[The Anniversary of the Polish Revolution of 1830]." In Karl Marx and Friedrich Engels, *Collected Works*. Vol. 6. New York, International Publishers, 1976.

————. "Draft of a Communist Confession of Faith." In Marx and Engels, *Collected Works*. Vol. 6. New York: International Publishers, 1976.

————. "Extraordinary Revelations, - Abd-el-Kader.- Guizot's Foreign Policy." In Marx and Engels, *Collected Works*. Vol. 6. New York: International Publishers, 1976.

————. "The Festival of Nations in London." In Marx and Engels, *Collected Works*. Vol. 6. New York: International Publishers, 1976.

————. "Free Trade Congress at Brussels." In Marx and Engels, *Collected Works*. Vol. 6. New York: International Publishers, 1976.

————. *The German Revolutions*. Edited by Leonard Krieger. Chicago: University of Chicago Press, 1967.

————. *Herr Eugen Duhring's Revolution in Science (Anti-Duhring)*. Translated by Emile Burns. New York: International Publishers, 1966.

————. "Outline of a Critique of Political Economy." In Marx and Engels, *Collected Works*. Vol. 3. London: Lawrence and Wishart, 1975.

————. "Outline of a Critique of Political Economy." In Marx and Engels, *Collected Works*. Vol. 3. London: Lawrence and Wishart, 1975.

————. "Principles of Communism." In Marx and Engels, *Collected Works*. Vol. 6. New York: International Publishers, 1976.

————. "Speeches at Elberfeld (February 8 and February 15, 1845)." In Marx and Engels, *Collected Works*. Vol. 4. New York: International Publishers. 1975.

[————.] Friedrich Engels to Karl Kautsky, February 7, 1882. In *Friedrich Engels' Briefwechsel mit Karl Kautsky*. Edited by Benedikt Kautsky. Vienna: Wiener Volksbuchhandlung, 1955.

[————.] Friedrich Engels to Karl Kautsky, September 12, 1882. In *Karl Marx* on *Colonialism and Modernization.* Edited by Shlomo Avineri. Garden City, NY: Doubleday, 1969.

Evans, Michael. "Karl Marx's First Confrontation with Political Economy: The 1844 Manuscripts." *Economy and Society* 13 (1984):115–152.

Fabiunke, Günter. *Zur historischen Rolle des deutschen Nationalökonomen Friedrich List (1789–1846): Ein Beitrag zur Geschichte der politischen Ökonomie in Deutschland.* Berlin: Verlag Die Wirtschaft, 1955.

Feinstein, Otto, ed. *The Two Worlds of Change.* Garden City, NY: Anchor Books, 1964.

Finkelstein, Joseph, and Alfred L. Thimm. *Economists and Society: The Development of Economic Thought from Aquinas to Keynes.* 2nd ed. Schenectady, NY: Union College Press, 1981.

Fischer, Wolfram. "Social Tensions at Early Stages of Industrialization." *Comparative Studies in Society and History* 9 (1966):64–83.

Fittbogen, Gottfried. *Friedrich List in Ungarn.* Berlin: Walter de Gruyter, 1942.

Fontenay, Elisabeth de. *Les figures juives de Marx. Marx dans l'ideologie allemande.* Paris: Editions Galilee, 1973.

Fox, Edward Whiting. *History in Geographic Perspective. The Other France.* New York: Norton, 1971.

Frank, Andre Gunder. *Dependent Accumulation and Underdevelopment.* New York: Monthly Review Press, 1979.

———. "The Political Challenges to Socialism and Social Movements." In *Socialism on the Threshold of the Twenty-first Century.* Edited by Miloš Nicolič. London: Verso, 1985.

Frankel, Viktor E. *Man's Search for Meaning.* New York: Washington Square Press, 1963.

Garver, Bruce M. *The Young Czech Party 1874–1901 and the Emergence of a Multi-Party System.* New Haven, CT: Yale University Press, 1978.

Gehrig, Hans. *Friedrich List und Deutschlands politisch-ökonomische Einheit.* Leipzig: Koehler and Amelang, 1956.

———. *Friedrich List. Wegbereiter einer neuen Wirtschaft. Hauptgedanken aus seinen Schriften.* Berlin: Erich Schmidt Verlag, 1966.

Gehring, Paul. *Friedrich List. Jugend und Reifejahre, 1789–1825.* Tübingen: J. C. B. Mohr Verlag, 1964.

Gella, Aleksander. "An Introduction to the Sociology of the Intelligentsia." In *The Intelligentsia and the Intellectuals. Theory, Methods, and Case Study.* Edited by Aleksander Gella. London: Sage Publications Ltd., 1976.

Gellner, Ernest. "Nationalism." *Theory and Society* 10 (November 1981):753–776.

———. *Nations and Nationalism.* Ithaca, NY, and London: Cornell University Press, 1983.

———. *Thought and Change.* London: Weidenfeld and Nicolson, 1964.

Gerschenkron, Alexander. *Economic Backwardness in Historical Perspective.* Cambridge, MA: Harvard University Press, 1979. (Original edition 1966.)

————. *An Economic Spurt That Failed*. Princeton: Princeton University Press, 1977.

————. *Europe in the Russian Mirror*. *Four Lectures in Economic History*. Cambridge: Cambridge University Press, 1970.

Giddens, Anthony. *A Contemporary Critique of Historical Materialism*. Vol. 1, *Power, Property and the State*. Berkeley and Los Angeles: University of California Press, 1985.

————. *A Contemporary Critique of Historical Materialism*. Vol. 2, *The Nation-State and Violence*. Berkeley and Los Angeles: University of California Press, 1985.

Gide, Charles, and Charles Rist. *A History of Economic Doctrines from the Time of the Physiocrats to the Present Day*. Boston: D.C. Heath, 1948.

Glaser, Hermann, ed. *The German Mind of the Nineteenth Century: A Literary and Historical Anthology*. New York: Continuum, 1981.

Golan, Galia. "Elements of Russian Traditions in Soviet Socialism." In *Socialism and Tradition*. Edited by S. N. Eisenstadt and Yael Azmon. Atlantic Highlands, NJ: Humanities Press, 1975.

Gouldner, Alvin W. *Against Fragmentation: The Origins of Marxism and the Sociology of Intellectuals*. New York and Oxford: Oxford University Press, 1985.

Graus, František. "Slavs and Germans." In *Eastern and Western Europe in the Middle Ages*. Edited by Geoffrey Barraclough. New York: Harcourt Brace Jovanovich, 1970.

Gray, Alexander. *The Development of Economic Doctrine*. 2nd ed. New York and London: Longman, 1980.

Gregor, A. James. *Italian Fascism and Developmental Dictatorship*. Princeton: Princeton University Press, 1979.

Grew, Raymond. "The Crises and Their Sequences." In *Crises of Political Development in Europe and the United States*. Edited by Raymond Grew. Princeton: Princeton University Press, 1978.

Griffith, Arthur. *The Resurrection of Hungary*. Dublin, 1918.

Hajdu, Tibor. "Socialist Revolution in Central Europe, 1917–1921." In *Revolution in History*. Edited by Roy Porter and Mikuláš Teich. Cambridge: Cambridge University Press, 1986.

Hamilton, Alexander. "Report on Manufactures." In *Papers on Public Credit, Commerce, and Finance*. New York: Columbia University Press, 1934.

Hammer, Darrell P. "N. V. Ustrialov and the Origins of National Bolshevism." Paper presented to the Third World Congress of Soviet and East European Studies, Washington, DC, 31 October–4 November 1985.

Hardach, Karl. *Nationalismus—Die deutsche Industrialisierungsideologie?* Cologne: Forschungsinstitut für Sozial- und Wirtschaftsgeschichte an der Universität zu Köln, 1976.

Haupt, Georges, Michael Löwy, and Claudie Weill, eds. *Les Marxistes et la*

*Question Nationale 1848–1914, études et textes.* Paris: François Maspero, 1974.

Hayes, Carlton J. H. *The Historical Evolution of Modern Nationalism.* New York: Macmillan, 1950. (First ed., 1931.)

————. *Essays on Nationalism.* New York: Macmillan, 1926.(New ed., New York: Russell & Russell, 1966.)

Heilperin, Michael H. *Studies in Economic Nationalism.* Geneva: Droz; Paris: Minard, 1960.

Heimann, Eduard. *History of Economic Doctrines. An Introduction to Economic Theory.* New York: Oxford University Press, 1964.

Henderson, William Otto. *Friedrich List: Economist and Visionary 1789–1846.* London: Frank Cass, 1983.

————. "Friedrich List and the French Protectionists." *Zeitschrift für die gesamte Staatswissenschaft* 138 (1982):262–275.

————. "Friedrich List and the Social Question." *Journal of European Economic History* 10 (1981):697–708.

————. *The Zollverein.* 2nd ed. Chicago: Quadrangle Books, 1959.

Herder, J. G. *Sämliche Werke.* Translated and edited by B. Suphan. Berlin, 1877–1913.

Hertz, Frederick. *The German Public Mind in the Nineteenth Century. A Social History of German Political Sentiments, Aspirations and Ideas.* Totowa, NJ: Rowan and Littlefield, 1975.

Hirst, Margaret E. *Life of Friedrich List and Selections from His Writings.* New York: Charles Scribner and Sons, 1909.

Hobsbawm, Eric J. *The Age of Capital 1848–1875.* New York: New American Library, 1979.

————. *The Age of Revolution 1789–1848.* New York: New American Library, 1962.

————. *Industry and Empire.* London: Weidenfeld and Nicolson; New York: Pantheon, 1968.

————. "Marx, Engels and Politics." In *The History of Marxism.* Vol. 1, *Marxism in Marx's Day.* Edited by Eric J. Hobsbawm. Bloomington, IN: Indiana University Press, 1982.

————. "Some Reflections on 'The Break-up of Britain'." *The New Left Review,* no. 105 (September–October 1977):3–23.

————. "Some Reflections on Nationalism." In *Imagination and Precision in the Social Sciences: Essays in Memory of Peter Nettl.* Edited by T. J. Nossiter, A. H. Hanson, and Stein Rokkan. London: Faber and Faber, 1972.

Hoselitz, Bert F. "Nationalism, Economic Development, and Democracy." In *The Two Worlds of Change.* Edited by Otto Feinstein. Garden City, NY: Anchor Books, 1964.

————. "Theories of Stages of Economic Growth." In *Theories of Economic Growth.* Edited by Bert F. Hoselitz. New York: The Free Press, 1960.

Hroch, Miroslav. *Die Vorkämpfer der nationalen Bewegung bei den kleinen Völkern Europas*. Acta Universitatis Carolinae Philosophica et Historica, monographia 24, Prague, 1968.

————. *Social Preconditions of National Revival in Europe. A Comparative Analysis of the Social Composition of Patriotic Groups among the Smaller European Nations*. Translated by Ben Fowkes. Cambridge: Cambridge University Press, 1985.

Ionescu, Ghita. "Introduction." In *The Political Thought of Saint-Simon*. Edited by Ghita Ionescu. Oxford: Oxford University Press, 1976.

Janos, Andrew C. *The Politics of Backwardness in Hungary 1825–1945*. Princeton: Princeton University Press, 1982.

Jaworski, Rudolf. "Nationalismus und Ökonomie als Problem der Geschichte Ostmitteleuropas im 19. und zu Beginn des 20. Jahrhunderts." *Geschichte und Gesellschaft* 8 (1982):184–204.

Johnson, Harry G. "The Ideology of Economic Policy in the New States." In *Economic Nationalism in Old and New States*. Edited by Harry G. Johnson. Chicago: University of Chicago Press, 1967.

————. "A Theoretical Model of Economic Nationalism in New and Developing States. In *Economic Nationalism in Old and New States*. Edited by Harry G. Johnson. Chicago: University of Chicago Press, 1967.

Kahan, Arcadius. "Nineteenth-Century European Experience with Policies of Economic Nationalism." In *Economic Nationalism in Old and New States*. Edited by Harry G. Johnson. Chicago: University of Chicago Press, 1967.

Kautsky, Benedikt, ed. *Friedrich Engels' Briefwechsel mit Karl Kautsky*. Vienna: Wiener Volksbuchhandlung, 1955.

Kiernan, V. G. "State and Nation in Western Europe." *Past and Present* 31 (July 1965):20–38.

Kitchen, Martin, The *Political Economy of Germany 1815–1914*. Montreal: McGill Queen's University Press, 1978.

Kitching, Gavin. *Development and Underdevelopment in Historical Perspective. Populism, Nationalism, and Industrialization*. New York: Methuen, 1982.

————. "Nationalism: The Instrumental Passion." *Capitalism and Class*, no. 25: (Spring 1985):98–116.

Klíma, Arnošt. "The Bourgeois Revolution of 1848–1849 in Central Europe." In *Revolution in History*. Edited by Roy Porter and Mikuláš Teich. Cambridge: Cambridge University Press, 1986.

Knei-Paz, Baruch. *The Social and Political Thought of Leon Trotsky*. Oxford: Clarendon Press, 1978.

Kobayashi, Noboru. *James Steuart, Adam Smith, and Friedrich List*. Tokyo: Science Council of Japan, 1967.

————. "Die List-Forschung in Ostdeutschland." Economic Series, no. 29. Tokyo: The Science Council of Japan, Division of Economics, Commerce and Business Administration, 1962.

Kohn, Hans. *Nationalism: Its Meaning and History*. Princeton: Van Nostrand, 1965.

Kolakowski, Leszek. *Main Currents of Marxism. Its Origin, Growth, and Dissolution*. Oxford: Oxford University Press, 1978.

Kolakowski, Leszek, and Stuart Hampshire, eds. *The Socialist Idea. A Reappraisal*. London: Weidenfeld and Nicolson, 1974.

Krejčí, Jaroslav, and Vitězslav Velimský. *Ethnic and Political Nations in Europe*. New York: St. Martin's Press, 1981.

Krieger, Leonard. "Nationalism and the Nation-State System, 1789–1870." In *Chapters in Western Civilization*. Edited by the Contemporary Civilization Staff of Columbia College, Columbia University. Vol. 2. 3rd ed. New York: Columbia University Press, 1962.

Kuczynski, Jürgen. "Friedrich List: Vorkämpfer der deutschen Einheit." *Der Aufbau* 3 (1947):418–423.

Kusín, Vladimir V. "Socialism and Nationalism." In *The Socialist Idea. A Reappraisal*. Edited by Leszek Kolakowski and Stuart Hampshire. London: Weidenfeld and Nicolson, 1974.

Laitin, David D. "Linguistic Dissociation: A Strategy for Africa." In *International Division of Labor*. Edited by John Gerard Ruggie. New York: Columbia University Press, 1983.

Landes, David. "The Industrial Revolution: 1750–1850." In *Chapters in Western Civilization*. Edited by the Contemporary Civilization Staff of Columbia College, Columbia University. Vol. 2. 3rd ed. New York: Columbia University Press, 1962.

Laski, Harold J. "An Introduction." In Marx and Engels, *The Communist Manifesto*. New York: New American Library, 1967. (New printing 1982.)

Lenin, V. I. "Better Fewer but Better" (1923). In V. I. Lenin, *The National Liberation Movement in the East*. Moscow: Foreign Language Publishing House, 1957.

———. "In Memory of Herzen." In V. I. Lenin, *Selected Works*. Vol. 1. New York: International Publishers, 1967.

Lenz, Friedrich. "Friedrich List und Grossdeutschland." In *Los von England. Der Deutsche Abwehrkampf gegen Englands wirtschaftliche Weltmachtstellung in der ersten Hälfte des 19. Jahrhunderts*. Edited by Wilhelm Ihde. Leipzig: Luhe-Verlag, 1940.

———. *Friedrich List's Staats- und Gesellschaftslehre: Eine Studie zur politischen Soziologie*. Neuwied und Berlin: Luchterhand, 1967.

———. *Friedrich List, die "Vulgärökonomie" und Karl Marx*. Jena: Gustav Fischer, 1930.

———. "Vom Pauperismus zum Proletariat: Friedrich List, die Arbeiterfrage und Karl Marx." In *Beiträge zur Wirtschafts—und Gesellschaftsgestaltung. Festschrift für Bruno Gleitze zum 65. Geburtstag*. Edited by Friedrich Lenz. Berlin: Duncker und Humblot, 1968.

Levin, Michael. "Deutschmarx: Marx, Engels, and the German Question." *Political Studies* 29 (December 1981):537–554.

Lewin, Moshe. "More Than One Piece is Missing in the Puzzle." *Slavic Review* 44 (Summer 1985):239–243.

Lichtheim, George. *Imperialism*. London: Allen Lane/Penguin, 1971.

————. *Marxism: An Historical and Critical Study*. New York: Praeger, 1962.

Lipiński, Edward. *Historia powszechnej myśli ekonomicznej do roku 1870*. Warsaw: Państwowe Wydawnictwo Naukowe, 1968.

List, Friedrich. *National System of Political Economy*. Translated by G. A. Matile. Philadelphia: J. B. Lippincott, 1856.

————. *Das nationale System der politischen Ökonomie*. Edited by Arthur Sommer. Basel: Kyklos-Verlag, 1959.

————. *The National System of Political Economy*. Translated by Sampson S. Lloyd. New York: Augustus M. Kelley, 1966. (A reprint of the 1885 edition.)

————. *Das nationale System der politischen Ökonomie*. Edited by Günter Fabiunke. Berlin: Akademie-Verlag, 1982.

————. *Das natürliche System der politischen Ökonomie*. Edited and translated by Günter Fabiunke. Berlin: Akademie-Verlag, 1961.

————. *The Natural System of Political Economy 1837*. Edited and translated by W. O. Henderson. London: Frank Cass, 1983.

————. "Petition on Behalf of the Handelsverein to the Federal Assembly, April, 1819." In Hirst, *Life of Friedrich List*. New York: Charles Scribner and Sons, 1909.

————. *Schriften. Reden. Briefe*. 10 vols. Berlin: Verlag von Reimar Hobbing, 1927–1935. Vol. 1, pt. 1, 1932; vol. 1, pt. 2, 1933; vol. 2, 1931; vol. 3, pt. 1, 1929; vol 3, pt. 2, 1931; vol. 4, 1927; vol. 5, 1928; vol. 6, 1930; vol. 7, 1931; vol. 8, 1933; vol. 9, 1935; vol. 10, 1935.

————. *Il sistema nazionale di economia politica*. Edited by Giorgio Mori. Translated by Helmut Avi and Paolo Tinto. Milan: ISEDI, 1972.

Löwith, Karl. *From Hegel to Nietzsche: The Revolution in Nineteenth-Century Thought*. Translated by David E. Green. Garden City, NY: Anchor Books, 1967.

Löwy, Michael. "Marx and Engels: Cosmopolites." *Critique* 14 (1982):5–12.

————. "Marxists and the National Question." *New Left Review* 96 (March-April 1976):81–100.

————. *The Politics of Combined and Uneven Development: The Theory of Permament Revolution*. London: Verso, 1981.

Ludz, Peter C. "Socialism and the Nation." In *The Socialist Idea. A Reappraisal*. Edited by Leszek Kolakowski and Stuart Hampshire. London: Weidenfeld and Nicolson, 1974.

Lukes, Steven, *Marxism and Morality*. Oxford: Clarendon Press, 1985

Luxemburg, Rosa. "Kwestia narodowościowa i autonomia." In Róża Luksemburg [Rosa Luxemburg], *Wybór Pism*. 2 vols. Warsaw: Książka i Wiedza, 1959.

————. *The National Question*. Edited by Horace B. Davis. New York and London: Monthly Review Press, 1976.

Lyons, F. S. L. *Ireland since the Famine*. London: Collins Fontana, 1973.

MacFarlane, S. Neil. *Superpower Rivalry and Third World Radicalism: The Idea of National Liberation*. Baltimore, MD: Johns Hopkins University Press, 1985.

McLellan, David. *Karl Marx: His Life and Thought*. New York: Harper and Row, 1973.

————, ed. *Karl Marx: Selected Writings*. Oxford: Oxford University Press, 1978.

————. *Marx before Marxism*. 2nd ed. London: The Macmillan Press, 1980.

Maddison, Angus. *Phases of Capitalist Development*. New York: Oxford University Press, 1982.

Maguire, John M. *Marx's Theory of Politics*. Cambridge: Cambridge University Press, 1978.

Mandel, Ernest. *Trotsky: A Study in The Dynamic of His Thought*. London: NLB, 1979.

Marshall, Howard D. *The Great Economists. A History of Economic Thought*. New York: Pitman Publishing Corporation, 1967.

Marx, Karl. "The Bourgeoisie and the Counter-Revolution." In Marx and Engels, *Collected Works*. Vol. 8. New York: International Publishers, 1977.

————. *Capital. A Critique of Political Economy*. Vol. 3. New York: Vintage Books, 1981.

————. "A Contribution to The Critique of Hegel's *Philosophy of Right*: Introduction." In *The Marx-Engels Reader*. 2nd ed. Edited by Robert C. Tucker. New York: Norton, 1978.

————. *Critique of the Gotha Program*. With appendices by Marx, Engels, and Lenin. New York: International Publishers, 1938.

————. *Critique of Hegel's 'Philosophy of Right.'* Edited by Joseph O'Malley. Cambridge: Cambridge University Press, 1978.

————. "Draft of an Article on Friedrich List's Book *Das nationale System der politischen Ökonomie*." In Marx and Engels, *Collected Works*. Vol. 4. New York: International Publishers, 1975.

————. "Draft Plan for a Work on the Modern State." In Marx and Engels, *Collected Works*. Vol. 4. New York: International Publishers, 1975.

————. "Karl Marks o knige F. Lista 'Natsional'naia sistema politicheskoi ekonomii.' " *Voprosy istorii KPSS*, no. 12 (1971): 3–27.

[————.] *Karl Marx: Selected Writings*. Edited by David McLellan. Oxford: Oxford University Press, 1978.

————. "On the Jewish Question." In *The Marx-Engels Reader*. 2nd ed. Edited by Robert C. Tucker. New York: Norton, 1978.

————. "Protectionists." In Marx and Engels, *Collected Works*. Vol. 6. New York; International Publishers, 1976.

———— "The Protectionists, the Free Traders and the Working Class," In Marx and Engels, *Collected Works*. Vol. 6. New York: International Publishers, 1976.

————. "The Revolutionary Movement." In Marx and Engels, *Collected Works*. Vol. 8. New York: International Publishers, 1977.

————. "Speech on the Question of Free Trade." In Marx and Engels, *Collected Works*. Vol. 6. New York: International Publishers, 1976.

————. "Theses on Feuerbach." In *Karl Marx: Selected Writings*. Edited by David McLellan. Oxford: Oxford University Press, 1978.

————. "Über Friedrich Lists Buch 'Das nationale System der politischen Ökonomie.'" *Beiträge zur Geschichte der Arbeiterbewegung*, no. 3 (1972):425–446.

————. "Zur Kritik der Hegelschen Rechtsphilosophie. Einleitung." In Marx and Engels, *Gesamtausgabe*, 1st series. Vol. 2. Berlin: Dietz Verlag, 1982.

————. "Letter to Vera Sassoulitch [sic]." In *Karl Marx: Selected Writings*. Edited by David McLellan. Oxford: Oxford University Press, 1978.

————. "Marx to the Editors of *Otechestvennye zapiski*." *Karl Marx on Colonialism and Modernization*. Edited by Shlomo Avineri. Garden City, NY: Doubleday, 1969.

————. Marx to Engels, October 8, 1858. *Karl Marx on Colonialism and Modernization*. Edited by Shlomo Avineri. Garden City, NY: Doubleday, 1969.

————. Marx to Engels, November 30, 1867. In *Karl Marx: Selected Writings*. Edited by David McLellan. Oxford: Oxford University Press, 1978.

Marx, Karl, and Friedrich Engels. *Collected Works*. London: Lawrence and Wishart; New York: International Publishers.

————. *The German Ideology*. Edited by C. J. Arthur. New York: International Publishers, 1978.

————. *Gesamtausgabe, vierte Abteilung, Exzerpte, Notizen, Marginalien*. Band 2. Berlin: Dietz Verlag, 1981.

————. *Historisch-kritische Gesamtausgabe*. Vol. 4. Edited by V. Adoratskii. Glashütten im Taunus: Detlev Auvermann, 1970. (Reprint of 1932 edition.)

————. *Ireland and the Irish Question*. New York: International Publishers, 1972.

————. *Kritik der bürgerlichen Ökonomie. Neues Manuskript von Marx und Rede von Engels über F. List*. Berlin: Verlag für das Studium der Arbeiterbewegung, 1972.

————. *Manifesto of the Communist Party*. Edited and annotated by Friedrich Engels. New York: International Publishers, 1948. (Reprinted in 1966.)

[————.] *The Marx-Engels Reader*. 2nd ed. Edited by Robert C. Tucker. New York: Norton, 1978.

————. "[On Poland]." In Marx and Engels, *Collected Works*. Vol. 6. New York: International Publishers, 1976.

Masaryk, Thomas G. *The New Europe (The Slav Standpoint)*. New ed. Lewisburg: Bucknell University Press, 1972.

Masaryk, Thomas G. *Světová revoluce za války a ve válce, 1914–1918*. Prague:

Čin and Orbis, 1925. English translation: *The Making of a State*. Edited by Henry Wickham-Steed. London: F. A. Stokes, 1927.

Matossian, Mary. "Ideologies of Delayed Industrialization: Some Tensions and Ambiguities." In *Two Worlds of Change*. Edited by Otto Feinstein. Garden City, NY: Anchor Books, 1964.

Mayer, Gustav. *Friedrich Engels. Eine Biographie*. The Hague: Martinus Nijhoff, 1934.

Mazlish, Bruce. *The Meaning of Karl Marx*. New York: Oxford University Press, 1984.

Meinecke, Friedrich. *The German Catastrophe: Reflections and Recollections*. Translated by Sidney B. Fay. Boston: Beacon Press, 1963.

Meusel, Alfred. *List und Marx: Eine vergleichende Betrachtung*. Jena: Gustav Fischer, 1930.

Meyer, Alfred G. "Eastern Europe: Marxism and Nationalism." In *The Politics of Ethnicity in Eastern Europe*. Edited by George Klein and Milan J. Reban. Boulder, CO: Eastern European Monographs, 1981.

———. *Leninism*. New York: Praeger, 1965.

———. *"Review of A Dictionary of Marxist Thought"* (edited by Tom Bottomore et al.). *Political Theory* 12 (August 1984):446–449.

Meyer, Henry Cord. *Mitteleuropa in German Thought and Action 1815–1945*. The Hague: Martinus Nijhoff, 1955.

Mommsen, Hans. *Arbeiterbewegung und nationale Frage*. Gottingen: Vandenhoeck and Ruprecht, 1979.

———. *Die Sozialdemokratie und die Nationalitätenfrage im habsburgischen Vielvölkerstaat*. Vol. 1. *Das Ringen um die supranationale Integration der zisleithanischen Arbeiterbewegung, 1867–1907*. Vienna: Europa-Verlag, 1963.

Mori, Giorgio. "Introduzione." In Friedrich List, *Il sistema nazionale di economia politica*. Edited by Giorgio Mori. Translated by Helmut Avi and Paolo Tinto. Milan: ISEDI, 1972.

Mosse, George. "The Mystical Origins of National Socialism." *Journal of the History of Ideas* 22 (1961):81–96.

Mumford, Lewis. *The Myth of the Machine*. London: Secker and Warburg, 1967.

Munck, Ronnie. "Otto Bauer: Towards a Marxist Theory of Nationalism." *Capital and Class* 25 (Spring 1985):84–97.

Nairn, Tom. *The Break-Up of Britain: Crisis and Neo-Colonialism*. London: New Left Books, 1977.

———. "Internationalism: A Critique." *Bulletin of Scottish Politics* 1 (Autumn 1980):101–175.

Namier, Sir Lewis. *Vanished Supremacies: Essays on European History 1812–1918*. New York: Harper and Row, 1963.

Neill, Charles Patrick. *Daniel Raymond. An Early Chapter in the History of Economic Theory in the United States*. Johns Hopkins University Studies in

Historical and Political Science. Vol. 6, no 15. Baltimore: Johns Hopkins University Press, 1897.

Nettl, J. P. *Rosa Luxemburg.* 2 vols. London, New York, and Toronto: Oxford University Press, 1966.

Notz, William. *Friedrich List in Amerika.* Hamburg: Broschek, 1925. (Offprint from *Weltwirtschaftliches Archiv*, vol. 21, no. 2, and vol. 22, no. 1 [April and July 1925].)

Nove, Alec. *Political Economy and Soviet Socialism.* London: George Allen and Unwin, 1979.

Oakley, Allen. *Marx's Critique of Political Economy. Intellectual Sources and Evolution.* Vol. 1, *1844 to 1860.* London: Routledge and Kegan Paul, 1984.

Obermann, Karl. *Deutschland von 1815 bis 1849.* Berlin: Deutscher Verlag der Wissenschaften, 1961.

Orridge, A. W. "Uneven Development and Nationalism: I and II." *Political Studies* 29 (1981):1–15, 181–190.

[Palacký, František.] "Letter sent by František Palacký to Frankfurt." *Slavonic and East European Review* 26 (April 1948):303–308.

———. "Manifesto of the First Slavonic Congress to the Nations of Europe." *Slavonic and East European Review* 26 (April 1948):309–313.

Parvus [Alexander Helphand]. "Die Handelspolitik und die Doktrin." *Die Neue Zeit* 19 (1900–1901):580–589.

Pelczynski, Z. A. "Nation, Civil Society, State: Hegelian Sources of the Marxian Non-theory of Nationality." In *The State and Civil Society: Studies in Hegel's Political Philosophy.* Edited by Z. A. Pelczynski. Cambridge: Cambridge University Press, 1984.

Pflanze, Otto. "Nationalism in Europe, 1848–1871." *Review of Politics* 23, no. 2 (April 1966):129–143.

Pipes, Richard. *The Formation of the Soviet Union: Communism and Nationalism, 1917–1923.* New York: Atheneum, 1968.

———. "Introduction: The Nationality Problem." In *Handbook of Major Soviet Nationalities.* Edited by Zev Katz. New York: Free Press; London: Macmillan, 1975.

———. *Russia Under the Old Regime.* New York: Scribners, 1974.

———. *Struve: Liberal on the Left 1870–1905.* Cambridge, MA: Harvard University Press, 1970.

Pokrovskii, M. N. *Russia in World History.* Edited by Roman Szporluk. Translated by Roman and Mary Ann Szporluk. Ann Arbor, MI: University of Michigan Press, 1970.

Polan, A. J. *Lenin and the End of Politics.* Berkeley and Los Angeles: University of California Press, 1984.

Potter, David M. "The Historian's Use of Nationalism and Vice Versa." In *Generalizations in Historical Writing.* Edited by Alexander Riasanovsky and Barnes Reznik. Philadelphia: University of Pennsylvania Press, 1963.

Pyle, Kenneth B. "Advantages of Followership: German Economics and Japanese Bureaucrats, 1890–1925." *Journal of Japanese Studies* 1 (Autumn 1974):127–134.

Raeff, Marc. *Understanding Imperial Russia: State and Society in the Old Regime.* Translated by Arthur Goldhammer. New York: Columbia University Press, 1984.

Randak, Harald. *Friedrich List und die wissenschaftliche Wirtschaftspolitik.* Basel: Kyklos-Verlag, 1972.

Ravizza, Andrea Johann. *Friedrich List und England. Ein Beitrag zur Analyse der politischen Haltung Friedrich Lists.* Mels: Sarganserlandische Buchdruckerei A.G., 1948.

Raymond, Daniel. *The Elements of Political Economy.* Vol. 1. 2nd ed. Baltimore, 1823.

Resis, Albert. "*Das Kapital* Comes to Russia." *Slavic Review* 29 (June 1970):219–237.

Riasanovsky, Nicholas V. *Nicholas I and Official Nationality in Russia, 1825–1855.* Berkeley and Los Angeles: University of California Press, 1967.

Rogger, Hans. "Nationalism and the State: A Russian Dilemma." *Comparative Studies in Society and History* 4 (1962):253–264.

Roll, Eric. *A History of Economic Thought.* New York: Prentice-Hall, Inc., 1946.

Rosa, Luigi de. "Economics and Nationalism in Italy." *Journal of European Economic History* 11 (Winter 1982):537–574.

Rosdolsky, Roman. "Friedrich Engels und das Problem der 'geschichtslosen' Völker (die Nationalitätenfrage in der Revolution 1848–1849 im Lichte der 'Neuen Rheinischen Zeitung')." *Archiv für Sozialgeschichte* 4 (1964):87–282.

———. "Worker and Fatherland: A Note on a Passage in the *Communist Manifesto.*" *Science and Society* 29 (Summer 1965):330–337.

Rosenberg, William G. "Russian Labor and Bolshevik Power After October." *Slavic Review* 44 (Summer 1985):213–238.

———. "Reply." *Slavic Review* 44 (Summer 1985):251–256.

Rostow, Walt Whitman. *The Stages of Economic Growth. A Non-Communist Manifesto.* Cambridge: Cambridge University Press, 1971.

Roussakis, Emmanuel N. *Friedrich List, the Zollverein, and the Uniting of Europe.* Bruges, Belgium: College of Europe, 1968.

[Rousseau, J. J.] *Rousseau: Political Writings.* Edited and translated by Frederick Watkins. Edinburgh: Nelson, 1953.

Rubel, Maximilien, and Margaret Manale. *Marx without Myth: A Chronological Study of His Life and Work.* Oxford: Blackwell, 1975.

Ruggie, John Gerard. "Introduction: International Interdependence and National Welfare." In *The Antinomies of Interdependence: National Welfare and the International Division of Labor.* Edited by John Gerard Ruggie. New York: Columbia University Press, 1983.

Ruggiero, Guido de. *The History of European Liberalism*. Boston: Beacon Press, 1959.

Russell, Bertrand. *Freedom versus Organization, 1814–1914*. London: George Allen and Unwin, 1949. (First edition, 1934.)

Saint-Simon, H. de. "On the Reorganization of the European Society." In *The Political Thought of Saint-Simon*, pp. 83–98. Edited by Ghita Ionescu. Oxford: Oxford University Press, 1976.

Saletore, Bhasker Anand. *Der Wert der Listschen Lehren für die Lösung der indischen Frage*. Leipzig: Universitätsverlag von Robert Noske, 1933.

Salin, Edgar. "Ein Nachwort zur List-Ausgabe als Vorwort für künftige List-Leser." *Mitteilungen der Friedrich List Gesellschaft* 3 (1960–1962):345–348.

Schippel, Max. *Grundzüge der Handelspolitik. Zur Orientierung in den wirtschaftlichen Kämpfen*. Berlin and Bern: Akademischer Verlag für sociale Wissenschaften, 1902.

Schnabel, Franz. *Deutsche Geschichte im neunzehnten Jahrhundert*. Vol. 3, *Erfahrungswissenschaften und Technik*. Freiburg: Verlag Herder, 1954.

Schulz, Erna. "Friedrich Lists Geschichtsauffassung. Ihre Gestalt und ihre Bedeutung für Lists Wirstschaftslehre." *Zeitschrift für die gesamte Staatswissenschaft* 97 (1937):290–334.

Schumpeter, Joseph A. *A History of Economic Analysis*. New York: Oxford University Press, 1963.

Sears, Dudley. *The Political Economy of Nationalism*. Oxford: Oxford University Press, 1983.

Seidel, Friedrich. *Das Armutsproblem im deutschen Vormärz bei Friedrich List*. Cologne: Forschungsinstitut für Sozial- und Wirtschaftsgeschichte an der Universität Köln, 1971.

Semmel, Bernard. *The Rise of Free Trade Imperialism, Classical Political Economy, the Empire of Free Trade and Imperialism 1750–1850*. Cambridge: Cambridge University Press, 1970.

Senghaas, Dieter. *The European Experience. A Historical Critique of Development Theory*. Translated by K. H. Kimmig. Leamington Spa/Dover, New Hampshire: Berg Publishers, 1985.

———. "Friedrich List und die Neue internationale ökonomische Ordnung." *Leviathan* 3 (1975):293–300.

Seton-Watson, Hugh. *Nations and States*. Boulder, CO: Westview Press, 1977.

Sewell, William H., Jr. "Ideologies and Social Revolutions: Reflections on the French Case." *Journal of Modern History* 57 (March 1985):57–85.

Shanin, Teodor. "Late Marx and the Russian 'Periphery of Capitalism.' " *Monthly Review* 35 (June 1983):10–24.

———. *Russia as a 'Developing Society': The Roots of Otherness: Russia's Turn of the Century*. 2 vols. New Haven, CT: Yale University Press, 1986.

Sheehan, James J. "What is German History? Reflections on the Role of the *Nation* in German History and Historiography." *Journal of Modern History* 53 (March 1981):1–23.

Siegel, Paul N. "The Style of the *Communist Manifesto.*" *Science and Society* 46 (Summer 1982):222–229.

Silberner, Edmund. *The Problem of War in Nineteenth Century Economic Thought.* Translated by Alexander H. Krappe. Princeton: Princeton University Press, 1946.

Smith, Anthony D. *The Ethnic Origins of Nations.* Oxford: Basil Blackwell, 1987.

———. *Nationalism in the Twentieth Century.* New York: New York University Press, 1979.

———. *Theories of Nationalism.* New York: Harper and Row, 1973.

Smith, Woodruff D. *The Ideological Origins of Nazi Imperialism.* Oxford: Oxford University Press, 1986.

Snyder, Louis L. *German Nationalism: The Tragedy of a People. Extremism Contra Liberalism in Modern German History.* Harrisburg, PA: Stackpole, 1952.

———. *Roots of German Nationalism.* Bloomington, IN: Indiana University Press, 1978.

Spann, Othmar. *The History of Economics.* New York: W. W. Norton, 1930.

Spiegel, Henry William. *The Growth of Economic Thought.* Rev. ed. Durham, NC: Duke University Press, 1983.

Stalin, J. V. "The Immediate Tasks of the Party in the National Question." In J. V. Stalin, *Works.* Vol. 5. Moscow: Foreign Languages Publishing House, 1953.

———. "Report on the National Question." *Sochineniia.* Vol. 4. Moscow: Gospolitizdat, 1947.

Stedman Jones, Gareth. "Engels and the Genesis of Marxism." *New Left Review,* no. 106 (1977):79–104.

Stokes, Gale. "Cognition and the Function of Nationalism." *Journal of Interdisciplinary History* 4 (Spring 1974):525–542.

———. "Cognitive Style and Nationalism." *Canadian Review of Studies in Nationalism* 9 (1982):1–14.

———. "How is Nationalism Related to Capitalism?" *Comparative Studies in Society and History* 28 (1986):591–598.

———. "The Underdeveloped Theory of Nationalism." *World Politics* 30 (October 1978):150–160.

Strösslin, Werner. *Friedrich Lists Lehre von der wirtschaflichen Entwicklung.* Basel: Kyklos-Verlag, 1968.

Struik, Dirk J. *Birth of the Communist Manifesto.* New York: International Publishers, 1975.

Struve, Petr. *Kriticheskiia zametki k voprosu ob ekonomicheskom razvitii Rosii.* St. Petersburg: Skorokhodov, 1894.

Szamuely, Tibor. *The Russian Tradition.* Edited by Robert Conquest. London: Secker and Warburg, 1974.

Szporluk, Roman. "Pokrovskii's View of the Russian Revolution." *Slavic Review* 26 (March 1967): 70–84.

———. *The Political Thought of Thomas G. Masaryk*. Boulder, CO: East European Monographs, 1981.

Talmon, J. L. "The Age of Revolution." *Encounter* 21 (September 1963):11–18.

Taylor, Charles. *Hegel*. Cambridge: Cambridge University Press, 1983.

Thaden, Edward C. *Conservative Nationalism in Nineteenth-Century Russia*. Seattle: University of Washington Press, 1964.

Tholfsen, Trygve. *Ideology and Revolution in Modern Europe: An Essay on the Role of Ideas in History*. New York: Columbia University Press, 1984.

Tilly, Richard Hugh. "Los von England: Probleme des Nationalismus in der deutschen Wirtschaftsgeschichte." *Zeitschrift für die gesamte Staatwissenschaft* 124 (1968):179–196.

Tipton, Frank B. "The National Consensus in German Economic History." *Central European History* 7, no. 3 (1974):195–224.

Tito, Josip Broz-. *The National Question*. Beograd: Socialist Theory and Practice, 1983.

Tocqueville, Alexis de. *Democracy in America*. Translated by George Lawrence. Garden City, NY: Anchor Books, 1969.

Tucker, Robert C., ed. *The Marx-Engels Reader*. 2nd ed. New York: Norton, 1978.

Ulam, Adam B. *The Unfinished Revolution: An Essay on the Sources of Influence of Marxism and Communism*. New York: Vintage Books, 1964.

Ustrialov, N. V. *Bor'ba za Rossiiu*. Kharbin: "Okno," 1920.

Vikor, Desider. *Economic Romanticism in the Twentieth Century*. New Delhi: New Book Society of India, 1964.

Vilar, Pierre. "Marx and the Concept of History." In *The History of Marxism*. Edited by Eric J. Hobsbawm. Bloomington, IN: Indiana University Press, 1982.

———. "Spain and Catalonia." *Review* 3 (Spring 1980):527–577.

Vollgraf, Carl-Erich. "Karl Marx über die Ökonomische Theorien von Friedrich List." *Wirtschaftswissenschaft* 25 (July 1977):991–1010.

Von Laue, Theodore H. *The Global City: Freedom, Power and Necessity in the Age of World Revolutions*. Philadelphia and New York: Lippincott, 1969.

———. *Sergei Witte and the Industrialization of Russia*. New York: Columbia University Press, 1963.

Wagner, Y., and M. Strauss. "The Programme of the Communist Manifesto and Its Theoretical Foundations." *Political Studies* 17 (December 1969):470–484.

Walicki, Andrzej. *The Controversy over Capitalism: Studies in the Social Philosophy of the Russian Populists*. Oxford: Oxford University Press, 1969.

———. *A History of Russian Thought (From the Enlightenment to Marxism)*. Translated by Hilda Andrews-Rusiecka. Stanford: Stanford University Press, 1979.

————. *Philosophy and Romantic Nationalism: The Case of Poland*. Oxford: Oxford University Press, 1982.

————. "Russian Social Thought: An Introduction to the Intellectual History of Nineteenth-Century Russia." *Russian Review* 36 (January 1977):1–45.

————. *The Slavophile Controversy*. Translated by Hilda Andrews-Rusiecka. Oxford: Oxford University Press, 1975.

Wandycz, Piotr S. *The Lands of Partitioned Poland, 1795–1918*. Seattle, WA: University of Washington Press, 1974.

Weinstein, Brian. "Language Strategists: Redefining Political Frontiers on the Basis of Linguistic Choices." *World Politics* 31 (April 1979):345–364.

Weippert, Georg. *Der späte List. Ein Beitrag zur Grundlegung der Wissenschaft von der Politik und zur politischen Ökonomie als Gestaltungslehre der Wirtschaft*. Erlangen: Universitätsbund Erlangen, 1956 ("Erlanger Forschungen," Reihe A, Band 7).

Wendler, Eugen. *Friedrich List: Leben und Wirken in Dokumenten*. Reutlingen: Verlagshaus Reutlingen Oertel und Spörer, 1976.

Whittaker, Edmund. *Schools and Streams of Economic Thought*. Chicago: Rand McNally, 1960.

Wilson, Charles, *Mercantilism*. London: Routledge and Kegan Paul, 1958.

Witte, S. Iu. *Po povodu natsionalizma. Natsional'naia ekonomiia i Fridrikh List*. St. Petersburg: Brokhaus-Efron, 1912.

Wright, A. W. "Socialism and Nationalism." In *The Nation-State: The Formation of Modern Politics*. Edited by Leonard Tivey. Oxford: Martin Robertson, 1981.

Yanaga, Chitoshi. *Japan Since Perry*. New York: McGraw-Hill, 1949.

Zacek, Josef F. *Palacký. The Historian as Scholar and Nationalist*. The Hague and Paris: Mouton, 1970.

Zimand, Roman. "Uwagi o teorii narodu na marginesie analizy nacjonalistycznej teorii narodu." *Studia Filozoficzne* 4 (1967):3–39.

Zwick, Peter. "The Marxist Roots of National Communism." *Canadian Review of Studies in Nationalism* 3 (Spring 1976):127–145.

————. *National Communism*. Boulder, CO: Westview Press, 1983.

# Index

Prepared by Ben Szporluk